THE
BIOTECH
INVESTOR'S
BIBLE

THE
BIOTECH
INVESTOR'S
BIBLE

GEORGE WOLFF

JOHN WILEY & SONS, INC.

New York • Chichester • Weinheim • Brisbane • Singapore • Toronto

ISBN 0-471-41279-1

Printed in the United States of America.

10 9 8 7 6 5 4 3 2 1

For Crystal Guthrie

A cherished memory
Cruelly stolen by Alzheimer's disease

Contents

Preface   ix

Acknowledgments   xiii

Part I The Investment Perspective

Introduction: Biotechnology's PC Paradigm   3

Chapter 1: At the Threshold   9

Chapter 2: Assessing the Biotech Market   26

Chapter 3: The Keys to Biotech Investing   50

Chapter 4: Going over Biotech Books   75

Chapter 5: Four Tiers of Biotech Companies   89

Chapter 6: Biotechnology and Portfolio Planning   113

Chapter 7: Decision Making   135

Chapter 8: The Sector in Perspective   155

Chapter 9: The Biotech Investor's Checklist   160

Part II The Scientific and Technological Perspective

Chapter 10: The Science behind the Industry   169

Chapter 11: The Language of Genes   186

Chapter 12: The Realms of Biotechnology (or Who's
Doing What)   193

Chapter 13: The Picks and Shovels of Biotechnology   204

Chapter 14: The New Biotech Therapies   216

Chapter 15: Special Sectors   238

Epilogue 257

Appendixes

A: A Breakdown of 185 Major Biotech Companies:
Alphabetically, by Market Cap, and by Tier 259

B: Resources 284

C: Glossary 289

Notes 303

Index 309

Preface

————•◦•————

Investing in biotechnology is a challenge, not a gamble. It requires research and commitment on the part of biotech investors, who face two key hurdles: recognizing great companies in a complex, poorly understood business, and committing hard-earned capital with long-term goals in mind. Success in this field has nothing to do with market timing and get-rich-quick stock plays. Old-fashioned investment practices are the most appropriate for this most modern of sectors.

The biotech sector is often called speculative and not without reason. The industry has a long history of dashed hopes punctuated by occasional, spectacular gains. But in 2000, the story of the industry was completely rewritten. The extraordinary growth potential that has drawn investors to biotechnology for the past two decades is finally beginning to bear fruit.

Now, as the lean years come to an end, time lines to profitability for many biotech companies are being measured in years and quarters instead of decades; important new drugs are awaiting FDA approval before coming to market; and the science behind the industry has matured to the point where a steady stream of new biotech products can be expected for many years to come. Finally, after a 20-year incubation, biotechnology has become less speculative and more product and profit driven.

By coincidence, current market conditions have turned the concept of speculative investing on its head. According to one astonishing estimate, the values of 50 percent of the companies on the Nasdaq exchange declined 50 percent or more between March and October of 2000. That is volatility and risk on a market-devouring scale. During a slightly longer period, January to October, the Amex and Nasdaq biotech indexes each gained more than 90 percent. Is this a fluke or a sign of a maturing industry? Over the course of this book, I explore industry trends and point out the milestones that mark the emergence of a major new sector of the economy.

Several dozen biotech companies have already achieved the accepted standards of corporate maturity, boasting annual revenues of several billion dollars and market capitalizations in the tens of billions of dollars. All mature biotech companies are involved in drug development, as are all emerging companies that have achieved valuations in the billion dollar plus range. Consequently, much of this book will center on the industry's current focus: human biological systems and medicine. But investors should be aware that there is much more to come from the biotech sector. No area of the economy, from insurance to hard rock mining, will remain unaffected by innovations in biotechnology in the coming decades. To date, industrial applications of biotechnology make up the least developed sector of the industry and offer considerable growth opportunities.

The biotechnology industry has unusual investment dynamics—never before surveyed comprehensively—and a new set of financial assumptions must be developed for it and for its investors.

In fact, the preparation of this book was driven to a large degree by the absence of widely accepted market criteria for biotech stock selection and valuation. The demand for comprehensive industry analysis and technical background became apparent when my clients in the financial industry began requesting copies of the research I had prepared for my own biotech portfolio.

I have divided this book into two major sections. Part I of *The Biotech Investor's Bible* focuses on the unique financial forces that drive biotech markets. By investigating the structure of the industry and its market underpinnings, I set the stage for an analysis of new parameters to guide investment decisions. Biotech investments are unique and the companies in this industry must be gauged according to novel criteria.

Part II of the book helps investors cope with the torrent of scientific and technical news generated daily by the industry. It is important not to be intimidated or enticed by scientific terms and industry jargon, and my intent is to demystify biotech terminology and methods. Investors need not be scientists to understand this science-driven industry. If that were a requirement, the sector would never have gotten off the ground.

I own shares in approximately 88 biotech companies, managed in three discrete portfolios. I own, or have owned, stock in a great many of the companies mentioned in this book. Because of this, I want to emphasize that none of the examples provided in *The Biotech Investor's Bible* should be construed as a recommendation to buy or sell any particular equity. The business, the science, and the market environment of the biotechnology industry change rapidly and no investment decision should be made without serious consideration of current conditions.

This is not a "get rich quick" book (despite the dazzling performance of biotechnology indexes in 1999 and 2000). Now that valuations in the biotech sector have risen across the board, investors will have to look a little harder to find bargains and be more careful to avoid setbacks. A primary goal of this book is to provide investors with cautions and strategies to reduce risk, combined with conservative investment techniques designed strictly for long-term gains.

Biotechnology is an industry based on breakthroughs in the understanding of living things. It is a knowledge industry and investors will not be able to make informed decisions without learning about it. *The Biotech Investor's Bible* is intended to serve investors who want to get in as close as possible to the ground floor of a great emerging industry. By taking the time to read this book and to explore the many recommended resources, you will be making your first and most important biotech investment. Failing to develop a base of understanding before entering this field is something like entering a broker's office empty-handed and asking him to turn a profit.

For investors who take the time to learn about the potential and the pitfalls of biotechnology investing, this is a golden moment. The mapping of the human genome has brought us to a watershed in history, a crossroads that will rival, in importance, discoveries from the likes of Newton, Einstein, and Copernicus. But, the decoding of the genome is only part of this story. The biotechnology industry as a whole has brought mankind to the threshold of revolutionary change in all of its endeavors.

Such sweeping assertions may be easily dismissed in this age of rampant hyperbole. The wild frenzy of speculation that surrounded the advent of the Internet has, I hope, inoculated many sensible investors against placing blind faith in grandiose claims and empty promises. Make no mistake. Biotechnology investing is still a speculative field. All great scientific discoveries have taken decades, sometimes centuries, to realize their potential.

Why then is biotechnology no longer a pure gamble? Why is it not empty rhetoric to claim that biotechnology has brought us to the brink of a revolution? The answers to such questions are the very nub of this book.

GEORGE WOLFF

Acknowledgments

While researching this book, I have been fortunate to meet with leading biotech executives and hear from many others at industry conferences. A number of biotechnology companies have been kind enough to invite me to tour their operations and others have generously taken the time to advise me in telephone interviews. I would like to thank the executives and staff of Advanced Tissue Sciences, Affymetrix, Collateral Therapeutics, Diversa Corporation, Neotherapeutics, and Sequenom for their thoughtful assistance. In the investment community, I must also thank Oscar Gruss & Sons and First Securities Van Kasper for making me welcome. Among authors, I must also pay tribute to Matt Ridley, Cynthia Robbins-Roth, Eric S. Grace, Susan R. Barnum, Arthur Kornberg, and William Bains who had the foresight to share their specialized knowledge about the biotechnology sector in print before its remarkable rise in the markets. Their keen insights have helped shape my opinions. I also thank BigCharts.com for the use of their statistical data and charts.

On the editorial side, I must thank Enid Guthrie, Allan Waters of Waters Risk Management, and Nelson Potter of Morgan Stanley Dean Witter for their diligence in checking my manuscript. Special thanks also to the staff at John Wiley & Sons, in particular, Joan O'Neil and Jean Glasser, who recognized the importance of biotechnology early on and supported this project long before the industry had demonstrated its extraordinary growth potential. Of course, no writer can hope to stay on course without the guidance of a talented editor, and I welcome this opportunity to thank Chris Heiser for his deft application of the editorial scalpel and his remarkably diplomatic suggestions for improvements. I must also acknowledge the enormous efforts of Sasha Kintzler at John Wiley and Nancy Marcus Land and Pam Blackmon at Publications Development Company of Texas who helped make my manuscript more presentable. Thanks also to Andrea Pedolsky of the Altair Literary Agency for her advice and counsel. Further thanks to my wife for sparking my interest in the stock market years ago and tolerantly supporting the rigorous demands made by this project.

I would be remiss if I did not conclude by paying tribute to the brilliance and dedication of the scientists who have brought the biotechnology industry to this pivotal point in its history. They have made the greatest investment of all, dedicating their minds and their careers to one of the greatest scientific pursuits in human history. If the twenty-first century does indeed turn out to be the biotech century, it will be the pioneers who toiled for many years in obscurity that all of us must be grateful to. One day cancer, Alzheimer's disease, and many other scourges will be curable because of their early efforts. No reward will ever measure up to their extraordinary contribution to human well-being.

G.W.

PART I

The Investment Perspective

Introduction:
Biotechnology's PC Paradigm

When Roy Whitfield, the C.E.O. of Incyte Genomics, one of the world's leading biotechnology research companies, stepped up to the podium at a biotech investment conference in New York last spring, he presented his audience with a fascinating and useful parallel. "Genomics," he declared, "is now where the computer industry was in the 1970s."[1] No comparison of this sort is ever perfect, but Whitfield's parallel provides a glimpse into the future as it appears to many biotech industry leaders today. Whitfield outlined his vision to an exclusive crowd of investment bankers, but his message also speaks directly to the ambitions of individual investors who are interested in the breathtaking potential of the biotechnology sector. It is, just as Whitfield says, a time very much like the period before the explosive development of the personal computer industry.

The pivotal event in the development of computers occurred during the 1940s when scientists at Bell Labs invented a compact, high-speed switching mechanism they called the transistor. By the early 1970s, a diverse array of sciences and technologies, including mathematics, electronics, logic, and materials sciences converged in the creation of a revolutionary transistorized device called the "very large scale integrated circuit" or VLSI. This chunk of silicon held thousands of transistors compressed onto a tiny slab, the forerunner of today's microchip processor (Intel's first microprocessor contained 2,300 transistors and performed more than 50,000 operations per second, a stunning speed at the time).[2] Mainstream computer developers combined the unprecedented speed and power of new integrated circuits with magnetic memory storage to develop increasingly powerful mainframe computers.

From the average investor's perspective, 30 years ago, there seemed to be few options to profit from the computer industry's development except to buy shares in established mainframe-oriented companies like IBM. In computer software, a company by the name of Wang was the dominant force in business word processing. The cutting edge of the industry appeared to belong to Seymour Cray, who was developing supercomputers. On the fringe, the Defense Advanced Research Projects Agency was creating a network of computers able to survive a nuclear holocaust—a project

3

that went by the awkward name of ARPAnet, now known as the Internet.

Biotech investors now face a strikingly similar scenario. The biotechnology industry's watershed moment occurred at Cambridge University in 1953 when James Watson and Francis Crick first discerned the double-helix structure of DNA (deoxyribonucleic acid).[3] In the following decades, scientists around the world struggled with the harrowing challenge of deciphering and manipulating the billions of molecular components that make up DNA, the master molecule at the heart of all living things. James Watson, one of the codiscoverers, later described DNA "the most golden of molecules" but decades would pass before any real gold emerged from the lab.

Now, almost 50 years later, biotechnology has finally achieved a number of breakthroughs comparable to those that made the transistor a practical tool for the creation of the personal computer industry. Biochips have compressed thousands of laboratory analyses onto tiny and ever-shrinking platforms. The manipulation and duplication of genes and genetic patterns (otherwise known as cloning and recombination) has become routine. The convergence of supercomputers, advanced mathematics and robotics has made possible another historic achievement: the mapping of the human genome. Still, society at large has not fully grasped the revolutionary changes that this important new technology will bring.

Back in the 1970s futurists predicted earnestly that computers would cause massive unemployment and a dangerous surplus of leisure time. They were wrong. Now, newsmagazines and commentators worry about the dangers of creating designer babies or a race of genetic superbeings although there is no evidence to suggest that any biotech company is actively pursuing such work. Not only are the technical challenges far beyond the capacity of current science; the goals are unappealing. Biotech industry leaders are well aware of ethical considerations affecting their work and have no interest in spending valuable research dollars for doomed ventures.

The futurists, true to form, are making imaginative, but somewhat impractical predictions about the long-range ramifications of the biotech revolution. One author estimates that the flow of new information generated by the biotech industry will grow exponentially to the point where the sum total of human knowledge will actually double every single day by the year 2016.[4] Hollywood has entered the fanciful fray with pessimistic films like *Jurassic Park* and *Gattaca* which portray nightmare visions of the consequences of genetic manipulation. (The title of *Gattaca* is a play on letters from the genetic code.) Even NASA Administrator Daniel Goldin has raised some eyebrows by predicting that in the year 2030 a biological spacecraft the size of a soda can will be sent to an asteroid where it will adapt to the environment and construct a starship from available materials.[5] Once again, this is reminiscent of the 1970s when films and books imagined computers developing independent powers and paranoid personalities, bent on dominating their masters.

Many people missed a great investment opportunity for a lack of meaningful information about what the future would bring. An investor who had a reasonable vision of the computer industry's actual future, a diversified portfolio within the sector, and the determination to stay the course for 10 years or more would have reaped an enormous return. Compaq, Dell, and even the badly shaken king of the mainframes, IBM, took advantage of the PC revolution to earn impressive revenues. Internet and software companies like Cisco Systems, Intel, and Microsoft created new industries more powerful and profitable than the most optimistic visionaries had predicted.

So it is now, for biotechnology. Most investors who wish to benefit from the impressive profit margins associated with drug development currently turn to the world's established multinational pharmaceutical companies, just as computer investors turned to IBM 30 years ago. But investors with a reasonable and practical understanding of this field share a momentous opportunity. The long-hidden mechanisms at the heart of all living things are yielding their secrets, and a global industry is emerging from the discovery process. Some biotech companies will fall by the wayside. Investor losses are inevitable in an emerging industry, but, as Dell, Cisco, Intel, and many others have proven, the profits from picking even one winner in a major emerging sector and sticking with it have a way of putting small losses in perspective. Buying $1,000 of Dell stock in 1989 and holding it for 10 years would have yielded a return of $400,000. Biotech investors, however, shouldn't forget the flip side of the PC parallel: buying $1,000 worth of Commodore Computer stock in 1980 could have yielded a near total loss, depending on when an investor decided to bail out.

The biotech industry's bargain basement days have already ended for some companies. Gains of several thousand percent enjoyed by companies like Medimmune and IDEC Pharmaceuticals during the late 1990s are far less likely to be achieved now because biotech indexes have risen substantially from their depressed levels at the end of the past century.

Nevertheless, the experience of the early PC industry provides an instructive model for biotech investing: Buy the very best emerging companies and hold them tenaciously to maturity. Instead of watching earnings and stock prices fluctuate daily, or from one quarter to the next, remain focused on an investment's long-term prospects. A great deal of diversification is needed to control risk in an emerging industry like biotechnology, and investors must learn as much as possible about the sector in order to make sensible buy-and-sell decisions. But, the risk and reward dynamics favor the investor who takes a position early in the emergence of a major industry.

FEW INVESTMENTS MORE VOLATILE

This is emphatically not a call to throw caution to the winds and bet the farm. The sector is far too volatile and risky for that. In the early months of 2000, the Nasdaq Biotech Index leapt from the low 800s in January to more than 1600 in March, then fell right back to the low 800s in April. Even that gut-wrenching level of volatility is merely an industry average. Most individual biotech stocks were rocked by even more violent swings on both the upside and the downside.

Consider the fortunes of an investor who bought a stock like Celera Genomics (the company that took the lead in mapping the human genome at the end of 1999) for less than $20. Between January and mid-March of 2000, Celera went off like a rocket, jumping some days by as much as $50 per share. For a brief moment our lucky investor would have enjoyed more than a 1000 percent gain. Had he been prescient enough to sell at the very peak, he might have turned every $20 invested into $250.[6]

But an investor who bought Celera at $250 a share near the peak of the biotech bubble in March 2000 would have suffered a staggering 72 percent loss as the stock plunged dizzyingly after the market bubble burst. Six months later, the sector's surprising recovery returned many biotechnology stocks to levels near their previous highs. But Celera remained down more than 50 percent (even during a White House ceremony to mark the company's historic role in mapping the human genome.) Caution is obviously the watchword.

How can anyone stomach an investment sector this volatile? Putting aside for the moment the increasingly erratic behavior of the wider markets, volatility in the biotech sector can be daunting. The exaggerated hopes that accompanied previous biotechnology stock surges were always followed by severe setbacks and long investment droughts. No responsible person would suggest playing on such wild volatility for profit. The risks are far too great and the rewards of investing for the longer term can be sufficiently attractive. Even in the Celera investment example, an investor who bought early and passively rode out the volatility would have enjoyed a respectable gain of more than 300 percent over the course of the year 2000.

The bedrock fact about the biotechnology industry, proven again and again, is that development time lines are exceptionally long and fraught with setbacks. Investment expectations should be set accordingly. Biotech investors will experience frequent disappointments unless they set realistic long-range goals and hold firmly to them.

It may be reassuring to keep in mind that the long-term view for the industry as a whole is exceptionally exciting. Biotech companies are finding hundreds of practical applications for groundbreaking scientific techniques, having learned to manipulate basic biological processes in virtually all life forms, including human beings. This broad front of scientific progress strongly suggests that the industry will ultimately subdue or conquer many catastrophic diseases as well as enhance human biological systems to increase the length and the quality of life. The potential dollar value of such power staggers the imagination.

Recognizing the industry's extraordinary promise and its market volatility, the biotech investor's most powerful weapons are patience, knowledge, and conviction. Volatility and long waiting periods for scientific and clinical results are an intrinsic part of biotech investing. Price fluctuations that cannot be traced to corporate news or performance reports are everyday distractions. Examine any biotech company that has risen from penny-stock status to a multibillion-dollar valuation, and a similar pattern usually emerges: a long incubation period, followed by impressive gains on the success of a new product or an IPO, and then a volatile period of uncertainty as the market tests new high and low values. The early, committed investor, not the volatility player, would enjoy the smallest risks and the greatest rewards.

Biotech investors who have bought wisely and stayed the course in this way have reaped enormous profits in the past. No one can guarantee such spectacular results for any given company, but vigorous growth seems to be a reasonable expectation for the industry as a whole for decades to come. The investor's task is to choose the companies that could become tomorrow's giants.

CAUTION IN UNFAMILIAR INVESTMENT TERRAIN

The forces driving this sector are unique. Stock markets are struggling to find realistic values for a diverse and unfamiliar group of pioneering enterprises. Because most biotech companies remain unprofitable, the formulas usually used for corporate valuation simply do not work. This book's obligation to the reader is to deliver a practical and usable understanding of the unconventional forces that move the markets in the biotech industry.

A conservative approach to biotechnology investment would have outperformed most conventional strategies and financial instruments during 1999 and 2000. In the first six months of 2000, biotech mutual funds were the hands-down winners among all other types of funds. The Lipper Company analyzed 72 funds that offered a combination of biotech and healthcare stocks and found they beat all other sectors, with average returns above 19 percent. By contrast, the average diversified equity fund gained only 1.3 percent in the same period. Pure biotech funds (those that are not cushioned against volatility with holdings in major pharmaceutical companies) made up 7 of the top 10 funds at midyear. Last year, the Franklin Biotechnology Discovery Fund returned 97 percent, a result that compared favorably with the performance of the Nasdaq and AMEX Biotechnology Indexes.[7]

Biotech investors need a sense of conviction about their investment decisions as well as the patience to see them through without much outside assistance or encouragement. Most retail brokers know very little about the industry and are loath to become involved because biotech is seen as too speculative and, these days, is often compared with Internet's dot-coms. A biotech investor's perseverance can only be maintained with considerable independent knowledge about one's holdings and an understanding of the field in general.

The self-directed investor who loses faith during market reversals and sells out instantly becomes a "buy high, sell low" victim. The good news is that the lows don't last as long as they used to. In previous decades, the sector's lows lasted four years or more. By contrast, the biotech stock implosion of 2000 dragged down prices in the sector for little more than two months.

Practical techniques to spot the greatest long-term potential in biotechnology investments are not widely understood or accepted, at least not yet. Market analysts are usually required to predict price changes from one earnings season to the next, but in the volatile world of biotechnology much longer time horizons apply. The day-to-day movements of biotechnology stocks are largely determined by institutional trades, wider market trends, and by the market's assessment of a company's potential for short-term gain compared with other investments that may be rising or falling. Such fluctuations are transitory and virtually impossible to predict. Only biotech investors who take the long view and focus on a company's realistic growth potential have a reasonable chance of making the gains commensurate with the industry's extraordinary potential. Investors who took a similar view of the computer industry's future 20 or 30 years ago have been richly rewarded.

CHAPTER 1

At the Threshold

We're on the verge of a revolution!
Dr. Stephen L. Hoffman, U.S. Naval Medical Research Institute

BIOTECHNOLOGY: ONE OF THE WORLD'S OLDEST EMERGING INDUSTRIES

Most investors regard biotechnology as one of the world's newest industries and, from a market perspective, that's true enough. But, from the historical point of view, nothing could be more incorrect. Using the simplest definition, biotechnology encompasses any technique that employs biological systems for a practical purpose, and by this standard, the industry is thousands of years old. Microorganisms were put to work turning sugars and starches into alcohol at least as early as 1700 B.C., when ancient Sumerians discovered how to make beer.[1] Selective breeding of livestock and agricultural techniques to enhance crop yields are also time-honored biotech disciplines. From bread baking and cheese making to running a sewage plant or managing a pharmaceutical company, the task is the same: harnessing living organisms and managing biological processes for practical results. Although some regard biotechnology as a junior cousin to the pharmaceutical industry, under this definition the opposite is true. Biotechnology is far more ancient and fundamental to human civilization than the much more narrowly focused business of creating and selling pharmaceutical compounds.

During the past two decades, biotechnology has advanced with astonishing speed, but the industry still serves the same wide mandate: to manage the machinery of living things for a useful result. The most immediate goal for the industry is the creation of an entirely new generation of drugs and medical techniques. Although biotechnology has much broader economic potential, medicine has emerged as the industry's main focus, and its most attractive investment opportunity, for both economic and historical reasons.

9

Almost 50 years ago, when Dr. James Watson realized that he and his collaborators had discovered the structure of DNA, he fought the urge to run to the nearest pub in Cambridge and declare he had uncovered "the secret of life."[2] In fact, his team had discovered *a* secret of life, and a very big one. Immediately, this discovery posed a web of closely related scientific questions: How exactly does DNA work? What role does it play in disease? What do its codes mean? Can DNA codes be altered?

Like any other major scientific challenge, the big questions could only be tackled by breaking them down into smaller problems of manageable size. Scientific specialties emerged as a result. Genomics evolved from the need to decipher the entire three billion-bit code of the human genome. Functional genomics arose from the desire to learn about the mechanisms and messages hidden within the genome. Scientists searched for ways to alter DNA by cutting and splicing molecular strands precisely. As the challenges multiplied and questions proliferated, a small army of academic researchers took up the pieces of this puzzle and eventually began finding solutions.

The world's leading universities have played a key role in bringing the industry to its current state. Biological science and research funding decisions are guided by a common desire to discover answers to the most compelling questions of our day. The desire to understand and control human disease has been a powerful uniting force, driving the biotech discovery process solidly in the direction of medical technology. The nature of cancer, for example, is a mystery that is important enough to draw research funding, and sufficiently challenging to engage the interest of many scientists.

This painstaking process of scientific discovery is at the heart of the evolution of the biotechnology industry. Each thread of scientific investigation has illuminated a small piece of the human biological puzzle, spawning the creation of equally specialized biotech companies, each intent on deriving a profit from the methods and insights of the pioneering researchers in their fields.

There are now more than 400 publicly traded biotech companies in U.S. markets and most of them are committed to discovering new cures for human diseases. Despite this apparent unity of purpose, the biotechnology industry is remarkably diverse, with many subsectors and a mind-boggling number of specialties. The reason goes back to the industry's scientific foundations.

Describing the difference between the traditions of the pharmaceutical industry and the biotech industry gives a clearer picture of what this means in practice. Pharmaceutical companies have searched the world for biologically active molecules, or drug targets as they are sometimes called. When a molecule is found to have interesting effects on biological systems, it is subjected to extensive experimentation intended to discover which bodily systems are affected by the drug, and how they are changed.

Aspirin was derived from a folk remedy that used an extract from willow tree bark to control pain, fever, and inflammation. More recently, the bark of the Pacific Yew tree yielded Taxol, which has proven useful in inhibiting some forms of breast cancer. As the chemical composition of the body has been further investigated, drugs have been discovered to inhibit biochemical reactions. For example, Prozac, the popular antidepressant, is the first in a family of relatively new drugs called selective serotonin reuptake inhibitors or SSRIs. After determining that depression was often characterized by low levels of the chemical serotonin in the brain, researchers sought to increase those levels by blocking the routine absorption of serotonin among neurons in the brain (or inhibiting reuptake). SSRIs have produced dramatic results in the treatment of many mental disorders, but they are not a panacea and they do generate undesirable side effects.

This traditional trial-and-error process of finding drug targets, modifying them chemically, and testing their effects on the body is imprecise by biotech standards. It is also severely limited because the pharmaceutical industry has largely focused on small molecule drugs, a term used to describe drugs that can pass easily through the walls of the intestinal tract into the bloodstream. Another key characteristic of traditional pharmaceuticals is their tendency to act mainly as blockers or inhibitors of biological processes involved in disease. This is an important limitation. Remarkably, the pharmaceutical industry's entire arsenal of drugs has only scratched the surface so far. It is estimated that the body is made up of 30,000 different kinds of proteins but existing drugs act on only 500 of these proteins.

By contrast, one of the most successful drugs developed by the biotech industry is Amgen's Epogen, an interesting product because it is so different from a traditional pharmaceutical. Epogen is a large molecule drug (a protein) that directly stimulates the production of red blood cells to treat a number of conditions. It is an exact, genetically engineered copy of an active component of the human body. As the initiator of a natural bodily process, Epogen has a positive, stimulating function that no conventional pharmaceutical "blocker" or "inhibitor" could be expected to equal.

The differences between drugs from biotechnology and conventional pharmaceuticals actually go much deeper but can be summed up in a single word: specificity. The biotech approach to drug development is based on detailed information about the operations of cells and molecules. Although this body of knowledge is far from complete, it has afforded biotech companies the ability to develop drugs that act in precise ways on biological functions. For example, Genentech greatly improved the safety of diabetes treatment many years ago by producing an exact copy of human insulin, rendering obsolete the side-effect-prone insulin previously derived from livestock.

Pharmaceuticals developed through trial and error typically cause a wide variety of undesirable reactions because their effect is not disease-specific.

Side effects are unpredictable and sometimes dangerous because the mechanisms and interactions of most conventional drugs within the human body are not well understood. For example, a narcotic painkiller like codeine affects the entire nervous system and can cause drowsiness, addiction, or death depending on the dosage. A more specific drug would act only on nerve cells or brain functions involved in the perception of pain. This is the test of specificity. If a new drug can be designed to affect only the cells or molecules involved in the disease process, it stands a much greater chance of being potent without creating undesirable side effects. Increasing specificity is the hallmark of advances in drug development and the goal of biotech companies engaged in drug discovery.

Because biotechnology is evolving from a foundation of new science, the industry is able to tackle problems that have remained far beyond the reach of traditional pharmaceutical development. For this reason, biotechnology is classified as a sector separate from the pharmaceutical industry, deeply involved in much more than conventional drug discovery methods. The industry is creating entirely new technologies, and the enormous scale of innovation in the biotech sector can be seen in a quick glance at its most promising approaches:

- *Therapeutic proteins.* Powerful medicines that were the first class of drugs to emerge from the biotechnology. Early protein drugs include fully humanized insulin, growth hormones, and Amgen's Epogen. The body makes thousands of proteins and that means many more protein-based drugs will be developed.

- *Monoclonal antibodies.* Copies of the body's natural defense agents. These new drugs make up a large class in development. Antibodies can be customized to attack infectious organisms or cancerous cells generated by the body itself.

- *Immune system modulators.* Molecules that regulate the immune system. In much the same way that Epogen triggers production of new blood cells, these molecules can bolster bodily defenses. They may also restrain the immune system if it becomes too aggressive and attacks the body itself, causing diseases like lupus.

- *Gene therapy.* Alteration of genes to fix the root causes of many diseases.

- *Angiogenesis.* Gene therapy to create new blood vessels for treatment of heart disease and other degenerative conditions.

- *Antiangiogenesis.* Starving of tumors by cutting off the creation of new blood vessels.

- *Tissue regeneration.* Rebuilding of damaged body parts by stimulating tissue growth.

- *Armed viruses.* Creation of customized viruses to attack cancerous cells.

- *Stem cell therapy.* Manipulation of the body's most basic cell types, able to assume any form and grow new tissues.

- *Drug delivery.* Novel systems to deliver medicines directly to the diseased area.

- *Curative vaccines.* Vaccines that attack diseases in progress. Once strictly preventives, now autologous vaccines made from a patient's own tumor cells are on the market.

- *Signal transduction.* Modification of cellular functions by sending instructions through cellular walls.

- *Photodynamic therapy.* The use of light to activate drugs in specific disease areas. The first such therapy is on the market for blindness caused by vascular degeneration.

- *Pharmacogenomics.* Genetic tailoring of drug therapy to match a specific patient or disease strain.

- *Telomeres.* The use of highly specialized DNA fragments to control aging and cancer.

Biotechnology research has progressed from the laboratory bench to industrial scale processes and to microminiaturized chips. Many technologies have been created to pursue increasingly precise and specific therapeutic agents. The fields of research include:

- *Genomics.* Deciphering the precise functions of genes.

- *Proteomics.* Discovering the workhorses of bodily systems, proteins.

- *Combinatorial and ADMET chemistry.* Developing new techniques to select promising drugs.

- *Assay development.* Prescreening drug candidates for their potential and for shortcomings in order to save time and money in human trials.

- *Computer modeling.* Pretesting drugs by developing computer models of drugs and their reactions in the body.

- *Bioinformatics.* Refining and managing the growing mass of data.

- *Gene shuffling.* Accelerating evolution by creating and testing entirely custom made genes.

- *High throughput machinery.* Automating and hugely accelerating drug discovery by testing thousands of chemical reactions in a miniaturized, automated chemistry lab.

- *Pharming.* Inserting human genes in animals to manufacture drugs or to conduct research.

Biotechnology is also producing new products that use genetic engineering, computer technology, and large molecule proteins in unexpected ways:

- *Biochips.* Microminiaturized chips for high-volume, high-speed testing of disease characteristics, patient DNA profiles, and laboratory research.
- *Nutraceuticals.* Foods modified to create therapeutic effects.
- *Cosmeceuticals.* Technologies to reverse the effects of aging.
- *Biometrics.* Security systems based on genetic traits.
- *Microrobotics.* Use of cellular and genetic molecules as machines.
- *Biocomputing.* Use of cellular and genetic mechanisms as computers.

Taken as a whole, this roster of new technologies and therapies shows enormous promise. The Pharmaceutical Research and Manufacturing Association (PhRMA) says we should expect "unprecedented progress in developing new medicines to conquer disease." History gives us some sense of what this might mean. The life expectancy of someone born in 1920 was only 54 years. Two fundamentally new biological technologies played a major part in extending life expectancy. Vaccines and antibiotics all but eliminated the prospect of death by whooping cough, measles, diphtheria, and polio in developed countries. By 1965, the life expectancy, at birth, of the average American had risen to 70 years. Vaccines and antibiotics can't claim all the credit for this phenomenon, but their importance is unquestioned. Now, more than a *dozen* new technologies that could rival the life-saving effectiveness of vaccines and antibiotics are being developed by the biotechnology industry.[3]

MEASURING BIOTECH INNOVATION

Figure 1.1, which depicts patents being issued by the U.S. Patent Office, can only suggest the growing scale of the industry's rate of discovery. The number of patents approved in the biotech field rose exponentially until 1998 when the number of approvals first exceeded 8,000. Then the industry hit a plateau, partly because the U.S. Patent Office is handling as many files as it can manage. Meanwhile, the number of patent applications has gone off the charts with the accelerating rate of discovery of disease-causing genes and therapeutic proteins.

Celera has filed a stunning 10,000 gene patent applications. Incyte Pharmaceuticals boasts that it holds more patents on genes than any other company: 500 patents granted and more than 7,000 applications.[4] Human Genome Sciences has received 200 patents and applied for 8,000 more. Millennium Pharmaceuticals has applied for 1,500 patents.[5] The sheer volume

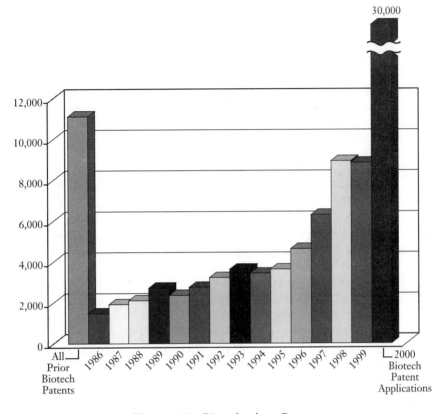

Figure 1.1   Biotechnology Patent

of patent applications is unprecedented in the history of the life sciences industry. The U.S. Patent Office says it now has a staggering 30,000 biotech patent applications pending, 20,000 of them gene related. Some of these applications may not be approved; nevertheless this is an unprecedented volume of claims on intellectual property for the biotechnology industry.[6]

The biotech knowledge explosion has already yielded an overwhelming number of new drug candidates, more than a thousand in total. Most of these new drugs are aimed at so-called big target diseases that will yield the highest revenue returns. For heart disease and stroke, 96 promising drugs are in development. For the many forms of cancer, 316 new treatments are in the works; 122 drugs are being developed to fight AIDS; 29 new approaches to treat arthritis are being tested. And, one of the most mysterious of diseases, Alzheimer's, may ultimately yield to one of the 17 new treatments in the pipeline.[7]

This flood of new treatments will capture a sizable chunk of existing drug markets and create entirely new opportunities in the treatment of diseases that currently have no effective form of therapy. And, as many observers have pointed out, the market will grow larger every year with the aging of the baby boom generation.

In March 2000, the *Wall Street Journal* put some exact numbers to the market potential for novel therapeutics. The newspaper reported that the pharmaceutical industry had generated revenues of $343 billion worldwide in 1999, an increase of more than 11 percent from the year before.[8] Although biotechnology currently accounts for a relatively small $20 billion portion of that revenue stream, the industry is poised to seize a much larger share of the worldwide drug market.

While the biotech industry is finally accelerating revenue growth, it also continues to ratchet up research spending. The Biotechnology Industry Organization, a Washington-based industry lobby group, reported that in 1999 American biotech companies spent more than half of the sector's revenues, $11 billion in total, on research. No other industrial group spends anything near that proportion of total revenues on research, not even the major pharmaceutical companies, which are usually named as the world's biggest R&D spenders.

After an incubation period of some 20 years, approximately four dozen publicly traded biotech companies have achieved substantial profitability, truly an extraordinarily low number in a sector made up of more than 1,300 public and private corporations in the United States alone. That gloomy picture is beginning to change, and analysts predict that the number of profitable companies will double by 2002.[9] But investors should always keep in mind that developing a new drug is a process that can consume 10 years, much of that time spent on clinical trials and government approvals. The discovery and early laboratory testing phase of the development process is being sharply compressed by new technologies that zero in on the best drug candidates and weed out those most likely to cause side effects. But, there is no way to speed up clinical trials. Human drug trials are conducted in three phases designed to test toxicity, optimum dosages, and effectiveness, a process which usually lasts more than 5 years. Certification of a new drug by the Food and Drug Administration may add another year to the process. The cost of the clinical trials and approvals process has been estimated (some say overestimated) at a half billion dollars.[10] At the end of this lengthy ordeal, it is not uncommon for the government to reject a drug, even if it has gone through all three phases of clinical trials.

More than 350 drug products and vaccines from the biotechnology industry are currently undergoing human clinical trials and many more are in development.[11] To put the impending explosion of new therapies in perspective, consider that major pharmaceutical companies typically bring only two or three major drugs to market in any given year and the entire pharmaceutical and biotech industry has historically brought fewer than 50 novel drugs out annually.[12]

This tally of pharmaceutical industry performance may seem low because it omits minor products and the many "me-too drugs" that pharmaceutical companies create to mimic a rival's blockbuster drug. The me-too process involves changing a few parts of an existing drug's molecular structure to alter its function slightly and to avoid patent infringement problems. What matters in this comparison is the volume of truly important new products created by the biotech industry.

THE POTENTIAL OF INDUSTRIAL BIOTECHNOLOGY

The biotech industry also has enormous opportunities outside the world of medicine in fields including agriculture, energy, plastics, pulp and paper, waste handling, chemicals, adhesives, fibers, and computer chips. The size of the potential market for industrial biotechnology is difficult to estimate because these industries are so large and the development of new technologies is still largely confined to the laboratory. For example, the worldwide chemical industry generates annual revenues of a trillion dollars. There is no doubt in the minds of scientists that biotechnology will assume an important role in the industry but it would be premature to estimate what portion of this revenue stream can be captured. Despite the lack of comprehensive dollar estimates for industrial biotechnology revenues, it may be helpful to illustrate some of the potential developments from this sector within a sector:

- *Energy.* Fast-growing plants being developed through genetic engineering may become a vast, renewable source of energy drawn from the sun. Hydrogen-generating microbes may become a source of the cleanest burning fuel possible.
- *Fibers.* Using the genetic codes for spider silk, fibers are being created that are stronger than steel. Many other innovations in the technology of industrial fibers are in the works.
- *Petroleum.* New enzymes, able to function in high temperatures, may make refining more efficient. Others may strip pollutants like sulfur from combustible fuels. There is also interest in developing enzymes that could loosen up billions of barrels of heavy oil that current technologies cannot extract from the ground.
- *Plastics.* Novel polymers are being developed with organic materials.
- *Pulp and paper.* The development of genetically engineered trees may reduce pollution and help save existing forests. The pulp and paper industry can limit the number of toxic chemicals used to break wood down into pulp by using trees that have been modified to disintegrate more easily. Fast-growing trees can reduce the need to cut existing forests.

- *Waste management.* Customized organisms will improve existing processes and may generate valuable by-products.
- *Environmental.* Cleanup of toxic waste and oil spills will be faster and more effective with the help of genetically engineered bacteria and enzymes.
- *Agriculture.* The agricultural biotechnology industry has the potential to greatly increase the world's food supply, but it faces serious environmental and political concerns.

A great deal more progress might have been made in these fields had it not been for decisions made during the early evolution of the biotech industry. Debates raged among the founders and financiers of the first biotech companies, including Amgen and Genentech, about diversifying widely into industrial and agricultural technologies. Scientists knew that huge advances in these fields were possible, but financing was tight forcing corporate boards to focus their goals on the most profitable targets. There was no question that drug development involved huge risks and a lengthy development process, but it was also clear that successful drugs offered the largest profit margins. In most cases, corporate boards of biotech companies opted for drug development as their organizations exclusive focus. In the case of Amgen, the decision to focus only on drug development was a huge success. But for Genentech, disappointing sales of a drug that had been expected to become a blockbuster cost the company its independence.[13]

MEASURING THE MARKET

Despite numerous disappointments in drug development during the sector's early years, the biotech industry doubled in size between 1993 and 1999 and it continues to grow rapidly. In the United States alone, more than a half million people now owe their jobs to biotechnology. Worldwide, the number of biotech companies is estimated at more than five thousand.[14]

From the swelling ranks of biotech contenders, new corporate powerhouses are emerging and older companies are rising in value. Amgen, founded in 1980, has achieved a valuation in the range of $65 billion (at this writing), based largely on the development of two drugs to stimulate the production of red and white blood cells. Biogen, a company established two years earlier than Amgen, has reached a valuation of $8 billion, thanks mostly to the drug Avonex, one of the few effective treatments for multiple sclerosis. Genentech, the first biotech to go public and the first to put therapeutic proteins on the market (recombinant insulin and human growth hormone) is valued by the markets at approximately $40 billion. The company was taken over by Roche in 1990 when sales of a heart drug failed to meet expectations. As Genentech's business prospects improved in 1999, the company was offered again as a publicly traded stock under the symbol DNA.

On the horizon, names like Millennium Pharmaceuticals, founded in 1993, and Human Genome Sciences, established a year earlier, are emerging as the next industry giants. The extraordinary thing about these companies is that they have been valued at more than $7 billion each although they have never turned a profit. In terms of corporate structure, what distinguishes these companies from other biotech firms is their high degree of diversification. Unlike many more specialized biotech companies, these two companies are committed to developing drugs from the early phase of genetic discovery through the process of development all the way to product testing and approval. Their expertise has been affirmed in collaborations with major pharmaceutical firms that have yielded hundreds of millions of dollars in research revenues.

BIOTECH'S REVENUE POTENTIAL

In March 2000, the *Harvard Business Review* surveyed the biotech industry's long-range potential and published a striking conclusion. Authors Juan Enriquez and Ray A. Goldberg wrote: "The ability to manipulate the genetic codes of living things will set off an unprecedented industrial convergence: farmers, doctors, drug-makers, chemical processors, computer and communications companies, energy companies and many other commercial enterprises will be drawn into . . . what promises to be the largest industry in the world." The largest industry in the world? Coming from any other publication, a prediction that sweeping might well be suspect. But the applications of biotechnology are so broad and the revenues garnered by the industries mentioned are so rich that the authors' prediction is credible if, and only if, one assumes a very long time frame for the industry to achieve its full potential.

Taking the U.S. market as an example, healthcare consumes approximately 14 percent of the country's gross national product, a total exceeding $1.1 trillion according to the U.S. Department of Commerce.[15] Prescription drugs presently account for only 8 percent of national healthcare expenditures, according to the Health Care Financing Administration (HCFA). Because so many diseases have no viable therapies, patients suffering from chronic untreatable conditions must often be institutionalized at great expense. The biotech and pharmaceutical industries would be able to justify a claim on a significantly greater portion of the healthcare budget if they can deliver new therapies to treat or prevent such chronic diseases. Here's one example.

In a single year, U.S. surgeons perform 600,000 heart bypass operations at a cost of approximately $45,000 per operation, a total cost of $27 billion a year. According to the American Heart Association, gene therapy may substantially reduce the need for repeat bypass surgeries. Currently, repeat surgeries account for 20 percent of the total number of coronary bypass operations, costing more than $5 billion annually.[16] New forms of gene therapy have the potential to reduce the need for first-time bypass surgeries by restoring blood flow to the heart through a process called angiogenesis, a technique that stimulates the growth of new blood vessels. Tissue regeneration technologies have demonstrated the ability to repair muscle damage caused by heart attacks. If biotechnology is able to produce therapeutic results as expected, the industry will access a multi-billion-dollar revenue stream.

New treatments will only be adopted if they provide significant savings to the healthcare system and real benefits to patients and many studies show cost-savings to the healthcare system from new therapies. A 1990 study for the publication *Hospital and Community Psychiatry* assessed the financial impact of new medications like clozapine on the cost of treating schizophrenics. These were estimated to cost $4,500 per patient every year. The price may seem exorbitant but not when compared with the cost of institutional treatment, which was then running at $73,000 per year.

Looking back even further, the savings to America's healthcare system from therapeutic innovations have been immense. The Centers for Disease Control in Atlanta estimates that every dollar spent on diphtheria-tetanus-pertussis vaccine saves the system $30. Every dollar spent on polio vaccine saves $6.[17]

If one projects a few years into the future, the industry's revenue potential becomes even larger. Using U.S. spending as an example again, the Heath Care Financing Administration in Washington estimates that national spending on healthcare will reach $2.2 trillion by the year 2008, more than 16 percent of the predicted gross national product (driven in part by the aging of the baby boom generation). Despite such tantalizing potential, it's important to avoid overoptimism. The coming generation of new biotech drugs does not appear to contain any magic bullets. But, although the first large wave of biotech therapies may not be perfect drugs, this does not negate their value. When treating major disease categories, a little progress goes a long way.

For a sense of perspective on the importance of incremental advances, consider the problem of diabetes. Insulin was discovered almost a century ago, and countless thousands of lives have been saved as a result. The production of insulin has been greatly enhanced by genetic engineering to produce a drug with entirely human characteristics. One biotech drug alone, Humalog, a genetically engineered form of insulin treats one million American diabetics. Unfortunately regular insulin injections are not a cure; diabetics suffer many complications from their illness including blindness, stroke, heart disease, high blood pressure, chronic open wounds, and other forms of tissue degeneration that can result in limb amputations or death. The American market for diabetic therapy products is expected to grow to $8 billion a year by 2002, as the incidence of the disease continues its sharp rise.[18]

Among the new technologies being brought to this market are greatly improved insulin delivery devices, including insulin pumps and insulin "pens" that eliminate the need for syringes. The use of needles might also be rendered obsolete by inhalable drug delivery systems that carry insulin to the lungs in tiny droplets called microspheres.

New drugs in the biotech pipeline also promise to improve the effectiveness of insulin by increasing the body's sensitivity. Chronic open wounds will soon be treated with recently approved artificial skin products and tissue regeneration stimulants. There are currently 20 biotech therapies in development for diabetics. Probably the most exciting achievement comes from the University of Alberta where researchers have successfully transplanted insulin-producing cells, called islets, into the livers of diabetic patients.[19] It appears to be inevitable that new therapies will take a significant share of the $8 billion market for diabetes treatments and reduce overall healthcare costs by keeping patients healthier longer.

The success story of Amgen is an excellent example of what is possible for a biotech company that brings a novel form of therapy to market. Amgen was founded some 20 years ago on the strength of an ambitious program to create synthetic human proteins. The study of erythropoietin (or EPO) resulted in the creation of *Epogen*, a drug that effectively treats anemia. Epogen was initially marketed to assist victims of kidney failure. The drug did not restore the health of kidneys, nor did it eliminate the

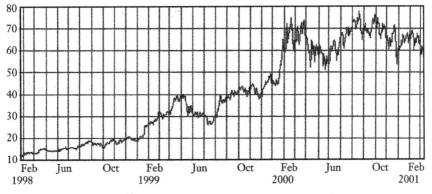

Figure 1.2   AMGEN (AMGN) Three-Year Performance

need for dialysis to remove toxic chemicals from the blood. But, Epogen did prove effective in treating the disabling weakness and loss of red blood cells caused by dialysis. With wider use of the drug, Epogen now generates revenues greater than a billion dollars a year, about half of Amgen's total revenue stream. The company's other lead product is called *Neupogen*, a drug that stimulates production of white blood cells.

The Amgen success story demonstrates the extraordinary impact of just two important products on the value of a young biotech company (see Figure 1.2).

THE SHAPE OF THINGS TO COME

Investment opportunities like the biotech revolution occur only rarely. Uniquely, we have the ability to take a careful look at a major new industry before it reaches maturity. Unlike the personal computer revolution, which saw new inventions rushed to market with amazing speed, biotechnology has evolved slowly in plain sight. After more than 20 years in the early development phase, industry watchers have had ample opportunity to discern the shape of these emerging technologies and pick the most promising contenders. Although relatively few biotech companies have actually delivered products to market, the industry has made a promising start. Carl Feldbaum, president of the Biotechnology Industry Organization, estimates that 270 million people worldwide have already benefited from biotech drugs and vaccines. He calls that "just the tip of the iceberg."[20]

In 2000, the U.S. Food and Drug Administration approved a record 32 new biotech drugs, vaccines, and other therapeutic innovations. The total number of successful biotech products on the market is now approaching 110. If this is the tip of the iceberg, what does the future hold?

The therapies emerging from biotech's first great wave of innovation will quickly be followed by increasingly advanced products as evolving technologies yield ever more sophisticated and more precisely targeted drugs. Some observers believe that the life span of a new prescription drug will begin to shrink from decades to years, perhaps even months as the tide of innovation accelerates.

Eventually, we may be awash in news of increasingly powerful treatments for the most intractable of diseases. It is one of the industry's fundamental beliefs that cures or effective treatments for heart disease, Alzheimer's, cancer, and other catastrophic, refractory diseases will eventually be brought to market. The question for investors is when? New investors have the benefit of being able to examine the track record of companies now approaching profitability. That is rarely the case with emerging industries and technologies. The investment community's experiences with dot-com companies are more typical: creative business plans supported largely by blind faith and sheer optimism.

Biotech IPOs are easier to judge. Most biotech companies go public with a history of commercial and scientific achievement. The number of privately owned biotech firms exceeds the number of public companies by approximately two-to-one and if such companies do go public, there is no need to buy a pig in a poke. A great deal of information is available on established firms.

The encouraging news for investors just entering this field is that commercial biotechnology remains accessible at prices that seem reasonable (for the most part) when viewed in a long-range perspective. Despite recent gains in the sector, stock prices are restrained by the memory of past disappointments and long, frustrating periods of waiting for revenues or profits. Finally, as more of biotechnology's innovations come to market, the sector is gaining credibility. Ken Kam, manager of the Marketocracy Medical Specialty Fund told CNNfn: "I believe we are now at a turning point in the birth of an industrial revolution."

Although the first wave of new biotechnology treatments will certainly improve the practice of healthcare, the industry has a very long way to go. The standard for an ideal drug would have two hallmarks: complete effectiveness and total specificity. It would target only the illness it was designed for and generate no side effects.

If we accept that all people are different, it follows that all disease processes and medicines tend to operate somewhat differently depending on the physical makeup of the patient. That's why patients often react in different ways to the same medicines. Therefore, an ideal medicine would likely have to be custom-made in order to be absolutely specific to the patient. As discussed later in this book, custom-made therapies are a practical approach. The first of them is on the market in Australia: a novel anticancer vaccine made from a patient's own tumor cells.

Genotyping is also a new and important new tool in the biotech industry's effort to create ever more specific drugs. Genotyping is the process of defining a patient's genetic structure to ensure that a medicine will be effective for that individual and that it will not cause side effects. The more precise these methods become, the more specific and effective new treatments will be.

Perfection in drug design may seem like an impossible goal for the industry, but it is no more unreachable than past impossible dreams such as the elimination of smallpox or the decoding of the human genome. Biological systems have proven to be staggeringly complex. But that does not mean they cannot be mastered. Living things are imperfect organizations of matter, energy, and information. Science has achieved a remarkable command over all three of these basic elements during the past century. In today's cutting-edge biotechnology, all of the technical powers and knowledge accumulated through physics, information sciences, chemistry, and medicine are finally brought together.

LESSONS FROM THE PC REVOLUTION

With the possible exception of the creation of the Internet, there is no undertaking as exciting as the worldwide race to find solutions to biological mysteries and discover novel cures for age-old diseases. It is precisely because solutions to some of the most daunting technical challenges facing the industry now appear to be within reach that biotechnology investment is flourishing.

Investors who currently own a diverse portfolio of stocks should consider it important to discern which industries will be affected by the emergence of biotechnology. Believers in diversification should also consider taking a position in biotechnology; just as an investor 20 years ago would have done well to consider carefully selecting some holdings in the computer industry.

The underlying question is the same now as it was at the dawn of the PC revolution: Where will great fortunes be made and where might they be lost? Today, the world's 10 great pharmaceutical companies seem as invincible as IBM did during the 1970s. Twenty years ago, many investment gurus were caught unprepared as IBM found its mainframe market being taken over by desktop and personal computers. IBM tried to gain dominance in PCs, but it took the company many difficult years to adapt. Xerox toyed with inventions like the "mouse" and "screen icons," only to see these inventions brought to market by upstarts like Apple Computer. Wang was decimated by the creativity and flexibility of brash newcomers like Microsoft. As memory, speed, and processing power grew exponentially, hundreds of innovators entered the field, building chips, PCs, drives, and software. There are now as many as 350 million computers in use worldwide.[21]

Consider the parallels between the biotech industry and the emergence of the PC. Big Pharma's dominance of the life sciences field is being challenged by five thousand biotech companies that have sprung up worldwide. Like the microelectronic innovators of the past century, biotech companies are putting highly advanced science and new technologies to practical uses.

The established powers in the life sciences, the huge companies that are often referred to as "Big Pharma" and the major chemical companies, churn relentlessly forward like great ocean liners. Already highly priced by the financial markets, they must run full throttle just to stand still. With market capitalizations in the hundred billion dollar plus range and P/E ratios running as high as 70, the future earning potential of Big Pharma companies has already been built into their stock prices. Most have been valued for endless double-digit growth. My worry, if I held stock in one of the "big ten," would be the downside risk. Eli Lilly was the first to demonstrate how real that danger is when it unexpectedly predicted lower, single-digit earnings until 2002 and instantly lost $35 billion in value.[22]

The total market capitalization of some 400 publicly traded biotechnology companies in the United States provides some perspective about the sector's growth potential. In 1998, the market cap of the entire biotech industry was a relatively puny $97 billion, less than the value of a single multinational drug company. The current market capitalization of the publicly traded biotech companies is approximately $400 billion, roughly the value of four or five large multinational pharmaceutical companies.[23]

As always during the early years, some biotech upstarts will founder. Some will be absorbed by competitors. And a few will become the Intels and Ciscos of a new industrial revolution. The challenge for the investor is to develop novel analytical tools to find tomorrow's leaders.

CHAPTER 2

————•◦•————

Assessing the Biotech Market

Maybe I don't understand this market. Maybe the music has stopped, but people are still dancing.

George Soros, legendary investment guru and billionaire, admitting to fallibility in an April 28, 2000, news conference after disastrous losses in high-tech funds.

WHAT DRIVES BIOTECH PRICES?

"Schizophrenic! Crazy! Insane!" that was the judgment of senior analyst Frank Capiello, when asked in a television interview about the chaotic state of the stock market during the turbulent month of July 2000[1]—a full three months after George Soros had spun his humble "musical chairs" metaphor during the Nasdaq's springtime plunge. The increasingly erratic behavior of the markets has baffled some of the most venerated analysts although few have shown the courage to admit their puzzlement quite so publicly as Capiello and Soros.

One week, a fast-growing economy is blamed by analysts for driving markets down. Next week, a slowing economy is fingered as the cause of a slump. Some experts blame the "Fed" and Alan Greenspan. And, a few even blame independent investors and day traders for volatility.

If conventional analysis is contradictory, how much more difficult will it be for the independent investor to make sense of the new biotech market? In some ways, it can be less confusing because there are fewer unsatisfying rationales, tirelessly delivered by the media to account for ups and downs on the broader markets.

Trends in biotech stocks are also unyielding to mathematical modeling and to most technical analysis. Because only a few dozen of the hundreds of publicly traded biotech companies are profitable, conventional guidelines such as P/E ratios rarely apply. Instead, biotech investment revolves around discovery, information, and innovation. Consider a statistical picture of Millennium Pharmaceuticals shown in Table 2.1 that provides a graphic example.

26

Table 2.1 Millennium Pharmaceuticals Metrics as of July 2000

Market Activity		Share Metrics	
52-week low	$22	Earnings	–$5.67
Current price/share	$112	Sales	$1.98
52-week high	$158	Price/earnings ratio	N/A
Average volume	1.8 million/day	Price/sales ratio	300
52-week change	+390%	Total sales (12 month)	$189 million
Change vs. S&P 500	+340%	EBITDA (12 month)	–$382 million
Market capitalization	$10 billion	Income	–$450 million
Shares on market	47 million	Shares short	4 million
Profitability		EPS growth	–25%
Profit margin	N/A	Beta	0.1
Operating margin	N/A	PEG ratio	N/A

Any analyst taking a cold look at the numbers behind a company like Millennium Pharmaceuticals without knowing anything else about the firm would have to wonder about the sanity of its investors. With no data on profit margin and operating margin, no price/earnings ratio, with a loss of $451 million dollars in the previous 12 months, how could such a company justify a market value that usually fluctuates around the $10 billion mark? Millennium's sales revenues are just over $180 million therefore the "price to sales" number (the ratio of stock market capitalization to sales revenue) is an eye-popping 56 to 1. For a company like Coca Cola, the price to sales ratio was a much more conservative 7 to 1 at the time. Nevertheless, after its second-quarter earnings report, Yahoo Finance listed seven major brokerages calling Millennium a "Strong Buy." The forces keeping Millennium's stock afloat, and making it volatile, are a mix unique to biotechnology.

To understand this perspective, it's essential to put aside, for the moment, the idea of "playing the market," that unsettling expression drawn from the vocabulary of speculators and gamblers. Biotechnology investing is based on a search for companies that have not yet realized their potential value—companies that will rise on the markets when they bring new products to the consumer. Naturally, some investors may want nothing to do with companies that have never realized a profit and that's entirely reasonable. But, if one is searching for companies with the potential to rise substantially in value, an investor must look beyond bleak quarterly earnings reports for companies that have room to grow and a good reason to expect growth.

In biotechnology, the search for value is more of an intellectual exercise than a process of mathematical abstraction from balance sheets and trend lines. Biotech companies are creating innovative and sophisticated products that take an extraordinarily long time to develop and test. It's hardly surprising that profitability typically takes many years to achieve when product development can consume 10 years or more. If and when these new biotech products finally prove successful, they will reach global markets and reap the kind of profit margins that have made pharmaceutical companies the envy of most other market sectors. The success of profitable biotech companies like Amgen, IDEC Pharmaceuticals, MedImmune, and Biogen, to name a few, demonstrates that the worldwide drug market is hungry for groundbreaking therapeutic products developed through biotechnology.

To borrow a concept from Warren Buffett, this is a form of value investing. The biotech investor is searching for companies with unrealized value, a quality that is relatively rare among stocks on the wider markets. The unrealized value in biotech stocks is not to be found in revenue sources that have somehow escaped the notice of the financial industry. Instead, the value of biotechnology must be judged in terms of promising products, intellectual property, corporate excellence, and scientific innovation.

Warren Buffett's idea of value investing did have a caveat that precluded the purchase of companies he didn't fully understand. That restriction kept his firm, Berkshire Hathaway, clear of both the perils and the profits realized by high-tech investors in recent years. Without question, biotechnology is relatively difficult to understand, but far from impossible. I would agree with Buffett's avoidance of companies that have an incomprehensible business plan, but I'd hate to miss out on the unrealized value of a growth industry like biotechnology because it requires a little extra effort and research to understand.

Sound investing depends on informed judgment and meaningful precedents. The rise in value of the profitable biotech companies mentioned previously provides one form of precedent. So does the multi-billion-dollar valuation pattern established by major pharmaceutical companies during takeovers of leading biotech firms:[2]

- Johnson & Johnson paid $4.9 billion dollars to acquire Centocor.
- Warner-Lambert paid more than $2 billion for Augouron.
- Roche paid more than $3 billion for Genentech and recouped much of its investment by spinning the company out with an IPO in 1999.

Recent takeovers of biotechnology companies by other biotech firms have also supported this level of valuation. These transactions provide empirical proof that unprofitable companies can be rationally valued in the billions of dollars.

Before getting down to specific investment and stock selection strategies, let's look at some of the basic forces driving the biotech markets. Eight key factors underlie the biotech sector as a whole. These are shifting forces, constantly affecting one another and driving change in the sector. Biotechnology is not immune to forces driving the wider markets, but the sector is also affected by these special considerations that are unique to the industry.

JUDGING BIOTECH VALUATION, RISK, AND UNCERTAINTY

Investing in biotech requires a whole new way of thinking about the word "value." One biotech executive painted this arresting picture during an interview: "Imagine a herd of ordinary-looking goats as valuable as a $100 million drug factory. Imagine a single corn stalk worth $30,000."[3] He was describing plants and animals that have been genetically engineered to produce humanized antibodies or proteins. Such customized organisms already exist, producing experimental medicines to treat human diseases. Their intrinsic value lies in the highly specialized genetic programming they carry.

Operating without profits, most biotech corporate valuations are supported by the most rarefied and hard-to-value of all assets: intellectual property and scientific expertise. Much of the industry's intellectual property, however brilliant, has yet to prove its worth. Market perceptions of such intangible assets are as mercurial as the flow of opinion on the Internet. Uncertainty about corporate valuation is, oddly enough, one of the constants in the industry—a driver of volatility.

Consider the valuation of companies in the field of genomics. How exactly does one put a price on companies like Incyte Pharmaceuticals or Celera, companies that are painstakingly investigating the components of DNA? A scientist might well say such knowledge is priceless, but an investor must make a reasonable judgment about market prices.

Incyte and Celera are two of the toughest investment calls in the biotech field. They have never made a profit and there's no telling when, or if, they will. Both have made impressive claims on intellectual property, but it's unclear whether the patent office will support them. The two companies are expanding their client bases and business partnerships but it would be fair to say that their time lines to profitability are measured in years and there is no general agreement on just how many years might be required. The longer investors must wait for profit, the greater the risk they assume. A sensible framework for valuation of Incyte and Celera has been debated at length without consensus among biotech investors and analysts. That's one reason the two companies went into a prolonged market decline after the initial excitement over the decoding of the human genome wore off. In the absence of a consensus about valuation, the safest bet is the lowest one.

All innovative biotech companies, even those with substantial profits, must contend with an unusual degree of uncertainty about their future profitability. No biotech company is exempt from speculation about the viability of its product development pipeline and its business model. The more exotic and specialized a company's research and development program becomes, the less investors can know with any degree of certainty about its true value.

Factors such as success in clinical trials for a new drug or "proof of concept" for a new technology will lower investor risk—the more a biotech company is able to prove its technology platform and demonstrate the practicality of its products, the more likely it is to achieve market stability and dispel investor doubt. But there are no absolutes in a field based on experimentation and discovery, only varying degrees of uncertainty among biotech companies.

Comparing three biotech companies with radically different profiles provides a useful demonstration; Celera, Human Genome Sciences (HGS) (HGS is the usual abbreviation, but HGSI is its stock symbol), and Amgen.

Celera has demonstrated extraordinary scientific and technical prowess by sequencing the human genome in a period of time no one had imagined possible. It is an industry leader. The company had revenues of $12.5 million and losses of $45 million in 1999. By the end of its fiscal year, June 2000, revenues were up to $42 million and losses were up to $92 million as the company expanded its research efforts. There is little likelihood that Celera will ever be allowed to fail because it has the backing of its very proud parent, the genetic equipment giant, Applera Corp. formerly known as PE Applied Biosystems. The market value of Celera more than doubled to the $3.5 billion range in a single year.[4]

But Celera surprised many investors when it substantially lengthened its time line to profitability by committing to a major new program of capital investment and research aimed at the immensely difficult problem of defining protein structures. The company's CEO, Craig Venter, said during one of his many television interviews following the company's success in the mapping of the human genome, "I didn't set out to make money. I would have been glad to do this experiment, not for the money." Spoken like a true scientist. But not exactly the careful words a CEO should use. Venter says a profit may appear in about five years.[5]

Both Celera and Human Genome Sciences are deeply committed to a broad program of discovery among genes, proteins, and SNPs also known as single nucleotide polymorphisms (pronounced "snips"). SNPs are subtle and seemingly random variations among the smallest components of genes (nucleotides). Some inherited SNP variations are believed to cause genetically based disease and others are responsible for genetically inherited characteristics like eye color. The SNP discovery challenge is to find the individual genetic building blocks (the single nucleotides) that correspond to various illnesses; this information may then lead to cures through gene therapy.

Although Human Genome Sciences didn't grab headlines, as Celera did, by mapping the human genome, HGS research appears to be more focused on practical products than Celera's efforts. Both companies have huge and growing research budgets and both are losing money, but HGS has already developed several promising drugs for clinical trials. Celera has customers subscribing to its database, but HGS has potentially valuable drug products in the pipeline, and collaborators. Lots of them. The HGS list of partners reads like a who's who of biotech and Big Pharma.[6]

Human Genome Sciences is sharply focused on narrowing the time line between genetic discovery and the development of new medicines. In a recent earnings announcement, the company took in revenues of $8 million during the third quarter of 2000 and generated a net loss of almost $13 million. (The annual revenue picture is somewhat distorted by one-time charges.) Currently, most HGS revenues are derived from research and collaboration fees, and the first drug in the company's pipeline is certainly more than a year from market.

The last subject for this comparison, Amgen, is currently the most successful company in the biotech sector with revenues of more than $3.5 billion and net income of more than $1 billion, based largely on the sales of two key drugs. Amgen's drug development pipeline appears to have similar potential to that of HGS.

Despite its profitability, Amgen's valuation, in the $65 billion range, is only a little more secure than Celera's $3.5 billion and HGS's $8–$10 billion price tag. Amgen's high valuation depends on investors' faith in its drug development pipeline as much as its revenue growth trends. Human Genome Sciences has insufficient revenues to support its market capitalization, but it boasts an outstanding business and scientific reputation, lending credibility to its drug development potential and its market value. In both cases therefore, investors are depending on the potential success of drugs in clinical trials to justify Amgen & HGS stock prices.

The most uncertain question of all is the true value of Celera. The company's scientific achievements are destined for the history books, and Celera still possesses a world-beating stable of scientific talent. One Celera executive boasted, during the company's early genomic investing frenzy: "There are only ten mathematicians in the world who can master the type of algorithms we use. Celera employs three of them."[7]

Scientific talent qualifies as an asset, albeit an intangible. In fact, until substantial revenues from database subscriptions appear, virtually all of Celera's valuation is based on such intangibles.

The higher the degree of uncertainty about the valuation of a biotech company, the higher its volatility. As perceptions of the industry change, just as they did in the case of Celera, the biotech market assigns new valuations, unrestrained by the usual metrics that connect conventional stock prices to profits. Celera's total market capitalization has rocketed wildly from $1.3 billion at the start of the biotech boom in late 1999, to a peak of approximately $14 billion and back down to less than $2 billion all in the space of a single year. Scientific excellence alone has not provided the company with market stability.[8]

Drawing on parallels between the growth of biotechnology and the emergence of the computer industry, an important lesson stands out in one example. The work of Seymour Cray in the development of early super-computers was groundbreaking science. Old Cray computers are still admired for their power and have recently been used to solve some of the complex mysteries of protein structure. Yet, scientific excellence alone did not ensure the company's success. (The Cray name was recently purchased from Silicon Graphics by the Tera Computer Company. Seymour Cray died not long after losing control of his foundering company.)[9]

In biotech investing also, scientific achievement alone guarantees very little. Even the best-run companies in this sector must manage their businesses in an environment of uncertainty about the outcome of product trials and rapidly changing science and technology. Perhaps, as greater revenues and more conventional balance sheets emerge among biotech companies, subjective judgments about stock prices will be increasingly stabilized by a meaningful financial track record. For the time being, it's more a matter of investor perceptions and risk management.

To diminish the sector's inherent unpredictability, practical criteria for investment decisions are essential. As the *Harvard Business Review* wrote, investment parameters for biotechnology have yet to emerge. Certainly, credible business plans and decreasing time lines to profitability are among the key investor criteria for risk reduction in biotech stock selection. Specific criteria for choosing companies as investment targets are set out in Chapters 3 and 4.

BIOTECH RISKS AND REWARDS

Among biotech companies developing new medicines, investors could be faced at any time by FDA rejection of a lead product. When the stock market receives news of a product setback for a biotech company, it is utterly unforgiving.

The story of Progenics Pharmaceuticals is a stark example of the downside risk. The company announced in May 2000 that a partner in one of its cancer trials was quitting the program due to reportedly lackluster test results from an experimental treatment for advanced skin cancer. The market slashed a stunning 70 percent from Progenics' share price in a single day.

The presence of many mitigating factors provided little support for the company's valuation. Progenics is in Phase II trials with another cancer vaccine and it is doing very promising work in the field of AIDS research. All that made no difference to the markets, which were in full flight.

For shareholders, the damage was done in an instant. Progenics' stock was immediately slashed from $23 to $10 per share.[10] On the day of that harrowing plunge, analysts at CIBC World Markets cut their rating on Progenics from "strong buy" to "buy," but they did maintain a degree of optimism, setting a 12-month price target of $40 on the stock, a prediction of a fourfold increase that did not happen. At this writing, Progenics is still languishing in the low double digits although the company reports that its disputed cancer vaccine is generating positive results in ongoing clinical trials (see Figure 2.1).[11]

The harsh dynamics underlying most biotech investments had come into play. Without established profits or "proof of concept," the value of Progenics stock had no fundamental supports. Only investors' hopes had kept it afloat. And, under a cloud of apparent failure, the perception of Progenics' in the marketplace changed from "potential blockbuster" to "loser" in a flash.

There are many developing biotech companies today with potential similar to that of Progenics, but they maintain a much higher market capitalization. One difference is that Progenics has delivered its first disappointment. In this subjective sector, a company that carries the burden of a public failure carries a greater weight of investor fear. Its scientific credibility has been called into question. Progenics has also become a much riskier investment because its next drug product is well back in the development pipeline. Longer time lines to profitability mean greater risk.

Most unprofitable biotech companies remain tenuously suspended somewhere between two powerful extremes. At one extreme is the prospect of multibillion-dollar gains from the development of a new drug. A successful

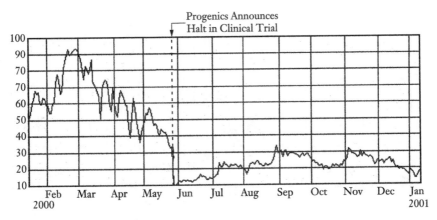

Source: © Copyright BigCharts.com.

Figure 2.1   Progenics

drug can quickly turn a penny stock into a major player. But, at the other extreme is the danger of sudden product failure that could all but wipe out share values. The slightest change in the balance of expectation and risk will trigger sharp price changes.

Biogen stands out as an example of the upside potential (see Figure 2.2). Company shares have grown from a split-adjusted value of little more than a dollar a share in 1987 to a peak in the spring of 2000 above $100. The decisive event in the company's history was the introduction of AVONEX, a drug for certain forms of multiple sclerosis. AVONEX sales are approaching $500 million per year. The company also collects license fees on a number of other products and has an ongoing research program. Total sales are in the $800 million range and the profit margin is 36.9 percent. With one major therapeutic success, licensing fees, and an ongoing research and development program, Biogen's market cap has briefly exceeded $10 billion . . . a stunning return for investors who got on board early.

Medimmune and IDEC Pharmaceuticals are two often-mentioned companies that grew in value more than 3,500 percent during the 1990s. The dream of achieving results like these is at the heart of a biotech investor's ambitions.

Kris Jenner, manager of T. Rowe Price's Health Science Fund coined the term "moonshots" for stocks that have the potential to yield at least 20-fold returns. Leverage is what makes a moonshot a practical possibility.[12] Hundreds of biotech companies are trading in single-digit share prices although they may be working on therapies that could be worth billions. Leverage like that on a single successful biotech investment can make up for many disappointments. More mature, highly valued biotech

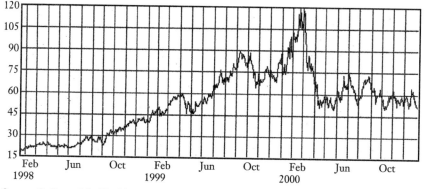

Source: © Copyright BigCharts.com.

Figure 2.2 Biogen Three-Year Performance

companies like Immunex may no longer have moonshot appeal. As share prices rise, leverage is reduced.

The degree of risk attached to an investment in a biotech company is partly related to the size of the organization. A major pharmaceutical company may release a new drug or discontinue a trial and see a comparatively minor change in its stock price because it has a number of successful products on the market to stabilize revenue projections. By the same token, the larger biotechs are less vulnerable to volatility because they are buttressed by revenue streams from existing products, a history of proven accomplishments, or a strong drug development pipeline. A solid track record lends extra credibility and stability to a biotech stock. Smaller, unproven companies offer far less assurance to investors and far more volatility.

Until this sector is fully mature, it will continue to be pushed and pulled out of balance, driven by its inherent extremes. Armed with a clear understanding of the sector and its harsh dynamics, the investor may choose to stay the course for the long run, enduring down cycles by believing that the best companies will ultimately deliver rewards. During boom cycles, investors may choose to take a profit when stocks are becoming overvalued. The important thing is to recognize these cycles and their underlying dynamics as a fact of life. By maintaining a sense of calm, and by recognizing these forces, it's possible to retain a pragmatic perspective and focus on realistic goals during the biotech market's inevitable gyrations.

THE "BIOTECH BUBBLE" PHENOMENON

Every few years, wild optimism gets the upper hand in this sector. Risk is ignored. But only temporarily, and always at the investor's peril.

Because biotech valuations are so subjective and the potential rewards so great, overvaluation is an ever-present danger. Biotech investors would be well advised to remain on guard for the signs of a bubble in the making. The most obvious signal is a simultaneous rise in the value of all biotech stocks, even marginal prospects, in the sector. Historically, bubbles have developed after long periods of stagnation in share prices, a problem so severe and prolonged in the past that some biotech executives routinely refer to it as a "nuclear winter."

Early biotech investors will remember all too well the biotech bubbles of 1984, 1987, and 1991. Biotech bubbles are typically set in motion by exciting developments in the field. Some veteran investors will recall the high expectations and media hype that surrounded the discovery of the first interleukins and interferons (agents of the immune system). Talk of a magic bullet against cancer became the rage in the media as researchers speculated about a single agent that might knock out all forms of this large family of diseases. No magic bullet has yet been found because all cancers have unique characteristics. Nevertheless, the excitement and speculation created unrealistic hopes and increasingly unstable markets that no single breakthrough could support. The same tide that lifted all boats in the sector quickly ebbed when the new discoveries delivered disappointing results.

As it turns out, there are more than a dozen important interleukins, so many that they have now been classified as a family of materials called cytokines. All have somewhat different functions, so it is small wonder that these first magic bullets were powerless against many types of disease and had unpredictable side effects. They are also very difficult and expensive to synthesize.

Biotech bubbles and nuclear winters may be two sides of the same coin. They are both temporary extremes. The difficulty biotech companies encounter in the pursuit of financing during a nuclear winter depresses the market value of all companies in the sector, pushing many to artificial lows. When a promising development thaws the markets, the companies involved in the breakthrough rise astronomically, as was the case when Celera rose from less than $20 a share to more than $250 during the initial excitement over the genome. Neither extreme appears to reflect the company's true value.

It is difficult to resist the temptation to join the frenzy of a biotech bubble. No investor wants to stay on the sidelines while huge paper profits are being made. It is sometimes difficult to ascertain whether one is in the grips of a bubble or participating in a long-overdue correction.

Before the most recent market bubble, biotech prices had been severely depressed for several years and higher values did seem justified for many companies. But two indicators suggested a bubble was in the works. The most obvious was the breathtaking speed of price increases. The other was the nature of buying patterns. Most biotech stocks shot up in tandem, suggesting that purchases were being made indiscriminately. Certainly a few critics were saying the sector had become overvalued, but no one could predict reliably when the cycle would peak. The wisest investors went to cash while prices were still rising (see Figure 2.3).

Biotech bubbles are often blown apart by seemingly unimportant events. From the start of the collapse of the 2000 biotech bubble, many analysts declared there was no cause for investor alarm. As one commentator put it, the biotech sector had merely become "a little too frothy." Others in the industry labeled the market implosion as misguided because it had been sparked by a joint statement issued by President Clinton and British Prime Minister Tony Blair that hinted at the possibility of more stringent standards for the granting of genetic patents. Analysts pointed out that a new standard for patents on genes would affect only a few biotech companies.

The day after the White House statement, analyst Michael King at Robertson Stephens issued "Strong Buy" upgrades on five biotech stocks: Affymetrix, Axys Pharmaceuticals, Gene Logic, Genset, and Millennium

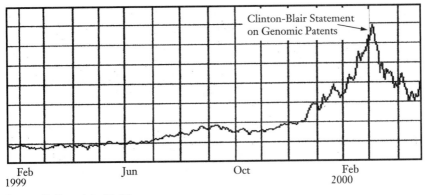

Figure 2.3   Biotech Index from January 1999 to April 2000

Pharmaceuticals. King said investors had misunderstood the news from Washington. CS First Boston reiterated its "Strong Buy" ratings on companies including Amgen, Biogen, and Incyte Pharmaceuticals, saying the sector's slump was unfounded and recent declines had created buying opportunities. Investors who followed such advice paid a heavy price.[13]

With the advantage of hindsight, we now know the implosion wasn't really caused by a few unclear words from the White House. Nor was it the fault of investors who failed to grasp the meaning of the presidential statement and panicked. The underlying reason for the sectorwide collapse of biotech stock prices was the preceding frenzy of speculation, momentum trading, and unreasonable optimism sparked by excitement over the mapping of the human genome. Many companies had become overvalued and all paid the price.

Rational markets are modulated by credible projections of a company's or an industry's growth potential. Extremes tend to be held in check in more mature sectors of the economy by a generally accepted foundation of experience and expectations. For example, it's relatively unlikely that a conventional company like Gillette will suddenly triple its revenues. Nor is it likely that the world will suddenly abandon the practice of shaving. There is little on the horizon that can violently upset the relatively stable equilibrium of expectations for such a company. (The stock did slump and gyrate during the year 2000 because of slowing growth rates but it was not a panic.)

By contrast, when biotech bubbles implode, prices plunge with lightning speed. To use George Soros' metaphor, the music stops and suddenly everyone is looking for a chair. In the absence of concrete parameters for biotech valuations, it's not just one chair that is suddenly missing but the whole floor. The sector's lack of financial substance permits extreme valuations on the high and the low end of the cycle.

The dynamics of boom and bust are amplified even further by the relatively low liquidity of the sector. Large buy orders have a greatly exaggerated effect on stock prices if the number of available shares is relatively small. By the same token, the sector's low liquidity squeezes prices into a nosedive during the bust phase of the cycle when too many sellers try to find buyers in a small and rapidly diminishing pool. Only by getting out of a bubble early will you have cash to invest after it bursts.

Watch out for these warning signs:

- Sharp daily stock price increases unconnected to corporate news (10% fluctuations are common; changes of 20% or more should be a cause for concern).

- SEC requests for explanations of sudden, unexplained price fluctuations.

- Daily price peaks that slack off before market closing indicate heavy day trader pressure on values.

- Sharp increases in trading volume indicate speculation by momentum players, likely not sustainable increases in value.

Always keep in mind that time lines for biotech product development are very long and there is rarely, if ever, any great hurry to take a position in these stocks if one is buying for value and holding for the long term. These long development periods tend to drive speculators away over time and prices drift downward in the interim between a burst of corporate news and the conclusion of product development. Although development time lines are being compressed, investors would be wise to wait for slumps in biotech stock prices to buy at bargain prices. This lag between innovation and production has been an important factor in biotech's nuclear winters.

Biotech bubbles offer unusual buying opportunities when they collapse, as they inevitably do. During the most recent sectorwide implosion, the best biotech companies fell just as sharply as any others, creating exaggerated lows that lasted for more than a month. It is difficult to time any market but, in the aftermath of a biotech bubble, good investments will be available for a fraction of their probable future value. Don't try too hard to find the bottom. Try to find the best companies and take a position with the perspective of several years rather than several months in mind.

THE RELATIONSHIP BETWEEN CREDIBILITY AND RISK

The announcement of the mapping of the human genome has little immediate practical value for medicine but it remains one of the cornerstones in the shifting fortunes of the biotech marketplace. Decoding the human genome was a scientific challenge so large that it seemed an unthinkable waste of time and money to many scientists a mere 15 years ago. Now it is history. More than three billion components of DNA, the fundamental building blocks of life have finally been mapped. Determining their functions and putting this knowledge to use will take more time.

The broad growth of biotechnology stocks, and the rise of biotech indexes during 2000, has been attributed to many factors. Probably the biggest influence remains the astonishing announcement back in November 1999 by Craig Venter, president of Celera Corporation, that his company would complete the mapping of the entire human genome during the upcoming 12 months. For biotech markets, which are inherently very forward-looking, the prospects of the entire sector seemed to change fundamentally around that time.[14]

The *New York Times* put the event into vivid perspective, writing: "It was as if private industry had announced it would land a man on the moon before NASA could get there. As if an upstart company intended to build the first atom bomb."[15] Venter intended to finish mapping the genome years ahead of the original target date set by the international public consortium known as the Human Genome Project. In fact, much of Celera's work was performed in the space of a single year by an army of analytical robots and a computer farm that has been called the largest civilian supercomputer in the world. The Human Genome Project, by comparison, had originally allowed itself 15 years to complete the task but was given a sharp push by Venter's audacious announcement. It's important to point out that the work completed by the Human Genome Project was a major contributor to Venter's breakthrough.

From a biotech investor's point of view, the most immediate result of the genome race is a change in the credibility and, consequently, the perceived potential value of the biotech sector. From the month of Venter's announcement, in November 1999, the biotech market underwent a sea of change. Gains in most biotech share prices were exponential. When the Human Genome Project announced that it too would complete the mapping of the genome during the year 2000, the sector began moving even more dramatically.

Significantly, it wasn't just Celera's stock that shot up during the months following Venter's announcement. Nor was the surge confined to companies working in genomics, like Celera. Instead, biotech companies with little use for the genome—companies which had languished in the single or low double digits for years—all began rising in tandem, doubling, and tripling in value, sometimes even more, over the space of four months. It is an uncanny experience to review the charts of biotech companies from that time. Almost without exception they show the same exponential growth curve and a simultaneous crash. But, the next few months showed that a fundamental change in the sector had taken place.

Very few biotech companies returned to their 1999 trading ranges. Share values in the sector stabilized during the two months after the crash and many began to rise again. By autumn, a number of companies rose again to levels very near their all-time highs. The broad strength of the sector's recovery after the crash is telling. Investor's didn't turn gun-shy as they had in the past, although they did become more discriminating.

Even now, few laypersons understand the full scientific meaning of the mapping of the human genome, but the basic importance of this milestone caught the imaginations of many investors. One of the great mysteries fundamental to human life had been unraveled by a commercial enterprise. The perception of risk had been moderated by a watershed achievement. The hope for reward had been buttressed.

In addition, the market's sudden realization that hundreds of drugs were in the industry's pipeline helped build the sector's credibility. "We stand on the threshold of a golden age of medical and scientific discovery," proclaimed one pharmaceutical industry publication. "Our ever expanding knowledge of the human body, the process of disease, and our genetic make-up will be translated into new medicines to prevent, cure, and treat diseases that now seem all but invincible."[16] Lofty hopes. Now, suddenly, more realistic.

The dizzying fall of the Nasdaq Biotech Index in March and April 2000, stopped more than two hundred points above the inflection point of the previous November. The moving average shows the bursting of the bubble caused only a brief downturn in the overall trend. Confidence had been shaken but, for the first time, not demolished by a speculative bubble. Both the Nasdaq and Amex Biotech Indexes continue to outpace the S&P 500 average for the remainder of the year (see Figure 2.4).

Biotech Mutual Funds, which had taken their place among the fund industry's top 10 performers during the first quarter, showed up in even greater numbers in the second quarter's top 10 list.

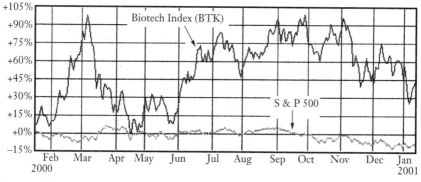

Source: © Copyright BigCharts.com.

Figure 2.4   Biotech Index versus S&P 500

Could the industry's second surge be another bubble? This time the sector's performance demonstrated two important differences. First, the rate of increase was more moderate. Second, the market had become more discriminating; driving up the values of certain companies while other biotech stocks remained relatively stagnant. Some of the biotech industry's recognized leaders, including Millennium and Human Genome Sciences, soared while others failed to keep pace.

The mapping of the human genome brought new cash as well as credibility to the sector. The brief boom had helped biotech companies in the United States and Europe raise a record $19 billion in public and private financing during the first quarter of 2000, an increase of 420 percent from the same quarter in 1999.[17] When I questioned industry executives about their fears during the March crash, none, except those contemplating future initial public offerings (IPOs) expressed concern. For the first time, many companies had been able to take the opportunity to fill their coffers with enough cash to last beyond a one- or two-year horizon—enough time to bring products in their pipelines to market. As the year progressed, the number of biotech IPOs worldwide set all-time records.

Among independent investors, the sensational stock surge of the first quarter provoked many to take a new look, or a first look, at a sector that had been slowly transforming itself during years of obscurity. The bursting of the bubble may have done some damage to investor confidence but the sector's speedy recovery demonstrates that biotech's credibility had become more sustainable even during the most volatile of years.

One of the most interesting aspects of the biotech sector's recovery was the relatively weak comeback of Celera itself. Even at the height of its scientific glory, Celera stock languished more than 50 percent below its peak value and critics of the company were questioning its ability to make a profit in the foreseeable future. Despite its great achievement, Celera's stock was not nearly as well rewarded as shares in companies with aggressive plans to market medical breakthroughs. It seems sadly ironic that Celera's achievement helped add enormous value to the entire industry but its stock has not shared in the sector's dramatic recovery.

CONVERGENCE AND SYNERGY IN BIOTECH DEVELOPMENT

Christopher Reinhard, President of Collateral Therapeutics, points to another key factor in the emergence of useful and profitable biotechnology. He calls it convergence. As Reinhard explains it, great synergy becomes possible when sophisticated new technologies mature and converge.

Reinhard's company is currently testing a form of gene therapy for heart disease. He sees his area of biotechnology at a convergence point of three overlapping industry technologies (see Figure 2.5).[18]

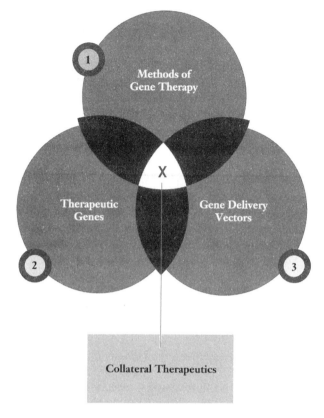

Figure 2.5   Converging Technologies

Each circle represents a broad area of expertise. Circle 1 represents methods of gene therapy: the nuts-and-bolts mechanics of snipping out or replacing a defective portion of DNA, or, perhaps, switching a particular gene on or off on a given chromosome. Such techniques have emerged from decades of institutional research and are slowly being commercialized by companies like Collateral.

Circle 2 represents therapeutic genes. Finding defective genes and creating therapeutic genes is an immense challenge, dominated by the industry segment called functional genomics. Some experts believe it will take more than a century to learn most of the truly valuable information to be gleaned in this field. (Industry competition and technological convergence may shorten time lines impressively.) Important names in this circle include Gene Logic, Maxygen, Double Twist, and Incyte.

Circle 3 represents gene delivery. This is a much tougher problem than most experts expected. Cells isolate and jealously guard the DNA master switches inside the nucleus. Delivering instructions to this switching center, or rewriting its code, involves the challenge of getting a chemical messenger through the door and to the right place so it can do its work. Important names in this the drug delivery circle include Gentronics, Alkermes, Hemispherix, Emisphere, Inhale Therapeutics, and Vical.

Collateral's Reinhard says the therapies his company is developing require the convergence of these three challenging disciplines. His job is to bring them together to produce the final product: a useful treatment for heart disease. Companies at the convergence point will reap the greatest rewards. Reinhard says it's something like being a baker. When all the ingredients are at hand, the recipe in mind, and the tools prepared, the final (and most valuable) product can be realized.

Collateral's technique involves injecting a messenger virus carrying a genetic signal directly to heart muscles. This therapy causes an effect called angiogenesis; it stimulates the growth of new blood vessels in target areas where the heart muscle suffers from restricted blood flow. The treatment has worked well in trials so far and the company claims lives have already been saved. It is one of several techniques that might reduce the need for heart surgery. Three disciplines: genetic discovery, drug delivery, and gene therapy converge in this one innovation. If proven, it has the potential to be much safer and less expensive than the surgeon's knife.

Convergence is also occurring at a more fundamental level in biotechnology. At a recent conference on biotech development, Monica Doss, the director of the Council for Economic Development of North Carolina noted the convergence of biotechnology and computer science was a noticeable trend. "These industries are coming together," she commented, "Especially in genomics. When you go into their businesses you see keyboards and computer screens, rather than test tubes."[19]

Computers have become powerful tools in genomic research because the genome has now been spelled out in a four-letter language, A, C, T, and G. These four letters represent the four molecules, or nucleotides, that are the building blocks of the master molecule, DNA. Just as computers are able to execute powerful programs by carrying out the instructions encoded in a linear stream of zeros and ones, it is a relatively easy task for a computer to translate the four-bit language of the genome into binary code. Suddenly the immense analytical power of the computer has been applied to human software. The effect could be compared to the digital revolution, which has transformed most electronic devices.

This breakthrough has been a long time coming. The basic workings of genetic inheritance have been known since the Austrian monk, Gregor Mendel, conducted his experiments with pea plants in 1866. The basic structure of DNA was explained almost 50 years ago, when James Watson, Francis Crick, and Rosalind Franklin discovered the famous double-helix structure of DNA. Only now is this knowledge beginning to reach a point of convergence between life sciences and advanced information technologies.

Electronic microchip manufacturing techniques have also been adapted to biological study, with the creation of "biochips." A single chip smaller than a quarter is currently able to screen thousands of variations (SNPs) in a DNA molecule. In effect, the chips (also called microarrays) are ultra-miniaturized laboratories, each containing the equivalent of 12,000 test tubes that will glow if a positive reaction takes place at any point. Biochip microarrays feed information directly into computers through laser scanning. In itself, the biochip is a revolutionary development, and the coupling of biochips with computers is a landmark technological convergence.

Now, IBM has begun work on a $100-million supercomputer project called "Blue Gene," which is intended to become the most powerful computer in history. Blue Gene will have its work cut out for it when it is tasked to crack the excruciatingly difficult problems of defining protein structures (called protein folding), a challenge even more complex than mapping the genome.

Computers are helpless without instructions and increasingly sophisticated biological software is being created to mimic the interactions of molecules such as proteins and DNA components in the human body. Hundreds of thousands, possibly millions of mock chemical interactions can be electronically synthesized in a day, resulting in new, highly specific drug development targets. The hot new research term for this kind of technique is *in silico*: the use of computers to isolate, manipulate, and test digital models of life forms. *In vivo* (tests in living organisms), and *in vitro* (biological testing in glass petri dishes) will never be completely obsolete, but in silico analysis and pretesting of drugs in computers is hugely accelerating the traditional, dogged work of the lab technician. As more advanced technologies converge, their power is not just added together. It is multiplied.

In its landmark article on biotechnology, the *Harvard Business Review* highlighted the importance of a previous industrial convergence: Binary computer code established a similar language for widely disparate industries including newspapers, broadcasting, music, and telecommunications. The language of zeroes and ones has transformed these industries and linked them together. The fusion of biotechnology with information technologies could be even more revolutionary. To quote a concise summary from the *Review:* "The ability to manipulate the genetic codes of living things will set off an unprecedented industrial convergence: farmers, doctors, drug makers, chemical processors, computer and communications companies, and many other commercial enterprises will be drawn into the business of life science. This transformation promises to be every bit as wrenching as the one set off by the Internet."[20]

BIOTECH'S EXPONENTIAL ACCELERATION

The first effect of the computer-biotech convergence has already appeared in the business of drug discovery. Not long ago, the pharmaceutical industry used to bemoan the bottleneck in the process of creating new drugs. The problem was the chronic shortage of viable drug candidates—a shortage of molecules that might have therapeutic effects. The convergence of genomics, chemistry, computing, and bioinformatics has put an end to that bottleneck. Promising drug candidates are pouring out of biotech companies using these new techniques and some drug development companies now complain of being awash in promising targets. As one pharmaceutical executive explained it, "We used to search for a needle in a haystack. All of sudden we have a lot more haystacks."

All sectors of the biotech industry are being swept forward by a powerful current of acceleration. Applera, one of the giants in the field of automated, computerized biological equipment predicts the speed and power of bioinformatics will do much more than help discover new drug candidates. By bringing together "high throughput screening" (industry jargon for ultrafast chemical analysis), powerful computer farms, and ingenious software, bioinformatics should be able to significantly compress the long time lines involved in picking out the best drug candidates and proving their worth.

The mapping of the genome was the most dramatic and public demonstration of the acceleration of this field. The Pharmaceutical Research & Manufacturing Association (PhRMA) points out that the discovery of the gene causing cystic fibrosis was achieved in the 1980s after a nine-year effort. In 1996, the discovery of a gene causing Parkinson's disease took nine days.[21] As mentioned previously, the patent office is now considering applications for patents on some 20,000 genomic discoveries.

Biotech scientists and researchers have brought Moore's Law, which states that computing power will double approximately once every 18 months, into the world of drug discovery.[22] Biotech equipment makers have built machines capable of a truly revolutionary rate of chemical analysis and this degree of acceleration shows no sign of slowing. Aurora Bioscience executive Douglas Harrell says his company has drug targets "coming out of our ears." Illustrating the acceleration of the process, he told a biotech investment conference that chemists used to do 36 assays of potential targets per day. "Now, we do 100,000 tests in a day. We do 12 years work in 12 hours."

Diversa Corporation of San Diego, which has been collecting genes from a huge variety of living organisms, claims it has the capacity to analyze more than one billion genes per day. "Using a fluorescence activated cell sorter we can sort 50,000 cells per second," Diversa executive Hillary Theakston enthused, "that's 10,000 times as fast as the previous standard in chemistry."[23]

Medarex, another biotech leader, says it has achieved a crucially important speedup in the time to take a drug candidate from initial research to clinical trials. Big Pharma companies claim that the process typically takes five years, but Medarex has announced that a new prostate cancer drug has gone into Phase I trials after a single year in research.[24] Moore's law is being proven all over again in the biological discovery process.

Equally significant in the acceleration of biotechnology is that this information explosion is being shared and processed in a way never before possible, using the networking power of the Internet. Years ago, Robert Metcalfe, the inventor of the Ethernet, enunciated a second law of the information age when he declared that the power of a network increases exponentially with the number of computers connected to it. Like Moore's Law, Metcalfe's law is also coming into play in biotechnology. One of IBM's projects is the creation of a networking hub called "Discovery Link" designed to unify the databases of the biotech, life sciences, and agricultural biotechnology industries.

Hundreds of companies have joined their new computing powers with networks of partners who have synergistic goals. The "Alliance for Cellular Signaling" is a consortium that brings together 50 scientists in 20 universities and researchers from several biotechnology companies as well as five major pharmaceutical firms. Myriad Genetics calls this alliance a massive scientific undertaking to discover how cells communicate. Using a broadband Internet connection, the partners will share in the creation of a "virtual cell," a computerized model that can be used to test new drugs in silico. Another group of biotech companies has launched the "Functional Genomics Consortium" to jointly discover the specific functions of genes. Yet another worldwide consortium of academics and corporations is creating a genomewide map of the genetic markers called SNPs (single nucleotide polymorphisms), single-letter variations in the master DNA molecule. Completion of the SNP map will greatly enhance the understanding of disease and the differing reactions to drugs among individuals. This growing store of data is freely available on the Internet.

One of the key factors in judging a biotech company is an assessment of its networking ability. Major universities including Harvard and Vanderbilt have networked with commercial genomic supercomputers.[25] The immensely wealthy companies that make up Big Pharma all boast of alliances with biotech collaborators. Thousands of discoveries registered for biotech patents in Washington are available for further study and development to researchers via the World Wide Web. As the players in this nascent industrial revolution share and analyze trillions of bits of data,

Metcalfe's law is proving to be as relevant as Moore's law. Bioscience is being transformed into a high-speed, highly networked global information processing industry.

One executive with a Big Pharma company recognized this transformation early and explained it in a novel way. In 1993, Jan Leschly, then CEO of Smith Kline Beecham signed a deal with Human Genome Sciences, agreeing to pay $125 million for gene-based data leading to drug discovery. He summed up the moment succinctly seven years later in an interview with *Worth Magazine*. "Suddenly we realized that we're an information company . . . because it's the software—all the research, the networking, marketing that's important. It's not the pill that costs so much. It's the software."[26]

If pills have become software, and if Moore's and Metcalfe's Laws continue to apply, biotechnology will be swept forward on an exponentially accelerating current of innovation similar to the computer revolution of the previous 20 years.

IGNORANCE IS RISK

"Smart Companies, Dumb Investors." That was the headline for a *Business Week* story written during the biotech market panic during March 2000. As mentioned, the trigger for the panic had been a joint statement by President Clinton and British Prime Minister Tony Blair that suggested patents on some genetic discoveries might be called into question. Almost instantly, billions of dollars were wiped from the value of the entire biotech sector. As *Business Week* pointed out, most of the companies being hammered by the market had no stake at all in genomics and gene patents and would therefore be unaffected by the White House statement. "Dumb Investors," the magazine concluded, were punishing all biotechs equally.[27]

In fact, investors who bailed out early turned out to be the smart ones. The "dumb" ones were those who bought indiscriminately near the peak, knowing little or nothing about the sector or the stocks they were buying. Biotechnology remains an enigma to the layperson, and buying into the sector without some knowledge increases the degree of risk.

Time and again, biotech executives have said they applaud any effort to improve public understanding. An investor-relations executive from Cura-Gen, a company using genomic analysis to create new drugs, described one exasperating situation. He told me he had received a call from a nervous investor who asked him: "Listen. I own twenty thousand shares of your company. Can you tell me exactly what it is you do?"

As biotechnology continues its advances on the scientific front, the industry is leaving many investors far behind. The field has always been difficult to understand and its inherently long time lines to profitability erode many an investor's inclination to accept arcane scientific projects on faith alone. The industry's increasingly exotic approaches to problem solving are difficult for any layperson to grasp. In an unintended way, quantum leaps in biotech science create quantum setbacks in public comprehension.

Although the parallels between the emergence of the biotechnology and computer industries generally apply, there is an important difference. Computers have become a household and business tool, familiar to millions of people who have developed a workable understanding of how their machines operate. Biotechnology has much less chance of becoming a familiar household tool and it will never be understood by the average investor as well as home computers are. After all, how many people really know how a pill as familiar as aspirin works?

Without a working understanding of the science behind the sector, biotech investors will have difficulty in getting a meaningful grasp of the value of the intellectual property they own. During a market downturn, investors may lose confidence in organizations they do not understand, especially if those companies are not turning a profit.

This "ignorance factor" will have much less power to drive markets up or down as biotech companies bring real-life products to market and increase their revenue streams. Finally they will be able to present balance sheets that can be analyzed by more traditional methods. As the sector becomes more profitable, scientific comprehension will become less significant to investors, compared with analysis of revenue flows.

However, only the early investors in this field will reap the gains to be realized by embracing an important new sector before the general investing public decides to get on board. Getting a workable grasp on the science and technology under development is essential to making wise choices during the industry's emergent phase. It is crucially important to learn which of the industry's many sectors and subsectors hold the greatest promise and which pose the greatest risk.

DIFFERING FROM DOT-COMS

The ephemeral nature of the biotech industry's valuation has created some unfortunate perceptions. Biotechnology investment is frequently compared with investing in dot-coms because the two sectors share several characteristics:

- In general, companies in both sectors are not yet profitable.
- Their value lies in ideas whose viability has not been proven.
- They are both volatile.

Such comparisons offend executives and scientists in the biotech world. Dr. Michelle Glasky, Vice President of Scientific Affairs for Neotherapeutics, colored visibly when I asked her if she resents firms in her industry being compared to dot-com companies. "We have intellectual property!" she declared emphatically. "There's an intrinsic value to what we're doing here."[28] Neotherapeutics (NEOT) is developing therapies for the regeneration of nerves, an approach that shows great promise in trials on Alzheimer's disease patients.

Glasky is categorical in pointing out critical differences between a biotech like Neotherapeutics and a dot-com. She allows, "It will be a long time—years before we have revenues." But that's where Glasky draws the line. "We're not going to disappear tomorrow and we're clear about risks!" she says. Pointing out that Neotherapeutics has substantial reserves of cash, she adds, "We're fiscally conservative, very careful about how we spend money." There's also the matter of a multibillion-dollar market anxiously awaiting an effective Alzheimer's treatment. Dot-com markets are always a mouse-click away from oblivion.

Glasky adds one last thought: "It's nice to invest in something that's good." She's right. True, most people have no understanding of the sector. But among those who do, there is an unspoken sense of excitement in being even a minor player in the realization of a truly historic scientific and technological goal. It is a field of science and industry that will ultimately, as Dr. Glasky said, "do good."

CHAPTER 3

———•◦•———

The Keys to Biotech Investing

If you think research is expensive, try disease.
Mary Lasker, "evangelist" for medical research,
as quoted by Nobel Prize-winning DNA scientist
Arthur Kornberg in *The Golden Helix*

WHAT TO LOOK FOR IN BIOTECH COMPANIES

Constant vigilance and research are the keys to picking biotech stocks and making buy or sell decisions. The industry generates a seemingly endless stream of technical and scientific innovation, and almost every day there is news of progress that could alter the development of an industry subsector.

The Internet has provided independent investors with unprecedented access to information and unique tools to guide decision making. Unlike previous periods of major structural change in the economy, this time the information is available to anyone with access to the Internet. Even better, it is often free.

Take a moment to log on to any of the following invaluable information sources.

- Certainly the most extensive and useful Internet resource for biotech investors is Biospace.com. BioSpace has a wonderfully large number of research options, covering the field by sector, by region, by disease—the list of choices runs to almost three pages on a computer screen. Push any button and begin exploring. Biospace.com also offers daily news bulletins delivered free of charge by e-mail.

- Another good source of e-mail alerts is qxhealth.com, which provides daily biotech news developments and options to customize the flow of information to the biotech subsectors that interest you.

50

- *Yahoo Finance/Multex* offers crisp corporate profiles and a deep pool of information about corporate financial and investment considerations, excellent research, and analytical tools. It is difficult to find more detailed corporate information available free of charge.

- *Recap.com* provides specific details about biotech clinical trials, research programs, and industry partnerships. This is the best source for these specifics.

If you take some time to look over these sites and sign up for e-mail bulletins offered by BioSpace, you'll soon realize one of the challenges facing biotech investors . . . a problem much like trying to take a sip of water from a fire hose. In a single week's news file, I routinely sift through more than 200 reports, many with important implications for major disease categories and sectors of the industry. To provide some sense of the news flow investors face, here's a small sampling of Biospace.com headlines from an ordinary, randomly chosen news week in mid-July 2000:

- *"Avax Becomes First to Commercialize Cancer Vaccine for Melanoma."* A new anticancer vaccine made from a skin cancer patient's own tumor cells goes on the market in Australia.

- *"Manipulating Simple Interactions to Create Artificial Bacteria."* Scientists discover a way to make chemicals assemble themselves spontaneously into microscopically small "tubules" that may be useful in drug delivery.

- *"Aethlon's Hemopurifier Removes 70 Percent of HIV Virus in One Hour."* A new, biologically active filter reduces patients' viral loads dramatically giving AIDS drugs a fighting chance.

- *"Maxim Submits NDA for Maxamine."* The Food and Drug Administration is being asked in a New Drug Application to permit the marketing of a drug for skin cancer patients whose disease has spread to the liver. Currently, a patient whose cancer has spread (metastasized) to the liver has virtually no treatment options and no chance of long-term survival. (Please see Epilogue for an update on this company.)

- *"Human Genes Turn Mice into 'Pharm' Animals."* A feature on Abgenix and Medarex, two companies breeding thousands of mice that have been genetically engineered to produce human antibodies for treatments against cancer and heart disease.

- *"Genzyme Seeks to Test Cystic Fibrosis Drug."* After a decade of research and repeated failures in gene therapy experiments, Genzyme believes it has discovered a novel approach to treat this fatal hereditary disease. Four competitors have abandoned the field in the past year, partly because gene therapy remains such a difficult challenge.

As extraordinary as such news reports seem to a reader like me, the mainstream news media have shown only sporadic interest in pursuing in-depth coverage of biotech breakthroughs. I have discussed the emergence of biotechnology with friends in the news departments of several major networks and the consensus among them seems to be "it's not ready for prime time." No problem. The greatest gains are made by those who are first in their field.

In the absence of wide coverage and consensus about biotech stocks, investors need to set some benchmark criteria to make informed decisions.

Drug development in biotechnology involves a time-consuming sequence of events. Typically, the process begins with the discovery of a biologically active protein or a gene responsible for the creation of important proteins. Researchers must then find a way to turn the gene in question on or off to start or stop production of the protein. Alternately, they must find a way to synthesize large quantities of the molecule under study for use in laboratory and animal testing. If these early tests show therapeutic potential, the Food and Drug Administration will consider an IND (Investigational New Drug) application for permission to begin testing of the new medicine in human subjects. Trials are conducted in three phases, described later in this chapter. If the objectives of these trials are met, the FDA then considers an application to permit sale of the drug.

The clock begins ticking backward on a drug development company's exclusive right to produce a new product from the moment a patent application is filed. Every delay in testing can be very costly. If a biotech company creates a drug that generates a billion dollars a year (e.g., Epogen), the loss of a year's marketing exclusivity due to early patent expiry can result in revenue declines of 70 percent or more ($700 million dollars a year), due to generic competition and price cutting.

The key tests of a biotech company's investment profile are:

- *The product pipeline.* It should be broad enough to support corporate valuation in case one product fails during trials.
- *Markets.* Products being developed should be valued in accordance with the size of market they serve.
- *Phased trials.* Because this is a lengthy process, companies are unlikely to generate revenues for many years unless drug trials are in the final (pivotal)phase.
- *Patents.* Patent protection for products and intellectual property should be clearly supportable.
- *Alliances.* Development partnerships provide revenues and scientific validation.

The Importance of the Product Pipeline

Few, if any, criteria are as important to a biotech company's future prospects as its product pipeline. That's always the first thing an investor should check. Look for companies that have a large complement of therapies in clinical trials. The more advanced these products are in the arduous trials process, the nearer they are to FDA approval, which means the company in question is that much closer to profitability.

Biotech investors frequently become interested in a company after reading news about important scientific progress or a major success in tests of a single product. But it is rarely apparent from reading news stories or press releases just how strong or weak a company's drug development pipeline actually is. Typically, a company's self-description in any news release will declare that the firm has several products in development, undergoing various phases of clinical trials—not very specific or helpful. The release will usually describe the company's disease targets with a "kitchen sink" approach. For example, a novel antiinflammatory agent might (one day) prove to be useful in a host of diseases including arthritis, asthma, stroke, heart disease, organ transplants, psoriasis, and lupus. The press release writer will typically name every possible disease target even though the company has no intention of trying the drug on more than one or two illnesses in the foreseeable future. (It sometimes turns out that drugs don't perform as hoped against a disease target during trials but show unexpected effectiveness against other conditions. Viagra is one example.) Such releases inevitably end with a glowing description of a company's prospects (followed by a disclaimer warning that anything and everything could go wrong).

Investors would be unwise to buy stock in a biotech company without obtaining much more specific detail about its development pipeline. Answers to the following eight questions are critical:

1. How many products are in development?
2. How many products have actually made it into clinical trials and how many of them are still being tested in the lab?
3. Of those drugs in clinical trials, what stage have they reached?
4. When did they enter their current phase and how much time remains in the trials process?
5. What diseases will these products treat?
6. How effective have they been in testing so far?
7. How many products are being tested against the same disease and how effective have they proven to be so far?
8. Among the competitors in the field, which is the most advanced in the trials process?

One would hope that a company's Web site would provide a complete picture of its pipeline, but that's not always the case. Investors need to know what stage each new therapy under development has reached in the trials process, and as much information as possible about a therapy's effectiveness. Many corporate Web sites contain only generalized statements and greatly condensed information, presumably to accommodate the short attention spans of many Web users.

Answers to the key questions about a biotech company's pipeline are relatively easy to find elsewhere on the Internet. But, before getting down to specific research techniques, it's important to define the various phases of biotech drug testing.

The Phases of Clinical Trials and Investment Pitfalls

Above all, keep in mind that there are many product failures during the three main stages of clinical trials. As has often been said, trials are not merely a part of the approval process; they are a part of the entire scientific experiment behind drug creation. A drug entering clinical trials may have shown spectacular results in preclinical testing on laboratory animals or in any number of other experiments, but drugs often act in unexpected ways in human subjects. On occasion, fortunately rarely, the experiment will kill the patient. In one notorious case, the entire technology of gene therapy received a setback when an 18-year-old patient died while undergoing an experimental treatment for a rare liver disease at the University of Pennsylvania in 1999.

The formal approvals process begins with an IND, Investigational New Drug application, which is intended to prove to the Food and Drug Administration that a therapy appears to be safe and that proper testing procedures have been followed. Approximately 85 percent of IND applications are approved. Unwelcome surprises can appear anywhere in the course of the clinical trials process. According to the Pharmaceutical Research and Manufacturers of America (PhRMA), a pharmaceutical industry public relations and lobbying organization, only one out of five drugs that enter clinical trials will ultimately be approved for market by the Food and Drug Administration.[1]

Phase I Trials

A Phase I trial is the first experiment with a human being, sometimes called a safety or toxicity test. The new therapy is usually tested on healthy volunteers and, sometimes, tested on the patients who are seriously ill and have failed to respond to other forms of therapy. The main objective is to learn whether a small dose of the drug will cause unanticipated adverse reactions.

Phase I trials also involve experiments to determine the optimum dosages of a new drug. Researchers must determine how a drug is absorbed, metabolized, and eliminated from the body. The duration of the drug's effectiveness is also calculated. Very few patients are exposed to this risky rite of initiation, usually less than 100. This process can last as long as three years and it often provides little of the information that investors require, an evaluation of a drug's effectiveness against disease.

Going to Phase II

Phase II trials should reveal more about the drug's effectiveness against a particular form of disease, its safety, and its mechanisms of action in the human body. A larger number of patients participate in Phase II, sometimes more than 300, as researchers experiment with various techniques and patient groups to determine the optimum therapeutic approach and dosage. The process lasts approximately two years.

Press releases issued at the end of Phase II trials often declare the drug under investigation has provided significant benefit to patients. Investors need to read between the lines as much as possible to determine just how beneficial the results have been. Relatively neutral phrases such as "significant benefit" may indicate only a moderately encouraging outcome. If other therapies are already on the market, a new drug must meet exceptionally high standards to gain eventual FDA approval. Therefore, look for detail showing dramatic outcomes among Phase II patients. Imprecise phrases and vague details about patient outcomes expressed in dense scientific jargon may conceal a mediocre result. Clear results are usually accompanied by clear language.

On the other hand, any benefit at all may be valuable in the management of previously untreatable diseases or some forms of cancer that do not respond to any other therapy. In the case of Alzheimer's disease, for example, no drug on the market offers much lasting improvement. It may be that the progress of Alzheimer's disease can be halted by a cocktail of promising new drugs now under development in much the same way a combination of drugs has sharply reduced the death rate for AIDS patients.

In the fight against cancer, an enormous variety of therapies is in trials against the many different forms of this disease. That fact affects my reading and analysis of cancer trial results. Drugs that are sent on to Phase III will invariably show some benefit, but the investor's problem is to choose among the many types of therapy under investigation. Investors should look for a high standard of effectiveness at the end of Phase II cancer drug trials, given the amount of competition and the significant chance of failure inherent in the upcoming trials and approvals process. I am not usually interested in making an investment in a company whose lead compound has demonstrated only a reduction in tumor size or a marginal increase in survival times among patients. "Remission" and "tumor free" are words I see increasingly often in reports from companies testing cancer therapies, and that kind of result gives me the greatest confidence when judging the value of cancer drugs in a product pipeline.

It's also an encouraging sign if severely ill patients participating in the trial are given permission to continue with a therapy after the end of any phase of the trial process. A decision like that provides compelling evidence that a test drug is providing important benefits to test volunteers without severe side effects. In such cases, it would be inhumane to suddenly discontinue treatment because a research stage has ended.

Phase III Trials

The decision to move on to Phase III trials is a significant endorsement of a drug's effectiveness because no company would dare to take the next step without reasonable confidence that it would justify the enormous costs involved. Phase III trials involve a large-scale, painstaking, and time-consuming process. The object is to prove conclusively that the new drug is not just effective but more effective and safer than current therapeutic options.

Typically, Phase III trials are conducted among more than 1,000 patients in a large number of healthcare facilities to avoid any errors or bias that might affect the result in a single institution. In medical parlance, it is called a *multicenter* trial. Often hospitals in several countries are involved. Phase III trials are *double-blind*, meaning neither patients nor doctors know if a placebo or the experimental drug is being administered. On rare occasions, some clinical trials are *open label* meaning both doctor and patient know they are receiving the experimental drug because it would be unethical or medically unwise to administer a placebo.

The object of a Phase III trial is to see how well the drug works in the largest possible number of test subjects over a long period of time, sometimes more than three years. Researchers will also attempt to find out if any important side effects appear in a larger patient population.

THE NEW DRUG APPLICATION

Assuming the drug eventually meets the efficacy and safety criteria set for Phase III testing, the results are then sent to the FDA for product approval (an NDA or new drug application). Even at this point the product may fail, if the FDA decides that a drug provides little therapeutic and cost benefit over the best existing treatments.

Approximately 10 to 15 percent of all NDAs are rejected. FDA approval usually takes about a year but it may require even more time if additional testing information is required from the applicant. The FDA sets high scientific standards, and it is not uncommon for a promising drug to be rejected because the scientific and statistical framework of a Phase III trial falls short of the agency's requirements.

On rare occasions, test results may have been distorted by overoptimistic researchers to give a drug an exaggerated appearance of effectiveness. When this is discovered, the effect on a biotech company and its share prices can be disastrous. The stock of a company called Gliatech fell in value almost 70 percent in just two days following allegations that inaccurate data had been submitted to the FDA. That wasn't all. A proposed acquisition by Guilford Pharmaceuticals was scrapped, the CEO was forced to resign, and a class action lawsuit has been filed on behalf of shareholders.[2]

Time lines in this process, already very long, may be extended even further by a unique medical and ethical problem. Vical, a company testing gene therapy, is approximately two years behind schedule for Phase III trials of a new treatment for skin cancer. The company's lead drug appears to be effective and safe, but it is still experimental. This presents doctors and patients with a dilemma. It may be that a new drug is very promising but, because Phase III trials usually involve the use of a placebo, patients who are critically ill face a difficult choice. Do they enroll in a clinical trial knowing that they may be given a worthless placebo instead of the new treatment? Many doctors and patients avoid the gamble involved in double blind clinical trials and opt for the most widely accepted therapy already on the market. In the case of Vical, Phase III trials have been delayed because the company has had considerable difficulty enrolling patients who are willing to take the risk of trying an unproven drug and, perhaps, being given a placebo.[3] Such concerns result in as many as 80 percent of clinical trials falling behind schedule due to enrollment problems.[4]

The Tufts Center for the study of Drug Development estimates that fewer than a quarter of all drugs entering the trials pipeline will finally make it to FDA approval. Even then there is some risk. As the recent controversy surrounding the combination of diet drugs called fen-phen showed, rare and dangerous side effects might not appear until the drug is in use among a great many people. When severe side effects do surface in the general population, drug companies face more than the failure of a key product. They also face immense liability risks if patients suffer adverse health effects. For the protection of patients and the company, Phase IV trial monitoring is required after a drug's release to monitor safety.

Often a drug will prove effective against conditions beyond the originally licensed disease target and doctors will prescribe it for "off-label" use, a practice that involves some risk for the patient but may also establish new markets for a product. A drug company is not permitted to encourage this practice but it may decide to initiate new clinical trials to gain approval for use of the drug in larger patient populations if off-label use is showing encouraging results.

The organization that speaks for major drug companies, the Pharmaceutical Research and Manufacturers of America (PhRMA), estimates that drug development is a 15-year process, fraught with risk every step of the way. By Big Pharma standards, the cost of bringing a new drug to market is $500 million or more. The industry claims as few as 1 in 5 drugs sent to clinical trials will make it to market. PhRMA goes on to paint an even gloomier picture saying only 3 drugs of the 10 that make it to market will recover their development costs.[5]

The pharmaceutical industry's report is deliberately sobering and is probably out of date. (We'll take a harder look at Big Pharma later.) As discussed, biotech companies are doing everything they can to shorten the time lines and reduce the risks of failure. Big Pharma estimates the initial discovery process, a step that typically produces 250 drug candidates, takes between 2 and 10 years,[6] but accelerated analysis and high-throughput screening technologies are cutting discovery times to a fraction of the previous standard. Preclinical screening of promising drug candidates, estimated by PhRMA to require several years, has been sharply accelerated. Human Genome Sciences recently announced that it had taken a drug from genomic discovery in 1999 to preparation for clinical trials in just over a year. (The drug is an immune system stimulant called BlyS and it's expected to enter trials as a cancer fighter and a treatment for immune deficiency in 2001.)

Among the products finally approved for testing, it is increasingly likely that the drug candidates of the future will have a much greater chance of success and fewer side effects because of the greatly improved powers of analysis that the biotech industry has brought to bear on the discovery and selection process.

Compressing the process even further, many early development phases can be overlapped as automated systems perform some of the complex processes involved in screening drug candidates simultaneously. Even the FDA has helped speed up the process of governmental oversight by adding 600 new reviewers to its staff, an innovation made possible by asking the drug companies to help fund the system. A report from the Tufts Center for the Study of Drug Development says FDA approval time for a new drug application has decreased sharply from two years required when the first recombinant protein was introduced in 1982. Now approvals take about a year.

There's no method, at least not yet, to compress the immense amount of time and money consumed in the three main phases of clinical trials. In fact, the Tufts study says that the clinical trials process has grown much longer: increasing from an average of 32 months during the 1980s to 58 months in recent years. One of the reasons, according to Tufts, is the increased sophistication of new biopharmaceutical products and a corresponding increase in the complexity of disease mechanisms the biotech industry is targeting.

This is the bottom line for biotech investors. On average, more than six years of effort and expense are required to bring a new biotech product from the laboratory to the public. It's important to keep this in mind when you hear exciting news about a revolutionary product going into Phase I trials. There's no good reason to buy in haste. Even if the market moves up dramatically on the news, the stock is very unlikely to remain at that level for more than half a decade.

ANALYZING A SAMPLE COMPANY

To bring this examination of the criteria for choosing a biotech investment down to a more practical level, consider the example of Millennium Pharmaceuticals. Millennium is widely regarded as one of the model companies emerging from the biotech field. The company is organizing itself, in its own words, as "the biopharmaceutical company of the future," a slogan that means integrating the drug discovery process from gene identification through drug discovery, trials, and approval, all the way to patient management. The industry calls this "vertical integration."

Millennium's pipeline seems promising.[7] The company's lead compound, *Campath*, is being considered by the Food and Drug Administration for licensing as a treatment against adult leukemia (chronic lymphocitic leukemia or CLL). *Campath* has passed all three trial phases and has been granted "fast track" status by the FDA, which means the drug is sufficiently promising to warrant an accelerated six-month priority review. It has also been granted orphan drug status, which will result in an extended period of market exclusivity. Approval is by no means guaranteed, but if *Campath* is licensed to go to market, Millennium will have its first major success. Please see the Epilogue for an update on this product. Twenty thousand patients are diagnosed with lymphocytic leukemia in the United States and Europe every year. Current therapies have no beneficial effect on half of the total number of the patients who try them. These patients will likely die within six months and all patients treated with existing therapies will eventually relapse.

Although *Campath* is no magic bullet, it appears to be effective and it is showing promise as a possible treatment for much larger groups of patients who suffer from other forms of leukemia, multiple sclerosis, and organ transplant rejection.

Interestingly, Millennium did not create *Campath*. It licensed the drug from Burroughs Wellcome, which had intended to develop this "monoclonal antibody" for the treatment of rheumatoid arthritis. The company was disappointed when arthritis patients suffered from low levels of lymphocytes—the infection fighting cells in the lymph nodes. CLL involves the overproduction of lymphocytes so *Campath* was an attractive candidate in Millennium's fight against CLL.

The next product in the company's pipeline is aimed at inflammatory bowel diseases, including ulcerative colitis and Crohn's disease. Other products in the Millennium pipeline show promise for treatment of stroke, heart disease, asthma, and cancer, but they are in earlier phases of clinical trials. Much more is in the works in laboratory testing. These drugs may not be perfect and it's unlikely that all of them will survive the rigors of clinical trials. But the potential for a major revenue-producing product in the foreseeable future is considerable. Millennium does a slightly better than average job of describing its pipeline in its Web site (www.millennium.com), but there are more comprehensive sources. Many writers suggest looking up annual reports, but there is a simpler and more up-to-date way to assess pipelines on the Internet.

Visit the recap.com Web site (www.recap.com), and you'll have free access to a comprehensive database of clinical trials for any biotech company stretching back many years. You can also get a list of products in preclinical development, in other words, drugs still being investigated in the laboratory, and you'll see a list of past trials that have failed. I'm not aware of any other source as informative about drug pipelines as recap.com (short for recombinant capital).

In the Millennium Pharmaceuticals example, simply go to the clinical trials portion of the recap.com site and type in the company name. The list of Millennium projects fills almost two pages. It's apparent here that Millennium's lead compound, *Campath*, is progressing well in trials against more than just one disease target. Other experimental drugs in the Millennium pipeline are also undergoing simultaneous trials against a variety of major diseases. From the sections of the page marked simply with an "L," meaning laboratory, it's apparent that Millennium is investigating treatments for other big targets including obesity and heart disease. The list is impressively large although the company is somewhat lacking in drugs that have made it as far as Phase III trials. On the other hand, Millennium is unusually diversified for an emerging biotech company. In total, it has six clinical trials underway and more than 10 drugs in preclinical testing. The company has other virtues among the important criteria that add value to a biotech's stock value and these are discussed later.

AIMING FOR BIG MARKET POTENTIAL

One criterion you'll often hear about is the "big target," shorthand for a major disease. Obviously, the more prevalent and serious a disease is, the bigger the demand for a treatment and the greater the potential reward.

Current drug sales give only a hint of the size of potential markets (see Table 3.1).[8]

In Table 3.1, I have noted a few major diseases for which the current market size is severely limited by the small number of treatment options or by the absence of treatments that provide substantial benefits for the patient. Cancer is the second leading cause of death in the United States with many disease subtypes. It is potentially a much larger target than the current $16 billion sales figure suggests because many cancers are not effectively treatable by any drug currently on the market. Similarly, for diseases like Alzheimer's, current markets have virtually no predictive value because available treatments have only marginal effects on the disease. A major advance in this field would be a multibillion-dollar breakthrough.

Although the potential rewards are large, several important factors should be weighed in any decision. As a rule, the bigger the target, the greater the competition. For example, 122 drugs are in development for HIV/AIDS; 316 drugs are in the works for cancer.[9] Choosing from the many companies engaged in this kind of work requires special consideration.

A simple guideline is to compare a company's progress in the development pipeline to its competitors. Those treatments closest to FDA approval have, in general, the greatest likelihood of gaining market dominance. Again, recap.com provides a valuable resource for those wanting to know

Table 3.1 Markets for Big Targets

Target Disease	Approximate Current Market
Arthritis	$6 billion
Asthma	$8 billion
Bacterial/Infection	$23 billion
Cancer	$16 billion (limited by current options)
Cardiac disease	$11 billion (limited by current options)
Depression	$7 billion
Diabetes	$6–7 billion
HIV-AIDS	$4 billion
High cholesterol	$11 billion
High blood pressure	$22 billion
Multiple sclerosis	$1 billion
Obesity	$1 billion (limited by current options)
Pain	$9 billion
Parkinson's disease	$1.5 billion
Schizophrenia	$3 billion
Thrombosis	$1 billion
Total	$129 billion

Data from qxhealth.com.

who's in the lead. Visit the recap Web site and go to the area focused on diseases. You will be presented with many possible criteria but, for the moment, it should be sufficient to enter the name of a disease and leave the other categories wide open. Start the search engine and you'll be presented with a list of every company working in that field. You will find the most interesting prospects, or the most serious competition, among the companies that are the most advanced in the process of clinical trials.

Of course, it may not be quite that simple. In the case of Alzheimer's disease, the characteristics of the illness are generally known but the mechanisms behind it remain a mystery. Many approaches toward a cure are in the works, but the drugs currently undergoing trials are emphatically not cures. Among the most interesting trials, Elan Pharmaceuticals of Ireland is testing a drug that could dissolve amyloidal plaques, the deposits that develop in the brain of an Alzheimer's patient. Neotherapeutics is developing a drug that stimulates the growth of nerve cells, which the disease progressively destroys. These therapies hold the potential for significant progress in the fight against Alzheimer's but again, neither is a magic bullet. Ultimately, one drug may prove to be more effective than the other or they may work synergistically if taken together.

The Alzheimer's example demonstrates the challenge facing anyone assessing a drug pipeline. It is essential to collect research about a disease and factor in the available knowledge about a drug candidate's mechanisms and effectiveness when making decisions. There is little incentive to invest if a drug's effects are marginal, as they are with most Alzheimer's treatments approved so far. It's also essential, after one has made an investment, to keep an eye on emerging competitors. News sources like Biospace.com and Qxhealth.com are valuable resources.

Turning back to our sample company, if we scrutinize the Millennium Pharmaceutical pipeline, an interesting and frequently used strategy can be seen at work. As mentioned, the company's lead compound, *Campath*, is going through Phase III trials against a comparatively small albeit important target: chronic lymphocytic leukemia. Simultaneously, *Campath* is undergoing earlier phases in the trials process against much bigger targets including multiple sclerosis and non-Hodgkin's lymphoma . . . targets with multibillion-dollar potential. That begs the question: why not go after the big targets with this drug first?

Millennium has apparently been cunning enough to understand that the trials process can be much faster and cheaper when bringing an "orphan drug" to market. Patients with CLL have essentially no long-term treatment options. Delay in bringing a viable treatment to market is a death sentence to many sufferers. That's why *Campath* was given "fast-track" and "orphan drug" status by the FDA. It can be given much faster review. Because the pool of patients is smaller, Phase III trials can also be more limited, therefore quicker and cheaper.

If *Campath* is approved and marketed in this relatively small patient population, it will effectively have an endorsement of its safety for other applications. And, if the drug is successful in treating chronic lymphocytic leukemia patients, it will simultaneously indicate potential for a larger patient group suffering from non-Hodgkin's lymphoma. Assuming effectiveness is demonstrated in practice and side effects are tolerable, this outcome will lower the burden of proof and accelerate trials of *Campath* for other diseases. Information from off-label use can also help in the testing and approval of an orphan drug for larger disease targets. By aiming at a small target first, Millennium has compressed the time and expense involved in tackling big target diseases.

THE IMPORTANCE OF ALLIANCES

Partnership agreements have helped biotech companies survive and maintain a degree of independence during the industry's leanest years. For investors, these partnerships have now become an important sign of strength in a biotech company.

Alliances in biotech take many different forms. One of the most common is an agreement between a smaller biotechnology firm and a major drug company to share the future profits from a promising new therapy in development by the junior partner in return for periodic cash infusions called "milestone payments." Typically, the Big Pharma partner pays the biotech ally a set amount when the smaller company achieves certain predefined goals in the discovery and drug-testing process. The biotech company benefits by receiving enough cash to carry on and the Big Pharma partner also stands to profit by gaining access to promising new developments without the enormous effort, investment, and risk involved in starting a discovery program from scratch. As Jim Moltz, chief strategist for the ISI Group put it during a television interview, "Biotech needs Big Pharma's deep pockets and Big Pharma needs biotech."[10]

Because clinical trials are extremely rigorous, an experienced partner can also lend a great deal of expertise to help the testing and approvals process go more smoothly. If the partner is a veteran of the trials process, it will be able to prepare a new drug application that is fit to undergo FDA scrutiny. If a therapy is approved, the biotech company may need help in large-scale drug manufacturing and it may require considerable marketing assistance. This is where the big pharmaceutical companies excel. The two groups have complementary strengths.

An investor should pay close attention to a biotech company's alliances in weighing the pros and cons of any decision to buy stock. Alliances mean much more to investors than mere assurances of subsistence revenue streams for money-losing companies. Most important, an alliance with a major partner is a stamp of credibility. The fact that an established drug company with its experienced scientific and managerial staff has examined a biotech venture and found it worthy of receiving millions of dollars in payments over many years is a strong endorsement of its potential. Alliances with major research institutions also demonstrate scientific credibility. Partnerships with other biotechs working in complementary areas of research may expand the potential of a small firm through networking and adaptability to cutting-edge technologies.

But beware, partnership agreements often allow pharmaceutical giants to withdraw their support at any time. The termination of a partnership can be a serious setback to biotech companies and to their investors. Inhale Therapeutic Systems lost more than 10 percent of its value, approximately $200 million, when Lilly decided to drop a joint project to develop a protein-based drug,[11] and another biotech ally of Lilly, Sepracor lost 40 percent of its value when the pharmaceutical giant decided to stop joint development of a successor to its blockbuster drug, Prozac.[12] In some cases, major pharmaceutical companies also pit biotech rivals against one another, assigning both a task, such as drug discovery, and reward only the firm that delivers results first.

Long-term revenue potential through alliances is also worth contemplating. Most biotech companies now require royalties from any drugs they have helped design or molecules they have discovered on behalf of a larger company. If the resulting drug makes it through trials and becomes a commercial success, its biotech creator will share a portion of the revenue stream. Given the length of the trials process, the silent biotech partner may receive a windfall many years after it has ceased work on a royalty-producing drug. As you read about some of the drug development deals already in place, you should consider the potential for future royalty streams from the many drugs being designed by biotech companies for major clients.

Lately, as financing has become more accessible, many biotech companies have been able to bring drugs all the way through the discovery and trials process by themselves. The later in this process a biotech company makes an alliance with a partner, the greater its share of the revenue stream. Drug discovery royalties generally provide the least revenue and require the smallest commitment of financial and technical resources from the drug's creator. Biotech companies that have taken a drug through the trials process with the help of a partner will likely agree on profit sharing. If a biotech company has borne all of the costs of preparing a drug for market, it may agree to allow a large pharmaceutical firm to handle marketing and distribution and will pay royalties to the multinational firm for this service. In a few cases, ambitious biotech firms will attempt to handle sales as well, thereby reaping all the profits but incurring the expense and risk of expanding a company into unfamiliar terrain.

Returning to Millennium Pharmaceuticals for an examination of partnerships, the company has completed two deals of truly major importance.

Back in 1998, Bayer paid $465 million for access to Millennium's expertise in gene discovery and drug development. The Bayer deal calls for Millennium to deliver 225 new drug targets. This is a remarkable validation of the biotech company's ability to decipher genes and design drugs, especially considering that the deal was concluded several years before the mapping of the human genome was completed. Beyond the initial payment, the long-term potential for revenues from a diverse number of royalty generating drugs is considerable.

More recently, Millennium clinched a strategic alliance with the pharmaceutical giant Aventis that allows Aventis access to the Millennium drug development technology in search of agents to treat inflammatory disease. Aventis had to come up with $450 million to clinch the deal. Few biotech companies can boast of such strong validation . . . backed up by cash.[13]

Checking information sources on Millennium's partnerships, the company's Web site shows a substantial number of alliances but much more detail is available at recap.com. Using recap's "alliance" search engine for Millennium, we find a detailed and comprehensive list of the company's linkages in the industry.

The Recombinant Capital database delineates more than thirty different kinds of corporate linkages (explained by a legend at the bottom of the screen). Each alliance is explained in point form, and in Millennium's case the record goes back to 1994. In total, Millennium's record runs to more than 50 items including collaborations, licensing agreements, acquisitions, and development contracts covering a broad spectrum of drug development activities. It's a good example of the networking that gives a small biotech start-up greater and greater potential.

Collaborations of this sort are vital engines of scientific and business development among biotech companies. Alliances, mergers, and other forms of partnership facilitate the sharing of knowledge and they lend credibility to the partners.

Takeovers are even better from the investor's point of view. When a company is acquired, shareholders can expect to be paid a significant premium over the going stock price. The number of biotech companies taking over other firms in the sector is currently on the rise and this trend is expected to accelerate as financial markets give larger biotech firms the capital they need to acquire synergistic partners.

THE POWER OF PATENTS

In biotechnology, patents are the ultimate form of property. No one in the industry has spoken more emphatically and clearly about the importance of patents than Dr. William Haseltine, chairman and CEO of Human Genome Sciences. "No one would develop a drug if you didn't have a patent," Haseltine said during the chaotic aftermath of the Clinton-Blair statement on genetic patents.[14]

The law says anyone who invents or discovers a new and useful process, machine, manufacture, or composition of matter may be granted a patent.[15] Sounds straightforward. But in biotechnology nothing is ever that simple.

If it were merely a numbers game, Celera Genomics might be considered the biggest of all biotech companies, boasting a roster of some 10,000 patent applications on human genes. Dr. Haseltine's company, Human Genome Sciences would be second with 7,500 applications for patents on gene sequences, followed closely by Incyte Genomics, which has 7,000 applications pending at this writing.

A U.S. Supreme Court decision in 1980 cleared the way for patents on living organisms, a decision that initially provided a considerable boost to industrial and agricultural biotech firms. The matter appeared to be settled until genomic data began pouring out of automated gene sequencing machines. Some genomics companies hurried straight to the patent office to stake a claim on any and all newly discovered genes without any understanding of their probable function. It has been alleged that some biotech companies routinely downloaded the freely available data produced by the Human Genome Project every night and filed a patent claim immediately, without making an effort to learn anything about the genes they were claiming intellectual property rights to.[16]

This practice brought the issue of patents on genes to a head. Patent law requires that an invention or discovery must be "useful" to be granted a patent. The kind of patent applications previously described may never meet that standard. To clarify the intent of the word *useful*, the patent office has added another qualification to its guidelines: applicants will have to describe a "substantial, specific and credible" use for the genes they claim. It is not enough to file a description of the structure of a gene. The applicant must know what the gene does and have some idea how to make use of it.

The patent office calls applications for rights to genes that have been deciphered by a computer without any further elaboration "naked DNA sequences." There's very little chance that "naked DNA sequences" will gain patent approval. That means some companies may be left holding worthless claims on genomic discoveries.

Dr. Haseltine of Human Genome Sciences supports the new restrictions and says his company is actively determining the natural functions and medical uses of genes. Other genomic discovery companies have been more ambiguous about the issue. Incyte Genomics has warned that the definition of usefulness shouldn't become so restrictive as to prohibit discovery. In an interview with the *San Francisco Examiner*, Incyte's president Randy Scott said, "It's not important that you understand the function of a gene." The only important thing, Scott believes, is that a gene can be shown to have commercial usefulness. It's a fine point but it is crucial to the intellectual real estate that many genomics companies claim to own.

Many patent applications may be accompanied by a potentially worthless analysis of gene functions. Using specialized software, genomics companies turn the problem of postulating a gene's function over to computers. The computer makes a guess about the gene's probable function and a patent application is filed. This process irritates many government scientists including Dr. Francis Collins, director of the Human Genome Project. Collins is urging the patent office to reject so-called in silico analyses because they are no more than a "hypothesis." The patent office believes that most of its current gene patent applications are based on computerized analysis. If so, thousands of gene patent applications may eventually be deemed invalid.

That's why investors would be taking a big risk if they judged the quality of a company's patent portfolio by sheer volume of numbers. In fact, the patent office believes the greater the number of gene patent applications filed by a single company, the greater the likelihood that they are in silico analyses, and therefore questionable.

There's another important reason for investors to be careful in judging how much importance to place on the gross numbers of patent applications held by a biotech company. Some companies file patent applications knowing full well that a number will be denied and that others are worthless. The only reason for this practice is to confuse competitors. Like a warplane scattering chaff to confuse enemy radar, biotech companies may file more patent claims than they need to disguise their objectives. Only a few of these applications are actually important to the company's drug development process, but they are well hidden in a blizzard of paperwork.

Other companies are wary of placing an important genomic discovery in the custody of the U.S. and foreign patent offices. The dissemination of patent data gives competitors a chance to create new drugs, based on a gene discovery, and apply for patents on the resulting drug without owning rights to the gene in question. The rules treat the drug as an entirely separate entity. As a result, some companies withhold data about their discoveries as long as possible to avoid giving competitors an undeserved advantage.

Equally unsettling to investors in genomics companies is the probability that the whole issue will be dragged through the courts for years, eroding the economic value of gene patents as long as their validity remains in doubt. Already my files are bulging with stories of patent suits in the biotech industry. The patent office is sanguine about the whole problem, saying this is a normal process among emerging industries and rules unique to a new sector take time to clarify.

One of the most interesting patent issues was the dispute between Amgen and Transkaryotic Therapies. Amgen holds a clear patent on the protein erythropoietin, which is the key ingredient in its biggest revenue generator, the drug Epogen. Amgen's drug is produced in the ovaries of genetically engineered hamsters. Transkaryotic found a way to induce human cells to produce the crucial protein in laboratory cultures. When

Transkaryotic took its newly derived drug to clinical trials, Amgen sued saying its patent had been violated. Transkaryotic argued that its process is new and could not have been envisioned when Amgen filed for its patent. Ultimately, the courts ruled in favor of Amgen.

No matter how many patents a company claims to hold and how firm its grip on intellectual property appears to be, there are few guarantees. It would be foolhardy to buy shares in a company with poor patent protection, but that's a difficult judgment call in the present legal and political environment. It would be especially risky to base an investment on a company's claim to hold more patents than any other.

VERTICAL VERSUS HORIZONTAL INTEGRATION IN BIOTECH BUSINESS PLANS

"We're not a biotech company, we're an information business!" Dr. Michael J. Brennan of Gene Logic told a group of investment bankers and venture capitalists last April.[17] Maybe it's just as well that the crowd was increasingly distracted that day by one of the most terrifying plunges in the history of the Nasdaq. It fell more than 500 points. Brennan was already swimming upstream as he told the crowd about the value of specialization, or "horizontal integration" in biotech business jargon.

Brennan was making a point that held sway in biotech circles for quite some time. Unable to match the enormous research muscle of Big Pharma, biotech companies made a virtue of specialization. From a discovery point of view, specialization has been a tremendous success. While the pharmaceutical giants carried on in the traditions of the industry, biotech innovators sprouted by the hundreds. Free to adopt new ideas emerging from years of research in institutional labs, biotech start-ups hired away top talents from the likes of Harvard, Berkeley, and Stanford.

University researchers themselves became more entrepreneurial as changes in patent laws allowed their institutions to reap the profits from original discoveries made on campus. The Bayh-Dole Act of 1980 allowed universities to patent discoveries derived from federally funded research. The Act was a government effort to inject new life into the stagnating American economy of the time by bringing academic discoveries out of universities and into the commercial arena. Other federal measures, including tax breaks, have helped forge stronger relations between institutional research labs and industry. The initiative worked. Independent biotech companies began proliferating soon after the government introduced the new measures. Many academics realized the commercial value of their research and began thinking about rewards larger than a professor's salary. Some founded companies based on their particular area of expertise.

While Big Pharma watched from the sidelines and occasionally dabbled in the field, new biotech companies embarked on one of the toughest challenges imaginable: to bring the potential of exotic new technologies like bioinformatics, genomics, and proteomics into the commercial mainstream. At the time, horizontal integration wasn't necessarily the best thing. It was the only thing. Early biotech companies barely had the money to survive and continue research, much less broaden their development programs and expand into traditional business disciplines such as sales and marketing.

At the time, no pharmaceutical giant had the stomach to take on such a vast amount of ground-up innovation. Saddled with institutional inertia and an unclear picture of which of the new biotechnologies would bear fruit, Big Pharma found it cheaper and safer to remain on the sidelines. Tossing a few million dollars to a promising upstart was a safe way to get a toehold in the new science without experiencing excessive risk and wrenching change.

The pioneers of biotechnology deserve credit for their ferocious tenacity as they methodically transformed scientific discoveries into usable technologies, all the while fighting to survive economically. Each individual enterprise recognized the value of its specialty and fought to bring it to fruition. Now, as the results of these labors finally emerge from the lab, diverse technologies are being interconnected. Companies are merging, developing partnerships, or buying one another out as they discover the need for complementary technologies. In effect, vertical integration is evolving spontaneously in the industry. Was Dr. Brennan correct when he portrayed biotechnology as a horizontally integrated industry? Perhaps he was at the time, but change comes rapidly when money is at stake.

The most graphic illustration of the relative values of horizontal and vertical integration can be found in stock performance charts. In the six months following the March biotech market crash, shares in Dr. Brennan's company have stagnated (see Figure 3.1).

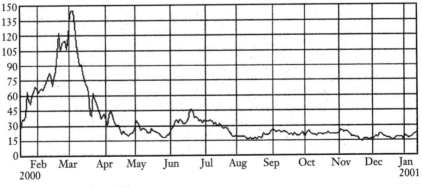

Figure 3.1 Gene Logic (GLGC) One-Year Performance

Without question Gene Logic is an organization with extraordinary scientific and research abilities. Unlike many functional genomics companies, Gene Logic employs a worldwide database of genomic information to produce highly specific analyses of gene functions. When Brennan described his company's work, I was very impressed. What happened to the stock?

After the implosion of the biotech bubble, the markets became increasingly focused on revenue potential. While Gene Logic expanded its stable of worldwide partnerships, the company retained its sharp focus on analysis of gene functions. Brennan's model of horizontal integration was put to the test. In July, the early results came from the company's quarterly earnings report.

Wall Street analysts had expected the company to trim its quarterly losses by 45 percent. Instead, Gene Logic reported a 16 percent increase in quarterly losses compared with the year before due to slow revenue growth. The company said the revenues were increasing but the timing of certain deals had led to the shortfall.

Was Gene Logic an isolated case? Compare its chart to that of another major genomics company, Incyte Pharmaceuticals (see Figure 3.2).

Incyte has a vast stable of patents and genomic patent applications. The CEO, Roy Whitfield, says his company is moving toward integration, and it includes many of the top 20 pharmaceutical companies among its database subscribers. Incyte may be more broadly focused than Gene Logic and its stock has recovered a little more than its competitor, but the trend line was less than encouraging in the third and fourth quarters of 2000.

To compare the market's valuation of a vertically integrated company holding a similar patent portfolio, look at the performance of Human Genome Sciences (see Figure 3.3).

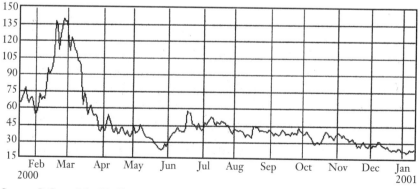

Source: © Copyright BigCharts.com.

Figure 3.2   Incyte (INCY) One-Year Performance

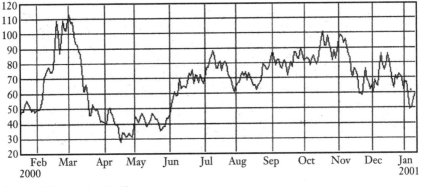

Figure 3.3   Human Genome Sciences (HGSI) One-Year Performance

The pattern is telling. Human Genome Sciences CFO, Steven Mayer, says his company's business plan calls for the creation of a new global pharmaceutical company, managing the discovery process "from genes to drugs." His words define the model for a vertically integrated biotech company.

Although all three of the charted companies have a strong program of genomic discovery, Human Genome Sciences has developed a much broader focus on drug development. The market has demonstrated a strong preference for this model.

Perhaps the most telling argument about the shape of the emerging industry was crystallized in the public discussion of Celera's business model. Not long after it had achieved the historic mapping of the human genome, critics began asking "Where's the profit?" How could this immensely expensive information factory ever make money? For several weeks, Celera issued press releases touting its expanding customer base, but the company's stock had begun to sink. The stock began to recover when CEO Craig Venter suggested that Celera was contemplating the possibility of putting its huge analytical power to work with an in-house drug discovery effort. Venter has since recanted, saying he wants nothing more than to be in the information business.[18] Celera's performance since that announcement has been unimpressive compared with vertically integrated biotechs (see Figure 3.4).

By contrast, it's worth returning to the chart of Millennium's stock. As discussed, Millennium has chosen to become a model of vertical integration, intent on managing every part of the drug development process except sales and marketing (see Figure 3.5).

Two months after the March biotech market crash, Millennium's stock began to recover strongly. Gene Logic, Incyte, and Millennium all had

Source: © Copyright BigCharts.com.

Figure 3.4   Celera (CRA) One-Year Performance

peaked earlier in the year in almost exactly the same range, just above
$150 per share. Six months later, Gene Logic and Incyte hovered down in
the $20 and $40 ranges, respectively. Millennium stands apart, having recovered much of its peak value near the end of 2000.

It's difficult to predict the future performance of any stock, especially
in biotech. But, the market's reply to Dr. Brennan's argument for horizontal integration is readily apparent from these charts. Although none of the
companies mentioned is making a profit, the market has demonstrated a
strong preference for the vertically integrated business model.

This may change but probably not until genomic discovery companies
demonstrate major increases in revenue flow and a convincing probability

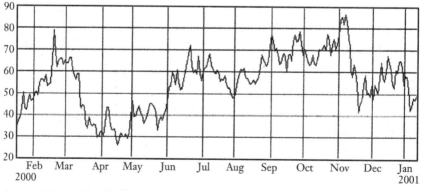

Source: © Copyright BigCharts.com.

Figure 3.5   Millennium (MLNM) One-Year Performance (Split Adjusted)

of emerging into the black. That may not happen soon for a simple reason. As a whole, the drug development industry has become engorged with raw data. A new bottleneck in the drug discovery process has been created by an overwhelming proliferation of "targets" (industry shorthand for molecules or genes that may be useful or biologically active). The markets have put their money on companies with expertise in using this flood tide of information. Companies developing drug targets from in-house genomic discoveries have earned the greatest credibility in the industry, as demonstrated by the enormous sums pharmaceutical giants have paid to vertically integrated companies like Human Genome Sciences and Millennium for research alliances. The market has also assigned a higher value to these companies partly because their drug development pipelines have the potential to produce large returns in a relatively short period of time.

The market's clear preference for vertically integrated biotech companies may change if genomic discoveries prove to have more commercial value than is now apparent. For the time being, I would prefer not to fight the market.

SUMMARY

The key criteria for judging a biotech investment are difficult to rate comparatively in importance. Most analysts put broad product pipelines in first place and often that is true. The exception to the rule is a big one.

Companies like Millennium and Human Genome Sciences do not boast the biggest pipelines in the industry but they do have the highest valuations among the biotech companies that have yet to turn a profit. One reason is the unusually wide scope of their drug development programs. Companies of this caliber have developed an impressive number of alliances backed up by very large payments and potentially huge royalty streams from multiple drug targets. The complete vertical integration of these companies has also helped them achieve high market capitalization.

Valuing a company according to the market potential of its disease targets depends greatly on the amount of competition and a judgment call about the relative effectiveness of the treatment being developed. It comes down to a matter of weighing a company's profit potential, and investors should consider the following guidelines in judging the attractiveness of a biotech investment:

- More drugs in trials mean a greater likelihood of profits.
- Shorter time lines to FDA approval mean lower risk of failure.
- More alliances reduce investor risk by validating the technology in development.

- Big dollar alliances generate cash and create the potential for royalty revenues.
- Widespread, serious, untreatable disease targets promise the greatest returns.
- Patents are important safeguards, but in genetics their value is unclear.
- Vertical integration increases a company's investment potential and may become a hallmark for the emergence of biotech's future giants.

CHAPTER 4

Going over Biotech Books

Intel is worth half a trillion dollars because they make great chips. If we make great medicines, we'll do just fine.

Jonathan Rothberg, CuraGen CEO, in a speech
to venture capitalists and investment bankers

MAKING INVESTMENT CHOICES

The guidelines in the previous chapter are intended to be commonsense methods for picking good companies in the biotech sector. But a great many biotech companies meet these criteria, leaving investors with a surplus of potential choices.

It's relatively easy to become overly excited about a company's prospects when one starts receiving a flow of news from Internet-based biotech news services. But it is essential to check a company's background and potential before making a purchase. Assuming the company meets the criteria set out in Chapter 3, is it always a good idea to make a buy? Not without further scrutiny and analysis.

ASSESSING BROKERAGE RATINGS

Biotech investors should take brokerage ratings with a grain of salt. One sobering example will make this point. Just before the implosion of the biotech bubble early in March 2000, Morgan Stanley issued an analyst upgrade on a company called Celgene.

Celgene is doing very promising work with drugs to control the immune system. The company's development pipeline is based largely on derivatives of thalidomide, the drug that caused terrible birth defects in some 12,000 infants when it was used to prevent morning sickness among pregnant women in Canada, Britain, and Western Europe during the 1960s. (Thalidomide was not licensed for use in the United States until recently when it showed effectiveness in the treatment of leprosy.)[1] Celgene

75

is aggressively developing the tumor-fighting power of thalidomide by evolving more advanced derivatives of the drug and testing them in 140 clinical trials around the world. The company has already achieved an income stream from drugs on the market.

Celgene stock had enjoyed a sensational run up from the $11 range to more than $170 in 12 months when it received the analyst upgrade (see Figure 4.1). On March 10, near the peak of the biotech bubble, Morgan Stanley issued a terse bulletin: "MORGAN STANLEY STARTS CELGENE AS STRONG BUY, SETS $212 TARGET."

Any investor unfortunate enough to make an investment based on that recommendation would have suffered severe losses. Within a month of the "Strong Buy" announcement, Celgene's stock value had been slashed to $101. As is often the case, the brokerage did not name the analyst making the call nor did it give any reasons for the upgrade. The fact that a number of analysts were warning that the biotech sector was in imminent danger of a major correction was apparently not a part of the firm's calculations. (Note: Celgene split three-for-one on April 11, 2000, but I have not split-adjusted the preceding numbers because I felt it was important to quote Morgan Stanley verbatim.)[2]

I spoke to a friend who works as a broker at Morgan Stanley and asked him how his company could have been so wrong. His answer was unsettling. "Part of my job," he said, "is to sort out B.S. from fact."[3] "The big investment houses," he explained, "derive their income from underwriting stocks. All of them will do this to get prices up. If they do investment banking business with a company they will promote that company." The remarkable thing is that "analyst upgrades" do not always disclose whether an investment house is in league with the company it is judging. When I suggested that this kind of behavior was a direct conflict of interest with a brokerage's

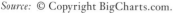
Source: © Copyright BigCharts.com.

Figure 4.1   Celgene (CELG) Chart Making Strong Buy Rating

responsibility to its clients, he waffled. "It's not flat-out lying," he said. "They may be hyping something. Maybe it's a bit unethical. It's my job to sort out the B.S.," he reiterated.

Motley Fool put the point even more bluntly in an article warning investors to ignore analysts' ratings. The writer raged that the same firms who issue the analyst ratings have built their business on financing the very companies they're analyzing, in his words a "blatant and unapologetic conflict of interest."[4] Can you count on your own broker to sort out the hype? Not necessarily. A veteran of another major brokerage tells me that he was often instructed in no uncertain terms by his employer which financial instruments his company wanted to sell. His performance ratings and commissions depended on how much he unloaded from this list of must-sell issues to his clients.

Making analyst ratings even more difficult to judge, most brokerages use different terms in their ratings and they attach different meanings to the words they use. But, no matter what language the brokers use, it is tough to find meaningful guidance among the terms "Strong Buy," "Buy," "Attractive," "Outperform," and "Accumulate." The most potentially useful prediction an analyst could offer investors, an outright "Sell" rating, is rare for obvious reasons.

In checking the histories of analyst ratings for biotech stocks, I have found that they tend to acknowledge a trend already in progress. As a predictive tool, they have little long-term value.

Occasionally, an analyst downgrade will trigger selling of a stock, but more often it amounts to an acknowledgment that a stock has already been doing poorly. Charles Hill, research director with First Call, decoded the language of the analysts concisely, telling *Investor's Business Daily* that "Strong Buy" really means buy. "Buy" means hold, and "Hold" means sell. After surveying a number of academic studies, *Investor's Business Daily* says flatly that analyst ratings are unreliable and investors should ignore them entirely.[5]

Perhaps not entirely. In assessing a biotech investment, I do look for *histories* of analyst ratings. These histories are interesting as an indicator of a stock's visibility to the investment community. If a great many stock analysts are covering a particular biotech issue, it may have reached its top market value for the time being. On the other hand, if only a few analysts have issued a rating on a company that I feel has great potential, it may indicate that the company I'm researching is an undiscovered gem. After all, the financial industry has relatively few biotech analysts covering a great many issues. Comparing a stock's actual performance to the history of analyst ratings can also give a measure of the objectivity and accuracy of current ratings.

Although it may be wise to take a jaded view of brokerage ratings and media commentary, there is one very good reason to pay attention.

Sometimes, instead of predicting markets, commentary may drive markets. For example, in November 2000 most high-tech sectors on the Nasdaq had taken a severe tumble except for biotechnology. *Barron's* published an article warning that biotechnology might "become the market's next dotcoms." The author, Michael Shaoul from the Oscar Gruss brokerage, noted that biotechs had generated impressive gains while "many of their brethren in other areas of the high tech universe had been battered." Shaoul argued that it was difficult for many investors to place a concrete value on poorly understood companies, but he firmly declared the sector "overvalued," publicly reversing his company's bullish outlook on biotechnology.[6]

In the five trading days that followed the article, the biotech indexes fell only slightly, but the companies Shaoul gave as examples of unrealistic valuation plummeted. Protein Design Labs dropped from $112 a share to $85 and Vertex Pharmaceuticals fell from $80 to $63 in one week.

Did *Barron's* make the market or predict it accurately? The evidence shows that in the short term the biotechnology sector as a whole did not fall sharply but the companies that were singled out as examples lost more than 20 percent of their value in a week. As time went on and the Nasdaq continued its broad slump, the biotech index was also dragged down, although many analysts noted that it was the last sector to be caught in the high-tech plunge.

As a long-term investor who believes strongly that the two companies singled out by *Barron's* are among the best companies in biotechnology, I chose not to sell my Vertex and Protein Design Labs shares. Perhaps a volatility player would have. In the long run, I would be genuinely surprised if these companies did not recover strongly.

Perhaps the basic difference between Wall Street analysts and many independent biotech investors is a question of investment horizons. Buying and selling for short-term gain is a Wall Street specialty, not a game for investors who buy quality firms with long-term growth in mind.

USING THE METRICS

The financial profiles of most biotech companies are completely unlike those for conventional stocks, which are measured by well-known formulas. The most popular is the P/E ratio, a simple formula that measures the price of a stock against company earnings. The higher the price-to-earnings ratio, the greater the market's expectations for growth. This common rule of thumb is only useful for a handful of biotech companies that have established a track record of profitability. Most biotech charts will show no P/E ratio, no operating margin, and no profit margin. So, if the usual yardsticks don't work, where does one look for perspective on a company's financial condition?

Generally I begin an analysis by going to a favorite financial Web site and inspecting corporate profiles. Yahoo Finance and Hoovers provide a wealth of information. Below the written summary describing a company is a table that provides a substantial amount of financial data. Assuming the company is currently losing money, compare negative income statistics to the sum of cash on hand. This gives some idea of the length of time a company can continue to function in the red without going belly up. Table 4.1 shows the statistics for Human Genome Sciences.

Under the heading "Income," the table shows a loss of $105 million. Under "Total Cash" the table shows cash on hand of $850 million. The company seems to have substantial funds to continue operations well beyond the two or three years it may need to bring drugs from its pipeline to market and begin profitable operations.

Because HGS has not yet marketed a major new drug, the sales total reflects mainly revenues from partnerships, license fees, milestone payments, and so forth. Fluctuations in a number so small, compared with the major criteria mentioned in Chapter 3, are not highly relevant. An increase in losses, the usual sign of disaster among conventional stocks, may not be cause for great alarm. Investors in Celera hardly blinked when the company announced that it was embarking on a major program of proteomic discovery. That meant the company would be spending hundreds of millions of dollars in coming years on the analysis of proteins, and losses would inevitably increase. The company's stock price remained relatively stable *at the time* as the investment community shrugged off the prospect of further losses and focused on the value of further expansion in Celera's vast database.

Returning to analysis of the Human Genome Sciences table, the "Market Activity" box demonstrates the underlying strength of the company. While many biotech companies have had difficulty recovering from the March 2000 price implosion, HGS shows a 52-week gain of 375 percent. Immediately below, the stock's gain relative to the S&P500 is equally impressive at 340 percent. The BETA, a measure of stock volatility, is a strikingly low .1.

Because HGS measures up well against the criteria discussed in Chapter 3, and because the company's 12-month stock performance is so strong, the company appears to be an attractive investment. But is there any more statistical evidence? HGS's performance can be charted by using a 50-day or 200-day moving average. The longer the moving average one selects, the less likely it is to be skewed by market volatility (see Figure 4.2).

Continuing the analysis of HGS, the company has produced one statistic that would set off alarm bells among conventional stocks. Earnings per share are declining. Sharply. How is it that the company's performance remains generally positive? The answer can be found by checking recent news or quarterly reports on the company. These are available by going more deeply into the news links attached to Yahoo's corporate profiles or by visiting the company's Web site.

On July 28, HGS announced that its second quarter loss had more than quadrupled because of increased spending on research. Shares declined

Table 4.1   Human Genome Sciences (HGSI) Statistics, August 2000

Market Activity		Share Metrics		Debt and Equity	
52-week low	$26	Earnings	–$2.10	Debt/equity	1.1
Current price/share	$129	Sales	.43	Total cash	$850 million
52-week high	$232	Price/earnings ratio	N/A	*Institutional*	
Average volume	1.8 million/day	Price/sales ratio	300	Strong buy calls	1
52-week change	+375%	Total sales (12 month)	$21.6 million	Moderate buy	5
Change vs. S&P 500	+340%	EBITDA (12 month)	–$53 million	Hold	3
Market capitalization	$7 billion	Income	–$105 million	Sell	0
Shares on market	54.5 million	Shares short	4 million	EPS surprise (recent)	27%
Profitability		EPS growth	–25%	*Top Mutual Funds Holding HGSI*	
Profit margin	N/A	Beta	0.1	Vanguard Specialized Health Care	
Operating margin	N/A	PEG ratio	N/A	Fidelity Growth Company Fund	

Source: HGSI Annual Report, BigCharts.com.

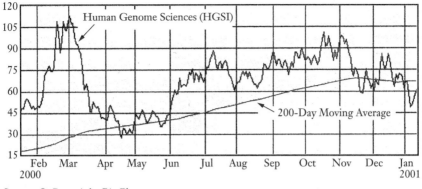

Source: © Copyright BigCharts.com.

Figure 4.2 Human Genome Sciences (HGSI) One-Year Performance with 200-Day Moving Average

following the report, but the damage was comparatively small. The news was balanced out somewhat by the company's announcement that it had achieved positive results in a test of a new drug for venous leg ulcers. Confidence was supported by the company's promising pipeline and its impressively high number of partnerships, which the market apparently takes as an assurance that the new research funds will probably be well spent.

Another good indicator of the investment community's high regard for HGS can be found by looking at its profile in the listings of institutional holders and mutual fund holders. The biggest institutional shareholder, Fidelity Management and Research holds almost $800 million worth of HGS stock. Janus, Invesco, and JP Morgan hold approximately a quarter of a billion dollars each. The big names in the mutual fund industry also hold substantial positions in the company. These two listings demonstrate the respect HGS commands among credible names in the financial industry.

Having passed even more of the tests for an emerging biotech company, the question then becomes: Is this a good time to buy? If we take the brokerage ratings with a large grain of salt, the answer is inconclusive.

FORMULAS, CHARTS, WAVES, AND PATTERNS

Many analysts have tried to come up with mathematical formulas to measure the value of emerging high-tech stocks. In surveying the books and articles on this subject, I've found very few formulas that provide substantially more guidance than rules of thumb already set out.

Michael Murphy, editor of the *California Technology Stock Letter* heavily advertises his expertise in biotech stocks. In his book *Every Investor's Guide to High-Tech Stocks & Mutual Funds* (Broadway Books, 2000), Murphy proposes using a P/GF ratio (price to growth flow). Murphy's theory may work among established high-tech companies, but it has limited use in biotechnology. Earnings are central to the calculation and, as often mentioned, earnings are negligible for most biotech firms.

For mutual fund investors, the book *How to Be a Sector Investor*, by Dr. Larry Hungerford and Steve Hungerford (McGraw Hill, 2000) suggests paying attention to the Sharpe ratio. This ratio involves complex mathematics developed by Nobel laureate William Sharpe and is intended to provide a measure of a mutual fund's performance on a risk-adjusted basis. The Sharpe ratio tells you how much a mutual fund's return has rewarded investors for the degree of risk they assumed. I have some reservations about making decisions based on past performance. In any event, biotech mutual funds have been market leaders for several quarters, which may skew calculation of the real risks involved by making them seem smaller than they are. For more detail on this form of analysis, check out William Sharpe's Web site at www.sharpe.stanford.edu.

Michael Becker, editor of the monthly newsletter *Beck on Biotech* (www.beckonbiotech.com), suggests using the MC/RD ratio. The formula divides current market capitalization by total research and development spending over the past five years. A ratio in the vicinity of 10 is considered normal for a biotech company although Becker writes that many small-cap biotechs have lately been showing numbers closer to 5. (The lower this ratio, the greater the R&D value one apparently receives per dollar of market capitalization, hence more value per share.) Three criticisms of this formula come to mind immediately.

The MC/RD formula assumes that all research and development has equal value. That seems like quite a leap. Some avenues of research spending may increase a company's cash burn rate without adding substantial value or profit potential in the foreseeable future. In addition, some pharmaceutical companies include marketing expenses as development costs by calling them "education costs." Becker himself acknowledges that many other considerations come into play, including the quality of management, cash levels, and competition.

A second objection: The MC/RD formula would suggest that an increase in R&D spending should boost the value of a stock. But, as discussed, increased R&D costs for Human Genome Sciences increased the company's losses and contributed to a small drop in share values. The MC/RD formula attempts to compensate for such short-term fluctuations by using a five-year research and development total in the equation. That requirement raises a third difficulty.

Finding and calculating the research and development spending of a company over a five-year stretch requires considerable sifting through old annual reports. The amount of digging involved may not be practical for an individual investor who wants to buy a fairly large variety of stocks to diversify a biotech portfolio.

The underlying intent of the MC/RD ratio is to establish that a company is spending enough on research and development to justify its stock price. I find this issue too subjective to squeeze into a mathematical formula. What's more, most emerging biotechnology companies spend everything they can on research and development, in amounts ranging as high as 70 percent of total budgets. In such a case, commitment to research is not in question. Demonstrating the value of biotech research in human trials, the so-called Proof of Concept is a much more important issue.

One other concept is the "q ratio." This formula attempts to measure the viability of stock prices by comparing them with the dollar cost of rebuilding the companies under consideration from scratch. If the differential is too large, the stock is overvalued and headed for a fall. It might be possible to calculate how much money has been spent in building a biotech company but what would be the point? Much of the intellectual property on which biotechnology is based is an outgrowth of decades of research in institutional laboratories. It is difficult to attach meaningful dollar values to the worldwide pursuit of pure science conducted by academia. Yet the fruits of such research underpin the commercial potential of most companies in the sector. Structural costs of this sort are customarily called *intangibles* and in biotech intangibles are the most important assets.

Using the same standard, it would also be meaningless to relate the total lifetime research and development expenditures of biotech companies to their stock values. As discussed, some avenues of research lead nowhere. What's more research spending can only be as valuable as the target market it is aimed at. I would value research that showed promise in the treatment of Parkinson's disease much more highly than a program of discovery in the treatment of a rare genetic disorder, although the two might be equivalent in terms of scientific challenge and overall cost. The valuation closest to a "q ratio" is the price paid during takeover of a similar biotech firm, an imprecise measure.

These formulas and ratios may have value in the assessment of profitable biotech companies, and I intend no disrespect toward their creators. But, applying such measures to the books of emerging biotech firms has so far proven to be largely an unproductive exercise.

One of the most useful Web sites for biotech analysis is marketguide .com, which can be found through Yahoo Finance. In its calculation of estimated earnings per share, Market Guide includes a category called the "Long Term Growth Rate." In theory, a stock's growth rate should closely match its P/E ratio. If they do correspond, it is often taken as a sign that a stock has been properly valued. The comparison of these two figures is a simple calculation that involves dividing the P/E ratio by the Long Term Growth Rate. If the two are the same, the ratio is one to one. This calculation is called the P/EG (Price/Earnings-to-Growth) ratio. If the ratio delivers a result less than one, it is assumed that a stock is growing more quickly than its P/E ratio has predicted, therefore the stock is undervalued.

If the figure is greater than one, the company's actual growth is lower than the current stock price can sustain, therefore it is overvalued. Although this calculation cannot be used for unprofitable biotech firms, it can set a standard for the valuation of the sector's few profitable companies.

The P/EG ratio can also be calculated using tools in the Motley Fool Web site. Motley Fool is also handy for keeping an eye on splits that occur relatively often among high-growth biotechs. Upcoming splits are conveniently presented in the form of a calendar that allows investors to scan a grid covering more than a month to see if one of their holdings is due for a split. It's worth checking out, not because splits affect corporate valuation, but because awareness of upcoming splits can prevent the needless shock of checking one's portfolio online and discovering that a stock has suddenly appeared to lose half of its value. Reverse splits also happen occasionally among foundering biotech companies whose value has fallen below $1. To avoid being delisted by major markets, companies that have become true penny stocks will sometimes decide to issue their stockholders one share for every ten they hold. The value of a share will increase tenfold and stockholders who are not aware of the change may be momentarily fooled into thinking that they have made substantial gains on companies that are obviously in serious difficulty.

Returning briefly to charting and formulas, I have found some interesting mathematical indicators among the exotic tools used by day traders. These traders routinely use sophisticated mathematical tools that were once the exclusive preserve of Wall Street technical analysts. These indicators can be accessed through Web sites such as WindowonWallStreet.com and BigCharts.com.

Charting Web sites offer as many as 25 technical indicators including Stochastics, RSI, Bollinger Bands, MACD, Volume by Price Charts, and Money Flow. All these formulas are applied to a chosen company and presented automatically on request so there is no need to spell out their elaborate mathematical detail. Explanations are readily available at the Web sites. Because these are technical indicators, they attempt to predict future price movements according to past trends and tend to be market timing rather than stock-picking indicators. I have found some indications of market-timing accuracy among Bollinger Bands, which display patterns of "mean deviation," in other words, how far a stock has strayed above or below its average price. When the upper and lower bands cross on a chart, it is taken as an indication to buy or sell, in accordance with the up or down trend of a stock's price. I would recommend such market-timing devices only in times of great uncertainty such as a suspected "biotech bubble," when investors need every tool at their disposal to provide a reality check. For the time being, I'd prefer to focus on other methods to increase the investor's selectivity in assessing biotech companies before getting to the thorny issue of market timing.

PAYING FOR ADVICE

Is there a source for more reliable analysis? Several biotech stock letters have earned the respect of the industry. The Medical Technology Stock Letter is edited by Jim McCamant, www.bioinvest.com. He was one of the first to warn that the market was badly overheated early in the year 2000 while brokerages were still issuing "strong buy" ratings. The California Technology Stock Letter at www.ctsl.com is edited by Michael Murphy who was once a partner with McCamant. Industry sources say there are several downsides for investors who subscribe to one or the other. The two letters are hotly competitive and may not cover stocks that the competing letter is following. Murphy attempts to cover Silicon Valley high-tech stocks as well as biotechnology, and his approach tends to be optimistic. McCamant covers only medical technology and has a somewhat more reserved approach, although he writes that he only picks stocks that he feels confident can appreciate by 200 percent in less than two years.[7]

You might also want to check out the BioVenture Consultants Stock report at www.bioventureconsultants.com. Another possible source is Beck on Biotech at www.beckonbiotech.com. Some of these sources, however, charge $200 or more per year for subscriptions.

For the frugal investor, Motley Fool pays more attention to biotech than most financial Web sites and can usually be counted on to take an interesting, contrarian point of view. However, Motley Fool tries to cover a huge range of sectors and subjects. Investment advice given on one day sometimes contradicts opinions published soon after. Motley Fool is increasing its focus on biotechnology and offering online investment courses for $75.

Greater depth can be found by going to the Signals Magazine Web site: www.signalsmag.com. Signals Magazine is a part of recap.com and is one of the best available sources of in depth analysis of the biotech companies from an investor's perspective.

BioSpace.com offers an enormous archive of published articles from various sources, as well as daily biotech business and technical news and excellent feature writing. Despite its high quality as a news and information source, BioSpace.com rarely offers independent opinions on investment strategy. Investors should be aware that BioSpace has signed an agreement with Celera to cooperate in information distribution.

Most large investment houses also offer industry or corporate analysis, paid for not by subscription, but per report. These run as much as 30 pages in length and are not cheap considering what they offer. Among those I've reviewed, I find a considerable amount of redundant background on industry technologies, with only a small portion devoted to discussing investment specifics. As a rule, the brokerages tend to cover the established majors in biotechnology and have little coverage of the many smaller players in the industry. Also, I have some qualms about the opinions they offer on equities that they might also be promoting.

The more opinion one gathers, the more contradictory it can become. I have collected reams of articles explaining why, for example, a company like Biogen is either a terrible or a wonderful investment choice. It is always difficult to assess which commentator is right, which is wrong, and who might be biased. Usually it comes right back to independent investor judgment, although a broad consensus among commentators should not be ignored entirely.

Here are some other approaches. The BioTech Sage report at www.biotechnav.com, has chosen to divide the sector into three groups: Aggressive Growth, Intermediate, and Stable Growth. BioTech Sage lists its buy recommendations for companies within these three tiers. A brief review of the site's advice back in January 2000 shows that investors would have profited had they followed BioTech Sage's recommendations. (Free sample reports are available at the Web site.) The site's usefulness is limited by the fact that many companies are not listed at all.

Salomon Smith Barney takes a different approach,[8] setting out three tiers of companies in the biotech world and naming them as follows:

- "Members of the Club" (companies with lead products available in growing markets).
- "The B List" (companies that have product sales but lack near-term pipelines or suffer from slowing markets).
- "The Fringe" (companies with no significant product sales and no near-term drug prospects).

In its March 2, 2000, report, Salomon called it right by advising against investing in the fringe companies, arguing that they were overvalued. Within two weeks of the report's release, biotech companies in this sector were decimated by the collapse of the market bubble.

On the other hand, Salomon's so-called Fringe companies had increased more than 76 percent from mid-January to mid-February of that year, better gains than Members of the Club produced. Salomon's rating system puts Human Genome Sciences among the Fringe players. HGS may have been overpriced at the time of the report, but it has since recovered robustly from the market correction. The Fringe designation does a disservice to companies of HGS's quality and potential. Brokerage ratings and analyses of this sort are generally available on the Internet for less than $100 per report.

When Salomon gave Amgen its top rating, the company had a price-to-earnings ratio of 52: substantially higher than many pharmaceutical giants. Earnings per share were also high and predicted to rise. Salomon argued that the company's astronomical valuations were "not excessive" because of Amgen's double-digit sales growth and the presence of promising drugs in the company's pipeline. Salomon's advice turned out to be sound during the following six months. Amgen shares rose substantially between March 2 and August 2.

Every investor who has watched the market's behavior during one of the quarterly "earnings seasons" knows how surprising the effects of an earnings report can be. Making a profit is not enough. Not by a long shot. Simply meeting the analysts' estimates for earnings usually means a drop in stock value. Most analysts are looking for a stock to meet or exceed the so-called *whisper number*, which is the more realistic figure shared by industry insiders and analysts in off-the-record conversations. Amazingly, even exceeding a whisper number can result in a drop in stock prices. Too much success can become a dangerous thing when excessively high expectations are attached to any stock.

P/E ratios are a measure of expectations, and ratios above 25 were once considered dangerously optimistic. Until recently, high-tech companies like Intel and Dell[9] defied this standard by producing steadily increasing earnings. But, the fall of the Nasdaq's star performers demonstrates how volatile markets become when companies are priced for perfection. Among profitable biotech companies, high P/E multiples may be even more dangerous because their revenue streams are generally built on a much narrower base of products than companies in most other sectors.

As for whisper numbers, several Web sites now offer a consumer version of this financial industry insider information. Whispernumbers.com collects earnings estimates on its Web site and surveys message boards for information. StreetIQ.com uses Web polling and an analysis of previous earnings surprises to arrive at an estimate. EarningsWhispers.com also uses information collected from the Web and claims to glean some information from financial industry insiders. The whisper number sites claim they're able to filter out manipulators, but it is difficult to recommend any form of information drawn from anonymous messages on the Internet.

Finding New Valuation Criteria

Valuations in biotechnology are rooted in intellectual property, on which it is difficult to put any kind of price tag. In conventional companies, such assets are marked up as intangibles and accountants do their best to price them in accordance with the return a company might realize if it were sold. Currently, biotechnology companies are sold at a premium during takeovers, with prices paid running at 30 or 40 percent above their valuation on the stock market.

Biotech stock prices are driven in the short term by transient factors. During the first quarter of 2000, genomic information was considered to be a prize asset. During the next quarter revenue stability was key. But, taking a long-range view of the industry, valuation will be driven by the quality of products brought to market and the speed at which they arrive.

That brings the valuation question back full circle. The final arbiter of product quality and quantity is still intellectual property. A biotech company's knowledge base, management focus, scientific and technological skill, its patent portfolio, and its ability to innovate are at the heart of a company's future and deserve first place in long-term assessments of biotech corporate valuations.

Without an abundance of these intangibles, even a company like Amgen, with its established revenue stream, would be worth much less. Remarkably, Amgen's market capitalization is almost twice that of General Motors, a company with annual sales above $180 billion and income of more than $5 billion. Amgen's total sales are approximately $3.5 billion and income is over $1 billion. Amgen enjoys an enormous profit margin but income alone can't account for the company's valuation. The market is expecting more. The company's P/E ratio demands growth and that depends entirely on intangible assets like intellectual property, products in development, and scientific talent.

In a field characterized by such enormous risk, volatility, and contradictory opinion, the biotech investor requires some kind of constant: a form of measurement that will provide a meaningful perspective on biotech stock prices. No instant formula is fully up to the task of providing long-term perspective for biotech investors. But a few financial yardsticks can assist in the formation of independent judgment about corporate valuations. These are discussed in Chapter 5.

CHAPTER 5

———•◦•———

Four Tiers of Biotech Companies

Genomics has helped make biotechnology seem like an attractive investment again.
It's more promising than the traditional goo in a test tube stuff.
John Taylor, Director National Venture Capital Association,
in an interview with the Associated Press, May 26, 2000

THE MARKET CAP YARDSTICK

Because the financial criteria for judging biotech companies are severely limited by their uncertain profit outlooks, one measure stands out among the parameters used by most analysts and writers: market capitalization. It is the simplest of all financial statistics, setting out in plain terms what the stock market believes a company is worth. This number is less subjective than most others because it is backed up by real money.

In most brokerage reports and published analyses of biotech companies, the level of market capitalization is the key tool for differentiation among the players. The analysis of biotech companies according to market cap commonly involves dividing the sector into three tiers. Ordinarily, Tier 1 includes companies with a market cap over a billion dollars. Tier 2 encompasses companies with a market cap between $500 million and a billion dollars. Tier 3 encompasses the smaller-cap companies valued at less than $500 million. Although this is the usual way of breaking the industry down, the substantial growth of the sector's market value calls for new criteria.

The few dozen biotech companies that are profitable have unique status because they yield to conventional metrics and systems of analysis. Therefore, the values and characteristics of these companies can be used to help set measurement standards for the rest.

The $65 billion market capitalization of Amgen is an important yardstick in the valuation system I use. Amgen's value remained relatively stable through the turbulent months that rocked most biotech shares in the first half of the year 2000. The company's market cap continued to be less volatile than that of other biotech firms into 2001. This unusual degree of

89

stability makes Amgen a useful reference point when gauging the potential of less mature biotech companies.

As mentioned in Chapter 4, revenues alone cannot support the company's stable valuation. Amgen's strong product development pipeline and corporate credibility play an important part in sustaining investor expectations. The Amgen example demonstrates that a biotech stock valuation can be projected from the dual elements of cash flow and pipeline potential. This helps explain the remarkably high valuations of some biotech companies that have yet to emerge from the red. Even when there are no profits to guide the investor, the market perceives a credible basis for valuing a stock according to a company's development potential.

The market capitalization of Biogen is another important yardstick, showing the potential of a company that has brought one important drug to market and derives income from other sources including royalties. Biogen has a far lower market value than Amgen, partly because revenues are considerably lower, and also because Biogen has a less robust drug development pipeline. These two mature biotech companies provide useful guidance in breaking the industry down into tiers and analyzing valuations.

I have found it useful to break down the categories of biotech companies into four tiers, based partly on market capitalization and partly on the criteria set out in previous chapters—the intangible assets.

DEFINING THE TIERS

Tier 1 companies are in a class by themselves because they have an established record of earnings. The metrics that apply to other revenue-generating high-tech stocks can be used to assess these issues, but their drug pipeline and revenue growth potential support higher market capitalizations than earnings flow alone would justify. All have successfully developed at least one important drug product and have brought it through the trials process to market. Companies in this tier have valuations well in excess of $5 billion.

Tier 2 companies have not yet established meaningful revenue streams, but they have managed to rise above the two billion-dollar market cap threshold. They have achieved their relatively high valuations because they meet or exceed so many of the criteria for a quality biotech company. They have a strong development pipeline, with a substantial number of drugs in development and at least one product in the final phase of testing before FDA approval. Companies in this tier have established credibility and long-term growth potential through excellent research programs, first-rate management, and impressive corporate alliances. Some Tier 2 biotech companies are not directly in the drug development business, but they have achieved high market capitalizations by establishing leadership in subsectors of the industry and by generating steady revenue growth.

Tier 3 companies have risen above $800 million in market value by developing either a promising near-term pipeline, or a highly credible R&D program for drug development. These companies often have at least one drug with blockbuster potential in the final phase of trials. No third-tier biotech company in the drug development business has achieved profitability, although some biotech equipment makers in this tier are approaching the breakeven point.

Tier 4 companies have market caps below $800 million dollars and their stocks typically trade in single or low double digits. They are very risky, but many offer investors significant leverage.

In the following sections, I describe the hazards and the potential rewards involved in making a biotech investment among the four tiers. My descriptions are illustrated with analyses of individual companies that were chosen because they exemplified important characteristics of their tier at the time of writing. My intention is not to recommend a particular company but to demonstrate an analytic process that I have found useful in assessing the quality of corporate valuations. Keep in mind, it is likely that business circumstances will have changed, affecting the position of these companies in the markets during the period between the preparation of this book and its publication.

THE FIRST TIER: JUDGING THE MAJORS

There's no arguing that Tier 1 biotech companies performed well during the year 2000. The names in this universe are relatively few but they have yielded exceptionally good market returns. Companies in this tier include Amgen, Genentech, Immunex, Chiron, Medimmune, and Idec Pharmaceuticals. All are drug development companies that have participated in bringing the first wave of biotech therapies to market, including complex proteins, monoclonal antibodies, and cancer treatments based on management of the immune system. These names come up repeatedly in brokerage evaluations of top-notch biotech investments. Analysts from the major brokerages and even the "rule-breaking" commentators from Motley Fool usually recommend such stocks as core holdings.

Because Tier 1 companies are generating substantial revenues, they have been relatively unshaken by biotech's boom and bust cycle. We are fortunate in having conventional metrics such as P/E ratios for first-tier companies, but the numbers they reveal give some cause for caution. Table 5.1 sets out some of the most important metrics and compares them with similar criteria for Merck, a pharmaceutical giant, and General Motors, an established industrial colossus.

As the table demonstrates, many Tier 1 companies have established extremely high P/E ratios, which means market expectations for earnings growth are enormous. The pharmaceutical giant, Merck, is generating the

Table 5.1   Tier 1 Biotechs versus Pharmaceutical and
Industrial Leaders, November 2000

Company	Approximate Market Capitalization (in Billions)	Price-to-Earnings Ratio	Earnings per Share and Earnings %/Share
Amgen	$ 67	56/1	$1.12 = 1.7%
Genentech*	38	*120	*NA
Immunex	21	174	$0.22 = 0.56%
Medimmune	12.5	145	$0.41 = 0.6%
Biogen	8	26	$2.12 = 3.7%
Chiron	7	43	$0.88 = 2.3%
IDEC Pharma	7	218	$0.57 = 0.4%
Merck	204	31	$3.81 = 3.2% plus 1.5% dividend
General Motors	31	6	$9.13 = 16% plus 3.5% dividend

* Genentech was subject to unusual accounting corrections in 2000 and its metrics are in flux.
Source: Data from annual reports, BigCharts.com.

most earnings per share among drug development companies in the table yet its P/E ratio remains lower at 31 indicating more limited growth expectations from the company. The P/E ratio of 6 for GM indicates even lower growth expectations despite very substantial earnings per share. The market anticipates great things from Tier 1 biotech companies. It is possible that the few biotech leaders showing an established earnings stream have been chosen by some investors because they appear to offer a measure of security against volatility. But some analysts are cautioning that first-tier biotechs have been "priced for perfection." That's a polite way of saying they have been "priced for disappointment" because no company can be perfect. Even large pharmaceutical companies are no longer a haven of security.

One needs only to remember what happened to the Eli Lilly company when it announced suddenly in August 2000 that it expected single-digit earnings growth until 2002 . . . a shocking disappointment to shareholders. Before the announcement, Lilly had a P/E ratio of 38. This valuation was based on the assumption that Lilly would continue to produce double-digit growth as it had for years. Such expectations have long been the norm among the major pharmaceutical companies. Within two hours of a court ruling that rebuffed the company's hopes of extending its patent on Prozac, Lilly's P/E ratio fell to the 28 range.[1]

Consider now how much more is expected of the first-tier biotechs. A P/E ratio above 50 suggests truly enormous growth expectations; much greater annual revenue increases and earnings-per-share requirements than

Lilly faced before its disappointing announcement. If the fall of Lilly contains any lessons for smaller biotech companies, the most important would have to be the danger of high P/E ratios and soaring market valuations.

Tier 1 biotechs do offer investors greater protection from market volatility because they have reliable revenue streams. Those with promising drug development pipelines have risen in the markets during a period when many other high-tech firms suffered severe setbacks. Nevertheless, investors should research companies in Tier 1 carefully to be confident that their revenue growth will live up to the stellar expectations indicated by their P/E ratios.

TIER 2: BIG CAP, SMALL REVENUES

Tier 2 biotech companies are, generally speaking, the most likely to emerge as tomorrow's industry leaders. Revenues or profits may be a mere trickle but cash flow has little to do with their remarkably high valuations. These companies are priced for their promise.

Among the major names in this group are Millennium Pharmaceuticals, Human Genome Sciences, Protein Design Labs, Vertex Pharmaceuticals, Affymetrix and Abgenix. Companies of this quality seem to defy the gravity of numbers. Despite small or nonexistent profits, they are valued in billions of dollars. How have such valuations been justified?

In a nutshell, Tier 2 companies meet the highest criteria for biotech investments except for substantial profitability. They have developed research capabilities that are widely recognized and proven by an extensive array of partnerships and alliances. Most have strong drug pipelines. (A biochip maker like Affymetrix does not develop drugs but holds a leadership position in a key field of biotechnology.) Second-tier companies hold impressive patent portfolios. Management is aggressive and focused. Their growth potential is enormous.

Companies in Tier 2 may have much greater growth prospects than Tier 1 companies. Although they are valued in the billions, they arguably have the potential to rise much higher. This is where the market capitalization yardstick comes in.

Consider the valuation of a company like Millennium Pharmaceuticals. After the March 2000 market bubble, Millennium's market cap rebounded to more than $11 billion. Because its earnings per share are negative (minus $3.59 at this writing), P/E ratios are meaningless. If Millennium's share price depended only on the success of the lead product in its pipeline, the company's valuation would be absurd.

The reason Millennium has such an enormous lead over other development-stage biotechs can be found most easily in its partnership and alliance profile. The company's extraordinary web of corporate connections (described in Chapter 3) was crowned in July 2000 when the pharmaceutical giant Aventis agreed to pay a whopping $450 million dollars for access to Millennium's drug discovery technologies and services. Millennium's many partnership deals give the company a royalty stake in the hundreds of drugs it is helping other pharmaceutical giants create. Although it has no drug revenues of its own yet, Millennium's research capability has been valued at almost a half-billion dollars by two of its major clients.

Now consider the market cap of a Tier 1 company like Amgen. A valuation of more than $65 billion has proven to be relatively durable through boom and bust cycles. As mentioned, Amgen's profitability rests largely on two drugs with approximately $3.5 billion in combined annual sales; the remainder of Amgen's valuation is based on its potential to develop new products. Therefore, the Amgen model sets a useful framework for the measurement of Millennium's potential valuation.

The widely recognized scope of Millennium's research platform suggests that the company will become a prolific generator of new drugs, even if its name is sometimes kept in the background as a royalty-collecting product developer for major pharmaceutical distributors. From this perspective, the company's $11 billion market capitalization becomes more comprehensible.

Using the market cap yardstick, Millennium's value could approach that of Amgen if its own drug products prove to be successful in coming years. Millennium's lead in-house product has the potential to become a blockbuster cancer drug, generating sales comparable to those achieved by Amgen's two drugs. Because the company's in-house drug pipeline has not been licensed out to its Big Pharma partners, revenues from these products will be substantially greater than royalties from successful products produced for the company's clients.

Examining the other major criterion for valuation, Millennium's research and development pipeline is easily comparable to that of Amgen, so both companies should enjoy a similar premium in stock valuation. On this basis, Millennium's potential market cap can be credibly projected, but, not guaranteed, to approach that of Amgen. In fact, Millennium has a stake in a much larger drug pipeline because of its external product development and royalty agreements; therefore it seems reasonable to expect that Millennium could become a larger company than Amgen sometime in the future.

Again, this is not a forecast. Drug trials are much too lengthy and unpredictable to permit any certainty about future valuations. This illustration explores the reasons for high market capitalization among unprofitable companies. Millennium may reach or exceed the Amgen market cap yardstick but the value of the stock also reflects some caution about the company's potential to fall short of that goal.

Another remarkable Tier 2 company is Vertex Pharmaceuticals. Vertex currently has one modestly successful drug on the market, an HIV/AIDS treatment called Agenerase which has yielded rather disappointing revenues because it was launched after other effective treatments had been adopted by the medical profession. Vertex has eight other drugs for a wide variety of disorders in clinical trials. Its balance sheet at this writing shows sales of $101 million and net losses of $27 million in the previous 12 months. Despite this negative income picture, Vertex has risen to a market capitalization of more than $4 billion.

Compare these numbers to those of Biogen, another Tier 1 yardstick, which has a market value of more than $8 billion. Biogen has one very successful drug on the market plus royalty income streams generating total revenues of more than $900 million. Biogen's after-tax profits are running at more than $300 million. How is it that a company like Vertex, which has chronically lost money in the past, is zooming upward on the stock market while Biogen is drifting downward?

Both companies' clinical trials programs show promise, but Vertex has a much larger drug development pipeline. Biogen has apparently achieved a peak value for its current income stream and its future growth is uncertain, dependent mostly on the outcome of clinical trials. But there's more to this comparison than drug pipelines alone.

Vertex is a unique company. Joshua Boger, its chairman and CEO, has built an organization with a laser-sharp focus on results. He has set an ambitious course, aspiring to shrink the time required to develop a new drug from the 15-year standard accepted by major pharmaceutical companies to as little as 5 years. Vertex's research and development program is driven by this challenging vision.

Unlike many biotech companies, Vertex has established a broad variety of scientific and technical platforms. Vertex integrates many new and older technologies in a coordinated manner. Evolving sciences like computational chemistry (the prediction of chemical interactions using advanced software) and chemogenomics (which relates the new understanding of genes to chemical interactions) are used concurrently with more established technologies such as crystallography (the determination of a molecule's shape by bombarding it with X-rays to see how energy is diffracted), spectrometry (the determination of molecular structure through measurements of mass), and combinatorial chemistry (a method to test the interactions of large numbers of chemicals by combining them en masse with a single target compound). However, the specific technologies aren't the point here. The key is the integration of diverse tools with a sharply defined purpose: the creation of small molecule drugs.

The company's choice of small molecules is a highly efficient technical and business strategy. Small molecules are easier to work with, and easier for the human body to absorb and use, compared with the giant molecular structures required for protein-based therapies. The active mechanisms of small molecules are also much easier to understand and simulate in computers. The small molecule is the traditional province of older pharmaceutical companies, but Vertex brings a high degree of technological innovation to the discovery process.

Vertex also demonstrates sharp focus in other aspects of its business. The company is constantly building new alliances with larger companies that will absorb much of the risk and expense of developing and proving new compounds, while permitting Vertex to maintain control of research and development. Vertex management drives a hard bargain, insisting on substantial royalties from any successful compound and ownership of drugs that may be abandoned by a client for any reason. The Vertex strategy was endorsed in a major way in May 2000. Until then, most of the company's alliances had been forged with midsize companies for relatively small upfront payments. Novartis changed the picture by signing a six-year, $800 million deal for the development of at least eight drug targets by Vertex. Like the Millennium deal with Aventis, the Vertex agreement with Novartis strongly validated the company's scientific and business model. The stock quickly tripled in value.

Compared with Biogen's market cap, in the $8 billion range, Vertex, which is trading in the $4 billion range, looks like a credible contender.[2] Measured against Amgen's valuation, Vertex is still tiny but there is reasonable cause to hope the company can eventually reach this milestone as well.

Vertex and Millennium display the kind of corporate management that investors should seek out in a Tier 2 contender. If one is to have confidence in a market capitalization above a billion dollars for a company with no profit history, the organization must display exceptional qualities to support its present valuation and to lend credibility to its potential. These qualities include ambitious drug development plans supported by highly focused and motivated management, as well as a large pipeline of drugs in clinical trials and support from major corporate alliances. If this potential is eventually realized through the delivery of important new drugs to market, then investors may consider the yardsticks provided by Amgen and Biogen valuations as credible goals.

Another kind of contender in the Tier 2 category is the biotechnology product company, not a drug developer. Affymetrix has a market capitalization of more than $3 billion on sales of more than $172 million and losses of less than $18 million.

Affymetrix has achieved a multibillion-dollar market capitalization by becoming the market leader in gene chip technology. These chips are the devices which have been described in countless magazine articles as they key to personalized medicine. In many writers' views of the future, patients will be able to send their doctors a small genetic sample, perhaps some saliva, for a total reading of their genetic makeup and health. Currently, gene chips (also called gene probe arrays or microarrays) are about the size of a postage stamp and are made with materials and processes first created by electronic semiconductor chip manufacturers. Thousands of tiny chemical markers, so-called gene-probes, are precisely piled in columns on the surface of a chip, as its silicon layers are deposited and etched with microscopic precision.

One Affymetrix executive suggested thinking of the strands of a shag rug to visualize the chip surface.[3] Each chemical strand is custom-made by layering the molecules that make up DNA (A, C, T, G) until a distinct genetic chain is laid out. Each strand, or probe, will bind only to the specific gene sequence it is designed to detect.

The use of these chips involves a process called *hybridization*. The surface of the chip is bathed in a solution containing genetic material of interest; for example, genetic matter from a cancer patient's tumor. Some of the genes will attach to (or hybridize with) the tiny probes on the chip, but only when their patterns match with a complementary genetic pattern. When scanned by a laser, these hybridized probes will fluoresce and the active points of light will be detected and cataloged in a computer. The resulting reading of active genes in the sample allows researchers to discriminate among many different kinds of cancer and tumor activity. With such a precise portrait of the illness, a physician is able to treat the patient more effectively with drugs specific to the diagnosed condition. Certainly there is a desperate need for drugs that are more specific than present-day chemotherapies, which have debilitating side effects on many parts of a patient's body. The chip could ultimately result in the creation of genetically specific therapies that could be much more precise and effective than the antibodies and immune system stimulants now being brought to market by the biotech industry.

So, will the magazine writers' vision of a quick genetic test for every kind of defect or disease ever be realized? Probably not, one Affymetrix executive told me. It simply wouldn't be efficient to create a chip bearing hundreds of thousands of probes for genetic variations and mutations, plus the genes for all known infective diseases in a one-shot test. Even if the "one chip fits all" vision isn't realized, the gene probe array will eventually become an indispensable tool of medicine. Most likely, a physician will have to analyze a patient's condition and select a gene probe array that has been designed to look for problems in that particular area, much like an Internet search engine, which works more efficiently if it is better targeted. Gene chips will also be used to read portions of the genetic code of individuals suffering from diseases that may be caused by an inherited genetic defect or mutations caused by environmental factors.

A study in the *British Medical Journal* predicts that assessing a patient's genetic drug sensitivity profile will eventually become routine for general practitioners. "One day," the authors say, "it may be considered unethical not to carry out such tests" because of the risk of exposing patients to harmful doses of drugs.[4]

The gene probe is already heavily used in genomic research laboratories, selling 100,000 units in the most recent Affymetrix annual report. Biochips cost anywhere between $45 and $2,000 each, depending on the degree of customization required by the client. A scanning platform, which is required to read the chips, can cost more than $100,000. Experts say the cost of a biochip must come down to about $5 before it can be adopted in everyday medical practice but if electronic chip-making is anything to go by, achieving this goal is just a matter of time.

Affymetrix has risen to the second tier partly because of the gene-chip's potential in medicine and partly because of the company's business profile. In the same way that Intel and Cisco staked out their turf in the personal computer and Internet spheres, Affymetrix is establishing a leadership position in gene chips. The product is constantly being miniaturized and adapted to increasingly specialized uses. Affymetrix is facing patent infringement lawsuits, but the company is defending itself aggressively. For the time being, legal expenses are holding the value of Affymetrix stock down. There are established competitors in this field, including Hyseq and Nanogen. Newcomers, including Motorola, Corning, and a Japanese consortium, have recognized the potential of biochips and entered the competition, but Affymetrix remains the industry leader.[5]

Tier 2 companies stand as the models for tomorrow's biotech giants. They have maintained multibillion-dollar market capitalization by striving for a leadership position in their respective fields. They are at once intensely focused on achieving specific goals yet broadly active in an array of technologies, partnerships, and potential markets. Because their valuations may have increased as much as 10-fold since 1999, there is little hope of achieving the investor's dream of buying a great company in this tier for pennies on the dollar. Nevertheless, it is reasonable for investors to hope that Tier 2 firms can reach the valuation parameters established by Biogen and Amgen. And, if they maintain their aggressive, expansionary visions after achieving their first successes, they have the potential to become much greater companies than the models I have chosen to measure them against.

Assessing a company's time line to profitability is the best way to estimate risk and growth potential among the multibillion-dollar contenders in Tier 2. Some companies in this category may not realize a profit for five years or more. Although I am inclined to be a long-term investor in this sector, the biotech industry is changing and emerging toward profitability very rapidly. Investors have many choices among companies that expect to produce profits within two years. By contrast, investment in a biotech business that cannot find a way to emerge from the red in less than five years promises to produce stagnant stock market returns at best. At worst, the business and scientific environment may change considerably over that span of time and the company may never deliver a profit. Imprecise business plans and foggy visions for the future are simply unacceptable in this high-priced tier, no matter how remarkable the degree of scientific achievement a company displays. The degree of risk is substantially increased by longer time lines to profitability.

Tier 3: Mid Cap, High Expectations

Tier 3 companies are the most difficult to value. With market capitalizations in excess of $800 million and no profits, they carry substantial risk, and, in many cases greater downside potential than Tier 2 companies. Companies in this category should be rigorously screened for two key risk factors: the danger of severe losses from a failed drug therapy and excessively long time lines to profitability.

The biotech boom early in the year 2000 was responsible for lifting many Tier 3 companies from penny stock status. Among those that have sustained their valuations, most are drug development companies nearing the conclusion of the clinical trials process with promising therapies for big-target diseases such as cancer, heart disease, Alzheimer's, and inflammatory disorders like lupus. Although the market has lifted Tier 3 companies to relatively high valuations, they often remain specialized in a single field of biotechnology, just as they were a year or two previously when they were struggling to survive while bringing a promising new idea from the lab to the marketplace.

The market value of such companies is balanced on a knife-edge. Profits and share-price increases could be tremendous, but only if their lead drug clears the clinical trials process, then secures FDA approval and is subsequently accepted by the medical community. However, if a company's first drug candidate fails at any point in this process, the consequences for investors are severe. Almost a dozen Tier 3 companies have experienced the failure of their most advanced drug candidates during 2000 and investors suffered losses in the 70 percent range as a result. At this writing, Cell Pathways is the most recent victim of such a setback, having had its lead anti-cancer compound rejected by the FDA (described in detail in Chapter 7).

Specialized Tier 3 companies, in the business of developing and selling genomic information to enable drug discovery, frequently suffer from the sector's other major risk factor, excessive time lines to profitability. Data banks and genomic analysis companies flourished on the markets during the early period of excitement over the decoding of the human genome. Many were assumed to hold priceless secrets about the genes that are at the heart of many diseases. But now, drug development companies have been swamped with information as the biotech industry pours out a tidal wave of data. It will be some time before the industry knows which companies in this tier hold the most valuable genomic discoveries and patents.

If soaring ambition and confidence could do the job, CuraGen's founder and CEO Jonathan Rothberg would probably take the prize. A highly charismatic man, Rothberg is surrounded on investment road shows by a throng of eager aides.[6] (His local newspaper in New Haven, Connecticut, labeled him "Rocket Man.") CuraGen's press kit is as slick as any produced by a Fortune 500 company, featuring images of the first footprint on the moon, the first flight by the Wright Brothers, and Henry Ford's revolutionary mass production assembly line.[7] His quote at the beginning of the previous chapter (comparing his company's future to that of Intel) is as bold as it could possibly be considering that CuraGen had no drugs in clinical trials at the time.

CuraGen is in the business of functional genomics and drug development. While Celera was busy mapping genomes, CuraGen applied itself to figuring out the exact functions of genes and proteins using the relatively simple genome of yeast as a model. Because there are so many similarities in the functions of genes and proteins among all living things, CuraGen's analysis of yeast has direct value in understanding human diseases.

CuraGen is valued at more than a billion dollars, and its market capitalization has risen more than 500 percent since late 1999. The company is losing more than $24 million a year on sales of approximately $20 million. It can afford to absorb these losses for some time, having built up a war chest of almost a quarter of a billion dollars during the market frenzy of the first quarter of 2000. CuraGen won't go broke any time soon, but is it a good investment?

Analysts have mixed opinions about CuraGen. There are no "strong buy" ratings I'm aware of at this writing. So, how did the company achieve such a high valuation? CuraGen has produced a scientifically impressive database of genetic functions. The company's expertise has proven useful to customers like Roche who need to know if drugs in development will have the desired effects. Morgan Stanley Dean Witter estimates that this intellectual property will raise the company's value to $14 billion by 2010.

Despite CuraGen's scientific skill, and despite Rothberg's pronouncements that his organization is "all about getting sick children out of the hospital," the company has yet to deliver hard proof that it can create viable medicines or profits.[8] A critically important test is now underway. CuraGen, and its partner Abgenix, have selected 24 antibody targets for possible development as cancer therapeutics. More than a hundred antibodies are also in development for inflammatory, autoimmune, and other diseases. From an investor's point of view, this achievement is remarkable compared with the rate of target development by major pharmaceutical companies. But there is no assurance that the company will realize profits before at least one drug candidate makes it all the way through the clinical trials process, potentially a six-year wait. In the interim, there is a possibility that some of the work CuraGen has performed for clients will bear fruit and the company will share in a royalty windfall (see Figure 5.1). There is also the possibility that the company's genomic database will prove its value, but there are many competitors in this field. (See Epilogue for an update on CuraGen.)

The prospect of holding an investment that has reached a development plateau in a field as volatile and fast changing as biotechnology is the equivalent of increasing risk. A volatile mix of high capitalization and narrow technical specialization is typical of many Tier 3 companies, and investors must exercise extra caution. Choosing among the many contenders in this category requires extra research, analysis, and greater comprehension of the technologies being developed. A broad pipeline, scientific diversity, and sharply focused management provide the only realistic assurances for investors assessing a Tier 3 company in the drug development business.

Cell Genesys is a Tier 3 company developing specialized expertise in gene therapy. Its lead products are two cancer vaccines, moving through Phase II trials. These vaccines are curative, not preventive like most of the vaccines we're familiar with. The Cell Genesys treatment involves removing tumorous cells, irradiating them and genetically modifying them. The modified cancer cells are then injected back into the patient with the hope of stimulating a disease-specific response from the immune system.

Results in trials so far have ranged from promising to outstanding. In some patients, the vaccine has produced apparent remissions in treatments for one of the most refractory of all tumors, pancreatic cancer.

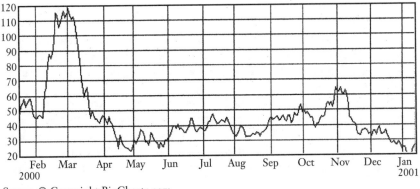

Source: © Copyright BigCharts.com.

Figure 5.1 Curagen (CRGN) One-Year Performance. (See Epilogue for update on Curagen.)

The company has also developed expertise in gene-delivery systems called viral vectors (the use of harmless viruses to deliver instructions for genetic modification to a cell nucleus). In addition, Cell Genesys has produced exciting results in the regeneration of damaged or degenerated nerve cells.

The company's listings of academic and commercial collaborators cover three full pages. It certainly has scientific credibility. Most of its corporate alliances are with other biotech firms. Cell Genesys is valued by the market at almost $800 million and its cash position is strong. All in all, it seems like a positive picture except for the company's relatively narrow drug pipeline. For the foreseeable future, Cell Genesys' profit potential relies largely on a single technology (called GVAX), which underpins the drugs in clinical trials.

What should a prudent biotech investor do? If, at the end of Phase II trials, Cell Genesys decides it is worth the risk to take the next giant step, Phase III trials, it might be time to share the company's confidence and buy in. But, four key factors weigh against a purchase decision, even at the Phase III stage:

1. The time required to bring a drug to market and the risk of failure remain considerable at the outset of Phase III.

2. The drugs in the Cell Genesys pipeline are based largely on a single technology and failure of one product could wipe out the value of the remaining drug candidates.

3. The company's relatively high market capitalization increases the risk of losses and limits upside potential during the development period.

4. Other companies are developing targeted, radiation-bearing vaccines that may be first to market, putting Cell Genesys at a possible commercial disadvantage.

Investors who got on board early deserve credit for recognizing a remarkable therapeutic innovation. But, at its current valuation and at this stage of development, Cell Genesys appears to present as much risk as reward potential.

One of the most interesting and attractive companies in Tier 3 is a company that is largely outside the drug development business: Diversa Corporation. Some have called Diversa a gene-mining corporation, a description that captures the most colorful portion of the company's discovery program. Diversa researchers literally go to the ends of the earth to dig up rare and potentially useful genes and enzymes. Company scientists have explored the jungles of Costa Rica, which are home to one of the greatest concentrations of diverse life forms on the planet. The team has found extraordinary microbes that thrive in the frigid and surprisingly arid environment of Antarctica. After some controversy, the Diversa team was allowed to visit Yellowstone Park to capture samples of the rare life forms that somehow survive in the bubbling mud holes and sulfurous pools that appear near geysers and other active volcanic features. Strange organisms have also been mined from the ocean depths where volcanic vents provide a habitat for sea creatures that proliferate among poisonous concentrations of harsh chemicals and sizzling water temperatures. As adventuresome as this quest may sound, it serves a more prosaic business need.

Diversa is looking for large molecules such as enzymes for use in industry. The company is building a collection of rare and exotic genes, proteins, and other molecules that have evolved in the harshest imaginable environments. To give life a toehold in these corners of hell, some organisms have become highly specialized by developing systems that can tolerate extreme environmental stresses and process toxic chemicals.

Discoveries among these rare genetic families promise to be useful to a wide variety of industries that employ chemical processes. Textiles, oil and gas, pulp and paper, detergents, food, and agriculture all are industries that use enzymes for a variety of applications. According to Diversa, fully 90 percent of all sales of industrial enzymes presently come from the production of just 30 products. The rate of innovation in the industry flattened out after the 1950s. The global demand for existing industrial enzymes is estimated at $2 billion. Capturing just a portion of this market would be a windfall and expanding the market by creating new enzymes would be an achievement of even greater value.

Several major companies including Novartis, Dow Chemical, Rhone-Poulenc Animal Nutrition, and Invitrogen have signed agreements with Diversa and the company's revenues are on the upswing although still comparatively small. Diversa has a market capitalization of more than $800 million and cash equity of $200 million. Its sales revenue stands, at this writing, at approximately $17 million and 12-month losses are almost $10 million. Major institutional shareholders include Putnam and New York Life.

In terms of its financial metrics and corporate alliances, Diversa is not much different from many other promising companies in the third tier. What makes it stand out is its time line to potential profitability. The industrial chemicals that Diversa is creating can be put into use without the years of clinical trials, and the many risks involved in the process of drug approval. The company recently formed a joint venture with Dow Chemical to develop industrial enzymes, and Diversa has created a number of chemical products that the two partners hope to commercialize in less than three years.

Diversa executive Hillary Theakston was bursting with enthusiasm when I visited the company's headquarters near San Diego. "Industrial genomics is the biggest resource imaginable!"[9] she declared. To demonstrate, she described a routine industrial process called "corn wet milling," which is used to turn raw cornstarch into high fructose corn syrup, a product used in vast quantities as a sweetener by companies like Coca Cola. (Coke permanently abandoned the use of high-priced sugar in the United States and many other countries when it launched the "New Coke.") The enzymes currently being used to break cornstarch down into sugar molecules operate only in a very acidic environment. Removing the residues of these acids and salts from the final product adds considerably to the cost of the process. Diversa has created a new enzyme that does the job in a much less acidic environment thereby saving the corn-wet-milling industry the cost of refining the residues from its corn syrups. Sound mundane? Diversa estimates that this one innovation is a $150-million product opportunity.

Because the genes and enzymes found and developed by Diversa operate far outside the usual range of temperatures, acidity, and toxicity that ordinary organisms and enzymes can tolerate, the company has created an opportunity to improve on the products of a multibillion-dollar industry. The company also has the potential to expand the industrial chemical industry by creating processes that previously seemed impossible. Diversa's innovations can be strongly protected by patents because they are not simply plucked from nature. The company's labs refine and evolve newly found genes and enzymes to optimize them for a given task.

This kind of biotechnology potential is hard to ignore, especially when it is backed up by considerable proof-of-concept, validated by highly credible partners and stoked by industrial markets hungry for cost-effective innovations. Not that I expect Diversa to make a killing overnight. The company's stock chart shows that many investors who bought in on the initial public offering did expect miracles and, for a brief time, the company was valued at more than $4 billion. But, despite the disappointment suffered by investors who paid IPO prices, the company has immense

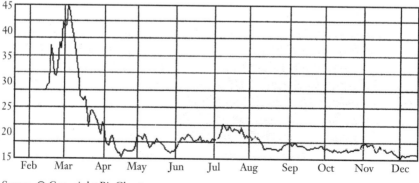

Source: © Copyright BigCharts.com.

Figure 5.2   Diversa (DVSA) from IPO

long-term potential. Furthermore, I think it is entirely reasonable to expect major growth within three years with limited downside risk (see Figure 5.2). That's a time horizon I'm comfortable with in a third tier investment. (Diversa and a leading competitor, Genencor, are also using discoveries from nature as an exciting resource for drug development. The rationale is that genes and other molecules which have survived the selective pressures of the evolutionary process will yield powerful new drugs.)

Investing in this tier wisely means watching and waiting. Not because anyone is able to time the market, but because testing takes time. Better to buy a good company a little late as it proves itself, than to buy early, at a premium price, and own a company that might prove to be a disappointment.

TIER 4: MICRO CAP, MACRO RISK

I have never enjoyed gambling, but I do enjoy investing in companies in the fourth tier more than any other. My delight in this sector has nothing to do with the thrill of risk and I don't believe in defying odds. The satisfaction of investing in fourth-tier companies is much like the delight a shopper experiences in searching for, and finally discovering, a great bargain.

Biotech companies operating with market capitalizations below $800 million are well under the radar for most large institutional investors. A huge mutual fund is unable to buy a meaningful position in a company of this small size. Consider the problem facing a diversified fund with $100 billion worth of assets under management. Buying into a small company generally requires limiting one's position to less than 5 percent of the company's total value to avoid various problems, including reporting regulations set by the Securities and Exchange Commission. Assuming the institution wants to go ahead and buy less than 5 percent of a $500-million company, the investment would be lower than $25 million. Compared with the fund's $100 billion capital base, this kind of investment would be relatively insignificant, even if the investment doubled in value over three years. Because of this size disparity, it would require dozens and dozens of micro cap success stories to make an impact on a large fund's total valuation.

For some institutional investors, that's a risky and an impractical strategy. Most large capital pools try to limit their holdings to something in the range of one hundred stocks. In addition, large capital pools often are bound by regulations that forbid their participation in stocks that trade in single digits.

Because the amount of trading in these shares is relatively low, large institutions also face a liquidity problem. They cannot operate in a small capital pool anymore than a large fish can hunt in a quiet pond without making waves. Major investment funds may be unable to buy a significant position in a small biotech firm without consuming the total number of shares available at the desired price. They will drive up their own costs if they buy too aggressively and even more worrisome is the problem of getting out. If a small cap company suffers a setback, the liquidity problem will have a greater effect. A large institution wishing to sell its position following negative news will find fewer buyers and even less liquidity. Dumping a huge volume of stock in a tight market will tend to drive the price down and amplify the institution's losses. These same liquidity dynamics already make the higher tiers of biotech stocks more volatile than the market as a whole. Among small or micro-cap biotechs, the large capital pools face prohibitive investment obstacles.

This odd dynamic gives individual investors one of the few advantages they can claim over the giants in the investment world. The little guy has freedom of movement while the major players are muscle-bound.

Tier 4 biotech companies are creating drugs and industrial technologies with large market potential just like biotech firms in any other tier. Generally they have low valuations because drug trials are at an early stage or because industrial products are not yet producing substantial revenues.

One of my first biotech investments may serve as an interesting example. Back in 1996, a friend of mine running a multimedia marketing business told me about work he had done for a small Canadian company called Vasogen. He had supervised the filming of patients who had been successfully treated with Vasogen's technology for a little-known condition called Reynaud's disease, an illness caused by poor circulation in bodily extremities such as hands and feet. Among the test subjects he had filmed in Scotland, my friend said the patients had experienced extraordinary recoveries. For the first time in their lives, he said, the test subjects had overcome the symptoms of chronic cold and stiffness in their fingers and toes. Patients were ecstatic.

At the time, Vasogen was traded only on the Montreal Stock Exchange and its price was little more than a dollar U.S. The risk of buying a few hundred shares was so small as to be negligible. It struck me that a company that had found a solution to the problem of opening constricted capillaries, veins, and arteries had exciting potential. Over the years I watched Vasogen with growing interest as the company's technology showed promising results in a wide variety of conditions, including atherosclerosis (hardening of the arteries), graft versus host disease (the rejection of transplanted tissue), transient ischemia (the most damaging effects of stroke), leukemia therapy, and a wide variety of autoimmune problems including psoriasis.[10]

Every time the company showed promise in a new field I bought a little more stock, but its value remained frustratingly low. Eventually the company was listed on the New York stock exchange and my small investment increased almost 10-fold. In late September 2000, the company was listed among the top five performers on the AMEX index after showing a 16 percent gain in a single week.

The company remains a micro-cap issue but I still hold it and so far I'm glad I did. There is a measure of security in Vasogen's diversity of disease targets and positive test results in major medical centers. If just one of its many promising lines of research makes it through the trials process, the company should realize substantial revenues and further market appreciation.

Enormous leverage is available to investors who find good biotech companies in the fourth tier. Taking a small position can be inexpensive, making the risk involved minimal. Reaping a reward, however, can require considerable patience. Many Tier 2 and Tier 3 biotech companies languished at extremely low market values for years until the sector began its rise from the doldrums in 1999.

One promising company that has tested the patience of micro-cap biotech investors is AVAX Technologies. Like Cell Genesys, Avax is using cell samples from the tumors of cancer patients to create curative vaccines. These cell samples are genetically modified to appear foreign to the body's immune system. When reinjected into the body, they stimulate an attack against similar tumor cells. In trials that began more than 10 years ago, the AVAX treatment, called M-Vax, was tested on 214 patients who suffered from advanced skin cancer: malignant metastatic melanoma. This is a deadly form of skin cancer and the AVAX treatment was used only on patients whose disease had metastasized—spread to the lymph nodes. The survival rate for such patients, treated with traditional methods including surgery and "alpha-interferon" drugs, was very poor. Only 20 to 25 percent of the patients treated conventionally were alive after 5 years.[11] Those treated with M-Vax showed a survival rate of 50 percent over a 5-year period and some patients were still showing an immune response against cancer after 10 years. This is a significant advance over present therapies for severely ill patients. As the company puts it, the vaccine trains a patient's immune system to attack their own cancer.

In June 2000, AVAX was rated a strong buy by analysts at Gruntal. M-Vax was going on the market in Australia while the rigorous trials process continued in the United States. The company had risen in value during the biotech boom early in the year, but it stubbornly remained at a valuation of less than $100 million.

This still seems like a model Tier 4 investment. The stock has maintained a price below $10 a share so it's not terribly expensive to take a position in. M-Vax is being subjected to unusually rigorous FDA testing in the United States because every dose of the drug is different, customized for the patient. Nevertheless, the therapy has earned orphan drug status, and it is showing exceptional promise in other areas, especially ovarian cancer. U.S approval for M-Vax is expected sometime in 2002, and the ovarian cancer treatment, O-Vax, is so successful in trials that it may be approved by 2003.

The largest institutional investor in AVAX, Paramount Capital holds $4 million worth of stock, a small amount in the world of giant financial institutions and less than 5 percent of the company's total value. There is room to grow and although the company is losing almost $9 million a year, it has sufficient cash to carry on for three years. The vaccine is no magic bullet but appears to be a safe and helpful addition to the arsenal of drugs targeted against a killer disease. Revenues are beginning to flow and the company's potential is bolstered by the apparent usefulness of this approach to other forms of cancer. Realizing a substantial profit from this investment may require further approvals in larger markets and a longer wait until additional therapies are brought to market. Because of the small size of such a Tier 4 investment, there is little to be lost by holding the stock and waiting patiently as a company, which has demonstrated the viability of its product in trials, achieves market recognition.

The intriguing thing about Tier 4 biotechnology companies is that they offer such a tantalizing variety of revolutionary products at seemingly low share prices. This presents both opportunity and risk. Alliance Pharmaceutical, for example, is a specialist in the use of perfluorochemicals (PFCs) and emulsion technologies, which may provide extraordinary medical breakthroughs. The most striking product is a compound called OXYGENT, which is now undergoing trials in the United States and Europe as a blood replacement. It has long been known that PFCs have extraordinary abilities to carry dissolved oxygen and other blood gases. The problem Alliance has apparently solved during 17 years of research is managing the highly oily nature of PFCs. These chemicals do not ordinarily mix with water, which means they cannot easily interact with biological systems. Alliance has solved the problem by creating an emulsion using chemicals called surfactants. (Emulsions are relatively stable mixtures of substances that repel each other. Surfactants act on the surfaces of oily and watery molecules to allow them to mix more easily. They are best known as the chemicals used to break up oil slicks after spills at sea.)

OXYGENT is being tested for use during surgeries that involve substantial loss of blood. Before surgery, much of the patient's own blood is removed for storage, and clear liquid OXYGENT is pumped into the body to take its place. This unusual chemical emulsion carries out the blood's task of delivering oxygen and absorbing waste gases such as carbon dioxide. If a patient bleeds profusely during surgery, he bleeds primarily OXYGENT, which can easily be replaced. At the end of surgery, the patient's own blood, containing many vitally important components, is returned.

Blood replacement is a promising alternative to existing methods. Banking a patient's own blood prior to surgery can result in the deterioration of important components when blood is drawn and then stored over a period of weeks. Drawing large amounts of blood for banking can also leave a patient weakened before surgery because of anemia. The advantages of blood replacement over the use of donated blood are also very compelling; there is no danger of spreading infection from unhealthy donors and no problem with blood shortages.

Alliance executives seem to enjoy startling investors by showing unsettling pictures of their products at work. The tactic certainly worked at a recent investors' conference when the company displayed images of a white mouse turning even whiter as its red blood was replaced with the clear PFC emulsion.[12] The last traces of color disappeared from the animal's pink feet and they turned light gray while the animal's red eyes went black. Even more bizarre was the demonstration of a product designed for inhalation. The photograph used to demonstrate this product showed a mouse, alive and healthy, while submerged in a container of liquid. It was breathing a PFC fluid, another of Alliance's products called LIQUIVENT.

LIQUIVENT turns out to be much more than a laboratory curiosity. It is a potential solution to the trauma that patients suffer from the use of mechanical ventilators to support breathing. LIQUIVENT is progressing through Phase II and III clinical trials, keeping desperately ill patients alive by filling their lungs with oxygen carrying fluids. (An Alliance spokesman assured me that the technique is not as uncomfortable as it might sound.) Yet another of the company's PFC emulsions is showing results by dramatically improving the clarity of diagnostic imaging procedures such as ultrasound. The FDA has indicated that it is ready to approve the product for market by issuing a so-called approvable letter.

The market for Alliance products could be enormous. The company estimates that 8 to 10 million surgeries requiring donated blood are conducted worldwide every year. The amount needed is usually between one and four pints. OXYGENT is expected to be priced at approximately $350 per pint. It's not difficult to calculate the potential market size for this lead product.

Only two analysts were on record as making recommendations for Alliance Pharmaceutical by the late summer of 2000, the most recent being a "Strong Buy" from Warburg on August 15. Phase III trials had then been conducted on 484 patients in Europe and an application for marketing authorization on the continent was being prepared (see Figure 5.3).

The European Medicines Evaluation Agency was reviewing Alliance's data from clinical trials when the excitement about OXYGENT and Alliance came crashing down. The trials showed a higher incidence of stroke among patients who had used the blood substitute, although Alliance argued that the number of strokes was within statistically normal limits. That was enough to halt clinical trials while researchers analyzed the data.

As if that wasn't bad enough, the company's shortage of operating capital led to a second major setback. Alliance had been pursuing a merger with

Source: © Copyright BigCharts.com.

Figure 5.3   Alliance Pharmaceutical (ALLP) One-Year Performance

another biotech firm in hopes of gaining enough capital to carry on. The merger took place on December 29, 2000, and Alliance announced the suspension of trials less than two weeks later. Now, Alliance is being sued by its new partner for several alleged securities violations, including the failure to disclose relevant data. The stock has taken a hammering, dropping from a high during the year 2000 of $18 per share to less than $3 per share in the early months of 2001.

No one can predict when the company's legal and technical problems will be fully sorted out. Alliance technology will undoubtedly prove to have some value to medical science, but for the time being the company's future is very much under a cloud. Investors who ignored the company's tight cash position during 2000 missed a key sign of trouble common to many Tier 4 biotechs. In addition, investors who became overenthusiastic about the potential of Alliance's blood replacement technology would have done well to spread the risk with investments in other companies that are developing competing forms of blood replacement. Above all, investments in Tier 4 companies, no matter how intriguing their technologies, should always be kept small. (See Epilogue for an update on Alliance.)

Summarizing the investment characteristics of Tier 4, it's obvious that the risk of losses in this sector is very considerable and bad news can come from some surprising sources. But, the degree of risk an investor faces can and should be moderated by keeping investments in this Tier so small and diversified that a serious setback will have little effect on one's overall portfolio.

On the other hand, the potential investment leverage from a few well-chosen fourth-tier companies can make up for many setbacks. After all, even the most profitable biotech firms, currently boasting multibillion dollar capitalizations started at this level. As an emerging sector, Tier 4 offers the fewest assurances of returns, yet, paradoxically, inspires the greatest hope for profits.

CHOOSING INVESTMENTS AMONG THE TIERS

The biotech investor is looking for companies that have credible potential to turn a profit or bring products to market within a reasonable time span. Target companies should have demonstrated that their products work as promised and that there is a substantial market for them. Investors must establish that the companies have not been overvalued and feel comfortable that the risk of a loss on the investment is tolerable.

Among Tier 4 companies, it is taken for granted that time lines to profitability will be the longest and risk of loss is greatest. As remarkable as their innovations may be, there are no guarantees and investors require enormous patience to enjoy the fruits of their decisions. In a diverse portfolio, some Tier 4 companies may languish at low values indefinitely and a few should increase in value several times over. These are the harsh realities of investing in emerging Tier 4 biotech companies, but my experience has been that the profits more than make up for the risks.

Third tier biotech companies are often the riskiest of all due to their high valuations. It is very difficult to find companies in this tier that have found credible strategies to shorten time lines to profitability or reduce the risk of product failure through broad diversification. When considering a purchase in this sector, try to imagine you are paying the full market capitalization value of the firm rather than the share price. Ask yourself if a money-losing company with a single technology or a single unapproved drug is really worth more than a billion dollars. If you can't be sure of the answer, you have already made the decision. Don't go near it.

Valuations of biotech companies in Tier 2 are highly subjective. Investors should look for exceptionally well-managed organizations that are likely to deliver profits in the near term and have the potential to become new industry leaders in the foreseeable future. Nothing less can justify multibillion-dollar valuations in companies with slim or nonexistent profits. The members of this select club are relatively few. Although I believe strongly in the potential of many second-tier firms, investors should be wary of high-priced companies that cannot deliver a credible business plan. If in doubt, think about dot-coms before opening your checkbook.

I suspect that many investors choose Tier 1 companies because they are the best known and they offer the appearance of security. Established revenue flows and products on the market are the goal of any biotech company. But, investors should keep an eagle eye on P/E ratios. The phrase "earnings disappointment" was invented for companies that are making money but not growing fast enough to support astronomical valuations. In today's overheated and volatile market, an earnings disappointment is just as bad as red ink on the bottom line if a company has been priced for perfection. Many Tier 1 biotechs are.

The profiles I have presented are intended to demonstrate a method for assessing companies among the four tiers of biotech companies. Business conditions may change substantially before this book reaches the reader. It is a process of analysis that I wish to convey, not a personal stamp of approval or disapproval on any company. Please check the Epilogue for late-breaking information on companies mentioned in this chapter.

CHAPTER 6

Biotechnology and Portfolio Planning

Biotechnology is revolutionizing medicine and agriculture in ways that were unimaginable just a few years ago, with far-reaching consequences for the quality of life not only in the United States but also around the world.

Federal Reserve Chairman Alan Greenspan
to the National Governors' Association, July 11, 2000

NEW VERSUS OLD STRATEGIES FOR INVESTING

No matter what sector one chooses to invest in, the goals of portfolio planning are similar:

- Maximize returns.
- Minimize risk.
- Control volatility.

The rules of the game have been repeated so often that every investor should know them by heart. Don't put all your eggs in one basket. Invest for the long term. Stay away from speculative investments (like biotechnology). Minimize risk as you approach retirement. And, above all, always consult your broker before trading. Why are so few people paying attention?

Perhaps because the behavior of the stock market has changed so radically in just a few years. The dramatic fall of Eli Lilly, mentioned earlier, was just one example. Other companies I have referred to as examples of conventional investments include Intel, General Motors, Coca-Cola, and Gillette. Shareholders in all of these companies have endured wrenching price swings. General Motors fell from more than $90 per share to less than $60 in just three months between April and July 2000. Gillette dropped from a high of $60 per share to less than $30 in 15 months between May 1999 and August 2000. Coke hit a high above $69 per share in December 1999 and fell to $43 four months later. And, of course, there is the Intel crash. A supposedly rock-solid investment, Intel shed more than

$220 billion in market value during less than a week. Not one of these companies is losing money. Yet many of their investors have.

In the same time frame, chronically unprofitable biotech companies have risen dramatically in value. The Amex Biotech Index (BTK) rose approximately 200 percent over a year and a half. Many individual biotech companies, especially those in Tier 2, have enjoyed much greater gains, some exceeding 400 percent. But, as everyone knows, it has been a volatile ride.[1]

Examining Biotech Volatility

Biotech stocks no longer have the market cornered when it comes to volatility. The small sampling of conventional companies just mentioned includes only secure, established multinational firms with consistent earnings, blue-chip holdings. Companies of the highest quality are now experiencing increasing extraordinary levels of instability. What has changed in the markets?

A recent study of market volatility by the Federal Reserve Bank and academics from several leading universities found two contradictory trends.[2] Measuring the volatility of a "typical stock," the authors found a significant increase over the years. Since 1960, the volatility of individual securities has risen by almost 100 percent. Surprisingly, the market as a whole during the 1990s was less volatile than it had been in previous decades. The study says the stock market of the 1990s was 31 percent less volatile than the market of the 1980s. But now, even marketwide stability is being shaken. A report from Bloomberg found that the Nasdaq composite index had become a daily "roller-coaster" ride in the first seven months of 2000. During that period the market shot up or down an average of more than 2.5 percent every day. Two years earlier, the average daily move was a little more than 1 percent. Investors of every stripe face a stock market that offers far less security and stability than it did only a few years ago.

By comparison, quality biotech stocks of the first and second tier are actually less volatile than blue-chip securities and high-growth companies like Cisco and Intel when measured by the most common standard: beta. Table 6.1 shows the "beta" of previously mentioned stocks from each sector. Beta is a widely used ratio that compares the volatility of individual stocks to the market as a whole, as tracked against the S&P 500. The market average of volatility is given a value of 1. A number higher than 1 shows proportionately greater volatility and a figure lower than 1 shows proportionately less volatility.

Common sense suggests this can't possibly be correct. How could a company like Gillette be five times as volatile as an unprofitable biotech firm like Human Genome Sciences? It's a question of perspective. Every biotech investor knows that 5 or 10 percent variations in the value of a biotechnology company from day to day are not uncommon. Over the

Table 6.1 Beta Figures for High-Tech, Biotech, and Industrial Stocks

Name of Stock	Beta
Intel	1.31
Cisco Systems	1.53
Vertex Pharmaceuticals	.73
Human Genome Sciences	.23
Amgen	.82
Medimmune	1.3
Gillette	1.12
General Motors	1.07

Source: Figures from S&P Comstock, October 12, 2000.

course of a month, it all tends to average out for a quality biotech holding. Day-to-day price changes are relatively large, but monthly volatility is surprisingly low which is why biotech beta figures seem to contradict common sense—price swings during the entirety of the year 2000 in the biotech sector have been extraordinarily high.

A one-year graph of biotech volatility shows how misleading statistical measures can be. Figure 6.1 demonstrates unmistakably that over 12 months the true volatility of a company like Human Genome Sciences is visibly greater than the market benchmark, the S&P 500. The beta statistic of .23 for HGSI may be a financial industry standard but it has limited relevance to the real dynamics of this stock.

A similar ratio of volatility appears in Figure 6.2. It shows a comparison of the entire Amex Biotech Index to the S&P 500. The charts leave little doubt that biotech has given investors a rough but rewarding ride.

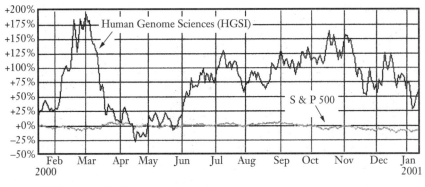

Figure 6.1 Human Genome Sciences (HGSI) versus S&P 500 during 2000

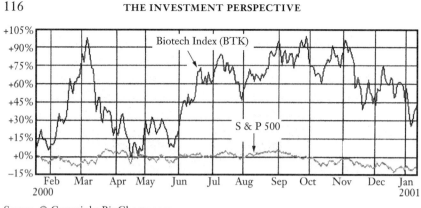

Figure 6.2   Biotech (BTK) Index versus S&P 500 during 2000

One of the key reasons for the volatility of biotech stocks is the liquidity issue. In terms of real volume, biotech stocks are more thinly traded on a daily basis than large cap issues. A company like Intel, for example, has more than 6.5 billion shares on the market and trades an average of 25 to 30 million shares daily. Human Genome Sciences has only 55 million shares outstanding and trades an average of 1.2 to 1.7 million shares a day.

Although the trading volume in Human Genome Sciences is a mere trickle compared with Intel, the proportion of shares traded every day compared with the total number available on the market is much higher for the biotech stock (less than 0.5% for Intel compared with more than 3.5% for HGS). When trading volume in the biotech sector rises sharply, as it did earlier in the year, biotech stocks may face a liquidity squeeze. If insufficient shares are available to meet buy or sell orders, the value of a stock can be forced up or down disproportionately. That's one of the technical factors driving biotech volatility.

The danger is that distorted price increases, artificially created by a liquidity squeeze, may be wrongly perceived as meaningful gains in corporate valuation. Investors should keep a sharp eye on trading volume before buying into a biotech stock during a sharp price increase. If trading volume is many times higher than usual, there's a good chance that a liquidity squeeze is pushing prices up artificially. They will likely fall back when volume decreases.

A sectorwide liquidity squeeze is one of the key factors in the dynamics of a biotech bubble. When a market as large as the Nasdaq, which routinely trades more than a billion shares daily, moves into a sector as thinly traded as biotechnology, the effect is greatly exaggerated. If the disproportionate effect of a sudden liquidity squeeze is mistaken for a sustainable industry trend, as it was during the excitement over genome mapping, trading volumes will grow ever more quickly. The squeeze will be intensified and a vicious cycle will begin, driving prices up in exponential leaps. When the market capitalization of companies in the sector becomes insupportable, the beginnings of a selling trend will reverse the liquidity squeeze very suddenly. Prices will be driven downward violently as the oversupply of sellers pushes prices into a panic-driven plunge.

A review of trading volumes for Human Genome Sciences during the March bubble shows a liquidity squeeze at work. During the buying phase, daily volumes rose above 5 million shares traded . . . almost 10 percent of the company was in play. During the subsequent panic, more than 12 million shares changed hands. If a company like Intel faced similar volumes it would be the equivalent of putting approximately 1.5 billion shares on the market. During its October plunge, Intel volume remained below 100 million shares.

It's apparent from the huge volume of trading in the months before the March biotech crash that HGS was in a speculative whirl. Volume was high enough to rotate the entire capital base of the company many times over (see Figure 6.3). Momentum players were buying in and selling out as often as they could to harvest a profit. Those left holding the bag in a downward squeeze may be long-term investors who bought during a period of overexcitement.

The danger of biotech bubbles will not abate until the industry has many more shares on the market and a larger sustainable capital base. For

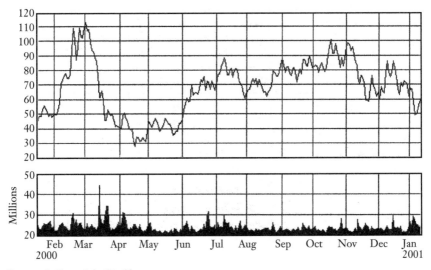

Figure 6.3   Human Genome Sciences (HGSI) Volume: One Year

the time being, the entire sector still operates from a capital base smaller than that of General Electric.

As a long-term investor, I prefer to ignore market volatility and allow my investment to grow with a company I believe in. When all is said and done, performance is the thing that really matters. In this comparison of two top-flight companies from the high-tech sector and biotech, there is no contest. Human Genome Sciences has outperformed Intel in all but three months, as shown in Figure 6.4.

Whether one measures volatility by the month, the year, or market movement, investors are likely to face sharp price changes no matter what kind of stock they choose.

Between May and October 2000, an index investor holding all of the Dow Jones Industrials' 30 blue-chip stocks would have lost approximately 9 percent. The fortress of the new economy, the Nasdaq, lost 33 percent in the same period. Investors who chose "Exchange Traded Funds" to follow major indexes would have done no better. Recalling the wild swings of the Nasdaq during the year 2000, it seems apparent that many index investors continued to experience substantial volatility while sacrificing potential performance.

Mutual funds provide another way to moderate volatility. America's 10 largest mutual funds showed an average loss of 2.7 percent during the first nine months of the year 2000 (without taking fund expenses into account). During a time of enormous productivity increases in the United States, mutual fund investment strategies have yielded modest results at best. Once again, biotech investors have reaped the biggest gains. One of the best mutual funds in the sector, the Dresdener RCM Biotechnology Fund gained 120 percent over the first eight months of the year.

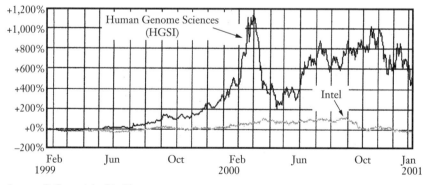

Source: © Copyright BigCharts.com.

Figure 6.4   HGSI versus INTEL: Two-Year Comparison

The harsh reality appears to be that the market now provides few safe havens from volatility. Depending on the time frame one uses as a measure, large price swings have shaken investors in almost every sector during one period or another. At least, biotech stock performance has generally made the experience a good deal easier to take.

Managing Volatility and Risk

Tier 1 Biotech companies, by definition, have the largest cash flows and, not surprisingly, experience the lowest levels of short-term volatility. Tier 2 and Tier 3 companies have little protection against volatility, no matter how strong their organizations and share price growth may be. Medimmune, a Tier 1 company with six products on the market and income approaching a half billion dollars shows substantially less volatility than a top-flight company from Tier 2, such as Protein Design Labs (see Figure 6.5).

An established earnings stream moderates short-term volatility among biotechs. Chart any company below Tier 1 and in almost every case, the apparent level of volatility will be much the same. The interesting thing, however, is the moving average.

Smoothing out the volatility for Protein Design Labs, a 200-day moving average shows a consistent rise in corporate valuation. In fact, the gains have been sensational, showing a 52-week increase of more than 450 percent with little long-term fluctuation in the growth trend, as shown in Figure 6.6.

This is one technique to help investors live with biotech volatility: Ignore daily fluctuations and keep an eye on the trend lines. Think in terms of moving averages, and, if you can't visualize them, call them up on the

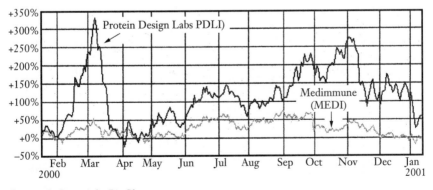

Source: © Copyright BigCharts.com.

Figure 6.5 Protein Design Labs (PDLI) versus Medimmune (MEDI): One-Year Comparison

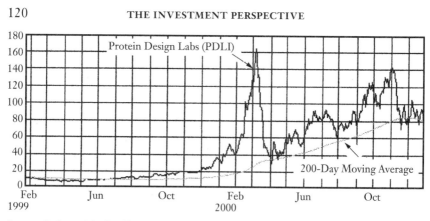

Source: © Copyright BigCharts.com.

Figure 6.6 Protein Design Labs (PDLI) Two-Year Performance with 200-Day Moving Average

Internet at services such as BigCharts.com. It can be difficult to sense trends in the blur of day-to-day volatility, 200-day moving averages may give investors a clearer sense of where a stock is headed.

One of the few parallels I discovered while trying to find patterns for biotech behavior was the semiconductor index (SOX). See Figure 6.7. Its pattern was remarkably similar to the biotech indexes. The fall of Intel dragged the semiconductor index down in September 2000 and biotech shares eventually followed. But for the first time, the much-admired SOX index plummeted below biotech.

Among the lower tiers of biotech stocks, there seem to be few useful patterns to be discerned in daily price swings. As a rule, Tier 2 and Tier 3

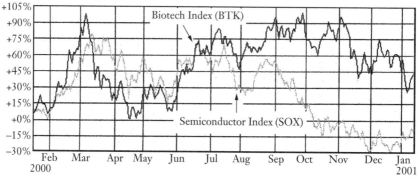

Source: © Copyright BigCharts.com.

Figure 6.7 Biotech (BTK) Index versus Semiconductor (SOX) Index

biotech stocks fluctuate more or less in tandem daily, suggesting that larger market forces are at work, rather than specific business factors. Apparently, these market forces are similar to those moving semiconductor share prices, but there seems to be little or no expert opinion about the nature of these wider-market undercurrents.

Price changes in Tier 4 companies seem to follow no discernable pattern at all on a daily basis unless there is significant corporate news. They oscillate within a trading range somewhat randomly, with one important exception. During periods of heavy upward or downward momentum in the sector, or in the Nasdaq, Tier 4 companies will be swept along by the current and may suffer exaggerated price swings.

On the whole, daily volatility should be of little concern to biotech investors who are confident about their stock choices. The trend lines, expressed by moving averages, are the most useful indicator of a particular stock's actual direction. Large price changes are cause to sit up and take notice. Do some research and find out if there have been fundamental developments driving the company up or down.

MANAGING RISK AND PORTFOLIO DESIGN

Diversification is the obvious answer to risk and volatility management no matter what field one is investing in. The independent biotech investor has a wealth of choices. The biotech sector is composed of some 400 publicly traded companies and many of them are approaching product launches and profitability.

The strongest opponent of diversification in investing I have come across is William O'Neil, the founder of *Investors Business Daily*. O'Neil advises against asset allocation in general, and recommends holding a very small basket of stocks. (Asset allocation involves spreading risk by diversifying among many different kinds of stocks and financial instruments, such as money markets, bonds, and foreign markets.) O'Neil says a person with $50,000 to invest should buy no more than four or five stocks.[3]

Mark Hulbert, editor of the *Hulbert Financial Digest* takes a radically different position. In a commentary for the *New York Times*, Hulbert says that a portfolio of 20 stocks was once considered the standard number of holdings required to limit volatility without diluting performance. Now, with the increasing volatility of the markets, Hulbert says he has come to the "melancholy conclusion" that an investor needs to diversify even further by holding a portfolio of 50 stocks to avoid sleepless nights. A portfolio of 50 stocks may involve a greater number of companies than most investors can keep track of, but long-term investors who have made good choices shouldn't need to track stock performance constantly. The most important safety net for biotechnology investors is quality stock-picking and broad diversification, a strategy that controls volatility and diminishes risk.

In scanning the available literature, I've found very few specific recommendations to suggest how much of an investor's total portfolio should be placed in the biotech sector. According to Michael Dauchot of the Dresdener RCM Biotech fund, no more than 10 percent of a portfolio should be devoted to biotech because of the sector's volatility.[4] His partner, Dr. Faraz Naqvi suggests no more than 5 percent. A decision of this sort is always based on personal goals, risk tolerance, and investor aggressiveness. My advice would be to examine one's existing holdings and decide what proportion is already dedicated to aggressive growth investments such as cutting-edge technology companies. If that portfolio percentage has proven to be comfortable in the past, I would suggest devoting half of that aggressive growth portfolio to biotechnology. The history of the biotech market over the past two years suggests that a diversified biotechnology commitment of this sort would have been no more risky and often more profitable than enduring the Nasdaq's plunge, a phenomenon now called the "tech wreck" by the pundits.

Risk tolerance is the most serious portfolio planning issue investors must address. Personally, I am willing to tolerate a greater than average degree of risk because I seek greater rewards and I'm fully prepared to do the investment research required. My solution to the problem of moderating risk is to choose the sectors I believe will be most rewarding and then to diversify very heavily within them.

I do not believe that all middle-aged baby boomers have had the opportunity to save sufficient funds for a comfortable retirement. Being in such a position is a risk like any other. Therefore it follows that aggressive (not careless) investment strategies may be appropriate after a family's housing and college expenses have finally been disposed of. Age should not be an automatic limitation on market participation, as the conventional rules of investment have suggested, especially when alternative strategies are underperforming and biotechnology is performing very well. My experience among middle-aged investors indicates that asset-allocation rules are already largely ignored by those who need to put their money to work. Right now, biotechnology is working best and the long-term view suggests the sector's growth and development will be sustainable over several decades.

RISK MANAGEMENT AMONG THE FOUR TIERS

There are many ways to control risk and avoid costly mistakes. The most important risk management tools for biotech investors are stock-picking disciplines of the sort outlined in previous chapters. Assuming one has chosen companies that satisfy these requirements, it is then time to winnow down the choices even further. The goal is to get the most for your money while achieving portfolio diversity. It's best to begin by dividing one's selections into the four tiers of biotech companies. In theory, the

objective is to select the best companies from each tier with an eye to taking a suitably sized position in all four levels:

- *Tier 1.* The high P/E ratios of most Tier 1 biotech stocks are the
  greatest concern in this sector. Medimmune (DNA) and Genentech
  (DNA) both experienced severe market setbacks in the third quarter
  of 2000, due, in part, to their high valuations. Medimmune lost 25
  percent of its value in a single day when one analyst downgraded the
  stock because of concerns about overseas sales growth. Genentech
  reported record growth but not enough to satisfy the market's expectations and share prices fell 20 percent during the third-quarter
  earnings season. Most biotech analysts recommend Tier 1 companies
  as core holdings, but the fate of these two companies illustrates the
  danger of excessive valuation in the Tier 1 group. If daily volatility is
  a concern, Tier 1 biotechs are usually the most stable. And, if an investor is uncomfortable owning companies in lower tiers with negative earnings, this sector may provide a greater sense of security. But,
  because Tier 1 biotech shares are highly valued, upside potential is
  more limited than in other tiers.

- *Tier 2.* Among the .best companies in this tier, investors can expect
  substantial long-term growth accompanied by significant daily volatility. Firms like Millennium, Human Genome Sciences, Protein Design
  Labs, and Vertex all enjoyed gains above 200 percent during the year
  2000. Because Tier 2 companies have appreciated very quickly and
  share prices frequently exceed $100, some investors may find it diffi-
  cult to buy enough companies within this group to hold a fully diversified position. The initial growth phase of Tier 2 biotechs may be
  reaching a plateau but their strong pipelines and royalty agreements
  will likely spark a second growth phase as products come to market.
  When deciding on the core assets of a biotech portfolio, investors
  would be well advised to give companies in the first or second tier a
  dominant position, no less than 60 percent.

- *Tier 3.* Among Tier 3 drug development companies, investors should
  choose only those with at least one highly promising product near the
  end of Phase III trials or awaiting approval. It goes without saying at
  this point that they should also have a substantial pipeline in reserve
  and the scientific validation that comes with major partnerships. Industrial genomics companies with relatively short time lines to profitability should be considered in this group. Because drug development
  companies in this tier carry considerable risk, no more than 25 percent
  of a biotech portfolio should be committed to this group.

- *Tier 4.* Approximately 15 percent of a biotech portfolio should be a
  safe amount to invest among inexpensive but promising companies in

Tier 4. The small investments in this portion of a portfolio offer enormous leverage, but volatility is high and price fluctuations are highly unpredictable. When picking companies in this tier, investors should be aware that setbacks will be inevitable, so it is crucial to take only small positions, no matter how exciting a company's prospects appear to be.

It is a great delight to hold a Tier 4 biotech stock when its potential is first proven to the market as a whole. Most recently, among my own Tier 4 holdings, Onyx pharmaceuticals rose suddenly from a $10 share price to $24 when the company reported significant results from Phase II trials for head and neck cancer. Onyx has found a way to create what the company calls "armed therapeutic viruses"[5] that are engineered to attack cancer cells. The company is now recommended by analysts including Ronald Garren, M.D., of the Biotech Insight Stock News Letter, and USB Piper Jaffray's Peter Ginsberg. I make no predictions or recommendations about Onyx in the future, and the stock has drifted downward considerably in the months since its announcement, a pattern typical of biotech market behavior following encouraging news. Nevertheless, the Onyx story makes the point that some very interesting companies are usually available in the fourth tier bargain basement.

The final step of the stock picking and portfolio building process involves narrowing down the number of selections while continuing to spread risk. The goal is to own a diverse selection of technological and business platforms among all tiers of biotech investments.

In Tiers 1 and 2, owning three drug discovery companies with different business and scientific strategies provides a substantial sense of security. Vertex Pharmaceuticals stands out from the rest because of its focus on small molecule drugs and quick product development. Protein Design Labs is a specialist in antibodies, and companies like Human Genome Sciences and Millennium Pharmaceuticals are internally diversified, pursuing drug development strategies from genomic discovery to patient care. For additional diversification, I suggest taking a position among so-called pick-and-shovel industries. For example, Affymetrix, an industry leader in the manufacture of biochips. Another example, Abgenix is a company that serves both ends of the business by taking part in drug discovery and supplying mice that have been genetically engineered to produce fully human antibodies. Like biochips, genetically engineered mice, goats, and plants have become an essential industry commodity for drug production and research. Investors should consider internally diversified companies like Abgenix or Genzyme Transgenics in their pick-and-shovel group among first and second tier biotech stocks.

In Tier 3, investors should seek diversity in disease targets among the companies that have met all other biotech investment criteria. I would also look for a variety of approaches to disease. Because companies in the tier tend to be specialists, the goal is to take several relatively small positions to achieve a wider breadth of growth opportunities. Industrial genomics companies like Genencor and Diversa should also be considered. It is not difficult to achieve diversification in Tier 3, but it is a challenge to find companies that have not been overpriced.

The fourth tier is the most diverse of all, offering a host of biotech companies with a staggering array of novel approaches to biological problem solving. Diversification is almost automatic when choosing companies in this sector. What's more, share prices are generally so affordable that one biotech author, Cynthia Robbins-Roth, calls it "investing for free."

Returning to the Tier 1, some companies in this profitable sector have had difficulty expanding their approaches to disease and product development since their initial successes. Many of biotechnology's first successful drugs are highly specialized proteins and agents of the immune system such as interferons. A desirable Tier 1 company would be an organization that has moved successfully into several technology platforms, including perhaps monoclonal antibodies, protein design, and genomic discovery. For example, Genzyme has achieved considerable internal diversification and was priced with a relatively reasonable P/E ratio of 30 at this writing. The key is to avoid one-trick ponies that may be unable to follow up on their first breakthroughs.

The same one-trick pony rule applies to companies in lower tiers. Single technology companies are just as risky as companies with extremely narrow drug development pipelines. For example, a new technology called antiangiogenesis (gene therapy to cut off blood vessel growth in tumors) has not yet lived up to the excitement that surrounded its discovery. Specialists in this field such as Entremed fell sharply in value when high investor expectations were disappointed by the technology's failure to deliver quick results.[6] Any company that relies on a single technology platform of this sort is no less exposed to failure than a company developing a very small pipeline of drugs. If a company's only technology disappoints, so will the stock. Tier 4 companies tend to have the least internal diversity because of financing limitations.

It may be impractical to expect a biotech investor to enter the field fully prepared to make many choices from a sheaf of promising stocks. Most will enter the field as I did, little by little. Nevertheless, the point of the scenario that has been described is to set out a pattern for portfolio design. Diversity among tiers, within all tiers, and within companies themselves will give biotech investors substantially lowered risk exposure without excessive dilution of profit potential. Choosing just a few favorites will remain a risky strategy as long as it is unclear which of the industry's many promising technologies will deliver the best results. Diversification is the likeliest way to participate in the sector's overall growth because the field itself is so varied.

Alternative Biotech Investment Strategies

"What you've got here is a mutual fund," one broker commented when looking at my own biotech portfolio. The man had a point. The strategy I've outlined involves a fairly large variety of holdings although not nearly as many as the standard for mutual funds, which often hold more than 100 different stocks. That begs the question: Why not just buy a biotechnology mutual fund and be done with it?

For some investors, that could be the best solution. It would be risky to purchase a portfolio of biotech stocks if one doesn't have the time or the inclination to become deeply interested in the sector. Other investors may feel they don't have enough capital to achieve a sufficient degree of diversification. Mutual funds provide a solution in either case by providing substantial diversification along with professional stock picking. During the first two quarters of 2000, biotech and healthcare funds made up 17 of the top 20 performers according to Morningstar, the best-known mutual fund rating service. Morningstar's biotech analyst, Emily Hall, told Reuters news service that the sector continues to show enormous growth potential because biotech firms are "at the forefront of medical discovery."[7]

Standard & Poor's rated the Nicholas Applegate Global Health Care Fund as America's top performing sector fund during the first two quarters of the year 2000, up 78 percent. Morningstar chose the Dresdener RCM Biotech Fund as the number two domestic stock fund overall with a gain of 27.3 percent during the second quarter of 2000 and an increase of 74 percent for the first half of the year.[8]

Dresdener's biotech manager, Dr. Faraz Naqvi, turned in exceptional results considering the degree of chaos in the biotech sector in the three months following the March crash. Even Naqvi admits he wasn't wise enough to foresee the coming correction and sell a substantial number of overvalued stocks before the market fell. Nevertheless, this physician turned biotech investor beat all but one of the veteran mutual fund managers.

Biotech fund investors should also be aware of other issues. Some mutual funds call themselves "biotech funds" even though they hold substantial positions in major pharmaceutical companies. This practice is not entirely misleading because Big Pharma is an important participant in the biotech industry's development. On the other hand, investors should know what they're getting and the market has chosen to use the word "biotech" to define a sector of the market that does not include established pharmaceutical giants. Strictly speaking, funds bearing the name "biotech" should be a "pure play," to use the market lingo. Mixed funds should properly be called "healthcare funds."

Fund managers who mix the two kinds of stocks have an entirely reasonable goal. They hope to decrease volatility in the portfolio through diversification, but they also risk diluting performance. Dresdener offers a "Global Health Care" fund as well as a biotech fund, both run by Dr. Naqvi. The mixed fund grew by 54 percent in the first two quarters of 2000, an excellent gain, but still 20 percent less than the pure biotech play. For investors who desire less volatility, a healthcare fund may be the way to go.

Buyers should check a mutual fund's prospectus or refer to Morningstar.com for information on a fund's contents. Some investors may decide it is wise to hedge their bets by mixing biotech and pharmaceutical holdings. Others may wish to avoid pharmaceutical stocks because these companies face serious challenges including patent expiries, political threats, and public relations issues. In any event, fund buyers should be told plainly what they're buying, and if the fund's prospectus isn't clear, it makes sense to do some checking and find out what kind of investments one is buying into (see Figure 6.8).

The other major drawback facing mutual fund holders is capital gains tax exposure. At the end of the year, mutual fund owners will receive an IRS form called a 1099 that declares capital gains. Investors who buy shares in a mutual fund are also buying shares of accumulating capital gains tax liability; even if they weren't holding the fund at the time the gains were made. Considering the large gains in biotechnology indexes and the heavy trading of these stocks during volatile periods, investors may be buying substantial exposure to past capital gains tax liabilities. Failure to check on a fund's tax overhang could be a costly mistake.

The market now offers a number of interesting alternatives to mutual funds for investors with limited capital. In addition to exchange traded funds like those tracking the biotech indexes, there are unit investment trusts (also called UITs) and a new online investing concept called Folio [fn].

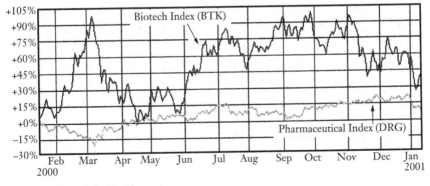

Figure 6.8   Pharmaceutical (PRC) Index versus Biotech (BTK) Index

Unit trusts are an old concept that has been adapted to current markets. In a sense, UITs are like shares of a corporation that holds a fixed portfolio of investments and eventually shares its profits or losses with investors who buy into the package. The corporation dissolves in a set period of time, usually one to five years, and delivers its returns to stakeholders. Unit trusts were long believed to be market underperformers because they dealt largely in mortgages and real estate. The new generation of unit investment trusts offers a small basket of stocks at a lower fee than most mutual funds charge. Shares in UITs can be bought and sold like stocks and several specialize in biotechnology. Investors are fully informed of all holdings. Companies like Niké Investments (nothing to do with the shoe company) and Salomon Smith Barney are able to charge lower fees because their portfolios are fixed for the duration of the trust. That means much lower management fees and no trading costs. Capital gains tax liability can be deferred by rolling over one's investment when a trust expires.

A new online trading company called Folio [fn][9] has come up with an original approach for investors who wish to buy a basket of stocks with limited amounts of capital. Put simply, an investor may choose a variety of stock purchases online without directly buying shares in the companies he or she selects. Folio [fn] accumulates buy and sell orders from its clients over the course of the day and trades the aggregate number of buy and sell orders from its clients near the beginning and the end of the trading day. It is an intriguing strategy for investors who seek broad diversification with a relatively small investment total investment. Suppose an investor wants to invest $10,000 in 20 biotech stocks. Purchasing them in the traditional way would be very inefficient. Folio [fn] allows investors to buy and sell stocks for a flat fee of $295 a year. Investors effectively own shares or portions of shares indirectly through the Folio [fn] holdings of their chosen stocks. This unusual system gives investors the opportunity to buy small positions in a wide variety of stocks without facing the practical problems involved in going directly to the market through a broker.

Margin and Biotech Volatility

Probably the biggest mistake an investor can make is to buy biotechnology stocks on margin. In the simplest terms, margin is a loan from your brokerage that allows you to buy more stocks than you could otherwise afford.

In a bull market, buying stocks on margin can amplify returns. To use a hypothetical example, an investor buying $5,000 worth of stock using his own money may be able to buy another $5,000 worth using money from a margin loan. Presuming the stock doubles in value over a period of time, the asset is now worth $20,000. After paying the brokerage back (not including interest) the investor is left holding $15,000 worth of stock. The stock has doubled in value but the investor has tripled his money.

Using the same hypothetical example, suppose that the $10,000 invest-ment suddenly lost money on a grand scale, perhaps 70 percent of its value. The investor now holds stock worth $3,000 but he owes the broker $5,000. His entire capital base is wiped out and the investor is suddenly in the red by $2,000. In reality, brokers will not allow the amount of stock collateral for their loans to fall that low.

Because biotech stocks are highly volatile, losses of more than 30 per-cent are not uncommon. An investor may have hedged against losses by di-versification but this provides no sure protection against a margin call. In the much-discussed March biotech crash, the entire sector lost approxi-mately 50 percent of its value in less than two months. Investors who used margin to amplify a biotech portfolio would have been utterly wiped out.

The problem with margin is that the downside risk is greater than the upside potential. In either case, the effect of a stock price movement has been doubled. There is no limit if the stock is increasing in value, but there is an absolute limit on the downside. If the investor has no more col-lateral and is forced to sell he will effectively lock in his losses. The broker is not a partner in the investment decision and will not wait for the stock to recover. Even if the stock's actual loss is only a temporary setback in the investor's opinion, he will have no choice but to accept sell and incur a dis-proportionate reduction in assets.

It is certainly easy to be caught up in the sense of excitement when biotech indexes rise. The temptation to use a margin loan is strong during heady times when every investment decision looks like a winner. Because margin loan positions can be increased as one's stock holdings grow in value, the temptation to use one's newfound "buying power" can seem ir-resistible. As the cycle of increasing success and increasing indebtedness accelerates, the risk exposure an investor faces grows exponentially. When the trend eventually reverses, margin-heavy investors soon discover that the system may be very forgiving on the way up but it is merciless on the way down.

WATCHING TRENDS FOR PROFITS

"The indiscriminate frenzy of biotech buying in the early months of 2000 was initiated, in part, by the market's realization of the sector's enormous promise. Since then there has been a marked and significant change in investor behavior. As Peter Ginsberg, a biotech analyst with U.S. Bancorp-Piper Jaffray, put it, "The sector is now based on product rather than promise."[10]

Genomics companies like Incyte, Gene Logic, and Celera were major players in an 80 percent rise in the Nasdaq Biotech Index during that ini-tial frenzy. Now investors have become much more discriminating. Com-panies with products in late-stage trials recovered well in the year's second biotech boom. Companies with products further back in the trials process and those with narrow pipelines did not recover nearly was well. Genomics research companies and other biotechs with long time lines to profitability have had very little to cheer about.

Looking back at the one-year chart for Millennium Pharmaceuticals, the vertically integrated drug developer, we see that stock rose strongly between May and November 2000, slacking off toward the end of the year in the powerful downdraft of the Nasdaq's slump (Figure 6.9). In addition to the many products in Millennium's development pipeline during this surge, the company had one new drug for lymphatic cancer awaiting FDA approval. That is why Millennium almost always outpaced the market averages despite the negative pull of the Nasdaq.

One of the peculiar characteristics of biotech stocks is their surprisingly sluggish responsiveness to positive news. On Thursday, December 14, 2000, the company announced that its drug for chronic lymphocytic leukemia had been recommended for approval by a committee at the Food and Drug Administration. The stock gained a little more than 10 percent on the day of the announcement and then fell sharply. As the five-day chart (Figure 6.10) shows, Millennium did rise strongly in the final hours of trading that week but it remained well below its high for the year.

Millennium's indecisive performance in the wake of positive news demonstrates two key characteristics of biotech stocks. Millennium's news was released during a week of severe losses on the Nasdaq. The stock's hesitant reaction to Millennium's positive news indicates that larger market forces exert a powerful pull on biotech companies, distorting their performance in unexpected ways.

It's also important to keep in mind that Millennium's performance on positive news is dramatically different from the probable outcome if the company's lead drug had faced rejection. This likely means that the market

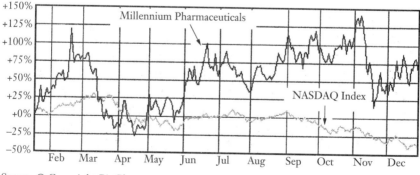

Figure 6.9 Millennium versus Nasdaq Index

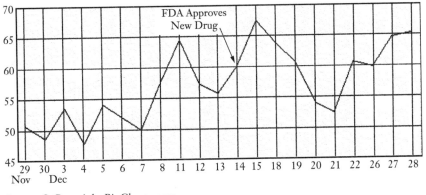

Figure 6.10 Millennium Stock Performance upon Product Approval

had already priced-in high expectations for success. Although these expectations cannot be represented by a P/E ratio (because of Millennium's unprofitability), it can be demonstrated by the contrast between the typically severe effects of product failure on any biotech stock, compared to the market's indecisive reaction to Millennium's success. Biotech companies directly involved in drug development walk a tightrope, highly valued for their potential but without the safety net provided by cash flow.

Millennium's one-year chart is remarkably similar in its profile to that of Amgen, even though the two companies have little in common in the biotech universe. Millennium is a Tier 2 company which has never earned a profit. Amgen is a Tier 1 industry leader with steady earnings and a market capitalization more than five times greater than that of Millennium (see Figure 6.11).

Comparing Figure 6.9 and 6.11, the moving averages and weekly price changes are very similar. Perhaps this is because the two companies have one notable characteristic in common. Both have the potential to increase cash flow with important new products about to reach the market. In the case of Amgen, the upcoming product is a new form of Epogen that requires less frequent dosing. This new version of an established drug will generate substantially increased revenues because Amgen will no longer be forced to share international profits with its partner in the offshore marketing of Epogen, Johnson & Johnson.

Compare the previous charts to the one for Incyte Genomics, shown in Figure 6.12. Incyte is a powerhouse in genomic discovery, boasting a partnership with IBM and a worldwide chain of distributors for its genomic data. Nevertheless, the Incyte chart shows some weakness.

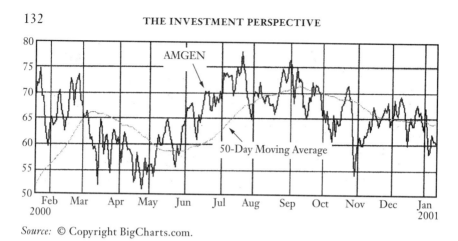

Figure 6.11   Amgen One-Year Performance with Moving Average

It appears from this chart, and others from similar companies, that ge-nomics fever is definitely cooling down. A closer look at the Incyte chart shows how short-lived the effect of major corporate news seems to be among genomics companies.

On September 11, 2000, Incyte announced the establishment of its al-liance with IBM. It was an important business development that greatly enhanced the marketability of Incyte's genomic data. The market re-sponded with a yawn, cutting Incyte's share price by 75 cents to $37 that day. Why? Partly because of the day's market pressures and partly because the company's profit potential remains uncertain. Over the two months

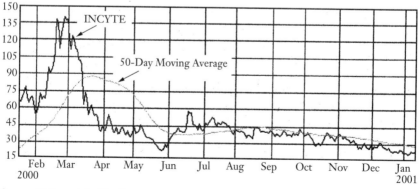

Figure 6.12   Incyte One-Year Performance with Moving Average

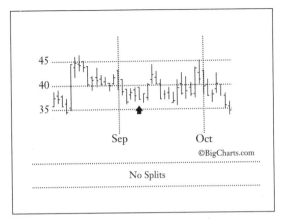

Source: © Copyright BigCharts.com.

Figure 6.13 Incyte Two-Month Moving Average

shown in Figure 6.13, Incyte did spike up for a brief period after the IBM partnership deal was announced but then continued to drift downwards, despite ongoing releases of positive corporate news. The news that would have made a difference, a projection of imminent profitablity, was not forthcoming.

Clearly, the market is now rewarding companies that demonstrate the greatest potential for profit in the shortest space of time. No longer would all biotech companies look the same to investors, full of promise and short on results. Now, new products and profits are imminent, and choices for biotech investors are increasing in number. During the previous two decades, only a few dozen biotech companies delivered viable products to market and earned profits, but now there are enough companies on the verge of profitability to fill a diverse portfolio.

Summary

The following investment lessons have emerged as the biotech market has become a more mature sector:

- Don't buy on the day positive news is announced. Markets sometimes overreact and the stock will likely cool down in a few days, making it available at a lower price.
- Don't be alarmed by a period of lower stock prices in the biotech sector. Volatility is the rule, not the exception.

- It may be better to buy a little too late than too early. Unprofitable companies that rise on good news usually sink substantially in value during the long product development period.
- Always consider the time lines to profitability. A company that is producing exciting results in early trials may experience a product failure. The company will still be an attractive investment several years later if it continues to show good results from clinical trials.

CHAPTER 7

———◆•◆•◆———

Decision Making

It is folly to forgo buying shares in an outstanding business whose long-term future is predictable, because of short-term worries about an economy or a stock market that we know to be unpredictable. Why scrap an informed decision because of an uninformed guess?

Warren Buffett, investment guru, in his 1994
Berkshire Hathaway Shareholder Letter

TAKING THE FIRST INVESTMENT STEP

The investor considering a first-time purchase in biotechnology faces daunting challenges. There are hundreds of publicly traded companies developing new products and technologies and, not surprisingly, press releases, Web sites, and annual reports universally project glowing optimism about corporate prospects. Critical analysis of individual biotech companies is as rare as news is plentiful. Risk and volatility are high, revenues thin, and time lines to profitability long. Before taking a position in a biotech stock, investors should assess their personal goals. Everyone desires maximum returns, but investors should govern their purchase decisions by gauging their tolerance for potential losses and their financial ability to diversify sufficiently to control risk.

For new biotechnology investors, the first step is not to go to a broker and not to make an investment. The safest beginning is to learn about the field through direct experience. Start by setting up a mock portfolio with an online charting service such as Raging Bull.com or BigCharts.com or a more sophisticated service like WindowOnWallStreet.com. Sign up for e-mail advisories from BioSpace.com and/or qxhealth.com. Get used to the heavy flow of information and try to become familiar with the stream of scientific jargon.

Go ahead and make purchase decisions in your mock portfolio with relative abandon. Then watch the outcome of these decisions over a period of time. After you've become familiar with the volatility of individual biotech stocks and the performance of your first selections, prepare to move on,

135

leaving this portfolio intact as a reference point. Set up a second mock portfolio and make a new round of purchases drawing on your initial experiences and adhering more closely to the criteria set out in this book, and any other investment guides you find useful. Compare the results. While monitoring your purchases, explore the Web sites recommended in the Appendixes. Check your portfolio against analyst ratings and against the performance of biotech indexes.

You'll probably have a good sense of when you've had enough preparation to make a few real investment decisions. In fact, you'll probably find it difficult to resist making actual biotechnology investments when you become interested in promising companies and comfortable with the sector's performance. Odd as it might sound, it is an important part of the learning process to become a bit jaded about the most remarkable developments. After growing accustomed to a daily flow of breathless e-mail bulletins, you will soon become aware that these news items are merely small pieces in a very large picture of an evolving industry. The key is to achieve a sense of this "big picture" to gain perspective on the merits and risks of purchasing a particular stock at any given time.

INTERPRETING HEADLINES—A SAMPLE STORY

Biotechnology generates more than its share of eye-catching headlines, and it's not uncommon to be drawn to a company by dramatic news headlines. But, exciting bulletins alone should not drive investment decisions. It is essential to decode news stories and scientific discoveries with an investor's eye, researching the meaning of news development for their financial meaning. Here's a sample analysis of a press release from Cytoclonal Pharmaceutics Web site:

Cytoclonal Obtains Gene for Telomerase— "Immortality"—Enzyme.

Sept. 6, 2000—Cytoclonal Pharmaceutics Inc. announced today the completion of an agreement with the Research & Development Institute Inc. (RDI) at Montana State University for worldwide rights to their Telomerase technology.

The Telomerase gene technology involves a gene which can be used to make variations of the Telomerase protein for treatment of degenerative diseases and optimization of the immune system. Telomerase is also a target for cancer and could influence the aging process.

"Telomerase is one of the most important proteins from the human genome," said Dr. Arthur P. Bollon, Chairman and Chief Executive Officer of Cytoclonal.[1]

Cytoclonal has acquired an important piece of intellectual property. But interpreting it from an investor's perspective requires some analysis of the gene's scientific background and its commercial potential. First, a brief sketch of the science behind the news.

Cancer researchers have looked long and hard for the universal factor in all cancers. The trouble is that every type of cancer features a distinct set of proteins, or markers on the surfaces of cancerous cells. These proteins are called tumor-specific antigens. Many conventional chemotherapies attack any cell that carries instructions or markers for rapid reproduction, including cells that grow hair, mucous membranes in the mouth, and the cells lining intestinal walls as well as tumors, hence the notorious side effects associated with current cancer treatments. Some new cancer medicines attempt to focus only on cancerous cells by locking on to a tumor-specific antigen and sending attack signals to the body's immune system. Like a red flag, these drugs send out the message "Attack here. This cell is foreign." Unfortunately, many new drugs using the immune system to attack specific markers for cancer have produced disappointing results, partly because cancers often change their surface antigens in the same way that bacteria can develop a resistance to drugs by changing its molecular coating.

Biotech researchers are seeking more universal therapeutic tools. The ultimate therapy for cancer would attack all cancerous cells by targeting a universal factor—something that must be present in all tumors. Telomerase is one such factor.

It is well known that one universal feature of cancer is its capacity for endless reproduction and this is where the "immortality protein" telomerase comes in. At the tips of every DNA strand are molecular caps called telomeres. Telomeres are like the front and back covers of a book, protecting the contents and marking the beginning and end. As the body ages and cells divide, telomeres become increasingly frayed. It is as if one photocopied a book many times and then tried to split the cardboard cover into thinner and thinner layers. Eventually the covers would become a shambles and the copied books would fall apart. In the same vein, telomeres can only be split a limited number of times during cell reproduction before they become so frayed that new copies of a cell cannot be made. When cells no longer reproduce and divide they eventually die off. Cancerous cells are called "immortal" because they all carry a protein called telomerase which stimulates the renewal of these vital telomeres, allowing cells to reproduce endlessly. The telomerase protein is therefore believed to be a universal marker for cancer.

In its news release, Cytoclonal Pharmaceutics points out that this key molecule is an important factor in aging, degenerative disease, and management of the immune system as well as cancer. The potential of such an asset could be spectacular. How could it not be a good investment?

Going beyond the press release and digging deeper can uncover some interesting background. Eli Gilboa, director of a study into telomerase at the Center For Genetic and Cellular Therapies at Duke University calls telomerase a "weak antigen"[2] that might need to be combined with other "universal antigens" to be effective. Discovering more universal cancer antigens will be no small task. Furthermore, there is competition. Geron Corporation, which specializes in diseases of the aging process, is also working with telomerase.[3] Because Geron does not necessarily require rights to the gene that creates telomerase in the body to develop specific drugs that control telomerase production, Cytoclonal has not acquired a monopoly.

Translating the science of telomerase into viable drug candidates may require years of effort. Subsequent clinical trials will consume even more time and more money. In the interim, other biotech companies are ignoring the search for universal cures and testing drugs that may soon prove to be highly effective in treating various types of cancer. Time to market is a key arbiter. Whoever is first to deliver an effective therapy has a tremendous commercial and regulatory advantage over late-arriving competitors.

It is true that Cytoclonal is doing promising work in several other areas and the company may be a sound investment choice for those reasons. But, one exciting headline such as Cytoclonal's acquisition of the telomerase gene should never be enough to drive a biotech investment decision.

It is essential to make investment decisions based on a biotech company's potential to produce practical results within the foreseeable future. The reason is plain enough. In this fast-moving field, important scientific discoveries and promising techniques may be beaten to market by more established, simpler, or cheaper technologies.

GOING IT ALONE?

Biotech investors who trade through a traditional retail brokerage may encounter several impediments. In some cases, your broker will try to dissuade you from investing in biotechnology because of its speculative nature. Investors may also suspect that their broker knows little or nothing about the sector. Clients need to determine whether a broker is able to contribute useful information to a biotech investment decision. Therefore, even if your broker does not challenge your decision, you should try to engage him or her in a discussion about the merits of your biotech investment choices. You will inevitably learn something, either about the investment or the broker.

Investors who use brokers should also take stock of the quality of their adviser's judgment. How well have past investment recommendations performed? It is possible that a broker may not be well informed about the biotech market but, nevertheless, displays good instincts and worthwhile judgment about market trends. Wise counsel is a surprisingly rare and valuable asset. Biotech investors who respect their brokers should not dismiss them lightly, not in a field this volatile.

Given the financial industry's limited focus on biotechnology, many investors have evidently made the choice to go it alone online. The impersonal and instantaneous nature of online trading has enabled investors to make rapid and sometimes impulsive decisions. Impulsive trading online in biotechnology could be an especially expensive mistake since buying a biotech stock immediately after receiving encouraging clinical or business news often delivers weak results. Also keep in mind that excessive buying and selling carries with it a hidden cost. During every transaction, the trader pays the spread: that is the difference between the going price for a buy and a sell, and in biotechnology the spread can be wider than average because of the low liquidity of many issues. More trades mean mounting spread costs paid by the investor on both the purchase and sale of a stock.

Trading costs aside, investors should think carefully before abandoning the counsel of experienced financial professionals. The fate of investors in a company called Cell Pathways illustrates why.

A CAUTIONARY TALE

During the first half of 2000, a biotech company called Cell Pathways released a flurry of news that strongly suggested that it had discovered a powerful new way to kill cancer cells. By putting out a high volume of press releases, averaging three every month,[4] Cell Pathways kept investors informed about dramatic results from a novel type of drug that selectively induces cell-suicide (also called apoptosis) in cancerous tumors while having no effect on normal cells. This family of drugs is called *SAANDs:* selective apoptotic antineoplastic drugs. The company's first SAAND compound went before the FDA for a New Drug Approval in 1999. Meanwhile, the company continued testing and development of its SAAND drugs and the more types of cancer Cell Pathways experimented with, the more effective and consistent the results seemed to be.

On September 23, 2000, the company announced that the FDA had decided that it would not approve the drug. Cell Pathways stock tumbled more than 70 percent, from approximately $30 a share to less than $8 in two days of trading. Raging Bull.com was peppered with postings from investors who came up with dozens of reasons to believe it was all a mistake. They remained convinced that the company had created a magic bullet against cancer and the stock would soon recover. But one very well informed writer rebuffed them all with a highly detailed, 14-point posting. He concluded that Cell Pathways' stock was dead in the water; at least until the next generation of SAAND drugs could demonstrate effectiveness.

The author of this extensive rebuttal argued passionately and authoritatively against the merits of holding the stock but ended on a sad personal note that said it all. He wrote, "I let myself get involved in this stock emotionally and now I am paying the price. I fear that my brokerage is going to sell me out Monday before I can get cash to them to cover my margin . . . and I have no one to blame but myself. I can't fully explain how disappointed I am in myself and this company. Farewell."[5] This conclusion is both poignant and intriguing because of the clarity and credibility of the author's previous corporate analysis. The writer obviously possessed the knowledge to comprehend the regulations and risks involved in the drug approvals process, yet he broke every investment rule in the book. He had become convinced that Cell Pathways possessed a magic bullet for cancer and he bet the farm. His stake in this one company was so great that a single product failure announcement threw his entire portfolio into a margin crisis. This was more than an investment setback; it was a love affair gone bad.

Every biotech investor will eventually be forced to confront the problem of emotional decision making. The prospect of a single cure for cancer can be as enticing to unwary investors as legends of El Dorado were to ancient Spanish explorers. Both are dreams in Technicolor. Decades of effort by the most brilliant scientists in the world with billions of dollars at their disposal have proven only one thing conclusively: that cancer is a disease of staggering complexity and unyielding aggressiveness. Perhaps Cell Pathways is still onto something. Possibly there is a common thread among the mind-boggling variations that cancer presents. (The company claims that its second- and third-generation drugs are respectively 10,000 and 20,000 times more effective than its previous lead compound. I hope this proves to be true. But, as a more cynical investor, such an extravagant claim leads me to wonder about the relative weakness of the company's much-touted lead drug.)

At its peak valuation, Cell Pathways was capitalized at more than a billion dollars. That put it in Tier 3 which is a very risky category. Reexamining the company's pipeline, it becomes apparent that a decision to buy Cell Pathways stock would have been an investment in a single technology platform. (The company is pursuing alternate technologies but they are at an early stage of development.) In effect, a billion dollars had been banked on one unapproved therapy! The degree of risk involved in buying an unproven single-platform company at such a high valuation was astronomical, no matter how great the potential reward.

The crash of Cell Pathways' stock is an important example of a speculative bubble at work in a single company. Biotech investors who go it alone, relying only on Internet advice, are taking a risk similar to a corporate executive who listens only to "yes men." Internet discussion tends to be dominated by "believers" and would-be experts whose comments may be self-serving, even corrupt. Biotech investors require a wider spectrum of opinion and critical analysis. Furthermore, sound advice about portfolio management, to avoid problems like a margin crisis, can be priceless. Good counsel of this sort requires no expertise in biotechnology, just investment experience. Even the best informed biotech investors, like the investor quoted earlier, can fall head over heels for a stock. For him, no amount of knowledge and common sense was enough to restrain his impulse to bet it all. Only a sober-minded and trusted adviser might have pulled him back from the brink.

If you don't want to hire a broker then tell someone else you trust and respect about your investment decisions. In some ways, it would be just as well if the person you chose to confide in does not have a compelling interest in biotechnology. When biotech gains are on the upswing, overenthusiasm about the sector can be infectious. The important thing is that your adviser have a good understanding of the market in general and a careful approach to investing. An impartial adviser can provide an invaluable dose of pragmatism when excessive optimism or intense volatility threaten to cloud a biotech investor's judgment.

MAKING BUYING DECISIONS

Start by buying quality companies, not quick cures. Companies like Human Genome Sciences, Millennium Pharmaceuticals, Vertex, and Protein Design Labs are "model" Tier 2 biotech firms with tremendous long-term growth potential. Despite gains of several hundred percent in recent years, the brief history of biotech investing demonstrates that much more is possible. To a first-time buyer, they may appear to be highly valued considering their negative earnings but firms of this quality have the potential to reach valuations greater than first-rate companies like Amgen. Even at current prices, good Tier 2 companies may deliver more than fivefold gains. As for the investor's downside risk, a second-tier firm's internal diversification and quality of management provides some degree of security. Portfolio diversification within this sector can provide additional protection against severe losses.

Perhaps, by the time this book reaches your hands, Tier 1 companies will seem more affordable. The exceptionally high valuation of most companies in this group currently allows little room for gains, and, because most are (at this writing) priced for perfection there is a considerable danger of disappointment. As mentioned earlier, the degree of risk involved in such highly valued stocks was graphically demonstrated when one of the companies in this tier, Medimmune (MEDI) fell 25 percent in October 2000 because a single analyst at Banc of America Securities downgraded the firm from a "buy" to a "market-perform."[6]

Billion-dollar valuations may be supportable for companies with highly diversified technological platforms and deep pipelines. But, in more narrowly focused biotech companies, like so many in Tier 3, such high valuations are usually driven by expectations that the first drug out of the pipeline will be a blockbuster.

On the day of Cell Pathways' spectacular plunge, two other biotech firms also announced failure of their lead anticancer compounds. Scotia Holdings, a Scottish firm, lost 61 percent of its value after the FDA rejected its anticancer drug, despite promising results from Phase III clinical trials. Another overseas firm, British Biotech, announced that its cancer drug had also failed.[7] The company's shares lost only 4 percent because previous drug candidates from British Biotech have failed during trials and investor expectations were very low.

The fate of these three cancer-fighting companies shows how important it is to keep an eye on a biotech company's current market capitalization. Cell Therapeutics and Scotia Holdings fell more sharply than British Biotech because they had been overvalued for their risk profile. The amount of risk and potential reward a biotech investor accepts when purchasing a stock is not set solely by the company and its technology. The market amplifies the degree of risk by bidding up corporate valuations. If you remember only one statistic after reading this book, make it this one: An average of more than 10 percent of all NDAs (New Drug Applications) are rejected by the U.S. Food and Drug Administration, despite successful completion of Phase III trials.

British Biotech's drug failures during clinical trials are a stark reminder that there are also many pitfalls along the way to an NDA. According to statistics from the Pharmaceutical Industry Association, as many as 90 percent of new drugs fail during the trials process.[8] That figure may be somewhat exaggerated by the industry lobby group, but nevertheless, it is difficult to overemphasize the importance of searching for a broad technology platform and a deep product pipeline when investing in a richly valued, profitless company.

PROFILE OF A TIER 4 CONTENDER

Earlier I mentioned a promising company called Vasogen and I'm happy to report that the news from this firm has been consistently positive for the five years I have held stock in this company. Having delivered a litany of cautions to biotech investors, perhaps it's time to remind readers of the remarkable scientific and investment potential of little known but carefully chosen biotech contenders.

In the years since I first purchased shares of Vasogen at little more than a dollar a share, the company's technology has demonstrated exciting and ever-increasing potential. First tested as a therapy against peripheral vascular disease, the technology has now shown effectiveness in five important disease categories. It is currently undergoing clinical trials in prestigious medical centers around the world in all of these areas:

- *Autoimmune disease.* This category includes rheumatoid arthritis, diabetes, multiple sclerosis, and psoriasis. The technology's ability to control the immune system will first be established in trials against psoriasis. Success in this field could lead to applications against many other autoimmune diseases.

- *Inflammatory disease.* Inflammation of the arteries and linings of vascular surfaces, called the endothelium, is a precursor to serious conditions including atherosclerosis, hardening of the arteries, and heart disease. Cardiovascular disease is the leading cause of death in the United States. Preclinical studies have shown that Vasogen technology significantly improves the function of the endothelium and reduces artery blockage.

- *Ischemia.* Diseases such as stroke and various surgical procedures damage cells through a process called ischemia. When blood flow to a part of the body such as the heart or brain is interrupted and then suddenly restored, cells often respond with an *ischemic* or inflammatory response that can be much more damaging than the initial, temporary loss of oxygen. Trials are showing Vasogen technology to be effective at moderating ischemia.

- *Congestive heart failure.* This disease involves an inflammation of the sac surrounding the heart, called the pericardium. As a result of this inflammation, the sac fills with fluid, putting pressure on the heart and impairing vital circulatory and respiratory functions. The company's technology appears to help control this life-threatening condition.

- *Graft versus host disease.* GVHD, as it is often called, involves the rejection of transplanted organs and tissues through an immune system attack. Although the company calls this a "niche market," the technology is showing potential to help prevent the rejection of transplanted foreign tissue.

This is a broad and important range of disorders for any biotech company to pursue simultaneously.

The Vasogen therapy involves an inexpensive procedure to extract a sample of a patient's blood and treat it with heat and light. This induces a stress response in the targeted blood cells. After treatment, the patient's blood is returned to the body, where it appears to modulate the inflammatory mechanisms of the immune system. Because no drug is involved, the FDA classifies this therapy as a "medical device." During a recent investor conference call, executives explained that medical devices can proceed through FDA approvals in 2 to 4 years, as opposed to a time line of 10 years or more for some drug therapies. Current drug alternatives such as steroids and cyclosporine are toxic. The Vasogen technique has shown no serious side effects. The therapy operates by manipulating an immune system agent called *interleukin-10*. I asked company executives about the possibility of competition from a drug that might also alter interleukin levels. According to their estimate, interleukin drug treatments could cost more than $10,000 a year because the protein is extremely difficult to synthesize in quantity.[9] By comparison, the Vasogen therapy involves a simple 20-minute office procedure.

The company has begun to pursue collaborations with major pharmaceutical companies and has received unsolicited offers. Vasogen has enough cash to go it alone for several years, which means its survival is assured for the time being, and just as important, it has no need to rush into a partnership and profit sharing with a pharmaceutical giant for ongoing support. This is a major advantage for investors because the later in the trials process a biotech company makes an agreement with a pharmaceutical distributor; the more favorable the deal will be for the junior partner. This type of arrangement tends to suit both sides. Big Pharma partners allow biotech firms to "de-risk" a new product, to use the industry argot. When the product has been proven, the pharmaceutical giant receives a lower return but it has risked nothing in the failure-prone drug trial and approval process.

The remarkable thing is that Vasogen remains a micro-cap stock, valued at approximately $200 million. I'm not aware of any source on the Internet or any brokerage firm that has prepared a substantial profile of the firm. For a new investor, this can also be very good news. As long as prices remain lower than competing biotech firms with similar potential, there remains an opportunity to buy a promising stock at rock-bottom prices.

This is a Tier 4 company that exhibits almost every virtue a biotech investor could hope for at the price. Its technology demonstrates effectiveness in a wide variety of important conditions. Trials have, so far, shown no side effects. The stock is relatively inexpensive and the company's therapy will be cheap and quick to administer. Competitive approaches will be far more expensive. Time lines to market are unusually short because it is a medical device. The only major downside is that the approach relies on a single technology and that makes Vasogen another single-platform company that has yet to prove its value through the entire trials process.

As always, it would be a serious error to invest more than a small percentage of one's biotech portfolio on this or any other micro-cap firm, no matter how good it might look on paper.

SELLING AND MARKET TIMING

The rules for selling are clear-cut in the eyes of some experts. William O'Neil, the founder of *Investor's Business Daily* says flatly, "If a stock falls 8% below your purchase price, sell it."[10] This is a reasonable strategy to prevent serious losses among low volatility stocks, but it may no longer work in fast-changing growth sectors. In particular, the exceptionally high volatility of biotech stocks would trigger "sell" or "stop loss" orders constantly if investors adhered to an 8 percent guideline. There is no arbitrary figure that I can suggest for biotech stocks due to their inherent volatility as well as their vulnerability to the current extremes of volatility on the wider markets.

Innumerable strategies are available in print to help investors time the sale or purchase of a stock. Most of these methods involve performance patterns on short-term charts that are believed to presage an important new trend in a stock price. The names of some chart patterns may be familiar to the reader: the "double top," the "cup and handle," or the "head and shoulders." All market-timing strategies, by definition, presume the ability to forecast the future by looking at the past. Biotechnology has a relatively brief history on the market and there are very few historical patterns with any predictive value, except the characteristic spike of a bubble. As an investor with an eye on the future, I cannot put much faith in formulas and numerical guidelines for selling. I own companies, not charts and statistics.

Some investors choose to profit on volatility, buying and selling aggressively on the basis of market timing. This is an approach I cannot recommend. As a long-term biotech investor, my goals are set on corporate achievement, not on short-term oscillations in the market. Often the biotech indexes rise and fall temporarily in sync with the Nasdaq, but unlike the Nasdaq they have recovered surprisingly quickly. In a volatile market environment, there is little to be gained by becoming alarmed over temporary setbacks providing an investor has been selective in making purchases. The important thing about biotech investments that decline in value is to judge them within a time frame of several years, not several months as most analysts and professional investors are mandated to do.

Two Investment Setbacks and a Decision Not to Sell

Because the biotech sector is often whipsawed by larger market moves, it's not uncommon for excellent companies to experience perplexing reverses, even when they are reporting extremely encouraging news. As an example, two first-rate industrial genomics companies, Diversa and Genencor were put on the market during 2000. An investor who took an interest in these companies and waited a month for IPO fever to die down before making a purchase would have experienced a loss of approximately 25 percent as the end of 2000 approached. Assessing these companies and deciding whether to sell them for a tax loss requires a bit of research but not a huge investment of time.

The question a long-term investor faces is very straightforward: What is the likelihood that these two firms will recover and show substantial gains within the foreseeable future? It turns out that corporate developments for the two companies have been very exciting since their market launch.

Genencor brought a new product to market in October, an enzyme that Procter & Gamble will use in a premium dish detergent. The enzyme (a protease which breaks up proteins) is being marketed as a new ingredient that delivers skin-softening benefits to consumers. Also in October, Genencor struck an important four-year agreement with Danisco A/S, a multinational food company. Danisco will pay $20 million for the discovery, development, and production of bioingredients including proteins, enzymes, and peptides (small protein structures) for use in worldwide markets. Genencor also struck useful commercial alliances with other biotech firms.

Diversa did just as well, establishing several major commercial agreements with Dow Chemical, Celanese, and Novartis.[11] The details are lengthy, but suffice it to say that Diversa has been engaged by three industrial giants in agreements with substantial revenue generating potential. Diversa also struck agreements to expand its search for novel genes and proteins throughout Russia and Alaska.

If there was any doubt that the potential of these two companies is both real and impressive, consider a prediction from the Oracle Partners hedge fund published by Barron's on November 18, 2000. Larry Feinberg,[12] who runs the Oracle fund, told Barron's that he expects shares in both companies to double because of positive developments in the industrial genomics field.

There seems to be little reason to be disturbed about short-term losses in the values of these two quality companies. The goals of Diversa and Genencor have been endorsed by multinational industrial firms. Because these are industrial biotech firms, they can bring products to market more quickly than biotech firms engaged exclusively in drug discovery. They may not grow as explosively as biotech success stories like Amgen, but they should show slower, steadier gains over a longer span of time.

The important thing about biotech investments that do decline in value is to review them according to expectations spanning several years, not 12 months or less, as many in the financial industry are required to do. A setback on the scale I have described for Genencor and Diversa is not unusual considering the sector's volatility and the market's impatience. Biotech markets are not always driven by positive news, but that fact should not discourage independent investors unduly.

It would have been preferable to buy these companies at their lowest prices but that would require a degree of market timing many experts believe to be nearly impossible to achieve. Instead, rely on growth through quality investments and don't worry excessively about timing. No mathematical formula is reliable enough to trigger the sale of a quality biotech stock. Paper losses may be troubling, but they do not become permanent losses until a stock is sold.

MARKET TIMING AND SELL INDICATIONS

Looking at the sector as a whole, biotech investing might be regarded as market timing on a macro scale. We know with a reasonable degree of certainty that the industry will be hugely important several years from now. At the moment, biotechnology is a relatively small niche. Therefore, now is the right time to buy low, while emerging biotech companies are still small enough to be considered niche players. The time to sell will arrive when the industry matures and its growth curve levels off. In effect, biotech investors are timing the market, but over a very long period.

Investors don't often have the opportunity to foresee an industrial revolution in the making but the emergence of biotechnology is one of those opportunities. By most reasonable estimates, we are still near the base of a growth curve which will extend for several decades.

It would be foolish to suggest that there is never a right time to sell a biotech stock. It's just that there are precious few times when it is wise to sell great companies in an emerging industry. Perhaps, if an investor recognizes a "biotech bubble" in the making, it would be sensible to take profits and wait for prices to fall. Sometimes it's also wise to sell holdings before tax time. Companies that have suffered massive losses on the failure of a lead drug may not recover their value for a very long time, if ever. Taking a tax loss will probably be much more productive than waiting for a lengthy and uncertain recovery.

A change in the business environment can be another good cue to sell. The climate surrounding pure genomics companies like Celera changed when the market moved from an atmosphere of excitement about the potential of genomic databases to a narrower focus on product delivery and profits. Celera delivered excellent returns during its growth phase, but there's no longer a compelling reason to suppose it will grow in value more quickly than a carefully chosen product-oriented company.

In general, if an investment is stagnating or its moving average is declining steadily, it is time to conduct further research to find out why. Should it turn out that the investment has more limited growth potential than first believed, consider selling and putting your money to work more productively.

Another significant sell signal can show up in the appearance of new competition. In the case of Affymetrix, a number of companies are challenging the company's lead in the manufacture of biochips. The most daunting of these competitors is a consortium involving Japan's top five biotech firms, including Mitsubishi Chemical Corp. The creation of the consortium follows an announcement from Mitsubishi Rayon Company that it had developed a low-cost technology to manufacture DNA chips. In the United States, Motorola and Corning have entered the fray. Affymetrix may still emerge as the industry leader, but its dominance in the field has been threatened at home and abroad, and its stock has fallen as a result. It is too early to tell if Affymetrix will lose its leadership position, but in a case like this, investors must be aware of new competitive threats and consider whether to tough out a period of increased risk.

SELLING BEFORE NEWS

Another selling consideration is unique to biotechnology companies involved in drug development. According to a much-quoted saying, investors should buy on anticipation and sell on news. The reasoning is that stocks will rise in anticipation of good news, such as an earnings increase, and market prices will reach a point where they have "priced in" the expected value of such news in advance. The stock will tend to slump when the news is finally announced, possibly because there is no immediate reason to anticipate more positive developments. In biotechnology, however, a unique risk-and-reward pattern operates.

During the last week of September 2000, shortly after Cell Pathways announced its failure to gain approval for a lead anticancer compound, a somewhat similar company called Cell Therapeutics (CTIC) announced a success in the fight against cancer. The FDA approved Cell Therapeutics' drug, called Trisenox for use in patients with a severe form of leukemia. Trisenox, or arsenic trioxide, is a highly toxic chemical and it was approved only for use in patients with acute myeloid leukemia who had failed to respond to other therapies. Despite these limited indications, Trisenox has produced complete cancer remissions during clinical trials and it is being tested for several other forms of the disease. FDA approval was a watershed moment for the company and the stock responded with a 14 percent increase in one day. Certainly, it was good news for all concerned but the stock's performance on the day of the announcement raises an interesting consideration.[13]

Cell Therapeutics' market value had risen to almost $1.5 billion before the announcement. Had the FDA decision been negative, it seems probable that the stock would have suffered the same disastrous fate as Cell Pathways' shares did. Consider the risk-and-reward issue this presents. FDA rejection could have meant a loss of as much as 70 percent. Approval yielded a gain of just 14 percent. An investor who had ridden Cell Pathways stock from its 52-week low of $1.31 to its high, before the announcement, of $55 would have comparatively little to gain and a great deal to lose by waiting for the FDA ruling. The risk of loss is still much greater than the potential reward for approval. Therefore, if a biotech stock has risen to the point where success has been "priced in," investors may be wise to sell during the time of highest anticipation and avoid the risk of waiting for uncertain news. Remarkably, in the case of Cell Therapeutics, the company's stock began to fall back during the week after the announcement, losing most of its gains (see Figure 7.1).

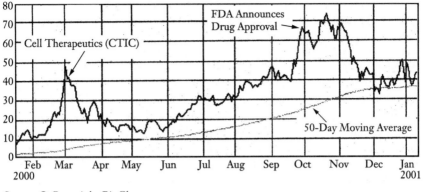

Figure 7.1   Cell Therapeutics (CTIC) One-Year Performance

Selling off a company with such potential is a tough call. Cell Therapeutics will continue to grow if Trisenox is approved for other indications. The drug's excellent results in trials give reason for optimism. On the other hand, the current FDA approvals for Trisenox are not adequate to support the company's $1.5 billion valuation. Failure to expand the usage of the company's lead drug could lead to severe losses for investors. My bias would be in favor of taking profits and reducing risk. The company has grown to the point where it displays a classic Tier Three risk profile: high valuation based largely on a single technology platform.

One last point on the issue of selling: Individual investors who wish to sell quickly are at a disadvantage compared with institutions that have invested in biotechnology. Institutional investors watch every position they hold every minute the market is open. Sell decisions can be made almost instantly on the release of negative news or on the dictates of mathematical models that trigger computerized trading. Individuals cannot respond with the same speed unless they are trading online and are glued to their screens at all times. Negative news will result in losses for all stockholders, but institutions will suffer less by responding more quickly. Even worse for individual investors, institutional sellers will tend to drive the market down disproportionately, as large blocks of stock are unloaded on biotech markets with relatively low liquidity.

TAKING PROFITS

It is imperative to review, periodically, one's success just as often as one's setbacks. Selling off a dead loser is a relatively simple decision no matter how uncomfortable it might seem at the time. But, deciding whether to sell a winner requires a thoughtful and detached analysis of the company's emerging profile. If it has become highly valued, ask yourself some questions: How sustainable is this valuation? How likely is it to grow further? Is its current valuation dependent on future achievements and if so, what is the likelihood of failure? The consequences of a setback become substantially greater when a company reaches new highs. If a Tier 4 company suddenly rises to a billion-dollar-plus valuation it may still have room to grow or it may have reached its full potential for the foreseeable future. At such a high valuation, its risk of losses has increased.

It is all too easy to become emotionally attached to the successes of a company that is delivering substantial shareholder gains and curing horrible diseases at the same time. It is especially easy to develop a proprietary feeling about a company if one has spotted it early and the company has rewarded the investor's faith. Review your winners with a cold eye. If you have earned money by investing in a company, there may well be no empirical reason to expect further growth.

Biotech companies are not like other advanced technology firms. Product development and approval consumes enormous amounts of time and money no matter how quickly fundamental scientific discoveries may appear. Companies like Intel and Microsoft and Dell Computer have far fewer limits on the number of new products they bring to market. Dell may decide to bring out a new and more powerful line of computers every year. Microsoft can generate sales by updating its Windows platform and developing new software in regular intervals. Intel is limited mainly by market forces and the speed of its scientific and technical innovation.

Biotech companies are severely restrained by long regulatory time lines. The time consumed by clinical trials is growing longer, and no drug development biotech company can escape these limits. Scientific and technical innovation are accelerating but it will be some time before the value of these discoveries is conclusively proven.

Expect no more from a biotech investment than realization of the goals that were reasonably within reach at the time you bought in. When those goals are met, consider selling unless compelling new prospects have appeared.

BIOTECH IPOs

Retail brokers rarely encourage their clients to buy into an initial public offering but online traders may be tempted to participate in the powerful price increases that often accompany biotech IPOs. There was an explosion in the number of biotechnology companies going public during the year 2000; between January and August alone, there were 46 IPOs, an unprecedented volume for an industry that used to rely on venture capital for financing.[14] Many of these offerings have performed extremely well. For

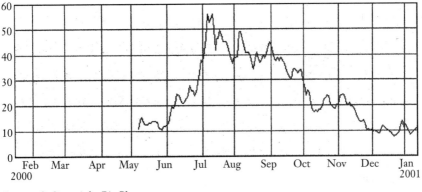

Figure 7.2 Orchid Biosciences from IPO

example, Orchid BioSciences opened in May, during the depressed after-math of the March crash. The offering price was $8 a share and the company rose 37 percent on its first day. By October it had risen more than 300 percent (see Figure 7.2 and Epilogue).

But other offerings have not performed nearly as well. Diversa Corporation opened in February at $24 and rose 213 percent on its first day as investors became excited about the prospects of industrial genomics. In a matter of weeks, it rose quickly to hit a 52-week high of $169 a share. When considering these statistics, keep in mind that if a stock jumps as sharply as Diversa did on its first day of public trading, very few investors are able to buy at the opening price (see Figure 7.3 and Epilogue).

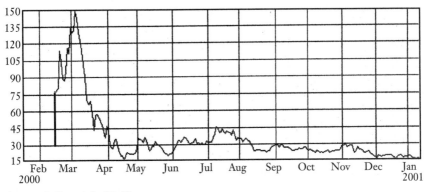

Figure 7.3 Diversa Corporation from IPO

The Diversa chart brings to mind one commentator's view of today's volatile IPO market. It can be much like a roller coaster, he said; you can lose your hat and your lunch during the ride but ultimately you wind up right back where you started. Diversa is a very promising company, but investors who have endured the ride from IPO to the present have very little to show for all the turbulence they have endured.

In general, investors who bought biotech IPOs during 2000 made money more often than not, but *only* if they were able to buy near the initial offering price. In such a volatile market, the odds in the investor's favor during a biotech IPO appear to be only slightly better than the flip of a coin. To some investors, these odds may be tolerable but the consequences of buying a weak offering at an early, inflated offering price may be dire. It is probably wiser to sit on the sidelines and watch a new stock's performance against the biotech indexes before making a purchase decision.

WAITING FOR RETURNS

The individual investor's biggest advantage is the ability to exercise patience. Financial industry professionals are driven to show results in short periods. But biotechnology investors can realize profits by recognizing that their sector is an industry that will require several decades to mature. Despite the massive acceleration of biotech systems, the sector is still harnessed to slow-moving external factors. The industry will speed up its rate of progress substantially, but not quickly enough to satisfy the institutional investment manager who is required to deliver market-beating returns in less than 12 months. The biotech investor who selects a strong emerging company and allows a longer time horizon to profitability has an advantage.

It has taken two decades of scientific labor for the first great wave of new products to be delivered. Early investors in the sector's first contingent of profitable companies have realized extraordinary gains by being patient and remaining confident during periods of low returns. Institutional investors have no choice except to put their money to work for immediate gains, hoping to switch positions just in time to get on board with the next big thing. Individual investors have the opportunity to own some of tomorrow's industrial giants if they are able to take a position early and outwait institutional and professional investors while the market gyrates and finally recognizes a great emerging company.

The waiting period for results differs greatly according to a biotech company's tier.

In the case of Tier 4 companies, there appears to be substantial market resistance to increasing their value in recognition of corporate and scientific achievements. The fourth-tier companies I have mentioned in this book are doing remarkable things, and given time, many will become great businesses. But the stock market rewards such companies only when larger financial institutions decide for their own inscrutable reasons that the time is right. Many such institutional investors are restricted from buying micro-cap stocks. As soon as one or two institutions make a move, others may rush to get on board and if they do, values will rise with breathtaking speed. Quantum leaps in corporate valuations happen far too quickly under current market conditions for the individual investor to spot a trend and take a position before the greatest gains have already been made. Patient stockholders have a far better chance of reaping gains.

Investors who become discouraged during a company's incubation period may decide to bail out, even though doing so may lock in losses. But those who choose well, invest early, and stay the course during setbacks will be among the biggest beneficiaries when the market engages in one of its periodic stampedes to embrace the companies of the future.

Long investment time lines also apply to companies that have risen to the third tier. Tier 3 companies have, by definition, typically achieved high valuations in anticipation of positive news. Because the market has already invested heavily in companies that are on the verge of delivering products to market, there is little to be gained by investing at peak prices. The next sharp rise in share prices for such companies may not appear until a new product or an expanded use for an existing product is about to be approved. In general, investors would be wise to wait on the sidelines, watching for a buying opportunity among companies in this category.

If the future is half as bright as I believe it to be among companies in Tier 2, substantial gains are only a year or two from appearing. These stocks have already appreciated enormously in anticipation of future gains. There is no way of predicting exactly when such companies will realize greater potential, but waiting on the sidelines could be a mistake. The most significant valuation increases can happen in a brief period. In this category, the biggest gains go to those who recognize a great company early and take a position before the market suddenly drives valuations into the stratosphere.

Tier 1 companies fluctuate roughly in sync with the Nasdaq index but only a few offer hopes for major returns because of their high valuations. The greatest gains have generally been made, and often future performance has already been priced in. The lowest P/E I have found among top-flight companies in this tier is Genzyme General which had a ratio of 25 at this writing. Investors looking for security and stability among these highly valued stocks should exercise patience and wait for a pullback.

SUMMARY

Choosing to invest in biotechnology qualifies as an aggressive investment decision from the outset. Much of what flows from that point on is about reducing risk. As much as one might dream of riding the next Microsoft from a dollar a share to four hundred (split-adjusted), the chances of this happening are still small. There is virtually no chance of discovering with any certainty a company that has an ultimate answer, such as the legendary magic bullet for cancer.

In the final analysis, investors must recognize and balance opposing goals and visions. Yes, the industry will emerge as one of the great industrial sectors of the twenty-first century, but there are no guarantees among individual companies. Certainly it makes sense to take a position in this sector, but the risk is high. Some companies will provide solutions to problems that have bedeviled humankind from time immemorial, but others will fail to live up to their initial promise. Diversification is the best solution.

The investor's challenge is to adhere to a strategy that will take advantage of a major turning point in human affairs while moderating the risk inherent in an emerging industry. The profit potential is huge and potentially mesmerizing. The investor's goal is to participate in this watershed development without being swept committed to just a few headline-grabbing biotech firms.

The less diverse one's position is, the greater the risk of disappointment. The more diverse, the better an investor's chances of participating fully in the emergence of an industry that could indeed become the largest in the world.

———◦•◦•———

CHAPTER 8

The Sector in Perspective

How can a business be valued somewhere between $5 billion and $50 billion? It's a crazy market.

> Joe Kernen, CNBC's unflappable analyst, comments on huge
> changes in corporate valuation during a plunge in the
> semiconductor sector

BIOTECH AND THE "GROWTH IMPERATIVE"

Although biotechnology investing is not for everyone, the evolving structure of the broader market should give all investors pause and reason to rethink some of their current investment assumptions. During the past five years, the markets have undergone enormous changes in structure and behavior.

Traditional investment strategies gave average investors a rough ride in 2000. In mid-April 2000, the Nasdaq suffered one of the worst weeks in history, losing approximately one trillion dollars in market capitalization. September of the same year also made history as the worst month for the Nasdaq since the dark days of the early 1970s when inflation, oil embargoes, and the Vietnam War were tearing the country and its stock markets to pieces. The Nasdaq lost 12.7 percent during in the September plunge while the Dow Jones Industrials and the S&P 500 both lost about 5 percent. How uncanny it seems that the stock market should be more unstable during a period of unprecedented growth, peace, and prosperity than it was during a decade of crisis. How remarkable it is that a largely unprofitable sector such as biotechnology should emerge as a star performer.

The emergence of biotechnology and other speculative growth stocks, including e-business, has been driven, in part, by basic changes in the structure and psychology of the stock market, a transformation that has been in the making for decades.

Before 1958, most common stocks paid relatively large dividends to shareholders on the assumption that the risks inherent in equity investment demanded some measure of steady, reliable returns. It is often forgotten that stocks once delivered greater dividend yields, as a percentage of the amount invested, than bonds. High dividend payments effectively lowered shareholders' need for growth in corporate valuations. Dividends began to decline as stock market performance improved, and risk appeared to diminish. The year 1958 marked a historic turning point when the average dividend yield from stocks fell, for the first time, below the return from bonds. The downward trend has continued ever since.

In August 2000, another milestone was reached when the average dividend yield of stocks on the Standard & Poor's 500 fell below 1 percent. Ironically, this occurred at a time when risk was sharply on the rise, as measured by both market volatility and individual stock volatility. Investors are now being offered less security than ever before at a time when they need it most.

The market's new profile compels investors to seek very high growth potential above all other considerations due to the absence of market stability and meaningful returns from dividends. This structural shift has gone largely unheralded because it has happened very gradually. The effect of dividend declines has also been masked, over the course of decades, by the market's performance. By staying invested in stocks for the long term, analysts assured stockholders, investors could expect returns averaging 10 or 11 percent a year through increases in share prices. Until recently, they have been proven correct. In fact, the booming markets of the 1990s delivered much better returns than expected. This boom further whetted the system's appetite for growth over income while creating extremely high, ultimately unsupportable valuations.

Investors of all stripes, biotech or otherwise, have learned the hard way that they ignore the market's imperative to pursue strong corporate growth at their own peril. I recall ruefully one aging broker's advice to an associate who held a large stock portfolio. He reassured her that it made good sense to maintain her considerable position in Philip Morris during 1998. In 2000 he persuaded her to purchase a substantial position in Microsoft. His rationale was that these were two "great companies" with enormous cash flows, therefore secure. In both cases, the investment decisions resulting from this advice had disastrous consequences. Philip Morris stock was cut in half by a corporate decision to reduce cigarette prices and by constant litigation. Microsoft was also thrown into sharp decline by antitrust litigation, and it is still falling at this writing. Both companies were then and still are very profitable.[1]

The fallacy at the heart of such seemingly sensible investment advice is the assumption that share values should be proportional to corporate revenues. That's not the case in today's market. Revenue fluctuations do affect share prices but not proportionately. Every market watcher has heard of stocks being pummeled because earnings per share (EPS) have fallen a penny short of analysts' expectations. In today's volatile market environment, investors lose a great deal more than a penny per share on such an announcement; they lose a substantial chunk of their equity stake in a company. Even small earnings disappointments are seen as a threat, not to the company, but to investors' expectations for endless expansion. Biotech stocks, by and large, are not valued according to earnings.

Because investor returns are no longer stabilized by meaningful dividends and are only loosely connected to revenues, shareholders depend on increasing corporate valuation for their profits. But, determining standards for corporate value is a much more subjective task than the simple measurement of revenues and profitability. The broader market has become almost as subjective as the biotechnology sector by basing valuation on the standards of investor expectations and market perception. Many large cap growth stocks such as Dell and Intel have fallen sharply in value despite strongly increasing revenues. Meanwhile, many biotech stocks that have never shown a profit have soared.

I would embrace the theories of any analyst who could explain this paradox satisfactorily. In the absence of generally accepted explanations, I will propose my own.

Put in the simplest terms, the markets have been structurally altered and distorted by increasingly untenable expectations of growth. Federal Reserve Chairman, Alan Greenspan, had it right when he expressed concern over "irrational exuberance" during the boom years of the 1990s. An investor stampede had pushed corporate valuations to extremes that could never be supported by actual revenue growth. A marketwide bubble was in the works, but no one in the financial community was about to object while everyone was making money. To his credit, Chairman Greenspan had the courage and wisdom to throw cold water on the festivities by ratcheting up interest rates. Many critics said this was a misguided effort to prevent inflation by cooling off an overheated economy, pointing out that there was never a credible threat of inflation during this period. There was, however, some danger of a market crash as growth expectations, expressed by P/E ratios, soared to unsustainable levels. Greenspan effectively reduced growth expectations and may have prevented a crash.

The markets fell into a period of severe turbulence as a consequence of Chairman Greenspan's actions. The biotech sector, having the most intangible basis for valuation and the most speculative growth curve, was the first to fall. Like a rolling wave, volatility shook sector after sector, as companies whose values had become alarmingly inflated were reevaluated. Even the mighty Intel shed more than $200 billion in market capitalization when the company hinted that its astonishing growth might ease off a little. Very few U.S. companies could support valuations that called for endless double-digit growth, even in a robust economy. By contrast, many biotechnology companies emerged from this shake-up with substantial gains for the year, suggesting that the market had determined that their growth prospects were convincing.

As Greenspan himself said several times, the biotech industry has enormous potential to add value to the economy. In today's financial marketplace, growth is everything, and somewhat paradoxically, the sector with the lowest cash flow proved to have the most credible growth potential.

With the erosion of stabilizing forces such as dividends and rational P/E ratios, investors who follow traditional strategies are experiencing levels of volatility that, ordinarily, only a speculator would be expected to endure. Even top-rank industry professionals are seeking alternatives. *Business Week* reports that managers of U.S. pension funds have placed 25 percent of their assets in simple indexed investments, a total amount exceeding $1.1 trillion. Individual investors are also turning to index funds, hoping to reap the performance of entire markets and market sectors rather than individual companies. But, even this cautious strategy is backfiring as increasing volatility takes entire markets and their index investors for a wild ride.

Against this unsettling backdrop, biotech investments may be seen in a new light. The sector is generally described as speculative and it will continue to be for some time, but the question now is, compared to what? Compared to Intel?

BIOTECH AND THE INVESTOR REVOLUTION

Biotechs are the kind of stocks your broker always warned you about, enticing, but a little too risky for the average, middle-of-the-road investor. Lately, however, investors occupying the middle of the road have become roadkill. *Business Week* magazine declared an "investor revolution" underway as the bluest of blue-chip stocks was whipsawed by volatility and pillars of steady growth took a beating. The flight of investors from retail brokers has become a stampede. The surge of new money into biotechnology has accompanied this trend.

Almost 16 million Americans have opened online brokerage accounts according to research from Piper Jaffray; nearly double the number from a year earlier. It's estimated that an astonishing 17 percent of all retail stock trades were conducted online in 1999 and volume surged by approximately 69 percent in the first quarter of the following year.[2] As online trading grew exponentially, so did biotechnology. Perhaps it is merely a coincidence, but the increasing volume of Internet information and online discussion about biotechnology suggests the biotech sector may well be one of the biggest beneficiaries of the so-called investor revolution.

The biotechnology revolution and investor revolution are ideal partners. Aggressive investors can now perform substantial amounts of research on their own, and make trades online without deferring to a middleman.

Among knowledgeable investors, it is almost a given that retail brokers will have little understanding of the highly specialized, complex, and rapidly changing biotech sector. Large brokerages do employ biotech analysts who provide research and opinions to retail brokers, but the opinions of analysts have become widely suspect because of possible undeclared conflicts of interest and because of the mixed results they have delivered.

Although investing in biotechnology is frequently dismissed as being too speculative for the average investor, readers should take a moment to reflect on the market as a whole. What should investors make of the extraordinary turbulence and fearsome losses suffered recently by so many mainstream stocks? Is there something to be learned from the beating taken by Nasdaq index investors? Perhaps it is confirmation that the mainstream market was badly overvalued.

If this seems to be a harsh assessment, consider one last time the fall of Intel. What could prove more conclusively that Intel had become a speculative play than the sudden disappearance of more than $200 billion in value? This company is widely considered to be one of America's finest high-technology firms, producing annual earnings increases reliably in the double digits. I can find only one brokerage that had the foresight to downgrade Intel in the month before this price collapse: USB Piper Jaffray. (Banc of America did downgrade the stock but then upgraded it again.) On the day the company announced that it might fall a few pennies short of earnings projections, nine analysts responded simultaneously by downgrading the stock, a move akin to closing the barn door after the horse has escaped. These analyst announcements tended to use words such as "Downgrade from Buy to Outperform," a professional opinion that does no justice to the terrible beating that so many individuals suffered by continuing to hold the stock as it fell. "Outperform" has a unique meaning on Wall Street compared with the rest of the English-speaking world.

THE BIOTECH INVESTOR'S ROLE IN THE MARKET

Biotech investors are doing exactly what investors are supposed to do: providing capital to help create and expand a promising business. By investing for the long term, rather than a quick profit, shareholders can properly expect a substantial reward when an industry they helped create realizes its stellar potential.

Investing in biotechnology involves the purchase of an intangible, but what an intangible! One is buying a stake in the most remarkable scientific and technological revolutions in history. This is the industry that will transform the human condition. That, I believe, has real value and growth potential.

CHAPTER 9

---•◆•◆•---

The Biotech Investor's Checklist

For you and me it means new, nearly unlimited hope against the ravages of aging and disease—plus another new path to nearly untold riches.
Michael Murphy, publisher of the *California Technology Stock Letter*

Michael is a mixed blessing for us. He's a big supporter but he's an extreme optimist.
Alan R. Engbring, Investor relations, Vical Corp.

The Key Factors

Even industry veterans sometimes get carried away by the extraordinary promise of biotechnology. When making investment decisions, try taking a glance at this list and considering whether your decision meets most of the conditions specified.

- *Development pipeline.* Always check a biotech company's product pipeline before making any decision. Ask the following questions:
  1. How advanced are the company's products in clinical trials?
  2. How long will it take for the lead product to reach market?
  3. Is the pipeline broad enough to provide security and a measure of stock price stability?
  4. What is the potential market size for a drug candidate?
- *Partnerships and collaborations.* Check a company's alliances at its Web site or by using recap.com:
  1. How many collaborations has a target company established?
  2. Do these collaborative agreements with major organizations add credibility to a biotech company's development program?
  3. How important are these collaborations? Milestone payments may generate small revenue streams that can be discontinued if a

company stumbles. Major cash commitments from a pharmaceutical giant are much more valuable.

4. What stake do the partners have in an approved drug? If a biotech firm is to receive royalty payments for an approved drug, the revenue stream will be smaller than a licensing or marketing agreement in which the biotech firm retains the major share of rights and profits.

- *Assess the competition.* Look for a list of competitors by entering the name of your company's disease target or methodology at recap.com:

  1. How many competitors are working toward the same goal?
  2. How advanced are they in clinical trials compared with the target company?
  3. What will be the effect if a competing company is first to market?
  4. Is the competition product more effective?
  5. Is it cheaper?
  6. Does it have fewer side effects?

- *Assess the technology.*

  1. How much proof is available to demonstrate that a technology is workable rather than theoretical ("proof of principle")?
  2. Is the technology novel or is the company entering a crowded market with a widely used technological base?
  3. Is the technology licensed from another source and, if so, will there be revenue consequences?

- *Analysis of tiers.* Assign your company to one of four tiers according to its profitability, structure, and market capitalization:

  1. If the target company is in Tier 1, is the market capitalization realistic or does the P/E ratio suggest unrealistic growth expectations?
  2. Is the company's revenue stream increasing?
  3. If the company is in Tier 2, how long will it take to realize profitability?
  4. Is it sufficiently promising and diversified to support its market capitalization?
  5. What is the probable effect on the Tier 2 company's market cap, if one assumes successful product delivery within approximately two years?
  6. If the company is in Tier 3, has it already risen to a maximum market capitalization in anticipation of product success?
  7. Is this a single platform technology company?

8. If it does operate from a single drug or technology platform, what would be the effects on stockholders from the failure of a lead product?

9. If the company is in Tier 4, how novel and potent is its product technology?

10. Does it appear to be undervalued, taking into account the company's progress in product development, trial results to date, time lines, and market potential?

- *Market considerations.* Print out charts on your target corporation and assess its performance:

  1. Has the company in question appreciated in value after biotech sector setbacks? If not, why not?

  2. Do the moving averages for 50 and 200 days show consistent patterns of progress or is there a weakness indicated by a slump in the moving average?

  3. If the company shows a dramatic rise in value, has it begun to taper off?

  4. Do you feel confident, taking all factors into account, that the company has not peaked, leaving new investors in danger of owning a stagnant or declining stock?

- *Financials.* Get corporate profiles from a site such as Yahoo Finance or Multex.com and scrutinize the company's financial performance:

  1. How much cash does a company have available compared with its annual expenditure or burn rate? How long can it survive before reaching profitability?

  2. If there is a profit, determine the company's P/E ratio and P/E growth rate. If the P/E ratio is higher than the growth rate, is it possible that the company is overvalued?

  3. If the company does appear to be overvalued, how much of its share value depends on expectations for delivery of future products?

  4. Do the pipeline and the competition profile support these expectations?

  5. If the company is not profitable, how tolerable is its volatility?

  6. Is there heavy short selling interest?

  7. Are there warning signs from increasing trading volume during a downtrend?

  8. Find the list of institutional shareholders. How much credibility does the reputation of these firms and the size of their holdings add to a company?

9. Consider the history, nature, and number of analyst opinions. How accurate have predictions been? How many analysts are covering the company? (A small number of analysts with very positive opinions may indicate an undiscovered gem, but consider the possibility of a conflict of interest in their opinions.)

- *Corporate history.* Call up previous news developments through financial Web sites and corporate Web sites:

    1. Have there been serious setbacks in product development in the past that cast doubt on the viability of the development program?

    2. Has the company made public predictions and then failed to meet its targets and time lines for revenues or product development?

    3. Has there been news of scientific or medical recognition of a biotech company's therapy?

    4. Is the company a takeover target or is management considering taking over another firm? If so, is there a potential profit to shareholders from a takeover or a risk of price declines if the target company takes over another?

    5. Has the company been the subject of wide media publicity and is there a possibility that this has pumped its stock value out of proportion?

- *Management.* Answering the previous questions will reveal a great deal about corporate management but there are also additional considerations. Check corporate profiles on company Web sites and financial sites such as Hoovers and Yahoo:

    1. Does the company appear to have a well-defined mission and strategy to deliver substantial profits?

    2. Is there a business plan that defines targets and profit goals?

    3. Does the company display management skill by harnessing scientific excellence to a clear business goal?

    4. Is there a corporate strategy to remain competitive by isolating large markets, developing novel technologies, and shortening time lines to product delivery?

    5. Has management shown aggressiveness in expanding its technical and business base through takeovers and collaborations?

    6. Has the company developed a specialty that makes it uniquely promising?

- *Personal goals.* Consider your risk tolerance and ability to meet the demands of investment in the sector:

    1. Can you devote the time and effort required to research your investments and stay up to date?

2. Do you enjoy the challenge of exploring new technologies and businesses or is it an unpleasant task?

3. Do you have sufficient resources to diversify within the sector or would it be wiser to explore other possible biotech investment avenues such as mutual funds, unit trusts, or online sites such as Folio [fn] or Buy and Hold.com?

4. Are you comfortable with volatility and prepared to live with the fact that some companies will deliver setbacks?

5. Are you prepared to wait through a period of substantial volatility for the delivery of a product to market?

- *Selling considerations.* It makes sense to review your portfolio periodically to consider if the time has come to sell any holdings:

  1. Has the stock achieved the goals you expected with no further growth prospects in the foreseeable future?

  2. Has the stock suffered a severe setback? If so, what are the prospects for recovery within the year?

  3. Is the benefit of taking a tax loss better than the prospect of holding a position?

  4. Has the competitive or business environment changed, putting your company in an inferior competitive position?

  5. Has the market changed? Is your stock likely to experience stagnation or decline because the market has shown a shift in valuation criteria such as the swing from enthusiasm about pure genomics companies to product-oriented companies?

  6. Do the chart trend lines demonstrate a chronically declining value for your holding indicating a lack of confidence in the company and a danger of continuing losses?

- *Research.* It's important to sift the daily flow of news and information to see if your company is experiencing change. Sign up for news services from Web sites such as Biospace.com and Drug Discovery Online. Search out the opinions of experts, commentators and, if you put faith in them, Web postings:

  1. Have external developments changed the competitive position of your holding?

  2. Is there internal news and if so, how has the stock responded?

  3. If you notice a sharp change in your stock price, can it be explained by the pull of general market movements, or does it require a search for news on the company Web site or elsewhere?

  4. Do you feel you have acquired sufficient information to be comfortable comprehending developments in the sector or is further reading required?

- *Business and regulatory environment.*
    1. How strong is your company's patent portfolio? Is it in danger of upset by a government decision affecting basics such as gene patents?
    2. Is the company embroiled in lawsuits and if so, how will this affect its future profit potential?
    3. Is there a danger of government-imposed price controls such as the threat facing the pharmaceutical industry?
    4. Are there ethical concerns that may affect an investment?
    5. Are there social concerns such as the backlash faced by the agricultural biotechnology industry?
    6. Are patents in danger of expiry?

Biotech Companies Not Involved in Drug Discovery

Many of the same criteria apply to companies that are not in the drug discovery business, but there are additional considerations.

- *Commercial potential.*
    1. Are there substantial markets willing to pay the price of a product? (E.g., some genomics discovery companies have had difficulty meeting revenue projections because of inadequate subscriptions to their databases.)
    2. How large are the markets for a product? (E.g., industrial genomics companies will capture huge commercial markets if they develop revolutionary money-saving biological and chemical processes.)
    3. Are there any regulatory hurdles?
    4. Are there political concerns such as those facing agricultural biotech?
    5. If there are no regulatory barriers, is there growth in sales volumes and/or profits? If not, why not?
- *Market leadership.* Consider the company's competitive environment and its response to competition:
    1. Has the company achieved market leadership and is it defending its turf aggressively?
    2. Have competitors created novel technologies that threaten to erode the target company's business? How credible are these threats?

3. Can the company defend its leadership position? (E.g., Celera has plans to become the leading genomics information company, but industry and government consortiums are creating alternative sources of information.)

4. How good is the product? (E.g., numerous companies are developing software to speed the screening of drugs through in silico (computer synthesized) chemical reactions.) Has this product been proven through customer subscriptions?

Thanks to the speed and convenience of the Internet, it won't take as long as it might seem to answer these questions. Much of the information you need is well summarized and concentrated in places like the Yahoo/Multex financial profiles Web site. Fifteen minutes of browsing through a company's history and profile with these considerations in mind can provide a wealth of crucially important information.

PART II

The Scientific and Technological Perspective

CHAPTER 10

The Science behind the Industry

This will symbolize to many people that we have the power to change human destiny. But the power is here and it's already being used.
William Haseltine, CEO of Human Genome Sciences
on the mapping of the human genome

WHAT YOU NEED TO KNOW

The most frustrating thing about starting out as a biotech investor is scanning a news release or annual report and finding it difficult if not impossible to understand. The industry liberally employs jargon and acronyms, and it presumes prior scientific knowledge in much of its literature. Most investors need to learn some fundamentals to stay abreast of what's going on in the biotech industry.

The challenge is not as insurmountable as it might seem. Any honest biotech executive or investment analyst would have to admit that the industry is far too complex to be grasped in every technical detail outside his or her own specialized fields. Biotech investors can be equally certain from the outset that they're unlikely to grasp the concepts of genomics, proteomics, and biology without help.

Biologists have labored for more than a century in relative obscurity to bring their science to the turning point marked by the mapping of the human genome. In the course of their research scientists, have developed a lexicon and a framework of understanding that took little account of the possibility that anyone outside their rarified circle would need to know about the details of their work. Still, the basic concepts of biotechnology can be refined and simplified to the point that they are well within the average person's grasp.

Without a rudimentary knowledge of the workings of DNA, RNA, proteins, and cells, investors will have difficulty understanding the biotech industry's many sectors. And, to make informed investment decisions, it is imperative to know about the sector you are buying into, and to be aware of the competition. In other industries, various subsectors may complement and serve one another. In biotechnology, most companies develop exotic specialties and then compete on two fronts: against other companies in their particular field and against companies developing other approaches. Biotech investors must be able to discern which approaches appear to be the most practical, the closest to reaching market, and the most profitable. That's why it's important to review a few fundamentals. Sound decision making is next to impossible without a sense of what the industry, and human life, is based on.

DNA: The Ultimate Software

As everyone likely knows by now, DNA (deoxyribonucleic acid) is the master molecule at the heart of every cell. This famous double helix contains every fragment of information required to build an exact copy of a human being. Perhaps the best way to understand DNA is to compare it to computer software. To a remarkable extent, bodily systems can be visualized within the framework of a computer's operations.

Using this comparison, DNA can be regarded as the fundamental code of an operating system, similar to the Windows, Macintosh, or Linux operating systems that drive a personal computer. The DNA instruction set is laid out, not in magnetic zeroes and ones on a hard drive, but in patterns of molecules strung together in a very long chain. DNA is software that also looks and acts like hardware (just like the first generations of mechanical computers, which worked with gears and punched holes in paper tape).

Four base molecules make up the DNA code: adenine, cytosine, thymine, and guanine, usually referred to by their first letters (ACTG). Just as the computer's binary code can be combined in an infinite number of variations for various tasks, DNA code can be equally versatile. The main difference is in the number of characters making up the two codes. For example, a precise reading of the operating system of your computer would yield a seemingly senseless stream of numbers such as 01001010111101010101010. DNA code reads out as an equally unintelligible stream of characters, looking something like this: ATACTCGTAGAGCTCTTGAGCTA.

The helical image of a DNA molecule is familiar to any high school student. The molecular letters of the DNA code are laid out in pairs suspended between two twisting backbones (made of sugar and phosphate molecules). The key thing about DNA's four base molecules is that they always seek to pair off with a matching partner. C and G always stick together. So do A and T. In some senses they operate like small magnets repelling or attracting one another.

The entire DNA molecule is often compared to a zipper. The teeth of the zipper can be made of only two possible molecular pairs, either "CG" or "AT." These are called "base pairs."

At first glance, this might appear to be a binary code because there are only two possible combinations. But there is also a structural variable. This is a small but important point in understanding the minute workings of the DNA operating system.

For the purpose of illustration I will demonstrate how the code would appear if the two molecules (called base pairs) had only a single orientation:

aggagagaggggagagagagagagagagagagaaaggagagggagaagagagaaagggagaaaaggggggagagagaga
tcctct . . . . etc . . . .

This is effectively a binary code, allowing for only two possible variations.

But the genome's four-letter code allows a DNA molecule to pack in considerably more information than a binary code would permit. This is possible because the orientation of a base pair (AT or CG) can appear one way or another on the supporting strands:

gatacacagatatagcctatagattcgttagagatctctgagagcttcgagagctagagacatggtagtcgagagctgagctcga
ctatg . . . . etc . . . .

Much more information can be compressed into this four-letter code.

The 24-letter code of the English alphabet allows many different meanings to be crammed into the comparatively small amount of space required to spell a word. If only two letters were available in the alphabet, then the English language would require immensely long chains of variables to distinguish the meaning of one word from the next. In Morse code, which is a sequence of dots and dashes, nine "dits" and "dahs" are needed to spell a three-letter message such as SOS. A four-part code like DNA could do the job with fewer characters.

Like any computer operating system, DNA code is prone to errors, most of them small and insignificant. But, as every computer owner knows, tiny errors in code or any damage to a hard drive can cause the entire system to crash. In DNA, coding errors are called mutations and most involve the "misspelling" of a single letter. Other, more complex, types of genetic mutation are described later in the chapter.

The technical jargon for a single-letter mutation or coding error is a "single nucleotide polymorphism." The abbreviation SNP, which is pronounced "snip," is used often in reports on genomic research. For practical purposes, a nucleotide can be thought of as any one of the four ACTG base molecules. Misspell just one of them and the sense of the DNA message is distorted, just as the sense of a word written in English can become gibberish with one letter out of place. The word TACT, for example, means nothing at all if it is accidentally spelled TGCT.

Any misspelled or misplaced base pair may qualify as a SNP but relatively few SNPs have a noticeable effect. Others are associated with genetic diseases and are the object of intense research and cataloging efforts. The DNA code of all human beings is 99.9 percent the same but SNPs can appear as distinct, inheritable traits, sometimes called "markers."

It is estimated that the entire human genome, a stretch of DNA three billion base pairs long contains 30,000 genes. Genes, very simply, are sections of DNA code that are known to have meaning. They carry operating instructions for the body. Genes show up on DNA as complex variations in the four-letter genetic alphabet, often beginning and ending with recognizable "start" and "stop" instructions. The much-publicized human genome carries all of the operating instructions for the body.

For reasons that are not yet understood, DNA is not densely packed with genes. Instead, there are long stretches of the molecule that look like extended stutters. These stretches have been given the controversial label "junk DNA" because some scientists assume they have no function. A length of stuttering DNA, between the genes, might read something like:

ACTACTACTACTACTACTACTACTACTACTACTACTACT

It would be a mistake to assume that the position of every base pair has been spelled out, despite the ceremony at the White House honoring the mapping of the human genome by Celera and the Human Genome Project. In fact, the term *genome* refers only to the genes in DNA, not to the long chains of stuttering molecules between them. These genes were considered to have been "sequenced" when the order of the letters making up each gene was determined. The genome was declared "mapped" when the positions of genes on the DNA strand were roughly determined. This picture is not complete because the definition of complete mapping of the genome allows a key exception. Technically, the job is defined as being complete when the map has been drawn as much as is possible within the limits of current science and technology.

One reason that human DNA has not been fully sequenced is the junk DNA problem. Current methods of sequencing are unable to read long repetitive strands. Celera Corporation is working to pin down the location of all three billion base pairs, in the belief that some of them may be important.

The quickest method of gene sequencing works (to use a simplified description) by breaking several strands of DNA into many small pieces of readable size. These chunks of code are then compared to millions of others in a computer's memory until a match is found. It is like a huge linear jigsaw puzzle. When enough overlapping patterns are fitted together, a full-length picture emerges:

TAGCTTACGATCGATCGAT
        GATCGATCGATCGACTCGATCGCAT
                GCATCGACTTTCGAGATA

Piecing the three overlapping sections together completes a longer sequence:

TAGCTTAC**GATCGAT**CGATCGATCGACTCGATC**GCAT**CGACTTTCGAGATAG

When matching patterns overlap, the known sequence of the gene is extended by the sequence in the next fragment. The process may seem tedious and arcane, but there is no existing technique to read the entire DNA strand at once.

The problem with so-called junk DNA is that a lengthy repeating sequence gives scientists no opportunity to match up unique portions. There is no variation, at least none in the small length of code current technology can cope with. The problem has been compared to the challenge facing a pilot flying over the ocean with no instruments. In his field of view, every wave looks just like the next so there is no way to judge the plane's position.

Perhaps stuttering DNA will prove to be junk, but some scientists maintain that the creation of junk is not nature's way of doing things. Huntington's disease is believed to be caused by a stutter some 258 letters in length within a gene. No matter who turns out to be right about junk DNA, it would be a mistake to think that the job of mapping the genome is entirely complete, or that this system is fully understood.

Mapping the genes of animals, plants, and humans is now a multibillion-dollar industry (in terms of market capitalization), and it has been highly automated and computerized. By learning the makeup and functions of our genes we can try to control them and, by extension, eventually hope to control the entire repertoire of bodily functions and dysfunctions. The medicines of tomorrow and some in development by the biotechnology industry today aim to modify genes or the all-important proteins they create.

THE DNA "FISHING" ROD

You will often encounter the term *expressed sequence tags* (ESTs). This acronym was coined by Celera's President, Craig Venter, to describe a step in the painstaking assembly of a complete gene map. ESTs are found by fishing in a pool of genetic fragments with a chunk of synthetic DNA called *complementary DNA* (cDNA).

To demonstrate, let's assume a researcher only knows the exact sequence of the middle section from the three small stretches of DNA used in an earlier example. DNA is said to be "expressed" when its code results in some observable activity within the body. This kind of DNA is easier to find and to sequence than inactive stretches of the molecule.

When using computer data to find overlapping DNA sequences, the researcher is looking for exact duplicates among the letters. But, when creating a gene probe, the researcher must make a physical chain of molecules with reverse (or complementary) codes. This is easily done by a machine that is operated like a typewriter and deposits a chain of genetic letters on demand. A researcher might simply type in the desired sequence of nucleotides, in this example GATCGATCGATCGACTC-GATCGCAT, and the synthesizer will deposit them in order and link them together. The catch in this scenario is that we're now dealing with physical chunks of code that attach only to their complementary opposites (A to T and C to G). Therefore, in looking for the extension of the sequence produced above, he will type in the opposite, or "complementary" DNA sequence.

Therefore, the length of code we wish to match:

GATCGATCGATCGACTCGATCGCAT

When typed out in terms of complementary nucleotides becomes:

CTAGCTAGCTAGCTGAGCTAGCGTA

Now the researcher has a physical strand of code that can find its natural complement. As mentioned, nucleotides are somewhat sticky, but selective about what they stick to, like opposite magnetic poles. Therefore, the gene probe will find and bind to its perfect match when it is placed in a solution that contains a complementary fragment. This is sometimes described in terms of fishing because the matching fragment will hook on to the probe and can be physically extracted for analysis:

The probe
CTAGCTAGCTAGCTGAGCTAGCGTA will bind to
TAGCTTACGATC**GATCGAT** or, at the other end, to **GCAT**CGACTTTCGAGATA.

Each end of the probe has found and stuck to an exactly matching opposite. These extensions are known as expressed sequence tags. As you can see by comparing the left and right extensions attached to the probe in the middle, they are the same as the extensions found in the previous example through computerized matching of known sequences in genomic databases. The description is a bit abstract, but ESTs are an important tool for biotech research that you'll encounter in investment news periodically.

One last bit of terminology from the genome: Chromosomes are formed when lengths of DNA are wound into tight formations with a characteristic X or Y shape. The human body has 23 pairs of chromosomes and it is the mixing of 23 chromosomes from a male and 23 from a female during conception that causes variations in genetic inheritance.

THE RNA DISK DRIVE

The main function of DNA is to hold the instructions for the manufacture of bodily components, mainly proteins, which are both the body's tools and its building blocks. But, like a computer's operating system, DNA has no power to act on its own. Instead, DNA instructions are carried by a mechanism called RNA (ribonucleic acid).

It may be helpful to think of RNA like a copying machine or a computer's floppy disk drive. The RNA molecule creeps along the length of a DNA strand, copying the sequences of nucleotides in genes. RNA skips over repeating segments of DNA, which is one of the reasons these portions have been called junk. Like a disk drive which has faithfully recorded a set of instructions from the hard disk onto a floppy, the RNA is then sent out of the nucleus to put cellular machinery to work. On arriving at the cell's protein-making factory, the RNA molecule is read out, much like a floppy disk that has been inserted into another computer. But the cell is not like an ordinary computer. It is more like an industrial robot that reads instructions and begins assembling, piece by piece, fantastically complex structures.

This form of RNA is called messenger RNA or mRNA because it delivers the genetic information.

The cellular protein factory is called a ribosome. Its draws on a warehouse full of materials to create exactly 20 kinds of protein building blocks called amino acids. These 20 amino acid molecules are then fused together in the precise sequence that was first prescribed by the DNA molecule and "messengered" over by RNA. The RNA code happens to be written in a slightly different alphabet from DNA and it is read in three-letter chunks called codons. Each codon is like a command, ordering the assembly of a particular amino acid. For example, the code CAC calls for the production of the amino acid histidine. There are 64 different codons, but only 20 amino acids that the body may assemble, which means that some codons are synonymous. There are other names for RNA with specific functions such as rRNA, which helps assemble the ribosome protein factory itself, and tRNA, which translates the message of codons into the language, that can build amino acids. As each amino acid molecule is constructed, it is joined to a chain of other amino acids in a precise sequence. It will become a protein upon completion. The resulting protein chain is called a polypeptide. (A peptide is a smaller protein unit.)

The process, to this point, involves many thousands of operations and errors can occur, but the system includes error-correction operations, much like a spell-checker in a word processing program. It is an elegant procedure, designed to keep the master DNA molecule safely detached from the cellular business going on outside the nucleus.

Comparing Gene Machinery to a Computer:

DNA = OS (Operating system and hard drive)
RNA = Floppy disk and message
Ribosome = Industrial robot (governed by the RNA message)
Protein = Final product

At this point, something truly fantastic happens. The chain of amino acids that has been extruded to create a protein goes into action, folding, twisting, and coiling following a precise, nearly perfectly choreographed dance to assemble itself into a huge molecular machine. This molecule is sensitive to fatty substances near the surfaces of the cell and watery substances nearer the nucleus that play a role in determining the final, all-important shape.

Protein folding, as it is called, is an operation of such exquisite complexity that it is currently beyond the limits of technology to decipher. Existing supercomputers have only begun to discern the cascade of events involved in protein folding, which is precisely the reason that IBM has dedicated approximately $100 million to build "Blue Gene," the most powerful computer in history, to sort out the mind-boggling intricacy of this self-assembly process.

PROTEIN MACHINES

To most people, proteins mean meat. Some people are aware that proteins make up inert materials like hair and fingernails. In fact, the body constructs approximately 30,000 different kinds of proteins and most of them are either the active tools, the messengers, or the building blocks of cellular systems. The all-important job of learning the functions of proteins is far from complete but some are well known:

- There are 3,000 proteins identified as enzymes, agents that rearrange molecules in many ways. They sometimes chop up fats from the digestive tract into manageable pieces, and sometimes perform more complex tasks like checking the DNA master molecule for spelling errors and making necessary corrections.
- Insulin is a key protein that enables the body to process and regulate sugars.

- Hormones are proteins that deliver complex messages to transform cells and entire organs in dramatic ways. They are most active during gestation when hormones switch genes on or off in the body of a developing fetus. The expressed portion of the genetic code (the genes switched on by the hormones) then manage the emergence of male or female characteristics.

- Nerves, muscles, and blood cells are made from complex structures of different proteins. Some proteins, like hemoglobin in red blood cells carry dissolved gasses into the body and waste gasses out. In nerves, they transmit electrochemical signals. In muscles, they enable contraction.

If we continue the line of thought that software can be made of hard physical components, then proteins are at the nexus between hardware and software, acting as both agents for information processing, and as active mechanical instruments.

LIVING CELLS

It requires an immense structure of many different proteins to build the smallest living thing in the human body: the cell. The body is composed of some three trillion cells and all contain exact, and complete copies of an individual's DNA (with the exception of blood and reproductive cells).

At the cellular level, there is again enormous diversity. Cells begin life more or less the same in the form called *totipotent stem cells*, meaning they can generate any kind of bodily cell. As cells mature and specialize in function, they are called *pluripotent stem cells*, which means they can produce cells with more precise and limited compositions and functions to make up particular organs of the body.

When the body interacts with its environment, cells are changed, sometimes permanently, by the signals they receive. For example, external stimuli affect the cellular receptors of the five senses, and the resulting sensory signals are then processed by brain cells to form coherent perceptions. Foods are processed to fuel the body's systems and toxic substances are isolated and eliminated. Infectious agents such as viruses and bacteria enter the body, and trigger the immune system to respond with cellular and chemical weapons. As cells go about their business, they signal one another to perform essential functions. For example, if the body is running low on oxygen, signals will be sent through nerves and by chemical agents to increase the heart rate and depth of breathing. A meal may result in a call for the production of insulin proteins to regulate the body's sugar levels. Signals may need to travel no further than the surface of a cell to achieve their purpose, or they may be transmitted more deeply inside by a chain reaction involving messenger proteins outside the cell, signal receivers on the surface, and proteins inside the cell that carry messages on to the nucleus. This message may result in certain genes being switched on or off. Gaining control of this signaling "pathway" is an important strategy in the science of managing disease.

DISEASE PROCESSES

In a system of such fabulous complexity, it is hardly surprising that things sometimes go awry. Despite the many mechanisms to control errors and repel invaders, the body may succumb to disease when some element in this process fails. If one considers the cascade of events involved in any bodily function, it should become apparent that there is opportunity as well as complexity and vulnerability. There are many mechanisms at many levels of bodily function where new technologies may intervene.

The variety of diseases that can affect such an immense and intricate system is too large to list here but a comprehensive database on disease can be found on the Web at www.mic.ki.se/Diseases/index.html which is the address of the Karolinska Institute (a Swedish University best known for its role in the awarding of the Nobel Prize for Medicine).[1] The following list describes the major families of disease:

- *Genetically inherited defects.* This large group of disorders may manifest itself anywhere in life, from the womb to old age. Deformations of the body may be obvious at birth, but other disorders such as Down's syndrome, sickle cell anemia, cystic fibrosis, or ALS (Lou Gehrig's disease) appear and take their toll at various stages of life. Some genetic conditions cause a predisposition to diseases such as cancer, although they may never manifest themselves as disease. Diagnosis in the womb through DNA testing is becoming more common, but workable gene therapies for this type of disease are still in the development stage.

- *Infectious disease.* This is a large family of diseases characterized by an attack on the body by a parasitic external organism. This group is generally broken down into four major categories:

  1. *Bacterial infection.* This type of disease is so common and well-known, that it needs no explanation. Its importance for biotechnology is that invading bacteria are becoming increasingly resistant to the most advanced forms of conventional antibiotics. New approaches to treat bacterial infection are urgently required and some promising avenues are discussed in the following chapters.

  2. *Viral infection.* This family of diseases runs the gamut from the common cold to HIV/AIDS. Viruses are extremely small invaders that blur the distinction between living and nonliving things.

Although generally considered to be nonliving because they are unable to function outside a host organism, viruses behave in many ways like any other life form. Viruses carry a distinctive genetic code that they insert into the DNA or RNA of a host cell. This set of instructions obliges the cell to manufacture new viruses that proliferate and spread the infection. In this way, the virus exhibits a mandate to reproduce, evolve, and to survive, all of which are unique qualities of living things (unique except for man-made computer viruses that function in a similar fashion). Conventional medicines have shown limited effectiveness against viruses but biotech approaches are showing more promise. Techniques involve the stimulation of the immune system and targeting the immune system's agents at distinct features or markers in the protein structure of a viral shell. Viral vaccines involve genetically engineering a virus to render it harmless and introducing it into the body to stimulate an immune system attack against similar invaders. Viruses are often used in biotechnology as *vectors*, carriers of genetic information for gene therapy.

3. *Fungal infections.* Fungi are responsible for a variety of conditions that usually occur in moist tissue, including thrush (or candidiasis) in the throat and mouth, and athlete's foot as well as eye and ear infections. Fungal infections are difficult to treat because they are complex living systems, resilient enough to be deadly in patients with a compromised immune system.

4. *Parasitic infection.* These organisms vary in size from single-celled structures to tapeworms more than 10 feet in length. The parasite uses the body's resources to feed and reproduce but does not always kill the host. Among the worst parasitic infections are malaria and "sleeping sickness." The biotech industry is decoding the genes of parasites such as malaria in an effort to find new weapons as these organisms become more resistant to conventional therapies.

- *Immune system diseases.* The symptoms of this complex group of diseases result from overactivity or underactivity of the body's immune system. There are many possible causes ranging from genetic malfunction to viral attack. The HIV/AIDS virus is responsible for the most notorious immune deficiency symptoms. By contrast, overactive immune systems mistake the body's own tissues for an invading organism and cause the body to attack itself. Rheumatoid arthritis, for example, involves an immune system attack on the body's own joints and some connective tissues. Allergies are a less severe form of overactive immune response. Management of the immune system is one of the major research avenues for biotechnology companies that are attempting to use the body's own disease-fighting mechanisms in ingenious ways, taking on illnesses ranging from heart disease to cancer.

- *Cancer.* This family of deadly diseases has one central feature: the runaway growth of mutated cells. Although the mechanisms that are responsible for the growth of a tumor are genetic, only a small fraction of cancers are caused directly by inherited genetic mutations. About 80 percent of cancers are believed to be caused by environmental factors, the most notorious being the carcinogens from cigarette smoking. Environmental factors can also trigger cancer in those with an inherited genetic predisposition to the disease. Two fundamental mechanisms can be at work (either singly or in concert) in cancer: oncogenes and tumor-suppressor genes. The effects of these two genetic systems on cell growth have been compared to the gas pedal and brakes of a car. An oncogene is like a gas pedal stuck at full throttle, driving rapid cell growth. A defect in the tumor-suppressor gene is like a broken brake pedal, unable to perform its usual function of halting excessive cell division. Gene therapy would appear to be the obvious answer to management of this disease but so far the technique has had limited success for complex reasons to be discussed later. Among the many other biotech approaches being developed are targeted radiation in which small isotopes are delivered directly to the tumor, also antiangiogenesis, which attempts to starve tumors of blood, and other approaches that involve both stimulating the immune system and helping it find the right places to attack.

- *Metabolic disease.* A family of diseases caused by genetic mutations that result in the body's individual cells being unable to break down (metabolize) materials necessary for cell function. The best known is Gaucher's disease. Current treatments are very harsh involving bone marrow transplants.

- *Endocrine diseases.* This important family of diseases causes the failure of vital glands. Endocrine glands produce complex chemicals and proteins, such as insulin, which are vital to the management of bodily systems. Disorders in this family include diabetes, obesity, growth disorders, hormonal imbalances, thyroid disorders, and osteoporosis. Many therapies are available for these diseases, most of which involve the replacement of missing glandular products, or suppressing the overproduction of these molecules. As the many complications of diabetes demonstrate, simply injecting a replacement protein like insulin falls short of a cure. Biotech strategies include the sensitization of the body to existing endocrine levels, management of the systems that malfunction as a result of endocrinal disorder and, possibly, tissue regeneration to recreate the products of malfunctioning glands. Biotechnology has already furnished fully humanized copies of growth hormones and insulin. Experiments with the transplantation of insulin-producing cells called islets are showing considerable effectiveness.

- *Aging and degenerative disease.* These are the diseases we are all heir to. It is suspected that all cells may contain instructions to cease reproducing, but genetic therapy using the telomerase gene and tissue regeneration may provide solutions.

- *Trauma.* Defined simply, trauma is physical damage to bodily tissues caused by an external force. Tissue regeneration technology is advancing medicine's ability to treat trauma. Also, techniques to control immune system and inflammatory responses may reduce the damage done by trauma. For example, the greatest damage in spinal injury is caused by posttraumatic inflammation.

- *Cardiovascular disease.* This disease family actually involves many different mechanisms and may not belong in a list describing disease functions, but the category is too important to be lost among the other disease types. The major afflictions in this group are hardening of the arteries, congestive heart failure, stroke, and heart attack. All involve immune system functions in some fashion. Atherosclerosis, or hardening of the arteries, is initiated by inflammation of the cells lining the artery wall and exacerbated by high blood cholesterol. Congestive heart failure involves inflammation of the sac surrounding the heart. Like atherosclerosis, stroke and heart attacks result from the buildup of plaque, cutting off oxygen supplies. Much of the damage in these conditions is caused by an inflammatory reaction called ischemia, which occurs when tissues are starved of oxygen and then suddenly resupplied. Control of the immune system's inflammatory mechanisms is a promising avenue of research and development. If heart tissues have been damaged by oxygen starvation, a gene therapy technique called angiogenesis, which stimulates the creation of new blood vessels, may help repair the damage.

- *Mental illness.* These diseases often involve the overactivity or underactivity of signaling systems in the brain. These diseases are not well understood, and there is ongoing debate about the roles of nature versus nurture. Conventional psychiatry once placed great emphasis on the role of parents (nurture) in creating psychiatric illness. New drugs to control signal processing have delivered important benefits in diseases such as depression, anxiety, schizophrenia, mania, and obsessive-compulsive disorders, leading many to believe that brain chemistry is more important in this family of diseases than previously assumed.

THE IMMUNE SYSTEM

As most everyone knows in the wake of the AIDS epidemic, the human body's immune system is the key to fighting off infectious disease. Its mechanisms are so powerful that they have been enlisted by the biotechnology industry to attack other forms of disease such as cancer. A basic understanding of immune system is essential to comprehend the details of biotech's disease-fighting strategies.

At its most basic level, the immune system is a mechanism with two key weapons: one is a living cell and the other a molecule that is carried in bodily fluids. "T cells" are, for the most part, the body's killing machines, designed to destroy any invader by direct assault. By contrast, free-floating antibodies could be described as custom-made attack proteins drifting through the blood and lymphatic system, ready to lock onto invaders and eat holes through them like a strong acid. The proper names for these two forms of attack are:

1. *Cell-mediated immune responses*, in the case of T cells.
2. *Antibody-mediated (or humoural) immune responses*, in the case of fluid-borne proteins.

The key to the operation of these two potent weapons is precise targeting. An immune response to infection is set in motion when roaming cells (called helper T cells) discover a foreign tissue. Unfamiliar organisms bear surface markers called antigens that the T cell reads and identifies as alien. Having recognized an infection, the T cell goes to work, creating molecules that interlock with surface antigens, trying to find those that fit best and bind most tightly to the antigen. (The molecules selected for binding to the antigen structure are called epitopes.)

The helper T cell then delivers the news of an infection along with a precise description of its antigens to so-called virgin T cells and B cells. Both begin multiplying rapidly and specializing to prepare for attack:

- B cells produce antibodies (attack proteins) that have been specially made to attach to the foreign antigens or epitopes.
- New T cells also proliferate, prepared to kill anything they stick to but customized to attach themselves only to the foreign invader (first recognized and described by the helper cell). These killer T cells bear a so-called T cell receptor (TCR), which might be described as a kind of grappling hook. The TCR will cling firmly to anything that is shaped like the object first mapped by the helper cell.

Once attached to an organism, these two weapons will set about destroying it. T cells will attempt to digest their prey while antibodies made by B cells will punch holes in it.

When the battle is over, the B cells stop producing large amounts of antibodies, and virgin T cells stop producing so many killer offspring. Both arms of the immune system then tuck away a few memory cells that contain all the information learned in battle so that a new attack can be mounted much more rapidly in case of a repeat infection.

The immune system's power does not always work properly. For reasons which have not been explained, the body occasionally mistakes one of its own parts for a foreign invader and mounts an attack. In the case of an organ transplant, foreign tissue is also subjected to attack unless drugs are taken to suppress the immune system. Immune system rejection of transplanted tissue goes by the name *graft versus host disease* (GVHD).

One point needs emphasizing. The agents of the immune system are inherently toxic but they should do no harm unless they are given a target. Once targeted, they will bind tenaciously to any organism bearing the enemy mark and the process of destruction will begin. The biotech industry's growing ability to direct the destructive power of the immune system gives researchers hope that antibodies and killer T cells can be harnessed to fight diseases like cancer.

THE LANGUAGE OF THE IMMUNE SYSTEM

You may encounter other technical terms when reading reports about immune system therapies:

- *Cytokines.* These are the molecules that direct the immune system's attack agents to the scene of trouble. Investors with a long memory of biotechnology will recall the excitement over the initial discovery of substances called interleukins, once thought to be potent cancer fighters. As it turns out, there are many interleukins with varying functions (at least 15), and they are often referred to by the family name, cytokines.

- *Macrophage.* Another name for a killer T cell.

- *Graft versus host disease.* Immune system rejection of transplanted tissue goes by this name and the acronym GVHD.

- *Granulocytes.* Another form of killer T cell.

- *Interferons (IFN).* These proteins also caused great early excitement in the field as a possible magic bullet against cancer. Interferons are now regarded as part of the cytokine family although their main function is to stimulate and direct an attack by macrophages. Three interferons have been discovered: Alpha interferon is sold by Biogen for hepatitis C. Beta Interferon may prove useful against cancer and multiple sclerosis (MS). Gamma interferon is a powerful stimulator, like adrenaline for macrophages.

- *Tumor necrosis factor (TNF).* This is the name given to the toxic agents expressed by killer T cells. Like any kind of poison, TNF destroys organisms indiscriminately and has no direct relation to tumors, aside from the possibility that it can be directed toward cancerous cells.

- *Colony stimulating factors (CSF)*. There are several of these agents, which stimulate killer T cells into action.

THE BIOTECH APPROACH TO TREATMENT

Conventional medical treatments rely on a relatively small arsenal of therapies to manage disease. Traditional pharmacology has concentrated on the development of small molecule drugs. As briefly described in Part I, small molecules are biologically active compounds that are robust enough to withstand an assault by digestive juices and small enough to be absorbed through cellular walls. By comparison, many biotech drugs are proteins, which are huge and complex molecules, unable to tolerate the rigors of the digestive tract and impossible to force through the lining of the intestine. A patient can recognize a protein therapy easily because it usually must be injected (although new biotech drug delivery systems will likely eliminate the need for injections).

Traditionally, small molecule drugs have been developed through a combination of scientific, technical, and trial-and-error techniques. In the past, pharmacologists began the search for new disease treatments by analyzing, as best they could, the chemicals at work in the relevant bodily system and testing the effects of similar chemicals on the disease process. Biotechnology typically approaches the task by discovering the functions of genes and the proteins created by them. If the activity (or the absence) of a gene or protein can be linked to a disease, then experiments are conducted to see if altering the gene or administering a protein substitute effects a cure.

The pharmaceutical industry's ability to create new small molecule drugs by traditional methods is nearing the end of its effectiveness and many multinational pharmaceutical companies are scrambling to find new ways to create drugs. Other therapeutic techniques are also running into difficulty. The administration of antibiotics for infection has been heavily overused, resulting in the evolution of disease-resistant strains of bacteria. Another time-honored therapy, vaccines, use killed bacteria and disarmed viruses to stimulate an immune response before the onset of disease. But many pharmaceutical companies have stopped the production of vaccines because of lawsuits resulting from adverse patient reactions. The arrival of new approaches to medical treatment could hardly be more timely.

Biotech therapies are typically targeted much more precisely than conventionally developed drugs. To draw a military analogy to the battle against disease, biotech therapies could be compared to cruise missiles and smart bombs. Older technologies are more like B-52 carpet-bombing, V-2 rockets or, in the case of cancer treatments, nuclear weapons. Today's medicines don't always hit the target and may cause a great deal of so-called collateral damage. Biotech's arsenal is intended to precisely target the weakest link in the chain of disease processes.

The following chapters include details about these promising new forms of therapy as well as the companies that are developing them. Biotechnology aims for a host of important improvements in medicine:

- To detect and diagnose diseases earlier through the use of microarrays. These biochips will be designed to locate defective genes or proteins involved in a disease process.

- To increase the precision of diagnosis and therapy through genotyping and phenotyping. Genotyping will show a patient's genetic makeup, enabling the detection of mutations and genetic disorders. Phenotyping involves classification of the expression of genetic traits, such as overproduction of a potentially harmful protein. In either case, this analysis will permit the clinician to choose a medicine that is appropriate for the disease and unlikely to harm the patient.

- Halting the progress of disease by controlling one or more of the mechanisms essential to its operation:

  1. Interception and destruction of infectious agents using techniques to recognize a foreign organism and mark it for attack. This could involve several approaches: targeting small molecules at vulnerable portions of the invader's genetic or protein structure or using antibodies, which are copies of immune system agents, for a direct attack against an invader.

  2. Halting a disease process by genetically modifying a patient's DNA or RNA.

  3. Creating vaccines, which are made from a specific disease strain, allowing for more precise and effective attack.

  4. Administration of proteins that can substitute for shortages or may be used as tools to manipulate diseased tissues.

- Restoring damaged tissues through tissue regeneration techniques.

- Slowing aging and degeneration through genetic manipulation of systems involved in automatic cell-death (apoptosis). Life and health might also be extended by stimulating the reproduction of cells that no longer have the potential to divide.

———•◆•———

CHAPTER 11

The Language of Genes

Nature will bear the closest inspection. She invites us to lay our eye level with her smallest leaf, and take an insect's view of its plane.

Henry David Thoreau

GENETICS AND GENOMICS

To better understand genomics, it may be helpful to briefly outline the science that gave birth to the industry: genetics. Genetics is all about the patterns of inheritance among offspring. Genomics is about the structure and specific functions of genes.

The science of genetics was first developed by an Austrian monk, Gregor Mendel, who carefully observed the generations of pea plants growing in his garden. Although Mendel had no inkling about the nature of DNA and chromosomes, he did postulate the existence of genes; in humans, genes are responsible for characteristics such as eye color and height, which may come from either parent. Humans have 23 pairs of chromosomes. Two sets of chromosomes are joined to create an embryo that derives genetic information from both parents. A recessive gene is expressed only when both parents contribute the same genetic information (or mutation in the case of genetic disease). Dominant genes are expressed in a child when either parent carries a copy of the gene in question.

As mentioned, some diseases are caused by the misspelling or omission of a single letter in the genetic code, a condition called *point mutation.* Some misspellings in the DNA or RNA chain have no effect at all and are called *silent mutations.* Other mutations involve the deletion of portions of the genetic code or the addition of meaningless letters. Many genetic diseases are caused by the mutation of a number of genes (an important complication for biotech researchers who may be unable to repair the entire array of mutations with gene therapy).

There are just a few more terms in the genetic lexicon that you may encounter when reading about biotech developments. The name *exon* has been assigned to the portions of a gene that have a known purpose in the production of proteins. Other portions of the gene do not have a role in protein production and are called *introns*. These are different from junk DNA because they do not have a well-defined stuttering pattern and they appear at various points between the coding portions of a gene. The meanings of the terms are easy to remember because they parallel the words "introvert" and "extrovert." The function of introns is largely unknown.

One more linguistic wrinkle: Scientists never say that a gene "produces" a particular protein because it is several steps removed from the manufacturing process. Instead, the usual terminology requires one to say that a gene "codes for" a protein because the gene merely carries the code responsible for a given function.

To this point, genes have been depicted as entirely passive, like a ROM (read-only-memory) chip in a computer. But DNA function varies according to which genes have been "switched on." This can be important in diseases processes if genes are incorrectly stuck in the on or off position. Oncogenes are an example of genes stuck in the on position, and tumor-suppressor genes may be switched off improperly. Some forms of gene therapy seek to throw these switches to the correct position.

Another peculiar genetic activity goes by the name of "jumping genes," or more scientifically, *transposons*. These transposons are genes that appear to move from one position to another on the DNA strand. Transposition of a gene doesn't often actually involve "jumping" to another location. Most often, a transposon is created when RNA runs a copy of a gene and then transposes this copy to another portion of the DNA chain.

Transposons are one of the tools bacteria use to create resistance against antibiotics.

Recombinant DNA

As daunting as the term *recombinant DNA* might sound, it means nothing more than cutting a DNA strand and inserting a new gene, possibly from a different organism. The cut DNA strand is spliced back together and it is "recombinant."

The biotech industry's methods for manipulating DNA are easiest to understand by going through a brief description of the process of cell division (mitosis). When a cell reproduces, the most important task is the creation of a perfect copy of the original DNA software/hardware. Imagine the process as separating the two strands of an enormously long zipper. The double helix is physically pulled apart by temporary mechanisms constructed by the cell for this purpose. The two resulting halves of the DNA molecule are genetic mirror images of one another. Where one shows an A, the other strand will show the matching nucleotide: T. The same with C and G.

Separated mirror image strands:

TAGCTTACGATCGATCGATGCATCGACTTTCGAGATA
ATCGAATGCTAGCTAGCTACGTAGCAGAAAGCTCTAT

These two strands are now free-floating in a solution that contains an abundant supply of raw nucleotides. These nucleotides are sticky but picky. Like magnets, the free-floating nucleotides will be eventually matched up with the proper partners on both strands. At the end of this process, both half-strands will have acquired enough base pairs to form a complete genetic mirror image of themselves. The end result should be two perfect copies of the DNA code.

Strand 1:

ATCGAATGCTAGCTAGCTACGTAGCAGAAAGCTCTAT
TAGCTTACGATCGATCGATGCATCGACTTTCGAGATA

Strand 2:

TAGCTTACGATCGATCGATGCATCGACTTTCGAGATA
ATCGAATGCTAGCTAGCTACGTAGCAGAAAGCTCTAT

To complete the process of division, the cell walls contract into an hourglass shape and eventually separate, with the new and old cell both containing the complete DNA code.

The first important step in putting DNA to practical use relied on the DNA molecule's very cooperative tendency to duplicate itself when split in half. Scientists found that the two halves of DNA fell apart naturally when heated just short of the boiling point. By cooling the two orphaned halves of the molecule in a bath of nucleotides, the strands gathered the pieces they needed to become whole again, just as in cell reproduction. By repeating this process, the two DNA strands could become four perfect copies, then eight and so on. One problem of working with a single copy of a microscopically thin molecule had been solved by multiplying the strand.

Unlimited numbers of copies of a tiny DNA sample can be generated using this so-called PCR (polymerase chain reaction) technique. PCR has become widely known through criminal investigations. A speck of blood or other tissue can be used to create a large sample of DNA that may verify the identity of a suspect. PCR was widely publicized but rarely explained during the murder trial of O.J. Simpson.

Another common, but slow, method of DNA analysis is called gel electrophoresis. The technique might be compared to a turtle race. Chunks of DNA are placed at the starting line, the bottom of a plate covered with gel. An electric charge draws pieces of DNA through the gel and the larger pieces slowly fall behind because they have more difficulty making their way through the gel. When the smallest pieces of DNA arrive at the finish line the larger chunks are arrayed behind them, the biggest pieces remaining very near the starting line. The result is a distinctive pattern of bars, similar to bar codes used in a grocery. This pattern varies from one individual to another and is a form of DNA fingerprint.

Two other key discoveries have proven essential to the manipulation of DNA. The first of these was the discovery of restriction enzymes, which are like molecular scissors. Restriction enzymes have a remarkable ability to snip a DNA strand into pieces at precise, known points. Because of this homing ability, restriction enzymes are important to gene mapping as well as splicing.

These enzymes are derived from bacteria that have no protective nucleus for their DNA. When a bacterium comes under attack from a virus (known as a phage), the bacterium defends itself against the insertion of foreign DNA by chopping it apart with restriction enzymes. In the lab, restriction enzymes have become tools to break the twin backbones of the DNA molecule after finding specific code sites that trigger the cutting action. The cut may be blunt, meaning the two DNA backbones are cut at the same place, or they may be staggered, with one backbone protruding, exposing its broken base pairs.

A blunt cut of a DNA sequence:

TAGCTTACGATCGATCGATG CATCGACTTTCGAGATA
ATCGAATGCTAGCTAGCTAC GTAGCAGAAAGCTCTAT

A staggered cut of a DNA sequence:

TAGCTTACGATCGATCGATG   CATCGACTTTCGAGATA
ATCGAATGCTAGCTAGCTACGTAGC   AGAAAGCTCTAT

This is where the second important discovery, called *ligase*, comes in. Ligase is effectively a glue that can join the broken backbone of the DNA molecule. With this tool, scientists are able to join an entirely new DNA sequence to the broken strand. The only requirement is that this new strand must have appropriate base pairs at the point of overlap. Therefore, if we were to join a new form of DNA to the broken molecule on the above left, the first five letters of the new strand must be complementary, genetic mirror images.

Splice Point
TAGCTTACGATCGATCGATG*CATCGC*TTTGACATAGACATACGG
ATCGAATGCTAGCTAGCTACGTAGCGAAACTGTATCTGTATGCC

The broken molecule is represented in bold type on the left and the new DNA is in plain type on the right. The common code used in the splice is in italics.

This is the heart of recombinant DNA. The operating systems of living creatures can be cut and edited in almost any way we choose. Because all living species share the same genetic language, it is possible for sections from the master molecules of two different organisms to be combined seamlessly. For example, if a human DNA fragment that codes for the production of insulin is attached to the existing DNA code from a mouse or hamster, then the rodent's body should produce fully human insulin.

The same technique could be used to cut out and replace defective portions of DNA in human beings, thereby curing genetically based diseases. The possibilities are virtually limitless, but realizing the promise of this technology will be a long hard road. Although the science has been proven, the technology has shown mixed results in practice, as described later in this book.

An Investment Perspective on the Science

Investors who expect miracle cures from biotech companies may have a very long wait. Mastery of the human genome and the body's protein mechanisms may take an entire century according to many experts in the field. During the first portion of the book, I urged investors to keep an eye on simple and inexpensive ways to combat disease. Simple techniques can be just as effective as advanced science while delivering results to patients much more quickly and at a fraction of the cost. The acid test for a great medical discovery hinges on affordability as well as effectiveness. Two new approaches to the control of malaria vividly demonstrate the importance of cost considerations as well as time lines for drug development.

Scientists at the Imperial College of London and the University of Washington reported two breakthrough discoveries in the battle against malaria during the year 2000. Both offer hope that a disease which affects 500 million people worldwide can be brought under control. The question for investors and disease victims is how soon and at what price?

Dr. Andrea Cristanti of London's Imperial College has found a way to insert a gene into the eggs of mosquitoes that could give the newborn insects resistance to malaria. The malaria parasite is transmitted to humans by female mosquitoes. Dr. Cristanti's breakthrough overcomes technical problems involved in inserting a new gene into a mosquito egg. Dr. Cristanti was able to prove the principle of gene therapy on mosquitoes by successfully splicing a fluorescence-generating gene into a mosquito. When exposed to ultraviolet light, the modified insects promptly gave off a green glow.

Dr. Cristanti says the next step is the insertion of a malaria-resistant gene into mosquito eggs; she predicts that within six years her team will create a mosquito that is physically unable to transmit the malaria parasite. By introducing such a genetically improved mosquito into the wild, she believes the disease-resistant gene will be transmitted to the species. Of course, it is impossible to be certain about several important issues until the following questions are answered:

- Will the transgenic mosquito resist malaria successfully?
- Will the malaria parasite develop a resistance to this form of protection, as it has to a number of drugs?
- Will the malaria-resistant mosquito successfully overtake the genetically unmodified strain?

Finding the answers to these larger questions will require much more than six years.

The other malaria discovery, from the University of Washington, is comparatively low-tech but no less brilliant. Uncanny as it might sound, Professor Henry Lai has found a way to attack malaria's falciparum parasite with low-energy magnetic waves. The mechanism takes a bit of explaining.

Malarial parasites feed on the oxygen-carrying protein in red blood cells called hemoglobin. They are able to consume most of the molecule but they cannot digest or expel the iron that hemoglobin carries. As iron builds up in the parasite's system, the organism might be poisoned by the metal except for a remarkable system it has developed that effectively converts excess iron into tiny bars. The parasite keeps these chunks of iron from harming its system by stacking and binding them together like a pile of bar magnets.

Dr. Lai found that by exposing a patient to a weak oscillating magnetic field, the iron stacks in a parasite's body are set in motion, causing substantial damage inside the organism. Tests with the deadliest strain of malaria have shown a reduction of as much as 70 percent in the number of parasites in the body of a patient exposed to the treatment. Dr. Lai envisions therapy on a wide scale using trucks that could travel from village to village in the third world, bearing relatively low-tech electromagnets. Patients could be treated harmlessly in a few minutes. The magnetic technology is simple, inexpensive, easy to administer, and quite effective.

These two technologies have not yet been commercialized, but it is not hard to figure out which would be the first to market. Cheap and simple treatments are often the best bet, and, in this case, much more likely to be adopted among impoverished countries. Dr. Lai's discovery has the potential to save millions of lives that would be lost while high-tech solutions are still in the lab.

There are many similar examples in the biotech industry. Ultrasound, heat, and light are currently being tested against diseases including cancer. The results of these tests are not yet clear-cut, but no approach, however simple, should be automatically discounted or ignored in favor of cutting-edge science. The human body is far too complex and the systems involved in the disease process too numerous to allow easy assumptions about the best avenues of attack.

CHAPTER 12

———◦•◦———

The Realms of Biotechnology
(or Who's Doing What)

An absolutely astounding change is taking place in the way drugs are discovered.
Douglas Harrell, Aurora Biosciences

THE DISCOVERY INDUSTRIES

Making an informed investment decision requires a base of knowledge about the biotechnology industry's many sectors. How do their technologies work and how effective are they? What is the profit potential? Who is competing? I have broken down the industry into many categories to simplify the answers to these questions.

Biotechnology has evolved from research projects conducted in universities and hospitals all over the world. Over the past 10 to 20 years, each field of research spawned highly specialized companies, all pursuing techniques that have varying degrees of profit potential, all requiring different amounts of time to achieve their goals.

The starting point of biotechnology is the search for knowledge among genes and proteins, industries called genomics and proteomics. Despite their fundamental importance to the future of the biotech sector, the investor honeymoon with companies in this sector appears to be ending.

GENOMICS: DECODING THE SOFTWARE

Genomics may be the primary field of discovery in the biotechnology industry but its dollar value is under considerable debate. No sooner had the audacious scientists at Celera Corporation announced their historic achievement mapping the human genome, than critics began crawling out of the woodwork. They pointed out that having the entire sequence of the human genome was about as useful as discovering the entire works of Shakespeare written in both a foreign language and an unknown alphabet. That

193

may be overstating the negative side of the argument from a scientific point of view but from an investor's perspective it merits consideration.

As described in Chapter 11, genomics involves finding the DNA code hidden in the cellular nucleus. The first complete genome sequence of a living organism was published in 1995 when the DNA code of bacterium less than two million base pairs in length was deciphered. It took only six more years for human genes, hidden among three billion base pairs, to be sequenced. The questions raised about the meaning of this discovery go to the heart of a biotech investor's dilemma. Yes, it is great science but what is it worth? After all, the entire sequence will be public property by the time this book hits the stands.

The next step for the genomics industry is crucial to its profitability. Having figured out the general makeup of the genome, scientists must find out what is normal and what causes disease.

Part of the solution involves decoding the genes of many other species and then drawing parallels to the human genetic code. For example, the smallest genome of a free-living organism ever decoded belongs to a bacterium called *Mycoplasma genitalium*. It requires only 580 thousand base pairs of DNA code to survive. Dr. Edward Purdue of the Mt. Sinai School of Medicine believes this obscure creature has just about the minimum amount of information required to sustain life. This may be a profound discovery. Here is a microbe which strips the functions of DNA replication, RNA transcription and protein synthesis down to the bare bones. Learning about the essential mechanisms of the simplest life form provides structure to our understanding of the most complex. (Put another way, a person completely unfamiliar with internal combustion engines would have an easier time understanding the workings of a Mercedes if he first figured out what makes a lawn mower run.)

Moving along the evolutionary chain, scientists at CuraGen have decoded the genome of yeast, and by looking for mutations in this code, it is possible to discern which functions of the organism are disrupted as a result. If knocking out a three-letter sequence disables a protein-producing function in yeast, we can look for a similar error and a similar outcome in a matching human gene. Yeast is simpler and safer to experiment with than a human being, so it is an excellent tool for genomic study.

To discover more complex operations, genomic scientists moved further up the evolutionary chain to decode the workhorse of biological science, the fruit fly. Yeast is a single cell organism and the fruit fly is a complex creature made of many different cells, but surprisingly, it has only slightly more than twice as many genes as yeast. (Yeast contains 6,200 genes and the fruit fly has approximately 13,600.) This means that a profound step in the development of life has been achieved through the evolution of only 7,400 genes. By comparing the two genomes, we can discover which ones they are.

As more creatures are decoded, more differences are discernible and by comparing the functions of various organisms, scientists are able to trace the functions of related genes. It is also essential to learn the genetic structures of creatures widely used in research, from the humble *E. coli* bacterium to the mouse. The mouse has become a standard tool in biological experimentation and drug testing because its genome is remarkably similar to that of human beings. A mouse DNA strand is believed to be 3 billion base pairs long, containing approximately the same number of genes as the DNA of humans. Decoding the genome of the mouse is especially important to biotechnology. Not only can it serve as a reference point for human genetic comparisons, it should also be useful in predicting the effect on humans of a drug first tested on a mouse. That's why Celera Corporation announced it would tackle this problem soon after completion of the human genome.

The decoding of the mouse genome is at the crux of a business problem for investors in genomics companies. Celera corporation has declared that it wishes to "become the Bloomberg" of biotechnology, which is another way of saying the company's goal is to become a central information bank. The question for Celera and all genomics companies remains: Who will pay for this information? For example, Celera knew that it could never have a monopoly on the human genome and that led to the decision to decode the mouse in a hurry. But Celera soon faced a serious competitive threat.

On October 6, 2000, the National Institutes of Health and three major companies, including the chip-maker Affymetrix announced that they too would sequence the mouse and make the information available free of charge on a public database. Days later, Celera announced that it had almost completed the mouse genome and promptly sued Affymetrix for patent infringement (relating to the production of oligonucleotides, short synthetic DNA chains used in analysis). By all appearances, Celera will lose its monopoly on mouse genome data within six months of its creation, a blink of an eye in the drug development process. The cost of decoding the mouse genome, according to the competing consortium, is $58 million.

Celera is also creating a database of SNPs, which are the one-letter variations in genetic sequences believed to be important in some diseases. Again, Celera faces competition from a public and private consortium that is also attempting to create a SNP database; because public money is involved, it is unlikely that this information will be kept secret.

The problem for all pure genomics companies is similar. The product they intend to sell is information, but any company with adequate resources can discover the same data. Celera hopes to make a profit by charging as much as $5 million for access to its database plus possible royalties on resulting drugs, a price high enough to give potential customers an incentive to form competitive consortia.

Table 12.1   Biotech Companies Involved in Genomics

Company	Areas of Specialization
Celera Genomics (CRA)	Supplier of genomic databases
Genome Therapeutics (GENE)	Genomics of disease organisms
Genset (France)	Genomics and gene shuffling
Human Genome Sciences (HGSI)	Genomics to drug discovery
Hyseq (HYSQ)	Genomic analysis and chips
Incyte Pharmaceuticals (INCY)	Genomics and functional genomics
Millennium Pharmaceuticals (MLNM)	Genomics to drug discovery
Orchid Biosciences (ORCH)	SNP discovery
Sequenom (SQNM)	Genomic analysis
Double Twist (private)	Genomic data and analysis
Variagenix (VGNX)	SNP discovery
Genaissance (GNSC)	SNP discovery

The problem facing a company in a field like genomics is that it can never be certain of controlling access to the information it discovers. This is a very important consideration for investors.

The competition is shown in Table 12.1. Celera is the leader in genomics. Most of its competitors have expanded their business fields beyond pure genomics. To give Celera its due, it's important to keep in mind that genetic data has become a software commodity and the Celera data system is gaining wide acceptance.

Functional Genomics

The problem with pure genomic information, aside from a lack of exclusivity, is the lack of certainty about the functions of genes. Biotech companies all over the world have developed an astonishing array of techniques to pin down the answers.

Most approaches involve statistical analysis that attempts to match an illness with a pattern of genetic variations. The story of a new company called deCode Genetics provides the simplest illustration. Based in Iceland, deCode is searching the island's population of 270,000 for the common markers of genetically based illness. Working in Iceland is an advantage because the population is largely descended from a small group of Nordic settlers who arrived there in the ninth century.[1]

Although 99.9 percent of all human DNA is the same, researchers still face a daunting number of variations and combinations of variations when trying to pick out a disease-causing gene in the general population. In Iceland, the similarity of DNA in the population is far greater than normal, a fact that makes variations much more obvious. What's more, Icelanders have kept genealogical records for a thousand years. This hugely simplifies the task of matching a genetic mutation to a specific disease. The deCode company has obtained access to genealogical records and the cooperation of the population to assemble a database of diseases that it has cross-referenced against the island's small gene pool. Already it has discovered genes involved in osteoarthritis and stroke for two major pharmaceutical firms. Two similar projects are underway in Canada where Newfound Genomics and Signal Gene are looking for disease-causing genetic variations among isolated communities in Newfoundland and Quebec. In the United States, Myriad Genetics is performing similar work among Utah's Mormon population. On a larger scale, Gene Logic is obtaining samples of diseased tissue from sources around the world and comparing them in hopes of finding matching mutations that could link a gene to a disease.

Companies like CuraGen and Lynx are pursuing more technical approaches to the problem using high-speed analysis of gene expression.

This is an enormously important field for the understanding of disease processes, but so far it has not been tremendously profitable. There are many competing approaches to functional genomics and customers appear to be waiting for breakthrough findings such as those from deCode Genetics before committing large amounts of cash.

All in all, the field demands close scrutiny by investors. It would be unwise to take a position in a functional genomics company or a pure genomics company that cannot demonstrate a growing client base and an increasing cash flow.

Table 12.2   Companies Involved in Functional Genomics

Company	Areas of Specialization
Axys Pharmaceuticals (AXPH)	Genomics, proteomics, and small molecules
CuraGen (CRGN)	Functional genomics and expression data
deCode Genetics (DCGN)	Population-based functional genomics
DeltaGen (DGEN)	Functional genomics and target validation
Diversa (DVSA)	Industrial genomics
Exelixis (EXEL)	Functional genomics and applications
Gene Logic (GLGC)	Functional genomics and bio-chips
Genzyme Molecular Oncology (GZMO)	Cancer antigens
Human Genome Sciences (HGSI)	Genomics to drug development
Incyte Pharmaceuticals (INCY)	Functional genomics
Lexicon Genetics (LEXG)	Functional genomics and knockout mice
Lynx Therapeutics (LYNX)	Comparative genomics and analysis
Millennium Pharmaceuticals (MLNM)	Genomics to drug development
Myriad Genetics (MYGN)	Genomics to drug development
Sequenom (SQNM)	SNP discovery and high-speed analysis
Tularik (TLRK)	Genetics to small molecule drugs

Some investors have profited in this field by cashing in on the early enthusiasm for genomic discovery. Now that the excitement has died down, investors should look at a stock's moving averages to see if a company is on a downward trend, and if that trend is justified by revenue shortfalls. Companies that leverage expertise in this area for in-house drug design may be the best performers.

The competition is shown in Table 12.2. Incyte is the biggest company in the field and holds the most genetic patents, plus thousands of patent applications. Revenues for Incyte and Gene Logic have not met expectations during the latter half of 2000.

ACCELERATED EVOLUTION

The human genome, however large, contains a limited number of genes and genetic variations. The same limitations apply to any other living thing. Occasionally genes may combine in novel ways and three outcomes are possible:

- A disease may result.
- A new trait may emerge to be tested in the evolutionary arena.
- There may be no effect at all.

A small number of companies have seized on the possibilities of combining genes, switching them on or off, or mutating them in forms never previously seen in nature. The process is called "gene shuffling," but there's a bit more to it than random cutting up and recombining of genetic material. Companies like Maxygen and Genset take the process to the next logical step and determine what each combination might produce. If the object is to create a new therapeutic protein, many thousands of shuffled genes will be sifted to see which is likely to code for the desired improvement in a protein.

The whole effort can sound a lot like the old argument about a thousand monkeys at a thousand typewriters trying to write a novel. They're not likely to succeed, even if the monkeys have a thousand years to work on the task. But, two factors make gene shuffling more practical. Rather than banging out random letters as monkeys might at a typewriter, gene shuffling companies use entire genes, or portions of genes, carefully cut apart by restriction enzymes. We know that three letters of a gene are the smallest number required to produce a coherent result because they create a codon in RNA and that results in the manufacture of an amino acid. If we think of a three-letter fragment as being a coherent phrase, and a larger chunk of DNA as a sentence, then an entire gene might be like a chapter of a book. If the gene is cut to maintain the syntax of its smaller chunks, then

Table 12.3 Companies Involved in Accelerated Evolution of Genes

Company	Areas of Specialization
Diversa (DVSA)	Gene shuffling and industrial genomics
Genencor (GCOR)	Genomics and industrial genomics
Genset (France) (GENXY)	Gene shuffling and screening
Maxygen (MAXY)	Gene shuffling and industrial genomics
Applied Molecular Evolution (AMEV)	Directed mutation and screening

the process becomes less chaotic. Gene shufflers effectively produce random combinations of genetic instruction sets.

Accelerated evolution is my own term to describe the heart of this intriguing process. Millions of genetic mutations are created and most of them are rejected immediately by the laboratory equivalent of natural selection. In successive levels of screening, only the fittest survive to become useful commercial products. This evolutionary creation of new genetic material is highly accelerated because new combinations can be tested and rejected at a rate of thousands per hour.

In the case of a company called Maxygen, some useful products have already emerged. Many laundry detergents contain an enzyme called subtilisin and Maxygen says it has found a way to improve on this commonly used protein. The company is involved in pharmaceuticals as well as industrial products and counts among its clients DARPA, the Defense Advanced Research Projects Agency, which created the Internet well before Al Gore. (In the case of Maxygen, DARPA appears to be looking for chemical agents to defend against biological warfare attacks.)

The problem, as usual, is the absence of profits. The good thing about companies in this business is that they produce products to order for clients and will share in the revenues from their inventions. The product is original and proprietary, unlike data about natural genomes, which might be reproduced by any competitor. There is also a greater likelihood of quicker returns on products produced for industrial clients because of the absence of regulations requiring lengthy clinical trials.

The competitors in the field of accelerated evolution of genes are listed in Table 12.3.

PROTEOMICS

This is "the next big thing" in the biotechnology industry, a challenge greater than the genome. As described earlier, proteins are the key mechanisms of organic function, carrying messages, rearranging other molecules, and building the structures of most of the body's parts. This is an awesome array of tasks and the current estimate that the body contains 30,000 different proteins may fall short of the mark.

At first glance, there might not appear to be too much mystery about proteins. We know that DNA presents its code to the messenger, RNA, and a cellular protein factory called a ribosome uses this information to extrude a chain consisting of no more than 20 different types of amino acids. This process has exquisite symmetry and is easy to understand compared with what comes next.

Imagine an airplane hangar strewn with thousands of bits of metal, cans of oil, chunks of wire, and pieces of plastic, but no more than 20 different types of material, all strung loosely together. This is much like a raw chain of amino acids emerging from a ribosome. Now imagine the entire repertoire of materials on the floor of the hangar suddenly springing into motion spontaneously. Pieces fly in every direction and begin hooking together, forming precise structures, bending into airfoils, coiling into instrument panels and sealing the windows and doors of what turns out to be a perfect Boeing 747. Now imagine this happening in a millisecond. If you can picture that, you have some idea of the mystery behind proteomics.

Somehow, the thousands of amino acid molecules that make up a large protein assemble themselves into an extraordinary structure in a mundane-sounding process called protein folding. These structures are so complex that they are rarely depicted in the familiar form used for ordinary molecules such as the Tinkertoy structures of balls and connecting sticks used in chemistry labs. In many cases, scientists have no idea where the individual atoms of a protein molecule are located after it has folded. Instead, "ribbon diagrams" are drawn using barrel shapes, strands, bands, and arrowheads to depict the gross features believed to exist in a protein under study. It's like drawing the blueprint for the aforementioned 747 with a paint roller.

Proteins interact with one another and the bodily environment in complex ways. The all-important shapes of proteins can be affected by interactions with watery or oily substances. (Proteins that are amenable to water are called hydrophilic and those that interact well with fatty and oily substances are called hydrophobic.)

Nothing expressed the complexity of the problem more crisply than an article from the Pittsburgh Supercomputing Center about the work of Professor Peter Kollman from the University of California.[2] Kollman and his colleagues tried to crack the mysteries of protein folding using a massively parallel (250 processors working together) Cray Supercomputer and software that would predict the motions of atoms in a relatively simple protein made of only 36 amino acids in a watery environment. They ran the computer for six months and simulated the movements of molecular self-assembly 100 times longer than anyone had before. This breakthrough resulted in a simulation one microsecond long. A complete simulation would have delivered somewhere between 10 and 100 microseconds of protein-folding . . . in other words, as much as 50 years of supercomputer time might be needed to simulate the entire folding process of a simple protein for 100 millionths of a second. As one proteomics research noted dryly, "This is big science."

To be strictly accurate, the supercomputer used in this experiment was getting a bit on in years, although the Kollman team souped it up by using 256 processors. The machine was recently sold on eBay for less than $100,000. As mentioned previously, IBM is building a supercomputer 100 times faster than anything now in existence to crack the protein problem.

The question is: Why make such a large investment? The short answer is that proteins are proving to be the best drugs in the biotech arsenal. A single protein, recombinant human erythropoietin, is at the heart of the Amgen fortune. More than 80 percent of the biotech drugs approved by the FDA are proteins, and most of them are both highly effective and very profitable generating more than $10 billion in revenues.

The reason it makes more sense to develop proteins, rather than DNA-based gene therapies, is effectiveness. As discussed later, results from gene therapy have fallen somewhat short of expectations. The problem is that DNA is twice removed from diseases processes because it must be translated into RNA and expressed through the cell's protein factory. The body lives or dies by what proteins do. Changing a protein's function changes everything with no intermediaries, as executives at Amgen can attest.

There are many different approaches to cracking the protein problem, but as the Cray Supercomputer story suggests, this business will be a long time in development. Computational chemistry of the sort Dr. Kollman and his team are developing will be a key tool. Current methods of understanding proteins include the use of X-ray diffraction and biochips of the sort used in genomic science, adapted to protein analysis. The methods used for functional genomics can also be applied to the protein problem.

Table 12.4 Companies Involved in Proteomic Analysis

Company	Areas of Specialization
Celera Genomics (CRA)	Proteomic analysis
Ciphergen Biosystems (CIPH)	Protein chips
Genomic Solutions (GNSL)	Automated gel analysis systems
Hybrigenics (France)	Protein interaction analysis
Large Scale Biology (LSBC)	Protein identification
Myriad Genetics (MYGN)	Protein interactions
Oxford GlycoSciences (United Kingdom)	Protein identification
Proteome Inc.	Protein identification
Proteome Systems (Australia)	Protein identification
Cytogen (CYTO)	Proteomic discovery

Not surprisingly, the aggressive team at Celera has been one of the first to jump into the fray, building a new proteomic analysis and computation center. It will take some time to determine the leaders in proteomic analysis, but companies like Amgen, Genentech, Human Genome Sciences, and Protein Design labs are not waiting for the final results of a universal understanding of the human proteome to emerge. They are developing drugs from the existing knowledge base.

Potential revenues from drug development are a key consideration when comparing competitors in this field. Table 12.4 lists major competitors.

THE DEADLY PROTEIN

One of the most disturbing findings about proteins emerges from studies of Britain's epidemic of "mad cow disease," properly known as bovine spongiform encephalitis (BSE). The word spongiform was coined to describe the structure of an afflicted animal's brain, shot full of holes like a sponge. The source of this disease was unknown for many years and it became highly alarming because it appeared to be crossing the species-barrier into humans.

The human version of the disease is called CJD, or Creutzfeldt-Jacob disease and its effect on the human brain is just as devastating as it is in cattle (or in sheep suffering from a related disease called scrapie). As a scientific debate raged over the cause of mad cow disease, herds of cattle were destroyed and people became terrified of eating beef. No bacteria, virus, or any other known infectious agent could be blamed conclusively. But a breakthrough theory by Dr. Stanley Prusiner of the University of California delivered a stunning answer. The infectious agent was a protein.

Never before has anyone recognized an infectious disease that acts entirely without genes or DNA of any kind. Even viruses, which may or may not be living organisms, carry a cargo of genetic code but this form of protein, called a prion, does not. The propagation of prion-based disease relies on a cascading change in protein structures. Prions exist normally in the brain and nervous systems of mammals although their function is not well understood. A protein-based infection begins when a few mutated prions enter the body, usually through the digestive system. These defective prions survive cooking and attack by stomach acids without effect, ultimately finding their way to the nervous system where an infection like no other begins. As we know, the shape of proteins is changeable but having the correct shape is essential to a protein's function. A malformed prion protein touches off a domino effect among similar molecules, causing them to distort in exactly the same manner. As the number of deformed prions grows, more and more normal proteins are exposed to the mutation. After an incubation period, which may last more than a decade in humans, the nervous system is ravaged.[3]

CJD is still a rare disease and the discovery of prions might have had limited importance if it weren't for the fact that these strange mutations clump together and contribute to the formation of amyloid plaques: one of the key markers of Alzheimer's disease. Prion infections have now been tentatively linked to a number of degenerative conditions beyond Alzheimer's including Parkinson's and Huntington's disease. The importance of this discovery was recognized when Dr. Prusiner was awarded the Nobel Prize in Physiology and Medicine in 1997.

Prion-based disease has emerged in a few years from a scientific theory to recognition as an important mechanism of catastrophic disease. If my earlier discussion about the importance of understanding protein folding seemed abstract and irrelevant, this is one compelling reason to think again. Science is a long way from learning how to manage this problem, but a central mystery of neurological disease is beginning to unfold.

CHAPTER 13

The Picks and Shovels of Biotechnology

The first Boeing 777 was built in a computer.
Michael Grey, President and CEO of Trega Biosciences[1]

MANAGING THE INFORMATION OVERLOAD

The explosion of information coming out of genomics and proteomics research has become something of a mixed blessing to the biotech and pharmaceutical industry. The overabundance of new data has utterly boggled some of the biggest potential customers. Major drug companies that once strained to find new targets for drug development now complain of being knee-deep in potential targets.

Functional genomics companies help drug companies and other clients find potentially valuable genes and, more importantly, refine their choice of targets. Most genomic firms also provide database management tools to help customers locate whatever they may be looking for. But, these services can't stem the tide of discovery or tame the flood of new information. Instead, genomic companies are commercially driven to increase the flow of new data.

The key to using this new wealth of drug targets efficiently is weeding out the least promising candidates before wasting money on laboratory development of dead ends. Thomas Klopack of "Drug Discovery Today" estimates that, on average, it takes $1.2 billion and 15 years of effort to bring a drug from target development, through clinical trials and FDA approval. Nothing could illustrate more sharply the importance of starting this process with the best possible drug target. The pharmaceutical industry desperately needs decision-making tools to reduce false starts in the lab and to decrease the risk of failures in clinical trials.

BIOINFORMATICS

One of the most promising approaches to the problem of weeding out an over abundance of potential drugs relies on computer analysis of a drug candidate's characteristics and probable effects. Although much of bioinformatics is concerned with organizing databases of raw information, the most valuable services are those that deliver real efficiencies to the entire drug development process. The criteria for this type of analysis are often summed up by the acronym ADMET. In just five letters, this term summarizes the make-or-break characteristics of a drug molecule under consideration.

- *A—Absorption.* Drug developers must know if a new molecule will reach its target intact. Many large-molecule protein drugs will be destroyed by the digestive system if taken orally. Some will not cross the blood-brain barrier (a system the body uses to keep toxic substances away from brain cells). Some gene therapies have great difficulty penetrating the cellular nucleus.

- *D—Distribution.* Assuming a drug has made its way into the bloodstream, the problem remains, will it go where it is intended? A protein designed to stimulate the production of red blood cells may never reach target organs such as the spleen and bone marrow in any quantity. Often, foreign agents will go straight to the liver and kidneys for immediate disposal.

- *M—Metabolism.* Presuming a drug has made it to the right place, the question remains: What will the body do with it? Will it be altered by the internal chemistry of the cell? Will it still be able to do its job effectively? Alternately, will metabolization change a drug from an inactive form into a useful one?

- *E—Excretion.* Researchers need to know how long a drug stays in the body. By learning how quickly a drug is excreted, and in what form, researchers will learn about the dosage levels and frequency required to maintain therapeutic levels of the drug in the system. They will likely also learn about how the body has used the chemical.

- *T—Toxicity.* The more researchers know about potentially toxic side effects in advance of human trials, the better they can predict the safety and likelihood for approval of their compound.

Much of this work used to be performed through so-called wet-bench science. This in vitro research requires experimenting with a target molecule in test tubes and petri dishes to discover unexpected chemical interactions. In vivo testing is a lengthy process that involves administering the drug to lab animals to see if it is effective or will produce toxic side effects. It is an expensive task, which, at its conclusion, cannot guarantee a positive outcome among human subjects.

The new frontier in this process is called *in silico* testing, meaning as much work as possible is performed through the manipulation of computer models. Any chemical process can be simulated in a computer as long as the available software adequately depicts the materials and interactions involved. One of the companies developing software to perform ADMET testing is Trega Biosciences of California. The company president, Michael Grey, predicts the time needed to test a drug candidate can be reduced from years to mere months through computer simulations of ADMET testing. If the company's software is a correct model of human reactions, then many unsatisfactory drug targets can be weeded out very early in the process, saving enormous amounts of money. Grey believes that animal tests are poor predictors of a drug's performance in humans and tremendous efficiencies can be brought to the problem of weeding out dead-end drug candidates by in silico testing.

Some information systems aim for narrower but no less challenging targets. The basis for the action of any drug, whether it is a small or large molecule, begins with its ability to attach itself to special areas on proteins called "docking sites." The drug and the body's protein hosts must fit together like lock and key, which is no small problem to predict, given the complexity of the huge molecules involved. Scientists then use computational chemistry of the sort described earlier to predict the effect of the drug on its target.

Some companies, like Trega, perform analysis to order, and others like CuraGen sell subscriptions to a database of protein interactions. Database management for genomics and functional genomics companies tends to be customized in-house from major software companies like Oracle.

Table 13.1   Companies Involved in Bioinformatics and Software

Company	Areas of Specialization
Ariad ARIA)	Small molecule regulation of proteins
ArQule (ARQL)	Developing ADMET systems
Caliper CALP)	Protein interaction chips
Compugen (Israel)	Web-based software
CuraGen (CRGN)	Protein interaction database
Cytogen (CYTO)	Protein interaction database
Double Twist (private)	Web-based software and SNP analysis
E-Bioinformatics (Australia)	Web-based access to software
Entelos	Pharmacology simulation
GeneBio	Protein Structure and function analysis
Genomica (GNOM)	Public and private database access
Informax (INMX)	Analysis of public databases
Pharmacopeia (PCOP)	Chemistry software
Silicon Genetics	Software for biochip Analysis
Spotfire	Drug discovery software
Trega Bioscience (TRGA)	ADMET predictive modeling
Tripos (TRPS)	3D visualization and databases

Analysis of the business prospects of such companies depends partly on their structure. A company like Trega is specialized and can be judged most easily by checking cash flow and growth. Others, like CuraGen, have diversified into drug development and testing as well as bioinformatics, so the broader criteria described earlier in the book come into play. Table 13.1 lists companies working on the development of biometrics.

ASSAY DEVELOPMENT

The tedious disciplines of wet-bench chemistry are quickly being overshadowed by machines that combine the powers of computers, lasers, optical reading systems, and robotics. The whole effort is wrapped up in a catchall term you'll hear very often: *high throughput screening* (HTS). Hundreds or thousands of chemical targets are arrayed on a tray or slide and subjected to very rapid analysis. For example, if a researcher wished to test hundreds of potential small molecule drugs, looking for those that bind to a docking site on a protein, a machine of this sort could do the job in hours. Each well of chemicals would be tagged with a fluorescent marker and the protein under study would be added to the miniaturized test tubes of the experimental array. A reaction would give off light that can easily be read electromechanically and translated into a computer database.

This should be regarded as a service industry and judged on cash flow unless a drug royalty agreement has been struck with a client or the company in question is developing its own drugs. Table 13.2 lists companies pursuing assay development.

PHARMACOGENOMICS

At its core, this discipline is all about predicting how patients will react to a drug. By comparing a patient's genetic and bodily structures (genotyping and phenotyping) with drug structures, researchers hope to predict the drug's effectiveness or potential side effects. This has obvious benefits for patients and will be useful in improving drug development. Clinical trials can become much more efficient if it is first established through pharmacogenomic testing that only certain patient populations will benefit from

Table 13.2 Companies Involved in Assay Development

Company	Areas of Specialization
Aurora Biosciences (ABSC)	Ultra-high throughput screening
Cellomics (private)	Genomic and proteomic screening
Cerep (CERXF)	Screening and customized assays
Igen (IGEN)	Specialist in chemical luminescence
Molecular Devices (MDCC)	Provides assay tools and materials

Table 13.3   Companies Involved in Pharmacogenomics

Company	Areas of Specialization
ViroLogic (VLGC)	Tests for drug resistance in HIV/AIDS
Visible Genetics (VGIN)	Genotyping for virus resistance to drugs
Affymetrix (AFFX)	Chips used for genotyping

the drug under investigation. Those who might be harmed can be excluded in advance. If the technology produces accurate predictions, then the number of toxic reactions can be reduced and the potential benefit of the drug can be emphasized in applications to the FDA. It may even be possible to convince the FDA to reconsider a rejected drug if test results are reconfigured to display the benefits among patients shown to be appropriate through genetic screening.

Pharmacogenomics has the potential to lead the way for the era of personalized medicine. By knowing which drugs are appropriate for a patient's genetic makeup, physicians can avoid the considerable expense, suffering, and wasted time that results from giving drugs which could prove to be ineffective or even harmful.

Visible Genetics is developing another practical use for pharmacogenomics. By profiling the genetic nature of a viral infection such as HIV/AIDS, physicians will be able to prescribe more effective medicines. Because this virus has undergone mutations, some drugs will be much more effective than others against a particular strain of the disease.

The major companies in this field could soon begin generating significant revenues from sales of their pharmacogenomic tests (see Table 13.3). The commercial viability of their products and the long-range investment potential may be apparent from early revenue flows. (Note: There is an ethical debate over genetic privacy that could delay the use of these systems. It is described in detail in Chapter 15.)

LEAD GENERATION AND OPTIMIZATION

Even the most vertically integrated biotech companies, like Millennium and Human Genome Sciences often derive revenue by putting their expertise to work for other clients. A major firm like Aventis might face enormous costs developing expertise in a specialized field like protein design, hiring staff in a tight market, setting up new labs, and building a meaningful database of experience. Not only is it more practical to hire out such development tasks, substantially less risk is involved.

Many companies in this field have developed special areas of expertise (see Table 13.4). Human Genome Sciences (despite a name that implies a

Table 13.4   Companies Developing Drug Candidates*

Company	Areas of Specialization
Abgenix (ABGX)	Antibodies
Human Genome Sciences (HGSI)	Genomics and protein drug design
Medarex (MEDX)	Antibodies for cancer
Millennium Pharmaceuticals (MLNM)	Antibody and small molecule development
Praecis (PRCS)	Ligands for cancer and pain
Protein Design Labs (PDLI)	Monoclonal antibodies
Vertex (VRTX)	Small molecule drug development

* See Appendix A for more complete listings.

focus on genomic discovery) has extended its knowledge of human gene functions into protein-based drug development. Vertex is a specialist in the design of small molecule drugs, and Millennium has a specialty in antibodies as well as small molecules. Most of the companies in this field are also testing drugs they have designed themselves.

These companies should be assessed according to two criteria. How numerous and potentially rewarding are their contracts with major partners? And, how successful and advanced are their own products in clinical trials?

Drug Improvement

Even a successful drug can be improved on in profitable ways. Amgen provides the best example of this potential. The company's lead drug, Epogen, is highly effective and profitable, but it faces profit-limiting dangers. In addition to the shrinking period of patent exclusivity, patient acceptance is a problem because the drug must be injected relatively often. A new, longer-acting version of this drug will address both of these problems and provide Amgen with an additional valuable benefit. Rights for international distribution of Epogen have long since been assigned to a major pharmaceutical partner Johnson & Johnson. But Amgen is now preparing to market the second-generation product worldwide on its own, eliminating its contractual obligation to share revenues.

Companies may also engage in so-called "Label Expansion." By finding other uses for an effective product on the market, revenues can be increased. Clinical trials are required to gain approval for new uses, but there are fewer hurdles because the drug's absorption, toxicity, and other criteria have already been established to the FDA's satisfaction. Label expansion can also extend the life of a patent on a drug.

Label expansion is usually conducted in-house. Drug improvement can be contracted out to specialists who can address a product's limitations.

PEGylation is one of the most efficient ways of expanding a drug's persistence in the body, allowing for fewer doses. PEG stands for polyethylene

Table 13.5   Companies Involved in Drug Enhancement

Company	Area of Specialization
Enzon (ENZN)	PEGylation to reduce dosage frequency
Sepracor (SEPR)	Improved Chemical Entities (ICE)

glycol, which can be used to build a shell around a therapeutic protein. This shell slows down the absorption of the drug and allows timed release as the shell breaks down. (See Table 13.5.)

Companies in this field cannot be judged by contract revenue streams alone because they are involved in developing or modifying drugs for their own pipelines.

DRUG DELIVERY

One of the least exploited opportunities available to the pharmaceutical industry is improvement in drug delivery systems.[2] PEGylation, described earlier is one of the older and more established technologies to gain improved performance from a known drug. There are many other advances in this field but several studies indicate that the pharmaceutical industry is turning away from such solutions after encountering technical difficulties. Not so, the biotech industry.

One of the most promising areas for the industry is in cancer treatment. Existing therapies and new gene-based treatments are limited by serious drug delivery problems. As everyone knows, chemotherapy can have devastating effects on a patient's entire body. Standard chemotherapies and radiation treatments may only be administered at certain levels beyond which the side effects could become intolerable or even fatal. One of the best examples of a technique to circumvent this problem is being developed by Coulter Pharmaceuticals (CLTR). Coulter is awaiting approval for a treatment for non-Hodgkin's lymphoma (NHL). The treatment, called Bexxar, addresses this problem through a drug delivery technology that precisely targets cancerous cells in the lymph nodes. The key to this process involves harnessing the immune system.

Every kind of cell is studded with unique arrays of protein structures that perform a variety of functions. The immune system is designed to find foreign agents in the body and deliver antibodies intended to kill cells bearing these markers. Coulter's Bexxar therapy (being developed with Smith Kline Beecham) is a combination of radioactive iodine and an antibody. The antibody has been engineered to attack cells that carry the unique markers of NHL. In the case of Bexxar, the antibody is also used to deliver a small, lethal dose of radiation to every tumor cell it can find and bind to. The FDA has given the product "fast-track" status and it may be on the market shortly.

This is just one example of a drug delivery technology that can significantly enhance a drug's effectiveness. A company called FeRx is investigating the use of magnetism to deliver radioactive isotopes to a solid tumor. By linking the radioactive element to molecules containing iron, researchers hope to draw the tumor-killing combination to a tumor site with magnetic fields. The treatment is more specific than chemotherapy and minimizes exposure of the rest of the body to lethal agents.

In gene therapy, one of the recurring problems is the challenge of getting recombinant DNA into the cell's nucleus. Gentronics is marketing a technique called electroporation, which promises significant improvements in the delivery of drugs through cell walls. The technique involves the use of pulsed electric fields that temporarily expand openings on cell surfaces, allowing drugs a greater chance of getting inside.

Many large molecules have difficulty making it into the body, much less into cellular systems. Injection has been the time-honored but widely unpopular way of dealing with the problem, as any diabetic using insulin will attest. Technologies are in development or on the market to overcome the difficulty of getting a macromolecule into the blood without going through the digestive system or using syringes. The most familiar is the transdermal patch, which is currently used to deliver hormones and nicotine through the skin, directly into the blood stream. Researchers are now testing the possibility of administering vaccines by patch, an achievement that might spare millions of children the fear of the needle. If a needle is required, a technique called ReGel may reduce the number of injections by mixing a drug with a substance that becomes a gel inside the body, allowing slow release of the active ingredient.

Drugs that might otherwise be destroyed in the digestive system can be delivered through the digestive tract unharmed if they are encapsulated in a protective coating. Liposomes are tiny spheres formed from fatty materials called lipids and liposomes have become one of the most promising tools for improving drug delivery.

Ligands are a dual-action molecular tool, currently being researched for several uses including drug delivery. The first job of a ligand is to find the appropriate markers on a cell's surface and attach itself. When that is done, the ligand may act as an agonist or an antagonist. An agonist will signal a cell to open structures called ion channels, and antagonists will close these channels to outside influences. A company, appropriately called "Ligand," is attempting to use this technique to move drugs inside cells where a host of previously unreachable cellular receptors can interact with the chosen therapy.

Other promising techniques involve encapsulating a therapeutic agent within a microscopically small sphere and inhaling it. The drug may be absorbed through nasal cavities, the mouth, or the lungs.

Despite their potential to improve existing therapies, analysts have been disappointed by the drug industry's reluctance to use these technologies.

Table 13.6   Drug Delivery Companies

Company*	Areas of Specialization
Cardinal Health (CAH)	Capsule technologies
Coulter (CLTR)	Antibody targeted radiation
Generex (Canada)	Oral drug delivery
Genetronics (GEB)	Electropororation to open cell walls
IDEA AG (European)	Regel injectable technology
Inhale (INHL)	Inhalable spheres for drug delivery
Ligand (LGND)	Ligands to enhance drug action.
Vical (VICL)	Developing "naked DNA" gene delivery
Alkermes (ALKS)	Inhalable, oral, and slow absorption drugs
Atrix (ATRX)	Delivery systems for cancer therapy
Endorex (DOR)	Liposome specialist
Vion (VION)	Prodrug delivery for cancer
Emisphere (EMIS)	Oral delivery (Heparin)
Bioject (BJCT)	Needle-free drug delivery systems
Alza (AZA)	Techniques for pain and cancer therapy

* Listings include symbols only for publicly traded biotechnology specialists.

Investors should look up partnerships, contracts, and other revenue sources through the database at recap.com (see Table 13.6 for a list of drug delivery companies).

TOOLMAKERS

A great many stockholders subscribe to the "picks and shovels" theory, which holds that only the people selling picks and shovels came away rich from the last gold rush. Internet investors have done well by this theory, sticking to the companies that enable the Internet, such as Cisco Systems, rather than backing the prospectors trying to strike it rich with dot-coms. Biotechnology also requires many toolmakers to build the expensive instruments central to the discovery process. Perhaps the best known are PE Applied Biosystems (now called Applera) and Affymetrix, the leading chipmaker. Chips are a highly specialized and increasingly competitive field, to be discussed later.

Applera and its chief competitor, Amersham Pharmacia Biotech (NYE) are the leading makers of DNA sequencing machines. Other companies in this sector sell sophisticated lab machinery that permits high-speed screening of drug targets. Mainstream computer companies have also recognized the importance of the biotech market and IBM estimates that the industry's budget for information technologies will rise to $9 billion during 2003.

Unlike drug development companies, which have the potential to realize sudden cash flows on FDA product approval, toolmakers are unlikely to

Table 13.7   Biotech Instrument Manufacturers

Company	Areas of Specialization
Aclara (ACLA)	Miniaturized lab equipment
Amersham Pharmacia Biotech (NVE)	DNA sequencing machines
Caliper (CALP)	Screening devices
Illumina	Fiber-optic microarrays
Invitrogen (IVGN)	Assay kit manufacturer
Applera (ABI)	DNA sequencing machines
Qiagen (QGENF)	Assay kit manufacturer
Quantum Dot	Microcrystals for gene analysis

realize sudden earnings breakthroughs. Accordingly they should be assessed largely on the growth rate of their revenues and standard P/E ratio assessment (see Table 13.7 for a list of companies).

BIOCHIPS

However large the biotech revolution turns out to be, very few pick-and-shovel companies will share the dynamic growth enjoyed by the Internet's toolmakers. The reason lies in the enormous specialization of the equipment used in biotechnology. Widespread, Internet-like applications are highly unlikely to evolve for products that are essentially lab equipment.

One possible exception to this scenario is the biochip. The sudden explosion of major corporations entering the field is a clear signal to biotech investors that biochips are expected to be an important industrial product of the future.

The current technology of the biochip was briefly described in a previous sketch of the industry leader, Affymetrix. To recap briefly, biochips are tiny glass or silicon platforms that contain thousands or tens of thousands of samples of DNA, RNA, or other so-called probes. Each probe contains a unique sample that will react with a target chemical, a process called hybridization in genetic chips. If a single probe finds a match in a sample fluid placed on the chip, it will give off light that can be interpreted and cataloged by a computer.

The biochip is currently a research tool, but it has obvious implications for the diagnosis of disease in doctors' offices. Even more compelling is the possibility that biochips will become sufficiently inexpensive and versatile to be used in the home. If that sounds far-fetched, keep in mind that an early form of biochip, the home pregnancy test, is already an established product. This form of chip looks for only one thing, hormones indicating pregnancy and gives off an indication by changing color. A more advanced home biochip might one day screen an ailing child for thousands of possible disease strains.

One of the problems limiting the use of biochips is their cost, running from more than $45 each to prices higher than $1,000, although there's every reason to expect these prices will come down in time. The other major problem blocking the adoption of chips in wider practice is the price of the instrument required to read them, as much as $100,000 each. This too will change, but for the time being the manufacture of chip readers is still an important part of the industry's revenue stream. Building a competitive platform is a difficult hurdle for industry newcomers to surmount.

The names of the competitors entering the field give some sense of the anticipated stakes. They include Motorola, Corning, Agilent, 3M, and a Japanese consortium led by Mitsubishi Rayon. Investors can expect to see a major industrial battle over the creation of an industry-standard platform for reading these chips (also called microarrays).

Adding to the competition is the belief that chip readers will generate enormous amounts of data to be analyzed and stored. Seeing this opportunity, Compaq Computer and Intel have begun actively exploring greater involvement and investment in biotechnology.

Faced with the high level of big-cap competition, biotech investors may have reason to worry about the viability of established companies in this field. Affymetrix has responded aggressively to the competition by expanding into genomic research and pharmacogenomics. Smaller companies like Nanogen may be takeover targets because they hold patents on innovative chip-making technologies.

The current market for these devices is approaching half a billion dollars and could increase almost tenfold in five years. Given this profile, investors should expect sharply increasing revenue streams in their chosen companies (see Table 13.8).

Table 13.8   Gene Chip Companies Currently in Production

Company	Areas of Specialization
Affymetrix (AFFX)	Industry-leading biochip maker
Amersham Pharmacia (NVE)	DNA arrays
Beckman Coulter (BEC)	DNA arrays
Caliper (CALP)	Screening devices
Gene Logic (GLGC)	Chip manufacture and genomics
Hyseq (HYSQ)	Chip design and manufacture
Incyte Genomics (INCY)	Chip manufacture and genomics
Lynx Therapeutics (LYNX)	Chip design and manufacture
Nanogen (NGEN)	Chip design and manufacture
Rosetta Inpharmatics (RSTA)	Whole genome arrays

COMBINATORIAL CHEMISTRY

The underlying principle of combinatorial chemistry is quite simple and biotech investors should be aware of its potential. In the most basic terms, combinatorial chemistry involves the large-scale synthesis of variations from a molecule that has therapeutic promise. To explain it more graphically, suppose that a popular antidepressant has shown a good degree of effectiveness and tolerable but significant side effects. A combinatorial chemist might use this compound or its molecular skeleton (called a scaffold) to search for improved versions of the drug. It is a trial-and-error process that involves attaching a huge variety of biologically active structures to the scaffold. Each combination is tested with high-speed, automated systems until the biggest improvement on the original drug structure appears. If this new drug is significantly different from the original molecule, patent infringement should not be a problem.

Drugs developed this way tend to be molecules that generally work by binding to a receptor site on a cell's surface and blocking an undesirable process, such as the production of too much cholesterol. The thousands of experimental variations produced in combinatorial chemistry can be tested and most of them rejected in the lab by trying them en masse against target proteins. The compounds that bind most strongly and interact most effectively will be selected for further research and development.

Orchid Biosciences is attempting to miniaturize this process to the point where it can be efficiently conducted on a chip. Other companies believe that much of the effort spent on combinatorial chemistry in the lab can be synthesized through a computer.

The technologies involved in combinatorial chemistry are evolving quickly. It seems premature to pick a winner and probably not useful to embark on elaborate descriptions of many technological approaches that may be automated out of existence. Investors should examine profitability and technical leadership, as well as potential revenues from the development of drug targets. Table 13.9 lists companies working with combinatorial chemistry.

Table 13.9 Companies Active in Combinatorial Chemistry

Company	Areas of Specialization
ArQule (ARQL)	Combinatorial synthesis and library
Axys Pharmaceuticals (AXYS)	Combinatorial synthesis and library
Pharmacopeia (PCOP)	Combinatorial chemical library
Symmyx Tech. (SMMX)	Industrial combinatorial chemistry
Trega (TRGA)	Combinatorial synthesis and computer simulation
Orchid Biosciences (ORCH)	Automation of combinatorial chemistry

CHAPTER 14

———◆◆———

The New Biotech Therapies

We're moving from an age of serendipity in drug development to one of specific design.

Dr. Steven Wolinsky, Northwestern University

THE STRATEGIES

Biotech investors should always keep in mind that every breakthrough in the evolution of the industry has followed a similar pattern: exaggerated hope followed by a long period of investor disappointment before the true potential of a discovery is eventually realized. That was the case with the first large molecule, protein-based drugs such as interleukins and interferons, compounds that turned out to be fantastically expensive to produce and difficult to administer without inducing side effects. A similar pattern is appearing again with gene therapy and other new technologies.

That's why investors need to have a clear idea of the practical realities behind biotechnology's new therapeutic techniques. Magic bullets for cancer and perfect cures for diseases like diabetes are not just around the corner, no matter what you might hear from the media or the Internet. The reason biotechnology has disappointed investors so often in previous decades has little, if anything, to do with the industry itself. The fault often lies in ourselves, the investors whose expectations routinely outstrip reality.

It is important to fully appreciate the exquisite intricacy of biological mechanisms because one can easily misinterpret news about the discovery of a new disease-fighting technology. Overexcited investors, in search of sudden riches, dig their own graves when they fail to recognize the long road between a breakthrough discovery and a useful drug.

MONOCLONAL ANTIBODIES

Monoclonal antibodies are emerging as one of the most promising weapons against disease in the biotech industry's arsenal. More than 70

216

monoclonal antibodies are in clinical trials for a variety of illnesses including cancer. Fewer than a dozen are on the market, a surprisingly small number considering how long the technology has been in development.

Antibodies are proteins with a purpose. When the body senses it is under attack, it creates highly specialized antibodies to destroy an invader. This much has been presumed since the first vaccines were created in the nineteenth century. Somehow, it was hypothesized the body recognized that the killed bacteria in vaccine injections were potentially dangerous and responded by creating an immunity to subsequent attacks. The mechanism was unknown for many years; nevertheless, the name *antibody* was given to these mysterious agents that repelled foreign bodies.

The first synthetic antibodies were produced in 1975 in an atmosphere of general excitement about the creation of magic bullets to fight disease. Early hopes were dashed by many complications that highlighted how much remained unknown about the operation of the immune system.

As mentioned previously, every cell carries identifying markers, and in the case of viruses and bacteria, these surface markers are called antigens. When the immune system encounters unfamiliar markers, it assumes the worst and goes on the attack. The antigens on the invading organism's surface are used as a mold (the technical term is *epitope*) for the creation of customized antibodies by the immune system's B cells. As antibodies are pumped out, these specialized molecules latch onto antigens like keys fitting into millions of identical locks. The antibody clinging to an invading organism then becomes a marshaling point for a counterattack by the full arsenal of weapons at the immune system's disposal. The heart of this process is the exact fit between an antibody and the antigen.

Two British scientists developed a deceptively simple way to make uniform antibodies more than a quarter of a century ago when they injected mice with the antigens of a disease they wished to treat. The mice obligingly produced antibodies from their B cells. The scientists then removed these cells and conferred immortality upon a select few of them by fusing B cells with tumor cells. The new type of cell was called a hybridoma and it continued to pour out a stream of antibodies that could then be separated and tested as a medicine. Because the hybrid cell was tumorous, it could reproduce endlessly, ensuring a steady supply of precisely crafted antibody molecules.

Hopes were high initially because monoclonal antibodies were so specific in their attack strategy. Scientists hoped that if an antibody could be designed to recognize a tumorous type of cell, it could direct an immune system attack on the cancer while leaving healthy cells untouched. The next two decades, however, presented more technical challenges than cures. The new technique of producing antibodies was extremely expensive and early experiments produced unexpected side effects without delivering the desired result.

The main problem was that the new antibodies were mouse proteins, which were immediately identified by patients' bodies as foreign. Allergic reactions developed and the treatments soon lost their effectiveness as human subjects developed new antibodies to destroy the unfamiliar mouse antibodies.

WHAT MAKES AN ANTIBODY MONOCLONAL?

Bacteria and viruses carry a variety of antigens that stimulate the creation of different antibodies, not all of them useful. Each B cell can create only one kind of antibody, so scientists must select the type of cell which produces the most effective type of antibody and clone many copies of this single strain. Hence the term: monoclonal antibody. Had scientists chosen to clone many different B cells to generate a number of antibodies at once, the product would be a polyclonal antibody but so far monoclonals have proven to be a more efficient tool.

Monoclonal antibodies have become more practical in recent years with the development of "humanized" strains. The best-known technique involves genetic alteration of mice. The genes responsible for the creation of antibodies in a mouse are deleted and replaced with human genes that serve the same function. The process is still expensive but it is producing a new generation of humanized drugs. Leading companies in the field of creating so-called transgenic animals for antibody production are Abgenix, Medarex, Genzyme Transgenics, and IDEC Pharmaceuticals. IDEC has used hamster ovaries to produce fully humanized antibodies and Genzyme Transgenics is working with goats.

Another technique involves a useful virus known as a phage, a strain known for attacking bacteria. By splicing human antibody genes into the genetic code of a phage, a variety of humanized antibodies will be generated by the virus itself. One of the leaders in this method, a British company called Cambridge Antibody Technology Group, has entered into a close collaboration with Genzyme General. Another leader in this technology is MorphoSys of Germany.

Monoclonal antibodies, known also as MAbs are now among the biotech industry's most important revenue generators. Therapies on the market include:

- Rituxan, a treatment for lymphoma by Genentech (DNA) and Idec Pharmaceuticals (IDPH).
- Synagis for infant lung infections by Medimmune (MEDI).
- Remicade by Johnson & Johnson for rheumatoid arthritis and Crohn's disease.

Table 14.1   Companies Involved in Monoclonal Antibody Development

Company	Areas of Specialization
Abgenix (ABGX)	Antibody production and development
Coulter (CLTR)	Antibodies with radioactive isotopes
Imclone (IMCL)	Cancer antibodies
Immunomedics (IMMU)	Antibodies with radioactive isotopes
Medarex (MEDX)	MAbs for cancer and autoimmune disease
NeoRx (NERX)	Antibodies with radioactive isotopes
Medimmune (MEDI)	Antibodies for wide variety of diseases
Immunex (IMNX)	Antibodies for wide variety of diseases
IDEC Pharmaceuticals (IDPH)	Antibodies for cancer and immune diseases
Immunogen (IMGN)	Antibodies and prodrugs for cancer
Gliatech (GLIA)	Control of scarring and inflammation
AVI Biopharma (AVII)	Anticancer antibodies
ICOS (ICOS)	Leukemia and stroke therapies
Protein Design Labs (PDLI)	Specialist in humanized antibodies
Cytogen (CYTO)	Cancer antibodies

Despite the progress made in this field and the number of drugs in development. MAbs still face limitations. They cannot enter a solid tumor, a problem that limits their effectiveness against most cancers except those in the blood or lymphatic system. Also monoclonal antibodies cannot easily pass through a cell membrane, at least not yet.

Monoclonal antibodies have overcome the biggest technical hurdles to their use and biotech investors will see increasing numbers of inflammatory diseases, immune disorders and forms of cancer coming under attack using this very promising weapon. Because these are drug development companies, the full set of investment criteria described in the first section of this book apply. Table 14.1 lists companies that are working on the development of monoclonal antibodies. (Note: See also the discussion on vaccines later in this chapter.)

PROTEIN THERAPIES

The production of therapeutic proteins is the biggest revenue generator for the biotech industry. Sales of recombinant human proteins are estimated at $20 billion dollars annually. Among the best known protein products are recombinant humanized insulin, growth hormones, and proteins to stimulate the production of white or red blood cells.

The proteins of interest in this section are those created for general use, not proteins customized for specific patients or for particular strains

Table 14.2   Protein Therapies

Company	Areas of Specialization
Lilly (LLY)	Humanized insulin
Genentech (DNA)	Human growth hormone
Amgen & Immunex (AMGN) (IMNX)	Blood cell production stimulants
Genentech (DNA)	Factor VIII (blood clotting agent)
Biogen, Genentech, Chiron (BGEN, DNACHIR)	Interferon
Cytogen (CYTO)	Researching new proteins
MYRIAD (MYGN)	Researching new proteins

of infectious disease. (The use of monoclonal antibodies is a therapy based on the customization of the immunoglobulin protein for a specific disease.) One of the earliest proteins of interest is called interferon, first recognized in 1957 as an immune system stimulant produced in response to viral attack. Production of interferon was made possible in 1980 by splicing human genes for interferon into bacteria. This breakthrough caused enormous excitement, but once again, the reality of interferon's effectiveness fell far short of some investors' expectations. Interferon is used to boost the immune systems of patients suffering from cancer and viral infections such as hepatitis, but it has never proven to be the panacea some had expected.

There is, however, no question about the effectiveness of replacement proteins like insulin and human growth hormone (HGH). But, again, they are not a panacea. Drugs of this sort must be injected regularly to maintain patient health, and in the case of insulin, dosages and timing are critical. New drug delivery methods will help alleviate some of the problems associated with constant dosing.

Because these are drug development companies, the full set of investment criteria described in the first section of this book applies. Many biotech therapies use proteins. Table 14.2 includes leaders in the field.

GENE THERAPY

No fact illustrates more clearly the enormous difficulty of making gene therapy work than the track record so far. Disease-causing genes were discovered more than 10 years ago for catastrophic illnesses including muscular dystrophy, cystic fibrosis, and sickle cell anemia. So far, no gene therapy for inherited genetic disease is on the market.

Gene therapy is the science of altering human DNA, equivalent to rewriting the operating system of a malfunctioning computer. In many cases, the objective is to trigger the manufacture of vital proteins that are sometimes missing in people suffering from genetically inherited diseases.

It's estimated that there are 400 diseases of this type. Gene therapy also has the potential to reverse the processes of many other diseases including cancer. It may be able to switch off oncogenes to stop them from promoting runaway tumor growth, or a similar technique could switch on tumor suppressor genes. If successful, gene therapy may be able to stimulate the production of new blood vessels for victims of heart disease and stop blood vessels from feeding a tumor. Ultimately, replacement of genes may promote the rebuilding of defective body parts; some of them as simple as the deformed blood cells characteristic of sickle cell anemia, others as complex as bodily organs.

Scientists now know the contents of the genome, and establishing the function of most genes within it is largely a matter of time. In light of such possibilities, why has so little progress apparently been made?

The biotechnology industry has finally advanced to the point where techniques are being tested in clinical trials, but it has taken a great deal of time and money to arrive at this point because the scientific and technical challenges are huge. At the heart of the problem is the fact that human genes are carefully protected within the nucleus of every cell. Getting a treatment inside this envelope and making it work has proved to be far more difficult than anyone had expected. Time and again, novel methods have been developed only to run into almost insuperable difficulties. Here's a list of methods of gene therapy and their attendant challenges:

- Simply injecting a corrected gene into a patient's body provides no assurance that the genetic information will reach the right kind of cell or that it will ever arrive at the cellular nucleus.

- Targeting a package of genetic information to the right kind of cell provides no assurance that it will splice into the existing genetic structure, or that it will arrive at exactly the right spot. If it is in the wrong place, its instruction set could be rendered either meaningless or harmful.

- When viruses are used to deliver DNA to the nucleus of a cell they are called vectors. Viruses are adept at injecting and splicing their DNA into a cellular nucleus, but, the most effective viruses may trigger allergic reactions. In one case, a viral reaction killed a patient undergoing experimental gene therapy.

- One class of viruses used as a gene therapy vector is the retrovirus, well known from the HIV epidemic. Retroviruses code their DNA signals into a cell's RNA, which is then transferred into a cell nucleus. These viruses have been engineered to be safe, but they may regain their power to cause disease. Retroviruses also are limited because they target only cells that are in the process of dividing, and they insert their genetic information in unpredictable places. (A new line of viruses called AAVs, adeno-associated viruses, may solve the infection problem because they are stripped of most viral genes.)

- Adenoviruses, which are associated with head colds, are less dangerous; but they can still trigger allergic reactions and may also replicate to cause disease. These viruses are highly effective in getting large amounts of genetic material inside the host cell's nucleus, but they cannot splice a gene into the chromosome. They can trigger the production of proteins in this free-floating state, but production gradually tapers off.

- So-called naked DNA technologies involve delivery of a raw gene sequence through the cell wall in fatty lipid containers called liposomes. The desired level of recombination and accuracy of the splice with the host DNA is not assured.

- Problems common to all of these approaches include the possibility that genes will be duplicated and copies placed in inappropriate sites, a phenomenon called "jumping genes" or, *transposons*.

- Even if the DNA has been delivered properly, cells often simply refuse to perform as intended. In some cases, cells containing recombinant DNA may not reproduce quickly enough, and the therapeutic line of modified cells appears to die out or lose effectiveness.

An alternative strategy is the *ex vivo* method. Cells from the portion of the body needing therapy are removed, genetically recombined in a laboratory setting and re-injected. However, there is no assurance that they will find their way back into place or reproduce in adequate numbers.

Another ex vivo method involves extraction of cells from bone marrow or other tissues and genetically modifying them. Stem cells from bone marrow are responsible for generating new cells for the blood and immune system. When they are genetically modified and returned to the body, they should trigger the production of many identical copies.

Ordinary (nonstem) cells, treated ex vivo, are injected under the skin in hopes they will thrive and generate certain needed proteins. This technique is called transkaryotic therapy, and a company that goes by the same name has had considerable success with the technique but has also been tied up in patent suits for years. The dispute arises over the fact that Transkaryotic has coaxed the bodies of its patients to make a desirable protein, but Amgen holds a patent on the protein in question and the courts have supported Amgen's claim.

Other experimental gene delivery methods involve the use of a "gene gun" that literally fires DNA-coated micropellets into a cellular nucleus. This technique has been most successful in modifying plant DNA, but it may also be useful in ex vivo gene therapy.

If this portrait of the problems surrounding gene therapy sounds bleak, it is not without hope. Among the many techniques described, some deliver

Table 14.3   Companies Testing Gene Therapy

Company	Areas of Specialization
Ariad Pharmaceuticals (ARIA)	Gene regulation for many diseases
Cell Genesys (CEGE)	Cancer, vascular disease, Parkinson's
Chiron (CHIR)	Cancer vaccines
Targeted Genetics (TGEN)	Wide variety of disease targets
Tanskaryotic Therapies (TKTS)	Stimulant for production of blood cells
Genetronics (GEB)	Techniques to deliver genes to nucleus
Genzyme Molecular Oncology (GZMO)	Cancer therapies
Genzyme General (GENZ)	Multiple disease targets
Avigen (AVGN)	Viral vectors
Tularik (TLRK)	Small molecules to control genes
Valentis (VLTS)	Stimulants for cytokine production
Vical (VICL)	Cancer therapies, "naked DNA"

better results when used against particular diseases (e.g., adenoviruses are showing promise in treating the lungs of cystic fibrosis patients). By adapting these gene therapy techniques and trying to ameliorate their negative effects, scientists have been able to launch more than 300 clinical trials and experimental procedures[1] that may prove certain methods of gene therapy effective against catastrophic disease. *Science Magazine* reports that gene therapy had its first unequivocal success during the year 2000 when Dr. Alain Fischer of the Hospital Necker-Enfants in Paris replaced the genes of several infants who were suffering a rare and fatal condition that had disabled their immune systems.[2]

The risks and potential gains associated with drug development described in Part I apply to the companies listed in Table 14.3.

BRANCHES OF GENE THERAPY

Antisense Therapy

Antisense therapy is aimed at defeating the instruction (or sense) given out by DNA. As discussed, DNA is constantly being copied and the message contained in this copy is a set of instructions to build a protein. The messenger is called mRNA.

Antisense therapy involves the synthetic manufacture of a small single strand of molecules that is expressly designed to bind to a complementary sequence of RNA or DNA. Suddenly, this portion of RNA or DNA is unable to deliver its message because the code has been blocked by a matching strand of anti-code. The sense of the RNA message has been obliterated, hence the name "antisense." This therapy has some limitations on its development possibilities because it is a blocking mechanism, not capable of stimulating protein production. The mechanism is analogous to throwing a monkey wrench into the machinery of a malfunctioning gene.

Table 14.4   Companies Using Antisense Therapy

Company	Areas of Specialization
Genta (GNTA)	Cancer therapy
Hybridion HYBN)	Solid tumor cancer therapy
ISIS (ISIP)	Virus therapy, cancer, immune system
Enzo Biochem (ENZ)	HIV therapy
Lynx (LYNX)	Cancer
Lorus Therapeutics (Canada) (LORFF)	Cancer
Atlantic Technology Ventures (ATLC)	Cancer, antisense against telomerase
Geron (GERN)	Cancer

Antisense drugs require the custom manufacture of DNA and RNA in the lab (sometimes called "synthetic DNA" or an oligonucleotide).

In its role as a DNA/RNA blocker, antisense gene therapy has the potential to arrest the effects of cancer-causing oncogenes. It may also be useful in blocking the activity of viruses that depend on RNA and DNA to function. Antisense therapy is already in testing against severe viral infections and is being tested widely, with some promise, against cancer. The Genta corporation's antisense therapy against skin cancer has been given fast-track status by the FDA.

One form of antisense therapy blocks functions on the DNA double helix, rather than the RNA strand. The technology involves a development called triplex DNA. It has been discovered that a short oligonucleotide, a synthesized single strand of DNA, can be bound to a complementary section of the double helix, blocking its message. Physically, it would be like having three strands of a zipper that could, with effort, be jammed together to create a triple stranded zipper. It wouldn't work very well, but that's the point of antisense therapy, to block out a part of the system.

The risks and potential gains associated with drug development described in Part I apply to the companies listed in Table 14.4.

Angiogenesis

Angiogenesis is simple in principle: Stimulate the growth of new blood vessels in patients suffering from blocked arteries, using gene therapy or protein-based growth promoters. The most optimistic definition of angiogenesis sums up the technique as a "bypass in a test tube." In practice, this promising strategy has run into development problems.

The most serious is the challenge of drug delivery because all the drawbacks described earlier for other kinds of gene therapy come into play. Some companies administering angiogenesis compounds to the bloodstream have achieved disappointing results accompanied by side effects such as lowered

Table 14.5 Companies Developing Angiogenesis Therapies

Company	Areas of Specialization
Collateral Therapeutics (CLTX)	Direct delivery of genes to the heart
Genentech (DNA)	Searching for improved drug delivery
Chiron (CHIR)	Searching for improved drug delivery

blood pressure. The company with the most direct approach (Collateral Therapeutics—CLTX) injects angiogenesis promoters directly into heart muscle. The company has not released an up-to-date report on the success of its trials at this writing.

Terminology you'll encounter while reading about this sector includes VEGF, which means vascular endothelial growth factor and FGF-2, fibroblast growth factor. Both are natural proteins involved in the growth of new blood vessels and may be administered directly or generated by genetically engineered tissues. One new approach, still in laboratory development, involves growing a matrix of blood vessels outside in a tissue culture and then transplanting them into the heart.

Assuming the technical problems are overcome, the overriding question is one of the treatment's ability to improve blood supplies. Angiogenesis stimulates the growth of blood vessels but heart patients may need an alternative to a much larger conduit, a blocked artery.

Incremental improvements in circulation using angiogenesis may be sufficient to restore blood supplies and outweigh the risks of heart surgery. The long view is even more hopeful as methods of drug delivery and gene therapy improve. The risks and potential gains associated with drug development described in Part I apply to the companies listed in Table 14.5.

Angiogenesis Inhibitors

Angiogenesis inhibitors are a novel form of gene therapy that sounded good in theory as a weapon against solid tumor cancers. This treatment, also called antiangiogenesis, blocks the mechanisms that create new blood vessels in and around tumors. Solid tumors have proved to be remarkably adept at building elaborate networks of new blood vessels to facilitate their explosive growth, and blocking this process was imagined to be yet another possible magic bullet against cancer. Many biotech companies have embraced the technique, but in practice angiogenesis inhibitors have, so far, delivered many disappointments.

Tumor development is a complex process involving the construction of a matrix of blood vessels, promoted partly by high levels of vascular endothelial growth factor (VEGF). Antiangiogenesis techniques employ different technologies including proteins, monoclonal antibodies, gene therapy, and small molecule drugs. All have the same objective: to block VEGF. Techniques include:

- Stopping production of the protein.
- Preventing VEGF from binding to cells.
- Blocking the protein's instructions or "signaling pathways."

There are four other types of angiogenesis inhibitors in development. MMP inhibitors, (metalloproteinase inhibitors) were among the first to be tried, mostly by larger pharmaceutical firms, with disappointing results. Surprisingly, the most promising is the least understood. Celgene's use of thalidomide has proven to be sufficiently effective to gain FDA approval. (Cell Therapeutics' approach to blocking signals from the VEGF proteins has also received the nod.)

Despite these successes, the consensus among analysts indicates that, for the time being, antiangiogenesis strategies are not the panacea they were sometimes believed to be after Dr. Judah Folkman first proposed the idea back in 1971. Most likely, the best of these substances will find use as adjuvants, meaning they will be used in concert with other anticancer drugs to enhance their effectiveness.

Despite this conservative view in the medical establishment, analysts at Decision Resources (a biotech analysis firm at www.dresources.com) has published a prediction that the market for these anticancer compounds will exceed $6 billion before the end of the decade. Table 14.6 lists companies that are developing angiogenesis inhibitors.

Table 14.6   Biotech Companies Developing Angiogenesis Inhibitors

Company	Areas of Specialization
Genentech (DNA)	Antibodies and VEGF inhibitors
Imclone (IMCL)	Antibody-based therapy
Ribozyme (RZYM)	VEGF inhibitors
EntreMed (EMED)	A specialist using many approaches
Magainin (MAGN)	Squalamine protein
CollaGenex (CGPI)	MMP inhibitor
Lorus Therapeutics (LORFF)	Antiangiogenesis for cancer
MedImmune (MEDI)	Integrin technology
OXiGENE (OXGN)	Naturally derived angiogenesis inhibitors
Cell Therapeutics (CTIC)	Signal transduction
Isis Pharmaceuticals (ISIP)	Signal transduction
Gilead (GILD)	VEGF inhibitors
Chiron (CHIR)	VEGF inhibitors
Gelgene (CEGE)	Thalidomide
Genzyme Oncology (GZMO)	Cancer treatments

Ribozymes

Ribozymes are molecular structures that offer a new approach to gene therapy. Until relatively recently, it was believed that only certain types of proteins such as enzymes had the power to cut apart molecules. But the discovery of a peculiar form of RNA called a ribozyme created a new avenue for therapeutic research.

Ribozymes are geometrically formed RNA structures that can bind to a complementary strand of RNA and physically pull it apart. This is especially promising in the treatment of RNA-dependent viruses such as HIV. A number of different ribozymes may be used in a single dose to tear apart the genetic codes of retroviruses at several points. Because of their unique shape, ribozymes are larger than antisense molecules and may be difficult to insert into cellular structures. This is a promising avenue of attack, still largely in the research stage (see Table 14.7).

Smart Viruses

Smart viruses are a little like the "smart bombs" that became famous during the Gulf War. These customized viruses cannot replicate in normal cells, but they grow vigorously in cancer cells that lack a tumor-suppressor gene called p53. Much like the cancerous cells that house them, these specially engineered adenoviruses multiply without limit and eventually burst the cell wall, spreading the anticancer virus to surrounding cells. This brilliant innovation has had setbacks that have been met with ingenuity by Onyx Pharmaceuticals, the company responsible for the new technique.

In trials, the virus did not always penetrate the entire mass of a solid tumor, despite direct injection into the site. Scientists believe this is because the virus could not penetrate layers of normal cells. Onyx took its virus one step further by engineering it to create a cancer-killing agent. To use the company's description, the virus was now "armed."

The technique is interesting to describe because it employs another novel technique that is emerging in the biotech industry. The technique involves an agent called a *prodrug;* Prodrugs are innocuous compounds that can be converted into active drugs by an external influence. In the case of Onyx, the new generation of viruses does not generate cancer-killing agents directly. Instead, it creates an enzyme that changes prodrugs into specific anticancer agents.

Table 14.7 Companies Developing Ribozymes

Company	Areas of Specialization
Ribozyme Pharmaceuticals (RZYM)	Anti-HIV therapy
Gene Shears/Johnson & Johnson (JNJ)	Anti-HIV therapy

In practice, the patient's tumor is injected with the improved virus and a small molecule prodrug is administered to the patient's body. This prodrug is nontoxic, but when it encounters the enzymes being churned out of tumors by armed viruses, it is converted into a powerful cancer fighter. Unlike standard chemotherapies that have side effects in many parts of the body, the Onyx chemotherapy is only toxic to cells that have been singled out by the armed virus. In trials, the technique has proved to be dramatically effective in shrinking and eliminating head and neck cancers (which are among the hardest to treat because of their strategic locations).

In Phase II trials, Onyx was presented with 30 patients who had been deemed incurable because they had failed to respond to surgery and radiation. Tumors disappeared completely in eight patients and 11 others experienced a reduction of their tumor size greater than 50 percent. Earlier trials indicated the virus was more effective when used in conjunction with chemotherapy and the company is now in Phase III trials using this combination.[3]

The results of trials so far have been sufficiently encouraging to triple share prices and briefly lift the stock from Tier 4 into the third tier of market capitalization. This therapy is most emphatically not a panacea. It can only attack cancers in which the tumor suppressor gene is missing or switched off and it cannot penetrate all solid tumors. Nevertheless, Onyx stands virtually alone in this field, with an apparent breakthrough technique that may become more powerful with the development of new drug delivery methods, better prodrugs, and expanded targeting of the virus.

PHOTODYNAMIC THERAPY

The idea behind prodrugs was initially rather limited. The first prodrugs were harmless agents that remained inactive until triggered by naturally occurring bodily enzymes. Consequently, this type of treatment was limited to organs that had specific enzymes already in place, such as the kidney and liver. Gancyclovir, for example, is a successful antiviral prodrug that is cleaved by bodily enzymes into two parts: an active drug and an inactive carrier.

Just as Onyx brought prodrugs into a new era by making the virus an enzyme carrier, companies involved in photodynamic therapy have taken the technique in new directions. One of the leading companies in this field is QLT Phototherapeutics of Canada.

QLT's first photodynamic therapy was called Photofrin, targeted at cancerous and precancerous cells in the esophagus. The treatment begins with the injection of a prodrug into a patient's bloodstream and, over the course of several days, it accumulates in tumorous cells as well as those which are in danger of becoming cancerous. A fiber-optic strand is then inserted into the esophagus and the prodrug is exposed to light. After a

Table 14.8 Biotech Companies Developing Photodynamic Therapy

Company	Areas of Specialization
QLT Phototherapeutics (QLTI)	AMD eye disease, skin cancer, psoriasis
Axcan Pharma (AXCA)	Cancer and dysplasia of the esophagus
Miravant (MRVT)	AMD eye disease, oncology, dermatology
Pharmacia (PHA)	AMD eye disease
Photogen Technologies (PHGN)	Laser and X-ray activated drug research
Pharmacyclics (PCYC)	Cancer and vascular disease

brief burst of light, the prodrug becomes an active destroyer of cancerous cells. QLT has sold this treatment to Axcan Pharma, and it is showing considerable effectiveness in Phase III trials.

QLT's main focus is now on a more prevalent condition called wet age-related macular degeneration (AMD), a leading cause of adult onset blindness. The disease involves the growth of excess blood vessels in the retina of the eye, which causes progressive scarring and ultimately, blindness. The company has received FDA approval to market a therapy that works in much the same way as Photofrin. A prodrug is administered and it accumulates in blood vessels. When a cool laser is aimed at unwanted vascular growths in the eye, they are destroyed without damage to surrounding tissues. Two other companies, Miravant and Pharmacia are developing similar photodynamic therapies. QLT is expanding its use of photodynamic therapy to skin cancers and psoriasis.

Like every new technique, photodynamic therapy is promising but limited by its intrinsic nature. The key issue is not so much in prodrug design as it is in getting the right kind of light to the right place. As is evident from the preceding profile, photodynamic therapy is effective in parts of the body that can easily be exposed to light. The expansion of this technique into areas requiring surgery is open to question. Other techniques, including prodrug activation by heat are being considered.

The risks and potential gains associated with drug development described in Part I apply to the companies listed in Table 14.8.

VACCINES

New Vaccines

For more than a century, the word vaccine has implied disease prevention. Immunization typically works according to the mechanisms described earlier in the section on antibodies. Genetic engineering may change the nature of the killed or attenuated bacteria and viruses to allow a single organism to confer immunity against many diseases if it carries the codes and proteins for these other illnesses. Fewer vaccinations would probably result in a decreasing number of side effects. This form of vaccine can only be expected to prevent, not cure disease. Therapeutic, or curative, vaccines are the next major step.

The core function of any vaccine is to provide an alert to the body's immune system using a characteristic of a diseased organism as a marker to target an attack. Vaccines to treat cancer have often failed because the body's immune system is somehow blinded to antigens on the surfaces of tumors. Autologous vaccines are designed to solve this problem by using a patient's own tumor cells to create a blueprint for an immune system attack. Samples of cancerous cells are extracted, genetically modified, and reinjected to cue the immune system to kill this type of cell. Such a treatment is already on the market in Australia, but it has not been approved for use in the United States because each dose of the drug is different, custom made for a patient's own tumor cells.

The treatment is elegant in concept but not sufficiently effective to be described as a cure. Although the autologous vaccine is directly injected into skin cancer tumors, it does not provide 100 percent effectiveness. This may be due to a problem common to therapies that use genetic engineering to spur the immune system into action. For some reason, the immune system responds more weakly than it ordinarily does to an assault by a foreign organism.

Until this problem is solved, it will likely dog efforts to design other cancer vaccines. Among these alternate vaccines, some researchers attempt to focus an immune attack on markers common to various cancers called epitopes. Biomira believes it has found an epitope for breast cancer and has taken a vaccine that targets an immune attack on this epitope into Phase III clinical trials. Existing breast cancer vaccines are believed to target markers contained in less than a third of all breast cancer strains. Finding a universal marker for all cancers is the ultimate goal, and researchers at Cytogen believe they have it in a genetic component called telomerase, which regulates cell duplication. Work with telomerase is still largely in the research phase.

Vaccines against viral infection are being improved by becoming more selective about the agents they use as markers. The era of injecting a killed organism, with its attendant potential for allergic reaction, is coming to an end. Instead, vaccine innovators are selecting specific proteins from infectious pathogens to be the key markers. In addition to being more specific to a particular disease, selecting a protein or gene that is central to the operation of a virus gives an infection fewer chances to mutate into a form that might defeat immune mechanisms. This gives a vaccine effectiveness against mutated forms of the infectious agent, and it gives the pathogen no opportunity to evolve away from an attack because it cannot survive without the molecule which has been chosen as a target for an immune system attack.

Table 14.9 Biotech Companies Developing New Vaccines

Company	Areas of Specialization
Aphton (APHT)	Antibody-based cancer vaccines
Chiron (CHIR)	Specialist in many forms of vaccines
Vical (VICL)	Naked DNA cancer vaccine
AVAX (AVXT)	Autologous cancer vaccines
Biomira (BIOM)	Breast cancer vaccine
Epimmune (EPMN)	Vaccines for cancer, viruses, malaria
Neurocrine Biosciences (NBIX)	Cancer vaccine
Corixa (CRXA)	Cancer vaccine
Geron (GERN)	Telomerase cancer vaccines
Cytogen (CYTO)	Telomerase cancer vaccines
Aviron (AVIR)	Viral vaccines
Trimeris (TRMS)	AIDS vaccine
Genzyme Oncology (GZMO)	Cancer vaccines
VaxGen (VXGN)	AIDS vaccine

The risks and potential gains associated with drug development described in Part I apply to the companies listed in Table 14.9.

DNA Vaccines

Vaccines usually operate by taking an imprint from an infectious agent and triggering the immune system to launch a custom-made attack. DNA vaccines turn the process on its head. Instead of waiting for an invader to arrive and going through the complex process of encoding the characteristic information, DNA vaccines attempt to go straight to the root of the problem.

Researchers begin by reading the genetic code of a target infection. The appropriate DNA code is then written to trigger a specific response. Using a DNA particle gun, it is possible to place the DNA that codes for an immune response into the skin. There is no intermediary. The immune system is given targeting instructions and it is prepared for attack. The nagging question is: What are the potential effects of making a permanent change of this magnitude to the human genomic structure? DNA vaccines remain in the research phase.

STEM CELLS AND TISSUE REGENERATION

Every human being begins life as a single cell. This simple fact is the root of an exciting field of research called stem cell therapy. The first human cell and those that descend from it in the early days of embryonic life can create any of the body's 200 cell types (as well as some animal cells in the bargain). This remarkable versatility has given rise to the name "totipotent stem cells." The word *totipotent* was coined to suggest that such cells could produce most anything. The term *stem* was drawn from the world of plant life in which stems can give rise to the numerous cell types that make up leaves, flowers, and other structures.

Stem cells have one other remarkable property: They are able to divide and differentiate into various cell types without any known limits. These are the factories that can generate endless supplies of new blood cells, and they are the basis for the creation of the entire organism. It doesn't take a lot of imagination to see how valuable such a cell type can be to the biotechnology industry.

Researchers and biotech executives foresee the day when the effects of many catastrophic diseases can be reversed. The damaged brains of Alzheimer's disease patients might be restored. Severed spinal cords may be rejoined. Damaged organs may be rebuilt. Stem cells provide hope that this dream will become a reality.

As always, there are many challenges. The heart of the mystery surrounding stem cells is summed up in a simple question: If a fetus is able to create any body part from stem cells, and, if adult bodies also contain stem cells, why do humans not regenerate any and all damaged tissues from their own stem cells?

The answer seemed fairly straightforward until recently. As an embryo matures, its stem cells differentiate into various types: some to generate neurons for the brain and nervous system, some to become muscle or skin and some to create organs. As the differentiation of cells becomes greater, stem cells also become more specialized. Early in the cell division process, totipotent stem cells become pluripotent stem cells, which are more limited, but still able to generate most of the body's tissues and organs. As the body matures, pluripotent stem cells are replaced by multipotent stem cells, which have the ability to generate a narrower range of cells such as various types of blood or skin cells. Adults carry relatively few stem cells, and researchers have found them very difficult to isolate and work with.

The versatility of embryonic stem cells made them a natural choice for tissue regeneration experiments. But the origin of these cells created an ethical and political problem. Research requires the use of tissues taken from aborted fetuses, or embryos destined to be discarded after in vitro fertilization. Despite a good deal of controversy and a protest from the Vatican, the U.S. government decided to permit federal funding of research using fetal stem cells. President Clinton summed up the argument in favor of stem cell research when he declared that the potential of this therapy to alleviate human suffering is "breathtaking." Indeed it is, but not without technical challenges.

The transplantation of stem cells from an unrelated fetus can result in rejection by the immune system. Genetic engineering is the most likely method to overcome rejection, allowing stem cells to be injected into a recipient's body near the site of tissue damage. Remarkably, stem cells appear to migrate to the places where they are needed most and go on spontaneously to become the kind of cell that is required.

Another technique is called somatic cell nuclear transfer (SCNT). By injecting the DNA-bearing nucleus of a potential recipient's cell into a foreign stem cell, the cell assumes the genetic identity of the new nucleus. This cell can then generate various tissues, such as heart muscle, in culture for transplant into the body. One experiment by Geron Corporation resulted in the creation of a chunk of heart muscle that began beating spontaneously in the laboratory. In a decade-long experiment conducted in Sweden, scientists injected stem cells from the fetuses of pigs into patients suffering degenerative brain disease. Most regained some brain function although somewhat less than researchers had hoped. (Tissue rejection is less of a problem in the brain because it is "immune privileged," meaning the blood brain barrier blocks the immune system from acting among neurons.)

Many of these developments suggest that stem cell research has a long way to go before it can be commercialized, but some scientists in the field believe it will yield results well before successful gene therapy techniques emerge from the lab. That's because some remarkable developments challenged established notions about stem cells.

Scientists at Canada's Ottawa hospital have found a protein that can direct a pluripotent stem cell to become a specific type of tissue. Using the Pax7 protein, researchers were able to direct stem cells to become muscles, an important development for victims of muscular dystrophy. Osiris Therapeutics is using stem cells to generate bone. Geron is generating human liver cells. (The company hopes to use them for in vitro experimentation to discover how certain drugs are metabolized.)

Even more remarkable than the tissues being generated with various "growth factors" is the possibility of using cells already present in the adult body. It has long been believed that multipotent adult stem cells are limited in the number of tissues they can generate. Blood stem cells have always been thought to have no potential beyond the creation of more blood cells, but animal experiments have converted these supposedly limited cells into nerve, muscle, and bone cells. Research at the University of Florida, Gainesville, astounded the medical community when mouse liver cells were grown from bone marrow stem cells. Ctyotherapeutics has also produced mouse liver cells from blood stem cells. If research of this sort continues to show potential, the problems involved in using stem cells from unrelated fetuses may be moot.

For all its scientific excitement, stem cell research has generated little in the way of corporate revenues so far. There is one interesting exception. Around the United States, entrepreneurs have set up facilities called "cord blood registries." These are tissue banks that store blood from umbilical

Table 14.10   Biotech Companies Involved in Stem Cell Research

Company*	Areas of Specialization
Aastrom (ASTM)	Stem cell research and development
Ariad Pharmaceuticals (ARIA)	Regulation of stem cell expression
CytoTherapeutics (CTII)	Stem cell research and development
Geron (GERN)	Stem cell research and development
Nexell Therapeutics (NEXL)	Cell culture and growth technology
StemCells Inc. (STEM)	Research and mass production techniques
Layton BioScience	Stem cell research and production
Diacrin (DCRN)	Neural stem cell therapy
Neuronyx	Stem cell research and development
NeuralStem Biopharmaceuticals	Stem cell research and development

* Listings include symbols only for publicly traded biotech specialists.

cords taken from a child at birth. This creates a reserve of stem cells that may prove to be useful to a child needing therapy later in life. Remarkably, stem cells from an umbilical cord may also have significant potential to assist other family members. For example, bone marrow transplants currently require exceptionally close tissue matching between donor and recipient. But a sibling receiving stem cells from a brother or sister's umbilical cord requires a much less precise match because much more versatile, immature stem cells can be used. These cells from genetically related donors may be able to grow new bone marrow without danger of tissue rejection.

For investors, shares in companies conducting stem cell research tend to be affordable, given the long time horizons that may be required to bring research to commercial use. Companies involved in such research are listed in Table 14.10.

GROWTH STIMULANTS

Earlier I mentioned VEGF, Vascular Endothelial Growth Factor, as a possible agent to create new vascular tissue in heart muscle. Growth factors are potent proteins with many other uses. Beyond directing the development of stem cells, growth factors can directly induce tissue development by throwing genetic switches in nearby cells:

- The best-known growth factor is Amgen's *Epogen* which stimulates the production of red blood cells and became notorious during the Sydney Olympics when runners used the drug to increase the oxygen-carrying capacity of their bloodstreams. The name used during the Olympics was EPO, the same as the scientific acronym for the relevant protein, erythropoietin.

Table 14.11 Biotech Companies Developing
Growth Factors for Tissue Regeneration

Company	Areas of Specialization
Amgen (AMGN)	Producing blood growth factor and testing stem cell, nerve, and wound factors
Regeneron (REGN)	Testing BDNF for brain disorders
Curis (CRIS)	Bone growth factor
Human Genome Sciences (HGSI)	Testing Repifermin for wound healing, BlyS for lymphocyte production
American Biogenetic (MABA)	Nerve cell regeneration
Guilford (GLFD)	Nerve cell regeneration
Neotherapeutics (NEOT)	Neuron regeneration

- Epidermal growth factor (EGF) is showing promise in wound healing by encouraging skin cells to divide and differentiate.
- Fibroblast growth factor (FGF) stimulates the growth of connective tissues and may be useful in healing forms of arthritis, scleroderma, bones, and tendons.
- Hemopoeitic cell growth factor (HCGF) stimulates production of bone marrow and blood cells.
- Various neurotrophic growth factors (NGF) stimulate the regeneration of nerves.
- Ciliary neurotrophic factor (CTNF) enhances nerve growth in embryos and may have human applications.
- Brain-derived neurotrophic factor (BDNF) is much like nerve growth factor but works inside the brain rather than in the nervous system as a whole.
- OP-1 is being developed by Curis for the repair of nonhealing bone fractures.

One need only look at the dramatic success of Amgen to realize the commercial potential of growth factors that emerge successfully from the clinical trials pipeline (see Table 14.11).

TISSUE REPLACEMENT

In the face of such progress among growth factors, the technology of direct tissue replacement may appear to be going the way of the buggy whip. Certainly there is a real threat to companies like Advanced Tissue Sciences, which has run its business for years with a revenue stream from the production of sheets of skin grown from stem cells in mass production

Table 14.12   Biotech Companies Involved in Tissue Replacement

Company	Areas of Specialization
Advanced Tissue Sciences (ATIS)	Skin, heart muscle, cartilage
Genzyme Surgical (GZSP)	Cartilage replacement
Organogenesis (ORG)	Connective tissue and skin replacement
ReGen Pharma (REGN)	Scaffolds for tissue replacement
Regeneration Technologies (RTIX)	Grafts of natural tissues

labs. These artificial skin products are important to burn victims and diabetics suffering from chronic wounds, but growth factors may overtake such therapies.

For companies of this sort, there is a great deal of work to do in the creation of complex and slow-growing bodily structures (see Table 14.12). Advanced Tissue Sciences is pressing ahead with an effort to develop a so-called ventricular tube—effectively, a cylinder of rolled heart muscle, complete with a valve, that might be grafted onto a failing heart to assist in pumping. The company also had a surprising success when it grafted a layer of its artificial skin onto a damaged heart muscle and sparked the growth of new muscle tissue.[4]

Genzyme is producing a therapy called Carticel, which involves taking a biopsy of a damaged cartilage and growing it in the lab for eventual replacement into the patient's body. Several companies are developing scaffolds that provide a form for the growth of new cartilage tissue in the precise shape required for a joint.

Even the most mature of these companies, Advanced Tissue Sciences remains unprofitable, therefore much depends on the success of new tissue replacement strategies.

SIGNAL TRANSDUCTION AND PATHWAYS

This somewhat intimidating terminology has a simple basis. No bodily process operates in isolation, and no therapy can be effective without triggering a chain of events. Signal transduction and cellular signaling pathways involve the analysis and management of a cascade of events involved in such processes. In the case of interactions between neurons in the brain, the transmission of signals is relatively well understood and somewhat similar to the processing of signals in a computer chip (although the processes of the brain involve chemicals as well as electrical impulses). Cellular signaling systems outside the brain are not believed to involve electrical impulses.

The surfaces of cells carry the molecular equivalent of sockets, called receptors. When a matching molecule, for example a hormone, finds an appropriate receptor, it inserts itself but goes no further inside the cell.

Instead, a chemical chain reaction moves from the surface of the cell and alters proteins on the inside.

Some researchers believe that signal transduction, the nexus where a chemical signal is received on the cellular surface and translated by a receptor, is a key point for controlling cellular functions (including cellular reproduction, which is essential to the spread of cancer). The understanding and management of signal pathways have the potential to affect many disease processes and are of fundamental interest to most biotech companies.

THE FUTURE OF BIOTECH THERAPY

In the long run, gene therapy appears to be the most powerful and versatile approach to curing disease. It is the only technology able to put the body's master control system entirely at our command. But there remains a great deal to learn about genes, proteins, and their myriad interactions. Gene delivery systems and splicing mechanisms remain primitive by the standards required to achieve complete control of the system.

Gene therapy may not capture a dominant portion of the biotech product market in the first part of this century but it will not be an insignificant player. Current gene therapies techniques are admittedly less effective than we might hope, but they are, after all, the first out of the pipeline. They are no less valuable and certainly no less revolutionary than the first vaccines simply because they happen to be earliest forms of this technology.

In fact, most of the innovations described here are still works in progress, and the cautions expressed in Part I of the book apply strongly. No one wants to own a company about to be taught a hard scientific and business lesson thanks to the unexpected complexity of disease systems. But, scientific dead ends and investment setbacks are inevitable. It is a reality shared by scientists and their backers—biotech investors who have chosen their place on the cutting edge of discovery.

CHAPTER 15

———•◆•———

Special Sectors

Genetic modification could lead to "zombie" farm animals programmed to feel no pain or stress. . . . The disturbing image of "animal vegetables" was painted by members of the new Agriculture and Environment Biotechnology Commission as part of an attempt to raise public awareness of the next GM battlefield—the Frankenstein Farmyards.

London Daily Mail, September 28, 2000

THE HYBRIDS

It is not a stretch to say that the stakes in the emergence of the biotechnology industry are above the trillion-dollar mark. So far I have focused largely on biotech companies involved in the creation of new medicines, but there are many other important sectors adding value to the industry. The agricultural and chemical industries have an enormous stake in the success of innovations from biotechnology. So do the textile, oil, cosmetics, and waste management industries. Even the Defense Department is sponsoring biotech projects, as is Big Pharma. There were more than 50 biotech IPOs during the year 2000, a figure that gives some idea of the breadth of this industry as well as its explosive growth.

The industry's reach is so great that it has provoked profound ethical and religious questions. Political considerations have also loomed large as agricultural biotechnology arrived on the scene with a thud heard around the world. No single book can cover it all, but this chapter gives a brief outline of the huge potential and inevitable challenges the industry faces in other fields.

AGRICULTURAL BIOTECHNOLOGY

Who could have imagined that the day would arrive when products able to save millions of lives, billions of dollars, and stave off disease would seem like a dangerous investment? That day, as every biotech investor knows, is here.

238

Here are some issues:

- One million children die every year and 300,000 go blind because of a lack of vitamin A. Genetically engineered "golden rice" from Monsanto could put an end to this tragedy, but the environmental lobby group called Friends of the Earth labels it a public relations exercise designed to gain acceptance for GM (genetically modified) crops.

- New genetically engineered strains of trees grow quickly enough to reduce the world's need to log existing forests. Their fast growth increases consumption of carbon dioxide which is a factor in global warming. Environmental opponents fear that genetically modified trees will become "Frankenforests," hostile to birds and insects. The World Wide Fund of Britain has called for a moratorium.

- Experimental trees are being grown that can be reduced to pulp without the need for tons of toxic chemicals now used by the paper industry. Environmentalists worry that genes from these trees will be transmitted to other strains, weakening the strength of wood.

- New strains of corn, potatoes, and soybeans are able to resist attacks from insects after genetic alterations that render them indigestible or toxic to certain insect species. Food supplies have been increased and pesticide use decreased. Recent reports indicate that genes from genetically modified corn have appeared in nearby fields where no GM corn was planted. The Food and Drug Administration has not permitted human consumption of genetically engineered corn, and as a result, millions of tons of corn have been rendered almost worthless.

- Genetically modified foods have lower spoilage rates and can be delivered to market in a ripe condition, unlike the tasteless vegetables now picked before ripening and given color by exposure to ethylene gas. Opponents have suggested that there may be health repercussions for consumers from genetically modified foods although there is no credible evidence to support such an argument.

- Genetic engineering and agricultural biotechnology have created more effective drugs to diagnose and cure animal diseases, reducing the need for antibiotic use on the farm. Faster growing farmed salmon have been developed, reducing the burden of overfishing among wild animals. Leaner, faster growing hogs have been developed, requiring lower feed consumption and potential benefits for human health. The environmental lobby response is summed up in the "Frankenfarm" headline quoted at the beginning of the chapter.

- Current worldwide food production is unlikely to be able to support population growth by the end of the decade according to the Hudson

Table 15.1   Companies Involved in Agricultural Biotechnology

Company*	Areas of Specialization
AstraZeneca (AZN)	Drugs and genetically engineered crops
Novartis (NVS)	Drugs and genetically engineered crops
Dow Chemical	Improved crops and industrial agriculture
Monsanto	Moved from chemicals into agbio

* Listings include symbols only for publicly traded biotech specialists.

Institute. Greenpeace campaigners have taken to destroying fields of genetically modified crops in Britain.

- Genetically engineered foods have been distributed in American supermarkets for over a decade without a single report of negative health effects. The Hudson Institute claims that thousands of consumers have been sickened and a few killed as a result of eating so-called organic foods.

From an investor's point of view, all of this is a lost opportunity. Food production is an $800 billion dollar industry in the United States alone. The worldwide forestry industry generates about $400 billion dollars a year. Monsanto saw the scale of potential profits in this field when it moved heavily into biotechnology. Now, the agricultural biotechnology industry is in full retreat. Gerber baby foods withdrew products with genetically modified ingredients even though its parent corporation, Novartis, is heavily invested in agricultural biotechnology. McDonald's has stopped accepting potatoes that might contain genetically engineered components. The list of similar decisions is very long.

Any depressed stock might become a good value some day, but that day does not appear to be approaching. Despite overwhelming evidence that the industry can deliver benefits, it will be powerless to act unless political and public concerns are addressed effectively. When that happens it may be time to take a second look at the companies in this sector (see Table 15.1).

NUTRACEUTICALS

Nutraceuticals are loosely defined as foods that provide some form of health benefit. By this definition, any food which provides a useful dietary supplement, such as enriched bread and iodized salt might qualify. But, the new generation of nutraceuticals stands apart because these foods have verifiable therapeutic effects. They straddle a gray area between nutritional supplements and pharmaceuticals. Nutraceuticals are not necessarily the product of genetic engineering, but they are very much a part of the biotechnology industry.

In the current environment surrounding genetically modified foods, it is difficult to predict the public's willingness to accept nutraceuticals. The first major product in this class to reach market, a spread containing stanol or sterol plant esters, appears to be holding its own despite premium pricing. These two products, under the brand names "Benecol" and "Take Control" have been shown in scientific studies to reduce blood levels of LDL, often called "bad cholesterol."

Some nutraceuticals currently under development lean even more toward an outright medicinal function. The University of Illinois is testing a genetically modified strain of cherry tomato that produces a protein similar to antigens on the surface of the deadly respiratory syncytial virus. When eaten, this protein elicits an immune response that creates a degree of immunity against infection by the real virus. The biotech industry is already selling a vaccine for this form of infection, a virus that strikes hardest at infants and the elderly, but researchers feel that edible vaccines might be preferable because they put the active agents at the site of infection, the mouth and throat.

Scientists at Cornell University have a more compelling reason for putting vaccines in food. They are engineering potatoes that elicit an immune response to the deadly Norwalk virus, the leading cause of foodborne illness in the United States. Researchers say such food-borne illnesses kill millions of people worldwide every year, but delivering hundreds of millions of doses of a traditional vaccine to developing countries may be financially unmanageable. A humble potato could solve this problem. Genetically engineered and easily reproduced, potato-based vaccines appear to meet the scientific criteria for a solution to the problem. The issue of public acceptance, especially in the politically charged environment of developing countries is open to question.

Nutraceuticals that act more specifically as food supplements may also be highly therapeutic. The FDA recently gave Orphan Drug status to a nutritional supplement containing the enzyme sold as UbiQGel (coenzyme Q10). The enzyme is important to patients suffering from rare cellular dysfunctions that degrade energy production in structures called mitochondria. In normal subjects, Q10 is produced by the body and found in some foods, but researchers are hoping that clinical trials will show UbiQgel is more easily absorbed by the body.

Other nutraceuticals in development include:

- Infant formulas that some claim is superior to mother's milk.
- Soybeans that produce heart-healthy oils.

Table 15.2   Companies Developing Nutraceuticals

Company	Areas of Specialization
Tischon Corp.	UbiQGel
Martek Biosciences (MATK)	Supplements to infant formula
Aquasearch (AQSE)	Astaxanthin antioxidant
McNeil Consumer Healthcare	Benecol, stanol ester spread
Lipton	Take control sterol ester spread
Neutraceutix (NUTX)	Health supplements and drug delivery
Cyanotech (CYAN)	Microalgae for food supplements

* Listings include symbols only for publicly traded biotech specialists.

- Tomatoes high in beta-carotene, which is processed by the body into Vitamin A.
- Astaxanthin derived from algae and believed to be a powerful antioxidant.
- Probiotics, bacteria that live in the human gut and promote digestion.
- Fiber that may have cancer-fighting properties in the colon.

Much of the research into nutraceuticals is still being carried out at the laboratory stage and it is premature to form an opinion on their commercial potential. Effectiveness will likely be less of an issue than consumer preferences and the ongoing debate over the role of biotechnology in food. Companies involved in developing nutraceuticals are listed in Table 15.2.

TRANSGENICS, FARMING, AND PHARMING

Humans have been tinkering with the genetic structures of plants and animals for 10,000 years now. It's only recently that we've gotten good at it. Archeological records show that almost any strain of farm life, from corn to cattle, has become dramatically larger and more productive as a result of selective breeding. This slow, evolutionary process has been dramatically accelerated by the science of genetic engineering.

In addition to the controversial advances in agricultural biotechnology, genetic engineering has used plants and animals to generate pharmaceuticals that might otherwise be horrendously expensive to produce in the laboratory.

The most basic transgenic organism is a genetically engineered bacterium. These organisms are relatively easy to modify because they are prokaryotes, meaning they are single-celled creatures with their DNA lying relatively exposed in a circular form called a plasmid. The important thing about a prokaryote is that it has no cellular nucleus. Recombinant bacteria that have been developed to express a therapeutic compound are grown in huge numbers by fermentation in vats called bioreactors.

Abgenix has made a specialty of producing transgenic mice, so much so that the company has created the trademark name "Xenomouse" for the technology involved. In addition to producing compounds such as monoclonal antibodies, transgenic mice serve a vital research function.

Typically, when a mouse is used for genomic study, the gene of interest is altered (generally in the egg) and a colony of mice with this new genetic trait is allowed to mature. These are called "knockout mice" because in most cases a gene has been knocked out of action. Because there are so many similarities between the human and the mouse genome, researchers are able to study the physical ramifications of a malfunctioning gene, suggesting similar mechanisms may be at work in humans. Therapeutic techniques can then be tested on the knockout mice to see if the injection of a protein or further genetic engineering can create a healthy animal. The effectiveness of this technique was proven dramatically recently in research into Parkinson's disease. It has long been believed that the symptoms of Parkinson's disease result from a lack of the neurotransmitter dopamine in the brain. Mice that were bred to lack dopamine suffered Parkinson-like symptoms but when their brains were injected with a factor designed to boost dopamine production, most of the mice recovered.

Goats have also become a favorite for transgenic production of medicines. Genzyme Transgenics is a specialist in this field. Goats can express special proteins in substantial quantities through milk. Cows might seem like a more logical choice due to their higher milk production, but concern over possible transmission of bovine spongiform encephalitis (also called mad cow disease) to human patients has made this approach unattractive.

Even rabbits have been drafted into the biotech industry. PPL Therapeutics is using milk from transgenic rabbits to generate a peptide (a small protein molecule) that has unique antibiotic qualities. The peptide, called p-113 is derived from a component of human saliva. The company sponsoring the research, Periodontix, believes the product will be useful in oral and lung infections.

Plants have also proven to be a viable medium for transgenic drug production. The introduction of foreign DNA to a plant is often performed with a gene gun, a device that fires a tiny gold or platinum pellet coated with DNA into a single cell. If the DNA is taken up by the cell, it can be cultured and a new transgenic plant grown from the cells formed in the lab. Tobacco and corn have proven to be especially amenable to genetic modification. The term *pharming* applies to the creation of transgenic animals but not to plants.

Companies in this field are difficult to judge on the merits of transgenic services alone, because many are also engaged in independent drug development studies (see Table 15.3). The usual criteria for judging a biotech

Table 15.3   Companies Involved in Transgenic Researc

Company*	Areas of Specialization
Abgenix (ABGX)	Mouse research and drug production
Genzyme Transgenics (GZTC)	Mouse research and drug production
Dow Chemical/Epicyte Pharmaceutical	Monoclonal antibodies from plants
Pharming (Netherlands)	Pharmaceuticals from transgenic milk
Monsanto	Transgenic corn for drug production
CropTech	Tobacco for drug production
Planet Biotechnology	Not disclosed, fears of vandalism
PPL Therapeutics	Transgenic rabbits
Periodontix	Rabbit production of human antibiotics

* Listings include symbols only for publicly traded biotech specialists.

drug developer apply in this case although extra revenues should be generated from transgenic contract research.

INDUSTRIAL BIOTECHNOLOGY

Considering the size of the market for improved chemical and industrial processes, it's a wonder that there aren't more companies moving aggressively into this field. The worldwide chemical industry currently generates more than a trillion dollars in sales and its growth curve is falling as innovation through conventional means slows down.[1] The best-known names in the business Dow, DuPont, and Monsanto have formed alliances with biotech companies but outsourced research revenues remain comparatively small.

Nevertheless, two publicly traded companies, Diversa and Genencor are among the first biotech companies to get their feet in the door with industrial chemical makers. As mentioned in Part I, Diversa is making important progress in developing enzymes, using DNA derived from the exotic creatures that inhabit strange places like undersea volcanic vents. The worldwide enzyme market is estimated to be worth more than $700 million dollars. That's what's attractive about the prospect of biotechnology in industry. The field is wide open to innovation and hasn't yet realized even a fraction of its potential. A small, early investment in an industrial biotech company has exceptional growth potential. Here is an example of a peculiar innovation that could become an important product.

A small herd of transgenic goats is currently producing one of the most intriguing products to emerge from the biotechnology materials industry: spider silk. The goats are using recombinant DNA, cloned from spiders, to assemble very long chains of proteins in their udders, the same protein chains that spiders use to spin their webs. The goats' spider silk produces a product stronger than steel but much lighter and more flexible. In the not-too-distant future, experimental bulletproof vests will be made with bioengineered spider silk, and, if they live up to their advance billing, the new vests will be lighter, safer, and more flexible than current products made with ceramic plates and Kevlar plastic fiber.

Another possible application for this rare substance: Surgeons require strong, flexible, and biodegradable materials for ultrathin sutures and for temporary replacement parts to be used in the body while healing is underway. One company producing "silk milk," Nexia, believes the medical market alone for spider silk products is enormous. But, importantly, this is only a starting point.

Every graduate knows the changes plastics have brought to the U.S. economy. Plastics are made from long chains of petrochemical molecules called polymers. Spider silk is a different kind of polymer, a protein chain. Researchers have identified at least half a dozen different types of spider silk,[2] each with varying degrees of tensile strength and stretching capability, dictated by the kind of structure a spider wishes to build.

The assembly of protein polymers can be changed during production and during the fine extrusion and spinning techniques that come naturally to spiders. As the study of silk milk demonstrates, an entirely new approach to the manufacture of specialized materials is emerging from the biotech industry's growing awareness of the versatility of proteins.

It's not likely that a vector as quaint as a herd of goats would be used for large-scale production of new materials. More likely, genetically engineered bacteria can handle many of the biomaterial industry's production tasks. Almost a dozen organisms have been used to produce biological polymers in laboratory settings. As unlikely as it may seem, biological processes hold the key to future industrial materials innovations.

Examining another sector, environmental protection is a growing industry, already generating more than a quarter of a trillion dollars. The use of bacteria in sewage handling is well established, but researchers hope to put single-celled organisms and specialized enzymes to work on much more challenging tasks.[3] For example, many waste materials such as heavy metals and chlorinated industrial chemicals are deadly poison to humans, but some single-celled creatures do survive in the presence of these toxins. In the case of poisonous metals like arsenic or cadmium, bioengineered organisms cannot be expected to destroy the pollutants themselves because such metals are base elements that cannot be divided. But, bioengineering of organisms that can survive in the presence of such toxins is expected to yield new microbes that can gather heavy metal waste and fuse it into new chemical compounds that can then be safely stored. Similar metal-loving bacteria may also find uses in mining, to extract minerals from ore and sulfur from coal slurries and petroleum.

Industrial enzymes and engineered organisms may also provide solutions to chronic pollution problems from carcinogenic chemical waste.

Toxic chemicals such as dioxins, PCBs are highly stable molecules that can be difficult or dangerous to break down. Current methods are less than ideal because the superheating of such chemicals creates new pollution concerns. Conventional chemistry is too costly to use with such durable, widespread pollutants. Engineered organisms have great promise because they can be mandated to seek out and gather pollutants as if they were food, and in the case of complex molecules, break them down into harmless fragments.

One more opportunity, currently going begging, is oil and energy. Biotechnology has several options to generate products of staggering value. For example, more than two thirds of the United States' oil reserves may never be recovered from the ground unless new techniques are found to free thick masses of petroleum from formations of sand and rock. Naturally produced xanthan gum is used at present, with less than ideal results. There is opportunity for the industry to create new enzymes and organisms to do the job. As for new energy generation, bacteria currently produce copious amounts of methane (natural gas) from waste in garbage dumps and independent energy companies are harnessing this resource to drive electrical generators. Scientists are considering expanding this approach to produce methane or hydrogen from other kinds of waste materials or from biomass, another word for organic materials produced in bulk.

Much of this kind of work remains at the laboratory stage because the biotechnology industry has, by and large, put its energies toward the development of pharmaceutical products. The demand for scientists is very high throughout the biotech industry, but many academics are often reluctant to bring their skills out of the confines of the university system, feeling they lose status by entering the world of commerce. The development of drugs is the most attractive field for talented researchers who choose to leave academia. It is much more difficult for industries such as waste management to attract the best brains in the business when opportunities to create lifesaving medicines also beckon.

With so many industrial giants dominating these fields, it is difficult to recommend biotech specialists beyond the few I have mentioned. Research fees alone will not suffice to make them great companies, but royalty agreements for breakthrough industrial processes may prove to be very lucrative in years to come.

COSMECEUTICALS

Cosmetic companies use the term *cosmeceutical* very loosely. The word suggests pharmaceutical health benefits, but does not require the manufacturer to meet any burden of proof. If these products were truly pharmaceuticals they would have to undergo the rigors of clinical trials under FDA supervision. The Food and Drug Administration is unequivocally clear about this.

It does not recognize the word cosmeceutical and explains its regulations as follows:

> The Food, Drug, and Cosmetic Act defines drugs as those products that cure . . . disease or that affect the structure or function of the human body. While drugs are subject to a review and approval process by FDA, cosmetics are not approved by FDA prior to sale. If a product has drug properties, it must be approved as a drug.

The message is clear. An investor should never buy into a company claiming to produce cosmeceuticals unless verifiable data, submitted to the FDA can be obtained.

It's hard to find a field of commerce more inclined to tossing around confusing medical jargon than the cosmetics industry. Many of the products on the market are little more than fatty compounds that diminish the appearance of wrinkles by causing water retention. Exaggeration of the benefits from cosmetics is so common that the industry has adopted the word "puffery" to describe the promotion of ingredients that are known to be mere sales gimmicks. A government Web page on the practice www.fda.gov/opacom/catalog/puffery.html provides a useful reality check.[4]

This might seem like a frivolous sector were it not for the amount of money that can be generated by effective cosmeceuticals. It is common for patients to pay as much as $800 for a botox treatment, involving the injection of highly diluted botulinum toxin to temporarily paralyze facial muscles, reducing the appearance of crow's feet and furrowed brows. High-priced, chemically simple cosmeceutical products such as retinoic acids and alpha hydroxy acids cause temporary inflammation, a process intended to increase the rate of skin cell replacement. The FDA is currently conducting complete risk assessments of several products including alpha hydroxy acids because they may worsen sun damage to the skin.

Even if a product is already on the market and appears to be successful, keep in mind that, without prior FDA approval, it can be recalled, classified as a drug, and subjected to lengthy clinical trials if it meets the previously quoted criteria. The government is reviewing the safety of diethanolamine (DHA), a common foaming agent in soaps and shampoos that may be carcinogenic, as well as aminophylline, an asthma medication often used in creams that claim to smooth out uneven fat structures under the skin (cellulite).

The industry's main target, the skin, is the largest and most exposed organ of the body but that does not mean it's a simple matter to alter its structure or halt its degeneration. As we age, collagen protein structures in the skin break down, especially when exposed to sunlight. The skin loses its firmness as a result. Skin cells stretch and form creases from repeated physical stress. Cells die and are replaced less frequently, further increasing the appearance of aging as the skin becomes thinner. Because these are changes at the cellular level—many of them natural biological processes—they are not amenable to simple solutions that involve smearing fatty compounds on the skin.

New drug delivery technologies are currently being developed to increase the absorption of potentially therapeutic substances. MIKA Pharma GmbH of Germany is producing liposomes, microscopically small spheres of fat that can penetrate the skin with relative ease. One problem is finding truly therapeutic ingredients to put inside the liposome, not just agents to increase swelling and water retention.

Companies involved in tissue replacement and regeneration (listed earlier) are making progress in cosmeceutical therapy. One of the first to take biotech methods to market is Advanced Tissue Sciences in partnership with SkinMedica, Inc. Advanced Tissue Sciences routinely grows patches of skin in bottles filled with a purple solution, containing nutrients, collagen, and growth promoters. Some time ago, the company discovered that this solution could have growth enhancing effects on normal skin. Dr. Richard E. Fitzpatrick of SkinMedica says early trials indicate that products made from this solution "demonstrate clinically important results, unlike anything seen before in the cosmeceutical market." This might be a bit of puffery, but during an interview, Arthur Benvenuto, chairman of Advanced Tissue Sciences, vigorously defended SkinMedica's claim about the effectiveness of the solution.

Copper peptides are being produced by a number of companies that tout their creams and lotions as being useful for wound healing, hair growth, and skin elasticity. The producers claim that these products perform many functions: promoting the development of new blood vessels, repairing damage to skin cells, and increasing the skin's collagen content. That's a pretty tall order. Although the inventor of copper peptide therapy cites many references about the effectiveness of the product, it is still not classified by the FDA as a drug, which says something about its biological efficacy.

What can one say about investing in an industry that makes a habit of exaggeration? Buyer Beware. Developments in cosmeceuticals are at an early stage and perhaps not sufficiently mature for investment at this time (see Table 15.4). Investors with a serious interest in this subject may

Table 15.4   Biotech Companies Developing Cosmeceuticals

Company	Areas of Specialization
Advanced Tissue Sciences (ATIS)	Compounds for skin regeneration
Biomatrix (BXM)	Biopolymers for skin care and therapy
Cellegy (CLGY)	Cosmeceuticals and prescription drugs
ProCyte (PRCY)	Copper peptide regenerative lotions

purchase a research report from Frost and Sullivan, at www.frost.com /verity/reports/chemicals_materials/rp713939.htm.

BIOLOGICAL COMPUTERS AND MACHINES

As incredible as it may sound, some observers believe that most computers will one day be biologically based machines, "wetware" as the scientists at Georgia Tech describe it. Experts believe that wetware biocomputers should be smaller and faster than any that current industrial manufacturing processes can create because chip-making technologies are reaching the limits imposed by the physics of atomic structures.

In an interesting first step, scientists have begun culturing networks of switchable neurons in hopes of breeding machines that might one day rival the enormous computing power of the human brain. Using neurons taken from leeches, highly compact, cellular mechanisms for biocomputing have been successfully tested in the laboratory. Leeches were chosen because they have unusually large, easily handled nerve cells. But, there is also research on a much smaller scale using DNA molecules and proteins as computer switching mechanisms and mechanical parts.

It's important to remember that proteins are much more than a food group in the eyes of biotech scientists. They are also more interesting and useful than any molecules previously produced in the chemist's lab. Proteins are nature's version of machinery, molecules of truly astonishing versatility and potency. If the body requires a cutting device, a building tool, a messenger, or almost anything else, usually a protein is created to do the job. That's why proteins appear to offer enormous potential to create micromachines and switching circuits.

High-speed molecular switching mechanisms made from proteins are now being studied at Northwestern University. These proteins, found in the inner ear are believed to be the body's fastest-moving parts. In nature, the so-called Prestin protein responds to sound vibrations by flexing as quickly as 20,000 times per second. Northwestern researchers have now discovered the gene responsible for manufacturing this protein and hope to use it initially to restore hearing. But biotechnology has long horizons and the industry's dreamers are already envisioning the day when biocomputers and Prestin proteins work together to perform the work of a surgeon. Imagine molecular machines traveling through the body to perform repairs like some imaginary device from the world of science fiction. It might sound like a far-fetched notion if it weren't that proteins and DNA already work together to perform tasks of exactly this kind in the body.

Scientists are also developing micromechanisms from the proteins that make muscles contract with astonishing power. One of the most unusual demonstrations of this highly miniaturized biological power in nature is a strange weapon used by some varieties of shrimp to stun their prey with a shock wave. By flicking a tiny appendage at high speeds, these shrimp send out underwater versions of sonic booms. Not only are small sea creatures rendered helpless by the shock, sonar systems on nuclear submarines are frequently deafened by schools of hungry shrimp. This obscure and somewhat bizarre biological mechanism gives some sense of the unusual powers available to researchers looking to exploit mechanical systems evolved over millions of years by nature.[5] In fact, a molecular motor the size of a bacterium has now been created at Cornell University. Researchers attached extremely small nickel blades to an energy-rich molecule and created a truly miniaturized submarine, a single molecule pushed along by its nickel propeller, revolving at eight revolutions per second.

Don't expect to see wetware-based computers in practical use anytime soon, but computer aficionados who understand neural networks may see the possibilities. Neural networks are self-organizing systems that are based on a set of fundamental operating instructions and a large amount of processing power dedicated to carry out a mandate. In a relatively simple experiment with a neural network, a small vehicle was commanded to drive on the roads of a university campus from one point to another without killing anything on its way. In its early excursions, the machine ran off the road, bumped into trees and usually lost its way. After many runs, the machine learned to stay within the white lines of the road and eventually found its way to the destination. With every trip, there were fewer mishaps and a quicker outcome. Learning this simple task requires internal architecture analogous to the brain, rather than the linear mechanisms of ordinary computers.

This illustration gives some sense of the possible application of computers and micromachines based on biological wetware. Conventional computers can only do what they are told, but neural networks can learn how to carry out a command. That defines the difference between a mere robot and a machine with artificial intelligence. All conventional computers are little more than high-performance adding machines. Neural networks have the power to learn and evolve.

When biotechnology makes its mark on the computer industry, it will bring a quantum leap in the capabilities of artificial intelligence. This is a distant horizon with no immediate investment potential.

BIG PHARMA

Major pharmaceutical firms have played an enormous role in the development of the biotechnology industry, making on average more than 500 deals with biotech firms and injecting in excess of $6 billion into the industry annually. The first successful drug made with recombinant DNA technology, fully humanized insulin, was sponsored by the Eli Lilly Company in partnership with Genentech. When Genentech hit a major snag in product development and faced financial disaster, it was bailed out by

Roche in a $3.5 billion takeover. Roche subsequently issued stock in Genentech with an IPO that raised almost $2 billion.

Big Pharma companies eagerly snapped up other biotech firms during 1999, spending well over $12 billion on acquisitions. These takeovers helped set new valuations on money-losing biotech firms that had been ignored by the markets for years. As the value of biotech companies skyrocketed, takeovers became more expensive and Big Pharma companies helped make the market once again by paying sums ranging from $300 million to $800 million for research alliances with companies like Millennium, Human Genome Sciences, and Vertex. Alliances of this sort provide investors with enormous benefits by providing cash flow and by validating the scientific credibility of emerging biotechnology companies. That translates into higher stock prices.

When the time comes to take a drug to market, Big Pharma will be an essential ally to companies that have no distribution and sales expertise. Only a few biotech companies have been bold enough to undertake the job of marketing the first drug out of their development pipelines, a huge gamble as Cell Pathways discovered when it began assembling a large sales force only to face product rejection by the FDA.

Tackling the peculiar disciplines of sales and distribution seems inappropriate and excessively risky for companies that have spent many years preoccupied with the dual problems of scientific discovery and financial survival. As an investor, my primary criteria for biotech companies include sharply focused scientific and management skills, not salesmanship. No industry that comes to mind can match the sales and distribution power of Big Pharma. Schering-Plough, for example, spent $137 million advertising the allergy remedy Claritin in 1999, increasing sales by 20 percent to more than $2.5 billion. The industry as a whole boosted advertising spending by half a billion dollars in 1999 and reaped a gain of $17 billion in sales of prescription drugs. Whatever one thinks of the practice of advertising prescription medicines to the public, it's clear that the pharmaceutical industry is very good at it.

Biotech companies in general have almost no track record that would inspire confidence in their ability to manage the task by themselves, no matter how effective their products might be. Therein lies a problem.

Big Pharma, by dint of its sheer aggressiveness, is rapidly creating a public relations nightmare for itself, and potentially for the biotech industry. Week after week, during the 2000 presidential election campaign, the *New York Times* and the *Wall Street Journal* have painstakingly exposed pharmaceutical industry practices that have appalled public interest groups and raised serious political, ethical, and legal concerns. Big Pharma may be a powerful ally to the biotech industry now, but the question is: for how long? The scope of the pharmaceutical industry's public relations problem encompasses almost every aspect of the business and threatens to engulf junior partners as well as industry leaders:

- The Federal Trade Commission is investigating whether Bristol-Myers Squibb and a small biotech firm called American Bioscience conspired to prevent a generic drug company from bringing a lower-cost version of the anticancer drug Taxol to market. The two companies under investigation deny the allegations by the generic drug maker, IVAX.[6]

- Two major pharmaceutical companies are being accused of "restraint of trade" for allegedly paying generic drug companies to keep competing drugs off the market.[7]

- The pharmaceutical industry charges Americans more for its products than consumers in any other country. A spokesperson for the industry says Americans have to pay more to fund research.[8]

- The industry justifies its pricing practices by pointing out the high cost of research and development. But, critics say, Big Pharma spends considerably more on marketing and administration than it does on drug development; three times as much according to the Kaiser Family Foundation.

- In Washington, the House Commerce Committee is investigating charges that Glaxo boosted sales of an antinausea drug by using methods which the committee chairman called "abusive" and an "outrage." The practice allegedly involved inducing oncologists to administer the Glaxo drug by increasing prices charged to Medicare without claiming reimbursement from doctors. In other words, doctors could pocket more money by prescribing a more expensive drug at government expense. The investigation continues and the Pharmaceutical Industry Association has not responded to the Chairman's accusations.[9]

- The industry has been accused of abuses of patent law and engaging in frivolous litigation to extend the period of marketing exclusivity granted under the Patent Act.[10]

The public interest group Congress Watch says the pharmaceutical industry spent $38 million to promote its cause during the last election and almost a quarter of a billion dollars on lobbying during the previous three years.[11] As the investigations continue, consumer groups are calling Big Pharma "an industry out of control."

Perhaps there is another way of looking at it. Put the whole picture together—the lobbying, aggressive advertising, the ferocious competitive practices and costly deal making with biotechnology—this appears to be an industry fighting for its life. How can that be at a time when most pharmaceutical companies racked up record profits? The answer lies in the very near future.

By the year 2002, pharmaceutical companies will face revenue declines of approximately $20 billion dollars due to the expiry of patents, according to research published by analysts at CMR International. By 2005, drug products that currently generate $34 billion in revenues may lose patent protection according to Banc of America Securities. It is small wonder that the pharmaceutical industry is doing everything in its power to extend the life of its patents while buying biotech companies at premium prices. Facing what one analyst calls an "innovation deficit," the industry is buying biotech drug pipelines to make up for a major decline in revenues when established blockbuster drugs lose patent protection.

In the short run, this trend has had a healthy effect on biotech stock prices. The question now is, what happens next? At a conference in San Francisco, Dr. Stelios Papadopoulos of S.G. Cowen predicted a radical transformation of the drug industry sparked by the biotech revolution.[12] "The pharmas missed the boat," he said. Papadopoulos says he expects biotechnology companies to dominate the industry within 10 years while major pharmaceutical firms and their large sales forces become obsolete. That is the most radical view I've encountered from any industry expert. The reality may be more modest.

As an investor, I subscribe to a more conservative view that envisages a change something like the transformation Hollywood movie studios went through years ago. Before the advent of television, a small cluster of studios held the film industry in an iron grip, dictating the terms of contracts to actors, directors, and exhibitors alike. The studio system broke down in the face of competition and the rising power of popular actors and creative talent.

Big Pharma faces a similar outcome. The collapse of the Hollywood studio system did not destroy the industry but it did transform the once all-powerful studios into distributors and deal brokers for an industry that had broken through its traditional boundaries. That seems like a credible model for the future of biotechnology. The power of major pharmaceutical companies will decline in the face of widespread competition from hundreds of biotech companies. But many biotech companies will rely on the marketing muscle of the pharmaceutical industry to bring their products to market.

As a whole, the biotechnology industry is too fragmented and specialized to take over all marketing and distribution functions from the established companies in the field.

As the flow of new products from the industry grows, the market life of new drugs will likely decrease substantially. Claude Vezeau, vice president of investments at BioCapital, told an industry conference in Montreal that drug companies once expected a five-year period of market exclusivity on a new product before competitors introduced a similar drug. Now, he believes, the time line for exclusivity may shrink to five months. In that kind of fast-changing environment, only very stable biotechnology firms with very large drug pipelines stand a chance of rising to dominant positions and staying there.

Smaller biotech firms would be foolish to spend their resources building marketing empires when their revenues could be unexpectedly decimated by unforeseen competition or scientific innovation. As an investor, I would be extremely cautious about selecting biotech companies with ambitions to go it alone, unless they first established an impressive base of scientific innovation and drug development.

It would be a mistake to assume that Big Pharma companies will sink quietly into the background. Most pharmaceutical giants have signed development deals that call for the delivery of dozens, sometimes even hundreds of drug targets from biotech partners. The big players may be suffering from an innovation gap now, but within the decade their investments in biotechnology will also begin to bear fruit.

The relationship between Big Pharma and biotechnology has usually been symbiotic. It would be unfortunate for investors in both arenas if the increasingly serious public relations issues raised during the past two years were allowed to become a political crisis causing radical changes in patent laws and drug price controls. No biotech investor should forget the market collapse that followed a relatively innocuous joint statement about genomic patents by President Clinton and British Prime Minister Tony Blair. Even companies in the business of saving lives are not immune to political consequences.

It says something important about the behavior of the pharmaceutical industry when politicians and the media compare drug companies to the tobacco lobby. Perhaps the only thing that would drive me out of biotechnology investments is the danger of a sweeping political backlash against all drug makers. If it comes to this, the pharmaceutical industry will have no one to blame but itself.

FUTURE CHALLENGES FOR BIOTECHNOLOGY

The most immediate dangers facing the biotechnology industry are broad ethical and legal concerns. Investors who dismiss the importance of the political and social climate should take a moment to consider the fate of agricultural biotechnology. The industry has been demonized in Europe by protesters, and public confidence has been undermined even in the most pragmatic of countries, the United States. Without making a judgment about the merits of the protesters' arguments, it's safe to say that for many years to come agricultural biotechnology will be hamstrung by political issues.

The fiasco that engulfed agricultural biotechnology was not ameliorated in the slightest by the enormous benefits the industry may bring to society. By the same token, medical biotechnology firms should expect no special consideration because they are upstanding corporate citizens engaged in a battle against disease. Unless the industry takes strong proactive measures to deal with ethical concerns, it could find itself fighting another desperate rearguard action.

The biggest ethical issue arising from the genome revolution is the privacy problem. There is no law protecting the privacy of genetic information from insurance companies and employers. Just as important, there are few laws that would force companies to obtain patient consent as a condition for genetic testing. Despite much public commentary when the genome was first mapped, the problem remains unsolved. Just before the genome announcement, Celera President Craig Venter urged the Joint Economic Committee in Congress to take action to prohibit discrimination based on genetic testing, saying such a law is "essential if the biotechnology revolution is to be realized." Venter is absolutely right.

Probably the first potential benefit from the genomics industry is improved medical diagnosis through genetic tests, conducted on a biochip and recorded by a computer. With the help of this information, doctors will be better able to prevent disease and prescribe appropriate therapies. Genetic tests for a patient's genotype will enable doctors to prescribe the right medicines for a particular patient, avoiding the adverse drug reactions that affect 100,000 people every year. Genetic tests will also reveal a patient's predisposition to disease, useful information for a physician but a matter that raises serious privacy issues.

In his testimony, Venter warned that it would be virtually impossible to defend the privacy of genetic records without government intervention. If the government has failed to act before genetic testing is more widely used, there is every reason to expect that patients, already hesitant to know in advance which diseases they may suffer from, would flatly refuse to cooperate with any form of genetically based treatment. The consequences for the biotechnology industry if this industry comes to a crisis point will be devastating.

If this all seems hypothetical, consider that Visible Genetics is currently building a factory to produce genotyping kits that will assist in the treatment of AIDS patients. Corning, Motorola, and Agilent have declared their intention to begin producing biochips. The widespread use of genetic diagnosis and genotyping is already imminent. It is incumbent on biotech industry leaders to defend their businesses by vigorously pursuing social issues of this kind. It would be foolish to expect the insurance industry to relinquish its ability to scrutinize genetic data any more willingly than it would give up the right to ask applicants if they are smokers or suffer from major preexisting health problems.

Elbert Barnscomb, director of the Joint Genome Institute (a participant in the Human Genome Project) has suggested that patient knowledge of their genetic makeup could effectively put insurance companies out of business because the industry depends on mutual ignorance about one's fate. The idea is rather extreme but it has a basis in fact. If some patients know that they have a predisposition to catastrophic disease and the insurer does not, the company will be at a disadvantage. People who know they have such predispositions will be much more likely to seek insurance than those who show lower risk. Unless the insurance industry has access to such information, it will find itself holding a disproportionate number of policies on clients who are likely to suffer serious illnesses and require expensive treatments. This issue will not be resolved without a struggle, and there is little time to lose before it comes to a head.

Investors should also prepare for the government to strike down thousands of genetic patent applications. Applicants who have not shown a valid understanding of a gene's function and demonstrated an ability to use this knowledge may be denied patent protection.

Looking somewhat further into the future, investors can expect considerable ethical debate about the use of stem cells derived from aborted fetuses and surplus embryos produced for in vitro fertilization. It's impossible at this distance to predict how serious this problem may become, but it would be unwise to ignore that the Vatican has already declared its opposition.

At the root of these ethical and social dilemmas is a deep instinctive opposition to the assumption of new powers over humankind's destiny. These are the stakes at the heart of the biotech revolution. Every biological process can ultimately be explained or even predicted by an analysis of genetic codes and protein interactions. This strikes deeply into religious and philosophical dogma. Dr. Francis Collins, director of the Human Genome Project, had this to say at a White House ceremony celebrating the mapping of the genome: "We have caught the first glimpses of our instruction book, previously known only to God." Collins was quick to say that he had no intention of usurping God's powers but he was among the first to put the issue on the table.

All of this might seem a little grandiose and irrelevant if it weren't that other issues which have pitted human powers against religious dogma, such as the abortion and euthanasia debates, have created serious political controversy. No one can predict how these issues will come to a head, but it seems most unlikely that debates over genetic privacy and agricultural biotechnology will be the last of the industry's ethical challenges.

Biotechnology has penetrated the core of our physical nature. The industry will play a role in the lives and deaths of millions of people. It will ferret out our most intimate physical secrets. And it will raise issues about the fundamental nature of humankind. Let's hope the industry is prepared for the high profile it will assume as it takes on unprecedented powers.

Epilogue

In the months between the completion of this book and it's final preparations for printing, a number of events have occurred which have changed the prospects of several companies mentioned—sometimes for the better and sometimes not. The following brief updates were marked by a note near the relevant section:

Maxim Pharmaceuticals. On January 19, 2001, the company received a *nonapprovable letter* from the FDA, rejecting its application to market the company's lead anti-cancer drug Maxamine. The company's stock value dropped from more than $30 to less than $8 and a lawsuit against Maxim on behalf of shareholders may be forth coming.

Millennium Pharmaceuticals. On December 14, 2000, a committee of the FDA recommended the approval of the company's CAMPATH drug (a monoclonal antibody) for chronic lymphocytic leukemia in patients who have failed other forms of therapy. The company's stock has not risen on the news as of February 2001 because of a severe slump in all Nasdaq stocks.

CuraGen. On January 16, 2001, CuraGen announced a major deal with Bayer, a German-based pharmaceutical giant. In the first of two agreements, CuraGen and Bayer agreed to develop 80 potential treatments for diabetes and obesity. In the second agreement, Bayer will draw on CuraGen's experience in genetics for the creation of experimental medicines. Some commentators believe this deal puts CuraGen in the same league as other leading Tier 2 biotech companies. Unlike other deals between major pharmaceutical companies and Tier 2 biotech firms, Bayer did not offer hundreds of millions of dollars as a payment. Instead, the two partners will share almost $1.5 billion in drug development costs and CuraGen will receive a larger than usual royalty stream from any resulting drugs. In the partnership agreement, CuraGen's royalty share and research costs will be 44 percent. CuraGen's stock is up approximately 60 percent from its previous 12-month low at this writing, but the company remains well below its one-year peak due to continuing downward pressure from the Nasdaq's decline.

Alliance Pharmaceutical. On January 9, 2001, Alliance Pharmaceutical stock tumbled 68 percent on news that the company had suspended testing of its blood substitute. The company says there were no obvious adverse effects from the treatment, but a control group showed a lower incidence of strokes. Two months later, testing was resumed and the company's stock rose 50%.

Orchid Biosciences. Orchid has apparently fallen from market favor as biotech analysts come to regarding genomic information processing more and more a commodity. Orchid's slump has continued into 2001 with a stock price at this writing just over $9 per share.

Diversa Corporation. Despite a constant stream of encouraging news, Diversa's stock has been drawn down in the slump affecting the biotech sector during the early months of 2001. The share price in mid-February 2001, is under $20.

A Breakdown of 185 Major Biotech Companies: Alphabetically, by Market Cap, and by Tier

Company Name (Symbol)	Industry Sector	Tier
Aastrom (ASTM)	Stem cells	4
Abgenix (ABGX)	Monoclonal antibodies, transgenic mice	2
Aclara (ACLA)	Biochips, micro-fluidics	4
Adv. Tissue Sci. (ATIS)	Tissue replacement & regeneration	4
Affymetrix (AFFX)	Leading maker of biochip microarrays	2
Agilent (A)	Biochip & equipment maker	1
Alexion (ALXN)	Immune system treatments	3
Alfacell (ACEL)	Cancer therapy through ribonucleases	4
Alkermes (ALKS)	Drug delivery	3
Allergan (AGN)	Established eye care company	1
Alliance Pharma (ALLP)	Blood substitutes, specialty chemicals	4
Allos Therapeutics (ALTH)	Small molecules for cancer	4
Alpharma (ALO)	Generic drug maker	2
Alza (AZA)	Pharmaceuticals & drug delivery technology	1
Amarillo Bioscience (AMAR)	Drugs discovery for fibromyalgia & hepatitis	4
Amer. Biogenetic (MABA)	Nerve cell regeneration	4
Amgen (AMGN)	Major drugs on market & protein discovery	1
Antigenics (AGEN)	Immune system therapies	4
Aphton (APHT)	Anticancer vaccines using antibodies	4
Applera (ABI)	Instruments, software for genomics & proteomics	1
Aquila Biopharm. (AQLA)	Immune system drugs for HIV & other disorders	4
Ariad Pharmaceutic. (ARIA)	Gene regulation, stem cell, small molecules	4
Aronex (ARNX)	Therapies for cancer & infectious disease	4
ArQule (ARQL)	Combinatorial chemistry & genomics	4
Atrix (ATRX)	Drug delivery	4
Aurora Bio (ABSC)	Genomic materials & equipment	3
Avant Immunother. (AVAN)	Immune therapies for cardiac & viral disease	4
AVAX (AVXT)	Cancer vaccines from patient tumor	4
AVI Biopharma (AVII)	Novel antisense antibiotics, cancer antibodies	4
Avigen (AVGN)	Gene delivery technologies, gene therapy	4
Aviron (AVIR)	Vaccines to fight viruses	3
Axonyx (AXYX)	Alzheimer's and memory therapies	4
Axys Pharma. (AXPH)	Drug discovery	4
BioChem Pharma (BCHE)	Drug discovery	2
BioCryst (BCRX)	Drug development for influenza & immune system	4
Biogen (BGEN)	Drug discovery & sales worldwide	1
Bioject (BJCT)	Needle-free drug delivery	4
BioMarin (BMRN)	Enzymes for genetic disease	4
Biomatrix (BXM)	Cosmeceutical, biomaterials	4
Biopure (BPUR)	Blood replacement	4
Biosite Diagnostic (BSTE)	Emergency diagnostics	4
Bio-Technology Gen. (BTGC)	Drug development & marketing	4
Boston Life Sciences (BLSI)	Broad scientific platform, 11 products in pipeline	4
Caliper (CALP)	Biochips & high throughput analysis systems	3
Cambridge NeuroSci (CNSI)	Drugs to treat nervous disorders & regeneration	4
Celera (CRA)	Genomics	2
Celgene (CELG)	Drug Development for cancer includes Thalidomide	2
Cell Genesys (CEGE)	Cancer vaccines & gene therapy	3
Cell Pathways (CLPA)	Novel anticancer drugs	4
Cell Therapeutics (CTIC)	Novel cancer & leukemia therapies	2
Cellegy (CLGY)	Cosmeceuticals & prescription drugs	4
Celltech (CLL)	British biotech-specialist in antibodies & genomics	2
Cephalon (CEPH)	Neurologically active drugs	3
Chiron (CHIR)	Vaccines for cancer, infectious & CV disease	1
Collateral Therap. (CLTX)	Gene therapy for cardiovascular disease	4
Connectics (CNCT)	Therapeutics for dermatology	4

Cap (mils)	P/E Ratio	EPS	Performance/12 mo.	Beta	Web Site
$ 50	N/A	($ 0.04)	150%	1.05	www.aastrom.com
1,500	N/A	(0.25)	110	1.33	www.aastrom.com
314	N/A	(0.28)	Since 2000 IPO −71	N/A	www.aclara.com
243	N/A	(0.09)	26	0.77	www.advancedtissue.com
3,300	N/A	0.01	24	1.5	www.affymetrix.com
2,100	28	1.68	26	N/A	www.agilent.com
1,100	N/A	(1.47)	304	1.13	www.alexionpharm.com
15	N/A	(0.02)	74	N/A	www.alfacell.com
1,700	N/A	(0.19)	39	0.55	www.alkermes.com
11,000	56	0.41	73	0.32	www.allergan.com
444	N/A	(0.29)	116	0.32	www.allp.com
196	N/A	(10.00)	Since 2000 IPO −22	N/A	www.allos.com
1,300	22	0.48	2	0.07	www.alpharma.com
9,000	60	0.23	72	0.61	www.alza.com
8	N/A	(0.80)	83	−0.17	www.amacell.com
55	N/A	(0.02)	177	1.23	www.mabxa.com
67,000	58	0.33	32	0.85	www.ext.Amgen.com
342	N/A	(0.94)	Since 2000 IPO −13	N/A	www.antigenics.com
444	N/A	(0.92)	103	0.75	www.aphton.com
33	N/A	(0.17)	210	0.71	www.aquilabio.com
196	N/A	(0.12)	390	0.19	www.ariad.com
127	N/A	(0.16)	41	0.81	www.aronex.com
370	N/A	(0.35)	275	0.44	www.arqule.com
231	N/A	(2.45)	178	−0.04	www.atrixlabs.com
725	65	0.55	210	−0.05	www.aurorabio.com
429	N/A	(0.24)	267	0.25	www.tcell.com
70	N/A	(0.89)	58	0.74	www.avax-tech.com
124	N/A	(0.52)	−8	−0.68	www.antivirals.com
588	N/A	(1.03)	20	0.75	www.avigen.com
1,180	N/A	(4.94)	203	0.96	www.aviron.com
108	N/A	(0.07)	Since 2000 IPO −13	N/A	www.axonyx.com
160	N/A	(1.12)	14	−0.04	www.axyspharm.com/index.html
2,300	11	2.06	1	1.18	www.biochem-pharma.com
170	N/A	(0.13)	−59	0.6	www.biocryst.com
7,900	25	2.12	−30	0.7	www.biogen.com
47	N/A	(0.88)	78	1.5	www.bioject.com
326	N/A	(1.02)	−36	N/A	www.biomarinpharm.com
450	26	0.21	−19	0.27	www.biomatrix.com/index.htm
663	N/A	(1.71)	147	N/A	www.biopure.com
426	82	0.13	160	2.2	www.biosite.com
431	49	0.16	−35	1.4	www.biogenerica.com
105	N/A	(1.08)	17	0.29	www.bostonlifesciences.com
959	N/A	(1.74)	18	N/A	www.calipertech.com
31	N/A	(0.19)	85	−0.85	www.cambneuro.com
2,500	N/A	(1.78)	54	N/A	www.celera.com
4,300	N/A	−0.13	2.17	1.1	www.celgene.com
764	6	3.39*	147	0.36	www.cellgenesys.com
160	N/A	(0.99)	−39	−0.8	www.cellpathways.com
1,300	N/A	(2.49)	1141	−0.1	www.cticseattle.com
93	N/A	(0.83)	67	0.33	www.cellegy.com
9,000	N/A	0*	17	N/A	www.celltech.co.uk
1,900	N/A	(1.57)	112	0.7	www.cephalon.com
8,400	49	0.88	32	0.9	www.chiron.com
379	N/A	(0.94)	60	1.2	www.collateralthx.com
151	N/A	(0.47)	−14	1	www.connectics.com
2,000	N/A	(0.44)	287	0.2	www.corr.com

(Continued)

262

APPENDIX A

Company Name (Symbol)	Industry Sector	Tier
COR Therap. (CORR)	Cardiovascular disease specialist	3
Corixa (CRXA)	Immune therapies for cancer & infectious disease	3
Cortex Pharma (CORX)	Drugs for brain dysfunction & degeneration	4
Corvas (CVAS)	Cardiovascular disease specialist	4
Coulter (CLTR)	Cancer therapies based on antibodies & isotopes	4
Cubist (CBST)	Specialist in fungal & microbial infection therapy	3
CuraGen (CRGN)	Genomic discovery & drug development	3
Curis (CRIS)	Cell regeneration specialist	4
CV Therapeutics (CVTX)	Cardiovascular disease specialist	3
Cyanotech (CYAN)	Nutraceuticals	4
Cypress Bioscience (CYPB)	Devices to treat immune disorders	4
Cytoclonal (CYPH)	Drug development from genomics	4
Cytogen (CYTO)	Drug discovery in antibodies and proteomics	4
deCODE Genetics (DCGN)	Genomics based on Icelandic population	3
Dendreon (DNDN)	Immune therapies for cancer	4
Digene (DIGE)	Pharmacogenomics & diagnostics for women	4
Diversa (DVSA)	Industrial genomics & gene shuffling	3
Elan plc (ELN)	Drug discovery & delivery	1
Emisphere (EMIS)	Oral drug delivery specialist	4
Endorex (DOR)	Drug delivery	4
EntreMed (EMED)	Antiangiogenesis cancer treatments	4
Enzo Biochem (ENZ)	Antisense therapy for viruses & immune regulation	3
Epimmune (EPMN)	Vaccines for cancer, viruses, malaria	4
Gene Logic (GLGC)	Genomics & functional genomics data	4
Genelabs Tech. (GNLB)	Small molecule drugs bind to RNA of viruses, lupus	4
Genencor (GCOR)	Industrial, agric., healthcare biotechnology	3
Genentech (DNA)	Engineering therapeutic proteins	1
Genetronics (GEB)	DNA Delivery through electropororation	4
Genome Therap. (GENE)	Genomics-based drug discovery	4
Genset (GENXY)	Genomics, pharmacogenomics, drug discovery	4
Genta (GNTA)	Antisense therapy for cancer	4
Genzyme General (GENZ)	Gene therapy, multiple disease targets	1
Genzyme Oncology (GZMO)	Vaccines, antiangiogenesis, cell path. for cancer	4
Genzyme Surgical (GZSP)	Devices, materials & therapeutics for surgery	4
Genzyme Transgen. (GZTC)	Humanized proteins from transgenic animals	4
Geron (GERN)	Anticancer & anti-aging stem cell therapy	4
Gilead (GILD)	Novel therapies for infectious diseases	2
Gliatech (GLIA)	Antibodies to control surgical scars	4
Guilford (GLFD)	Nerve regeneration, cancer, drug delivery, prodrugs	3
Hemispherx (HEB)	RNA-based drugs for HIV & CFS	4
Hollis Eden Pharma (HEPH)	Novel AIDS & antiviral therapies	4
Human Genome S. (HGSI)	Drug discovery from genes to proteins	2
Hybridion (HYBN)	Antisense technology: cancer, viruses, eye diseases	4
Hyseq (HYSQ)	Genomic discovery & drug development & biochips	4
ICOS (ICOS)	Small molecules, antibodies, anti-inflammatories	2
IDEC (IDPH)	Antibodies & isotopes for cancer & immune disease	1
Ilex Oncology (ILXO)	Contract cancer research	4
Imclone (IMCL)	Antiangiogenesis, cancer vaccines, growth blockers	2
Immtech Int'l (IMMT)	Pnuemonia & antiparasitic drug development	4
Immune Response (IMNR)	Immune therapies for HIV, gene therapy	4
Immunex (IMNX)	Antibodies & immune control for arthritis	1
Immunogen (IMGN)	Antibodies & prodrugs for cancer	3
Immunomedics (IMMU)	Antibodies targeted at cancer with radioisotopes	3
Incyte (INCY)	Genomics & functional genomics data	3
Inhale (INHL)	Oral drug delivery specialist	3
Interneuron (IPIC)	Drug dev. for neural disease: stroke & anxiety	4

Cap (mils)	P/E Ratio	EPS	Performance/12 mo.	Beta	Web Site
738	N/A	(2.83)	103	0.5	www.corixa.com
46	N/A	(0.08)	235	0.2	www.cortexpharm.com
500	N/A	(0.54)	554	0.7	www.corvas.com
660	N/A	(3.18)	100	1.8	www.coulterpharm.com
950	N/A	(1.22)	225	0.7	www.cubist.com
1,600	N/A	(0.71)	210	1	www.curagen.com
400	N/A	(15.00)	Since IPO −13	N/A	www.curis.com
1,300	N/A	(1.71)	395	−0.36	www.cvt.com
19	N/A	(0.26)	95	1.1	www.cyanotech.com
33	N/A	(0.16)	−66	0.5	www.cypressbio.com
125	N/A	(0.51)	31	0.59	www.cytoclonal.com
332	N/A	(0.27)	169	0.5	www.cytogen.com
761	N/A	(0.23)	Since IPO −37	N/A	www.decode.com
326	N/A	(9.03)	Since IPO −12	N/A	www.dendreon.com
561	N/A	(0.48)	85	1.1	www.digene.com
800	N/A	(0.81)	Since IPO 26	N/A	www.diversa.com
14,000	91	0.56	78	0.56	www.elan.ie/home/.com
488	N/A	(1.92)	64	1.9	www.emisphere.com
25	N/A	(0.59)	6	−1	www.endorex.com
440	N/A	(3.24)	7	0.47	www.entremed.com
940	148	0.25	44	0.75	www.enzo.com
21	N/A	(0.50)	5	0.3	www.epimmune.com
434	N/A	(1.01)	162	0.9	www.genelogic.com
251	N/A	(0.29)	42	0.2	www.genelabs.com
1,100	N/A	(0.54)	Since IPO −21	N/A	www.genencor.com
38,000	N/A	(0.41)	62	N/A*	www.gene.com
30	N/A	(0.38)	−62	N/A	www.genetronics.com
284	N/A	(0.13)	230	1.5	www.genomecorp.com
323	N/A	(1.05)	16	0.8	www.genxy.com
370	N/A	(1.19)	78	1.1	www.genta.com
7,000	30	2.61	114	0.8	www.genzyme.com
177	N/A	(1.74)	132	N/A	www.genzyme.com
102	N/A	(2.89)	34	N/A	www.genzyme.com
136	N/A	(0.70)	136	0.44	www.genzyme.com
446	N/A	(1.93)	75	0.36	www.geron.com
3,290	N/A	(0.81)	42	1.6	www.gilead.com
41	N/A	(0.70)	−59	0.9	www.gliatech.com
460	N/A	(1.53)	30	0.7	www.guilfordpharm.com
200	N/A	(0.28)	−22	−0.69	www.hemispherx.com
64	N/A	(2.09)	−65	0.64	www.holliseden.com
8,200	N/A	(2.27)	136	0.21	www.hgsi.com
12	N/A	(0.83)	0	−0.56	www.hybridion.com
261	N/A	(1.56)	168	0.76	www.hyseq.com
2,200	N/A	(1.01)	30	0.73	www.icos.com
8,000	226	0.78	154	1.4	www.idecpharm.com
680	N/A	(0.83)	61	0.85	www.ilexoncology.com
3,100	N/A	(0.83)	131	0.05	www.imclone.com
68	N/A	(1.57)	−55	N/A	www.immtech-international.com
122	N/A	(0.52)	−1	0.7	www.imnr.com
2,200	183	0.22	71	1.7	www.immunex.com
1,100	N/A	(0.14)	700	0.02	www.immunogen.com
1,000	N/A	(0.20)	890	2.33	www.immunomedics.com
1,900	N/A	(0.47)	94	0.5	www.incyte.com
2,000	N/A	(2.03)	212	0.45	www.inhale.com
65	8	0.19	25	1.5	www.interneuron.com
3,900	2100	0.04	163	?	www.invitrogen.com

(Continued)

Company Name (Symbol)	Industry Sector	Tier
Invitrogen (IVGN)	Genomic & biological research supplies & services	1
Isis Pharmaceuticals (ISIP)	Antisense drug development for cancer & viruses	4
Kos Pharmaceutical (KOSP)	Drug discovery, development, drug delivery	4
La Jolla Pharma. (LJPC)	Humanized antibodies for lupus, thrombosis	4
Large Scale Bio (LSBC)	Gene expression analysis & drug development	4
Lexicon Genetics (LEXG)	Genomics & functional genomics, mouse clones	4
Ligand Pharma. (LGND)	Drugs for specialty uses, wide range of targets	3
Lorus Therapeutics (LORFF)	Antisense & antiangiogenesis for cancer	4
Lynx Therapeutics (LYNX)	DNA analysis technologies & equipment	4
Magainin (MAGN)	Antiangiogenesis, respiratory genomics, infection	4
Maxim Pharma (MAXM)	Cancer therapy by immune system management	3
Maxygen (MAXY)	Molecular breeding or gene shuffling	3
Medarex (MEDX)	Monoclonal antibodies for cancer & immune disease	2
Medimmune (MEDI)	Antibacterials, antibodies & antiangiogenesis	1
MGI Pharma (MOGN)	Cancer & rheumatology drug development	4
Millennium (MLNM)	Vertically integrated: genomics to drugs	2
Miravant Medical (MRVT)	Photodynamic therapy, multiple targets	4
Molecular Devices (MDCC)	Bioanalytical devices, combinatorial chemistry	3
Myriad (MYGN)	Genomics & proteomics for cancer therapies	3
Nanogen (NGEN)	Biochips integrating chemical & electric function	4
NeoPharm (NEOL)	Cancer diagnostics & treatment, drug delivery	4
NeoRx (NERX)	Cancer therapies: internal targeted radiation	4
Neotherapeutics (NEOT)	Small molecules for nerve regeneration: Alzheimer's	4
Neurobiological Tech (NTII)	Drug development for neurological disorders	4
Neurocrine (NBIX)	Psychiatric, degenerative, inflammatory, cancer drugs	4
Neurogen (NRGN)	Drugs to regulate cellular communication	4
Nexell Therapeutics (NEXL)	Stem cells from immune system to fight disease	4
Onyx Pharma (ONXX)	Developer of "armed virus" technology for cancers	4
Orchid Biosciences (ORCH)	Bioinformatics, SNP analysis & SNP products	4
Organogenesis (ORG)	Living & connective tissue replacement	4
Oxis International (OXIS)	Therapies to limit damage done by free radicals	4
Pain Therapeutics (PTIE)	Developing novel drugs for pain management	4
Pathogenesis (PGNS)	New antibiotics & inhalable drug delivery systems	4
Pharmacopeia (PCOP)	Lead discovery for drugs & high throughput analysis	4
Pharmacyclics (PCYC)	Photodynamic therapy, cancer, & vascular disease	4
Pharmos (PARS)	Drug discovery in steroids, angiogenesis	4
Praecis (PRCS)	Developer of cancer & pain drugs, Ligand-based	3
ProCyte (PRCY)	Cosmeceuticals for aging & hair loss	4
Progenics (PGNX)	Developing drugs for cancer, HIV & other viruses	4
Protein Design Lab (PDLI)	Specialist in humanized monoclonal antibodies	2
Protein Polymer (PPTI)	Biomaterials for surgery & wound healing	4
QLT Inc. (QLTI)	Photodynamic therapy for eyes & immune disease	2
Quest Diagnostic (DGX)	Leader in diagnostic & information services	1
Regerneron (REGN)	Antibodies & designer proteins, genomics	4
Repligen Corp. (RGEN)	Drugs for autism, organ transplant, cancer	4
Ribozyme Pharma. (RZYM)	Ribozyme therapy to destroy viruses & cancer	4
SangStat (SANG)	International transplant medicine specialist	4
Sepracor (SEPR)	ICE pharmaceuticals: "improved chemical entities"	2
Sequenom (SQNM)	Genotyping & SNP analysis for industry & drug dev.	4
Shire Pharam. Plc (SHPGY)	International specialty pharmaceutical developer	2
Skye Pharma plc (SKYE)	Leading company in drug delivery	4
SuperGen (SUPG)	Acquires & develops promising drugs from innovators	4
Targeted Genetics (TGEN)	Gene therapy for multiple targets	4
Techniclone (TCLN)	Targeting methods for cancer therapy	4
Titan Pharma (TTP)	Drug development for Parkinson's, schizophrenia	3
Transkaryotic (TKTX)	Gene therapy, gene activated proteins, proteins	3

Cap (mils)	P/E Ratio	EPS	Performance/12 mo.	Beta	Web Site
417	N/A	(1.69)	−29	0.9	www.isip.com
456	N/A	(2.23)	360	−0.13	www.kospharm.com
168	N/A	(0.53)	560	−0.3	www.ljpc.com
325	N/A	(1.66)	Since IPO −49	N/A	www.lsbc.com
660	N/A	(0.88)	Since IPO +35	N/A	www.lexicon-genetics.com
803	N/A	(1.31)	39	1.7	www.ligand.com
175	N/A	(0.06)	344	0.5	www.lorusthera.com
142	N/A	(0.31)	9	0.35	www.lynxgen.com
119	N/A	(0.40)	168	0.5	www.magainin.com
800	N/A	(5.17)	150	−0.14	www.maxim.com
1,100	N/A	(1.73)	Since IPO −9	N/A	www.maxygen.com
2,700	N/A	(0.28)	575	0.5	www.medarex.com
13,000	150	0.41	41	1.3	www.medimmune.com
330	N/A	(0.12)	66	0.5	www.mgipharma.com
1,100	N/A	(3.59)	138	0.3	www.mlnm.com
310	N/A	(1.25)	48	1.4	www.miravant.com
857	N/A	(0.20)	73	1.6	www.moldev.com
1,600	N/A	(0.41)	395	−0.2	www.myriad.com
253	N/A	(0.98)	71	1	www.nanogen.com
325	N/A	(0.07)	Since IPO +41	1.6	www.neophrm.com
214	N/A	(0.55)	367	0.01	www.neorx.com
44	N/A	(5.10)	−63	1.6	www.neotherapeutics.com
90	N/A	(0.22)	Since IPO +60	N/A	www.ntii.com
732	N/A	(1.07)	121	1.2	www.neurocrine.com
493	N/A	(1.09)	100	0.85	www.neurogen.com
87	N/A	(1.95)	−17	−0.6	www.nexellinc.com
287	N/A	(0.44)	85	1.1	www.onyx-pharm.com
421	N/A	(0.27)	Since IPO +20	N/A	www.orchid.com
275	N/A	(0.75)	−10	1.6	www.organogenesis.com
8	N/A	(0.41)	73	1	www.oxis.com
517	N/A	(2.90)	Since IPO +19	N/A	www.paintrials.com
640	N/A	(0.13)	164	1.2	www.pathogenesis.com
19,000	N/A	0.94	124	N/A	www.pecorporation.com
572	N/A	0.03	46	0.8	www.pharmacopeia.com
690	N/A	(1.80)	26	0.8	www.pcyc.com
138	N/A	(0.11)	64	0.45	www.pharmoscorp.com
1,100	N/A	(0.90)	Since IPO +67	N/A	www.praecis.com
11	N/A	(0.26)	−9	0.17	www.tricomin.com
324	N/A	(0.17)	−7	1.6	www.progenics.com
4,290	N/A	(0.15)	376	0.9	www.pdl.com
13	N/A	(0.23)	228	−2.5	www.ppti.com
3,900	N/A	(0.06)	6	1.2	www.qltinc.com
5,000	84	1.30	263	0.2	www.questdiagnostics.com
960	N/A	(0.45)	239	−0.04	www.regeneron.com
132	N/A	(0.20)	14	−0.59	www.repligen.com
250	N/A	(0.98)	106	0.69	www.rpi.com
148	N/A	(2.58)	−62	1.4	www.sangstat.com
5,600	N/A	(2.71)	55	0.6	www.sepracor.com
473	N/A	(6.34)	−10	N/A	www.sequenom.com
4,800	N/A	0.00	76	0.4	www.shire.com
481	N/A	(0.71)	6	−0.7	www.skyepharma.com
664	N/A	(1.15)	−39	0.5	www.supergen.com
389	N/A	(1.05)	215	0.29	www.targetedgenetics.com
247	N/A	(0.16)	418	−2.67	www.techniclone.com
970	N/A	(0.74)	169	0.2	www.titanpharm.com
1,000	N/A	(1.90)	−2	1.5	www.tktx.com

(Continued)

Company Name (Symbol)	Industry Sector	Tier
Trega Biosciences (TRGA)	Drug development services, information, chemistry	4
Triangle (VIRS)	Specialist in developing antiviral drugs	4
Trimeris (TRMS)	Vaccines to prevent viral infection from HIV/AIDS	3
Tularik (TLRK)	Gene expression control via small molecule drugs	4
Unigene (UGNE)	Oral delivery of therapeutic peptides	4
Valentis (VLTS)	Gene delivery & therapy to stimulate cytokines	4
Vasogen (MEW)	Devices to treat immune system disorders	4
Vasomedical (VASO)	Mechanical counterpulsation angina therapy	4
VaxGen (VXGN)	Developing AIDS vaccine	4
Vertex (VRTX)	Small molecule drugs in-house & contract	2
Vical (VICL)	Gene delivery "naked DNA" for cancer	4
Vion (VION)	Cancer drugs, prodrugs, drug delivery	4
Viropharma (VPHM)	Antiviral pharmaceuticals target RNA viruses	4
Visible Genetics (VIGN)	Genotyping, pharmacogenomics, gene sequencing	4
Vivus (VVUS)	Sexual dysfunction treatments	4
Xoma (XOMA)	Drug production technologies & drug development	4

Cap (mils)	P/E Ratio	EPS	Performance/12 mo.	Beta	Web Site
37	N/A	(0.54)	30	0.6	www.trega.com
239	N/A	(3.04)	−67	0.2	www.tripharm.com
1,000	N/A	(1.91)	203	−0.3	www.trimeris.com
1,500	N/A	(1.02)	42	N/A	www.tularik.com
70	N/A	(0.24)	126	0.39	www.unigene.com
255	N/A	(1.24)	75	−0.02	www.valentis.com
275	N/A	(0.15)	40	N/A	www.vasogen.com
181	N/A	0.02	221	0.6	www.vasomedical.com
339	N/A	(1.70)	111	N/A	www.vaxgen.com
4,300	N/A	(0.53)	465	0.7	www.vpharm.com
356	N/A	(0.30)	−15	1.1	www.vical.com
204	N/A	(0.57)	43	1.4	www.vionpharm.com.com
282	N/A	(2.46)	−23	−0.16	www.viropharma.com
391	N/A	(2.53)	68	0.84	www.visgen.com
89	5.4	0.51	29	1.8	www.vivus.com
709	N/A	(0.46)	286	0.83	www.xoma.com

* Indicates unusual accounting circumstances.
Source: Data from WindowsOnWallSt.com as of November 2000.

Company Name (Symbol)	Industry Sector	Tier
Amgen (AMGN)	Major drugs on market & protein discovery	1
Genentech (DNA)	Engineering therapeutic proteins	1
Applera (ABI)	Instruments, software for genomics & proteomics	1
Elan plc (ELN)	Drug discovery & delivery	1
Medimmune (MEDI)	Antibacterials, antibodies & antiangiogenesis	1
Allergan (AGN)	Established eye care company	1
Alza (AZA)	Pharmaceuticals & drug delivery technology	1
Celltech (CLL)	British biotech-specialist in antibodies & genomics	2
Chiron (CHIR)	Vaccines for cancer, infectious & CV disease	1
Human Genome S. (HGSI)	Drug discovery from genes to proteins	2
IDEC (IDPH)	Antibodies & isotopes for cancer & immune disease	1
Biogen (BGEN)	Drug discovery & sales worldwide	1
Genzyme General (GENZ)	Gene therapy, multiple disease targets	1
Sepracor (SEPR)	ICE pharmaceuticals: "improved chemical entities"	2
Quest Diagnostic (DGX)	Leader in diagnostic & information services	1
Shire Pharam. Plc (SHPGY)	International specialty pharmaceutical developer	2
Celgene (CELG)	Drug development for cancer includes Thalidomide	2
Vertex (VRTX)	Small molecule drugs in-house & contract	2
Protein Design Lab (PDLI)	Specialist in humanized monoclonal antibodies	2
Invitrogen (IVGN)	Genomic & biological research supplies & services	1
QLT Inc. (QLTI)	Photodynamic therapy for eyes & immune disease	2
Affymetrix (AFFX)	Leading maker of biochip microarrays	2
Gilead (GILD)	Novel therapies for infectious diseases	2
Imclone (IMCL)	Antiangiogenesis, cancer vaccines, growth blockers	2
Medarex (MEDX)	Monoclonal antibodies for cancer & immune disease	2
Celera (CRA)	Genomics	2
BioChem Pharma (BCHE)	Drug discovery	2
ICOS (ICOS)	Small molecules, antibodies, anti-inflammatories	2
Immunex (IMNX)	Antibodies & immune control for arthritis	1
Agilent (A)	Biochip & equipment maker	1
COR Therap. (CORR)	Cardiovascular disease specialist	3
Inhale (INHL)	Oral drug delivery specialist	3
Cephalon (CEPH)	Neurologically active drugs	3
Incyte (INCY)	Genomics & functional genomics data	3
Alkermes (ALKS)	Drug delivery	3
CuraGen (CRGN)	Genomic discovery & drug development	3
Myriad (MYGN)	Genomics & proteomics for cancer therapies	3
Abgenix (ABGX)	Monoclonal antibodies, transgenic mice	2
Tularik (TLRK)	Gene expression control via small molecule drugs	4
Alpharma (ALO)	Generic drug maker	2
Cell Therapeutics (CTIC)	Novel cancer & leukemia therapies	2
CV Therapeutics (CVTX)	Cardiovascular disease specialist	3
Aviron (AVIR)	Vaccines to fight viruses	3
Alexion (ALXN)	Immune system treatments	3
Genencor (GCOR)	Industrial, agric., healthcare biotechnology	3
Immunogen (IMGN)	Antibodies & prodrugs for cancer	3
Maxygen (MAXY)	Molecular breeding or gene shuffling	3
Millennium (MLNM)	Vertically integrated: genomics to drugs	2
Praecis (PRCS)	Developer of cancer & pain drugs, Ligand-based	3
Immunomedics (IMMU)	Antibodies targeted at cancer with radioisotopes	3
Transkaryotic (TKTX)	Gene therapy, gene activated proteins, proteins	3
Trimeris (TRMS)	Vaccines to prevent viral infection from HIV/AIDS	3
Titan Pharma (TTP)	Drug development for Parkinson's, schizophrenia	3
Regerneron (REGN)	Antibodies & designer proteins, genomics	4
Caliper (CALP)	Biochips & high throughput analysis systems	3
Cubist (CBST)	Specialist in fungal & microbial infection therapy	3

Cap (mils)	P/E Ratio	EPS	Performance/12 mo.	Beta	Web Site
$67,000	58	$0.33	32%	0.85	www.ext.Amgen.com
38,000	N/A	(0.41)	62	N/A*	www.gene.com
19,000	N/A	0.94	124	N/A	www.pecorporation.com
14,000	91	0.56	78	0.56	www.elan.ie/home/.com
13,000	150	0.41	41	1.3	www.medimmune.com
11,000	56	0.41	73	0.32	www.allergan.com
9,000	60	0.23	72	0.61	www.alza.com
9,000	N/A	0*	17	N/A	www.celltech.co.uk
8,400	49	0.88	32	0.9	www.chiron.com
8,200	N/A	(2.27)	136	0.21	www.hgsi.com
8,000	226	0.78	154	1.4	www.idecpharm.com
7,900	25	2.12	−30	0.7	www.biogen.com
7,000	30	2.61	114	0.8	www.genzyme.com
5,600	N/A	(2.71)	55	0.6	www.sepracor.com
5,000	84	1.30	263	0.2	www.questdiagnostics.com
4,800	N/A	0.00	76	0.4	www.shire.com
4,300	N/A	(0.13)	217	1.1	www.celgene.com
4,300	N/A	(0.53)	465	0.7	www.vpharm.com
4,290	N/A	(0.15)	376	0.9	www.pdl.com
3,900	2100	0.04	163	?	www.invitrogen.com
3,900	N/A	(0.06)	6	1.2	www.qltinc.com
3,300	N/A	0.01	24	1.5	www.affymetrix.com
3,290	N/A	(0.81)	42	1.6	www.gilead.com
3,100	N/A	(0.83)	131	0.05	www.imclone.com
2,700	N/A	(0.28)	575	0.5	www.medarex.com
2,500	N/A	(1.78)	54	N/A	www.celera.com
2,300	11	2.06	1	1.18	www.biochem-pharma.com
2,200	N/A	(1.01)	30	0.73	www.icos.com
2,200	183	0.22	71	1.7	www.immunex.com
2,100	28	1.68	26	N/A	www.agilent.com
2,000	N/A	(0.44)	287	0.2	www.corr.com
2,000	N/A	(2.03)	212	0.45	www.inhale.com
1,900	N/A	(1.57)	112	0.7	www.cephalon.com
1,900	N/A	(0.47)	94	0.5	www.incyte.com
1,700	N/A	(0.19)	39	0.55	www.alkermes.com
1,600	N/A	(0.71)	210	1	www.curagen.com
1,600	N/A	(0.41)	395	−0.2	www.myriad.com
1,500	N/A	(0.25)	110	1.33	www.aastrom.com
1,500	N/A	(1.02)	42	N/A	www.tularik.com
1,300	22	0.48	2	0.07	www.alpharma.com
1,300	N/A	(2.49)	1141	−0.1	www.cticseattle.com
1,300	N/A	(1.71)	395	−0.36	www.cvt.com
1,180	N/A	(4.94)	203	0.96	www.aviron.com
1,100	N/A	(1.47)	304	1.13	www.alexionpharm.com
1,100	N/A	(0.54)	Since IPO −21	N/A	www.genecor.com
1,100	N/A	(0.14)	700	0.02	www.immunogen.com
1,100	N/A	(1.73)	Since IPO −9	N/A	www.maxygen.com
1,100	N/A	(3.59)	138	0.3	www.mlnm.com
1,100	N/A	(0.90)	Since IPO +67	N/A	www.praecis.com
1,000	N/A	(0.20)	890	2.33	www.immunomedics.com
1,000	N/A	(1.90)	−2	1.5	www.tktx.com
1,000	N/A	(1.91)	203	−0.3	www.trimeris.com
970	N/A	(0.74)	169	0.2	www.titanpharm.com
960	N/A	(0.45)	239	−0.04	www.regeneron.com
959	N/A	(1.74)	18	N/A	www.calipertech.com
950	N/A	(1.22)	225	0.7	www.cubist.com

(Continued)

Company Name (Symbol)	Industry Sector	Tier
Enzo Biochem (ENZ)	Antisense therapy for viruses & immune regulation	3
Molecular Devices (MDCC)	Bioanalytical devices, combinatorial chemistry	3
Ligand Pharma. (LGND)	Drugs for specialty uses, wide range of targets	3
Diversa (DVSA)	Industrial genomics & gene shuffling	3
Maxim Pharma (MAXM)	Cancer therapy by immune system management	3
Cell Genesys (CEGE)	Cancer vaccines & gene therapy	3
deCODE Genetics (DCGN)	Genomics based on Icelandic population	3
Corixa (CRXA)	Immune therapies for cancer & infectious disease	3
Neurocrine (NBIX)	Psychiatric, degenerative, inflammatory, cancer drugs	4
Aurora Bio (ABSC)	Genomic materials & equipment	3
Xoma (XOMA)	Drug production technologies & drug development	4
Pharmacyclics (PCYC)	Photodynamic therapy, cancer & vascular disease	4
Ilex Oncology (ILXO)	Contract cancer research	4
SuperGen (SUPG)	Acquires & develops promising drugs from innovators	4
Biopure (BPUR)	Blood replacement	4
Coulter (CLTR)	Cancer therapies based on antibodies & isotopes	4
Lexicon Genetics (LEXG)	Genomics & functional genomics, mouse clones	4
Pathogenesis (PGNS)	New antibiotics & inhalable drug delivery systems	4
Avigen (AVGN)	Gene delivery technologies, gene therapy	4
Pharmacopeia (PCOP)	Lead discovery for drugs & high throughput analysis	4
Digene (DIGE)	Pharmacogenomics & diagnostics for women	4
Pain Therapeutics (PTIE)	Developing novel drugs for pain management	4
Corvas (CVAS)	Cardiovascular disease specialist	4
Neurogen (NRGN)	Drugs to regulate cellular communication	4
Emisphere (EMIS)	Oral drug delivery specialist	4
Skye Pharma plc (SKYE)	Leading company in drug delivery	4
Sequenom (SQNM)	Genotyping & SNP analysis for industry & drug dev.	4
Guilford (GLFD)	Nerve regeneration, cancer, drug delivery, prodrugs	3
Kos Pharmaceutical (KOSP)	Drug discovery, development, drug delivery	4
Biomatrix (BXM)	Cosmeceutical, biomaterials	4
Geron (GERN)	Anticancer & anti-aging stem cell therapy	4
Alliance Pharma (ALLP)	Blood substitutes, specialty chemicals	4
Aphton (APHT)	Anticancer vaccines using antibodies	4
EntreMed (EMED)	Antiangiogenesis cancer treatments	4
Gene Logic (GLGC)	Genomics & functional genomics data	4
Bio-Technology Gen. (BTGC)	Drug development & marketing	4
Avant Immunother. (AVAN)	Immune therapies for cardiac & viral disease	4
Biosite Diagnostic (BSTE)	Emergency diagnostics	4
Orchid Biosciences (ORCH)	Bioinformatics, SNP analysis & SNP products	4
Isis Pharmaceuticals (ISIP)	Antisense drug development for cancer & viruses	4
Curis (CRIS)	Cell regeneration specialist	4
Visible Genetics (VIGN)	Genotyping, pharmacogenomics, gene sequencing	4
Targeted Genetics (TGEN)	Gene therapy for multiple targets	4
Collateral Therap. (CLTX)	Gene therapy for cardiovascular disease	4
ArQule (ARQL)	Combinatorial chemistry & genomics	4
Genta (GNTA)	Antisense therapy for cancer	4
Vical (VICL)	Gene delivery "naked DNA" for cancer	4
Antigenics (AGEN)	Immune system therapies	4
VaxGen (VXGN)	Developing AIDS vaccine	4
Cytogen (CYTO)	Drug discovery in antibodies and proteomics	4
MGI Pharma (MOGN)	Cancer & rheumatology drug development	4
BioMarin (BMRN)	Enzymes for genetic disease	4
Dendreon (DNDN)	Immune therapies for cancer	4
Large Scale Bio (LSBC)	Gene expression analysis & drug development	4
NeoPharm (NEOL)	Cancer diagnostics & treatment, drug delivery	4
Progenics (PGNX)	Developing drugs for cancer, HIV & other viruses	4

Cap (mils)	P/E Ratio	EPS	Performance/12 mo.	Beta	Web Site
940	148	0.25	44	0.75	www.enzo.com
857	N/A	(0.20)	73	1.6	www.moldev.com
803	N/A	(1.31)	39	1.7	www.ligand.com
800	N/A	(0.81)	Since IPO 26	N/A	www.diversa.com
800	N/A	(5.17)	150	−0.14	www.maxim.com
764	6	3.39*	147	0.36	www.cellgenesys.com
761	N/A	(0.23)	Since IPO −37	N/A	www.decode.com
738	N/A	(2.83)	103	0.5	www.corixa.com
732	N/A	(1.07)	121	1.2	www.neurocrine.com
725	65	0.55	210	−0.05	www.aurorabio.com
709	N/A	(0.46)	286	0.83	www.xoma.com
690	N/A	(1.80)	26	0.8	www.pcyc.com
680	N/A	(0.83)	61	0.85	www.ilexoncology.com
664	N/A	(1.15)	−39	0.5	www.supergen.com
663	N/A	(1.71)	147	N/A	www.biopure.com
660	N/A	(3.18)	100	1.8	www.coulterpharm.com
660	N/A	(0.88)	Since IPO +35	N/A	www.lexicon-genetics.com
640	N/A	(0.13)	164	1.2	www.pathogenesis.com
588	N/A	(1.03)	20	0.75	www.avigen.com
572	N/A	0.03	46	0.8	www.pharmacopeia.com
561	N/A	(0.48)	85	1.1	www.digene.com
517	N/A	(2.90)	Since IPO +19	N/A	www.paintrials.com
500	N/A	(0.54)	554	0.7	www.corvas.com
493	N/A	(1.09)	100	0.85	www.neurogen.com
488	N/A	(1.92)	64	1.9	www.emisphere.com
481	N/A	(0.71)	6	−0.7	www.skyepharma.com
473	N/A	(6.34)	−10	N/A	www.sequenom.com
460	N/A	(1.53)	30	0.7	www.guilfordpharm.com
456	N/A	(2.23)	360	−0.13	www.kospharm.com
450	26	0.21	−19	0.27	www.biomatrix.com/index.htm
446	N/A	(1.93)	75	0.36	www.geron.com
444	N/A	(0.29)	116	0.32	www.allp.com
444	N/A	(0.92)	103	0.75	www.aphton.com
440	N/A	(3.24)	7	0.47	www.entremed.com
434	N/A	(1.01)	162	0.9	www.genelogic.com
431	49	0.16	−35	1.4	www.biogenerica.com
429	N/A	(0.24)	267	0.25	www.tcell.com
426	82	0.13	160	2.2	www.biosite.com
421	N/A	(0.27)	Since IPO +20	N/A	www.orchid.com
417	N/A	(1.69)	−29	0.9	www.isip.com
400	N/A	(15.00)	Since IPO −13	N/A	www.curis.com
391	N/A	(2.53)	68	0.84	www.visgen.com
389	N/A	(1.05)	215	0.29	www.targetedgenetics.com
379	N/A	(0.94)	60	1.2	www.collateralthx.com
370	N/A	(0.35)	275	0.44	www.arqule.com
370	N/A	(1.19)	78	1.1	www.genta.com
356	N/A	(0.30)	−15	1.1	www.vical.com
342	N/A	(0.94)	Since 2000 IPO −13	N/A	www.antigenics.com
339	N/A	(1.70)	111	N/A	www.vaxgen.com
332	N/A	(0.27)	169	0.5	www.cytogen.com
330	N/A	(0.12)	66	0.5	www.mgipharma.com
326	N/A	(1.02)	−36	N/A	www.biomarinpharm.com
326	N/A	(9.03)	Since IPO −12	N/A	www.dendreon.com
325	N/A	(1.66)	Since IPO −49	N/A	www.lsbc.com
325	N/A	(0.07)	Since IPO +41	1.6	www.neophrm.com
324	N/A	(0.17)	−7	1.6	www.progenics.com

(Continued)

Company Name (Symbol)	Industry Sector	Tier
Genset (GENXY)	Genomics, pharmacogenomics, drug discovery	4
Aclara (ACLA)	Biochips, micro-fluidics	4
Miravant Medical (MRVT)	Photodynamic therapy, multiple targets	4
Onyx Pharma (ONXX)	Developer of "armed virus" technology for cancers	4
Genome Therap. (GENE)	Genomics-based drug discovery	4
Viropharma (VPHM)	Antiviral pharmaceuticals target RNA viruses	4
Organogenesis (ORG)	Living & connective tissue replacement	4
Vasogen (MEW)	Devices to treat immune system disorders	4
Hyseq (HYSQ)	Genomic discovery & drug development & biochips	4
Valentis (VLTS)	Gene delivery & therapy to stimulate cytokines	4
Nanogen (NGEN)	Biochips integrating chemical & electric function	4
Genelabs Tech. (GNLB)	Small molecule drugs bind to RNA of viruses, lupus	4
Ribozyme Pharma. (RZYM)	Ribozyme therapy to destroy viruses, & cancer	4
Techniclone (TCLN)	Targeting methods for cancer therapy	4
Adv. Tissue Sci. (ATIS)	Tissue replacement & regeneration	4
Triangle (VIRS)	Specialist in developing antiviral drugs	4
Atrix (ATRX)	Drug Delivery	4
NeoRx (NERX)	Cancer therapies: internal targeted radiation	4
Vion (VION)	Cancer drugs, prodrugs, drug delivery	4
Hemispherx (HEB)	RNA-based drugs for HIV & CFS	4
Allos Therapeutics (ALTH)	Small molecules for cancer	4
Ariad Pharmaceutic. (ARIA)	Gene regulation, stem cell, small molecules	4
Vasomedical (VASO)	Mechanical counterpulsation angina therapy	4
Genzyme Oncology (GZMO)	Vaccines, antiangiogenesis, cell path. for cancer	4
Lorus Therapeutics (LORFF)	Antisense & antiangiogenesis for cancer	4
BioCryst (BCRX)	Drug development for influenza & immune system	4
La Jolla Pharma. (LJPC)	Humanized antibodies for lupus, thrombosis	4
Axys Pharma. (AXPH)	Drug discovery	4
Cell Pathways (CLPA)	Novel anticancer drugs	4
Connectics (CNCT)	Therapeutics for dermatology	4
SangStat (SANG)	International transplant medicine specialist	4
Lynx Therapeutics (LYNX)	DNA analysis technologies & equipment	4
Pharmos (PARS)	Drug discovery in steroids, angiogenesis	4
Genzyme Transgen. (GZTC)	Humanized proteins from transgenic animals	4
Repligen Corp. (RGEN)	Drugs for autism, organ transplant, cancer	4
Aronex (ARNX)	Therapies for cancer & infectious disease	4
Cytoclonal (CYPH)	Drug development from genomics	4
AVI Biopharma (AVII)	Novel antisense antibiotics, cancer antibodies	4
Immune Response (IMNR)	Immune therapies for HIV, gene therapy	4
Magainin (MAGN)	Antiangiogenesis, respiratory genomics, infection	4
Axonyx (AXYX)	Alzheimer's and memory therapies	4
Boston Life Sciences (BLSI)	Broad scientific platform, 11 products in pipeline	4
Genzyme Surgical (GZSP)	Devices, materials & therapeutics for surgery	4
Cellegy (CLGY)	Cosmeceuticals & prescription drugs	4
Neurobiological Tech (NTII)	Drug development for neurological disorders	4
Vivus (VVUS)	Sexual dysfunction treatments	4
Nexell Therapeutics (NEXL)	Stem cells from immune system to fight disease	4
AVAX (AVXT)	Cancer vaccines from patient tumor	4
Unigene (UGNE)	Oral delivery of therapeutic peptides	4
Immtech Int'l (IMMT)	Pneumonia & antiparasitic drug development	4
Interneuron (IPIC)	Drug dev. for neural disease: stroke & anxiety	4
Hollis Eden Pharma (HEPH)	Novel AIDS & antiviral therapies	4
Amer. Biogenetic (MABA)	Nerve cell regeneration	4
Aastrom (ASTM)	Stem cells	4
Bioject (BJCT)	Needle-free drug delivery	4
Cortex Pharma (CORX)	Drugs for brain dysfunction & degeneration	4

Cap (mils)	P/E Ratio	EPS	Performance/12 mo.	Beta	Web Site
323	N/A	(1.05)	16	0.8	www.genxy.com
314	N/A	(0.28)	Since 2000 IPO −71	N/A	www.aclara.com
310	N/A	(1.25)	48	1.4	www.miravant.com
287	N/A	(0.44)	85	1.1	www.onyx-pharm.com
284	N/A	(0.13)	230	1.5	www.genomecorp.com
282	N/A	(2.46)	−23	−0.16	www.viropharma.com
275	N/A	(0.75)	−10	1.6	www.organogenesis.com
275	N/A	(0.15)	40	N/A	www.vasogen.com
261	N/A	(1.56)	168	0.76	www.hyseq.com
255	N/A	(1.24)	75	−0.02	www.valentis.com
253	N/A	(0.98)	71	1	www.nanogen.com
251	N/A	(0.29)	42	0.2	www.genelabs.com
250	N/A	(0.98)	106	0.69	www.rpi.com
247	N/A	(0.16)	418	−2.67	www.techniclone.com
243	N/A	(0.09)	26	0.77	www.advancedtissue.com
239	N/A	(3.04)	−67	0.2	www.tripharm.com
231	N/A	(2.45)	178	−0.04	www.atrixlabs.com
214	N/A	(0.55)	367	0.01	www.neorx.com
204	N/A	(0.57)	43	1.4	www.vionpharm.com.com
200	N/A	(0.28)	−22	−0.69	www.hemispherx.com
196	N/A	(10.00)	Since 2000 IPO −22	N/A	www.allos.com
196	N/A	(0.12)	390	0.19	www.ariad.com
181	N/A	0.02	221	0.6	www.vasomedical.com
177	N/A	(1.74)	132	N/A	www.genzyme.com
175	N/A	(0.06)	344	0.5	www.lorusthera.com
170	N/A	(0.13)	−59	0.6	www.biocryst.com
168	N/A	(0.53)	560	−0.3	www.ljpc.com
160	N/A	(1.12)	14	−0.04	www.axyspharm.com/index.html
160	N/A	(0.99)	−39	−0.8	www.cellpathways.com
151	N/A	(0.47)	−14	1	www.connectics.com
148	N/A	(2.58)	−62	1.4	www.sangstat.com
142	N/A	(0.31)	9	0.35	www.lynxgen.com
138	N/A	(0.11)	64	0.45	www.pharmoscorp.com
136	N/A	(0.70)	136	0.44	www.genzyme.com
132	N/A	(0.20)	14	−0.59	www.repligen.com
127	N/A	(0.16)	41	0.81	www.aronex.com
125	N/A	(0.51)	31	0.59	www.cytoclonal.com
124	N/A	(0.52)	−8	−0.68	www.antivirals.com
122	N/A	(0.52)	−1	0.7	www.imnr.com
119	N/A	(0.40)	168	0.5	www.magainin.com
108	N/A	(0.07)	Since 2000 IPO −13	N/A	www.axonyx.com
105	N/A	(1.08)	17	0.29	www.bostonlifesciences.com
102	N/A	(2.89)	34	N/A	www.genzyme.com
93	N/A	(0.83)	67	0.33	www.cellegy.com
90	N/A	(0.22)	Since IPO +60	N/A	www.ntii.com
89	5.4	0.51	29	1.8	www.vivus.com
87	N/A	(1.95)	−17	−0.6	www.nexellinc.com
70	N/A	(0.89)	58	0.74	www.avax-tech.com
70	N/A	(0.24)	126	0.39	www.unigene.com
68	N/A	(1.57)	−55	N/A	www.immtech-international.com
65	8	0.19	25	1.5	www.interneuron.com
64	N/A	(2.09)	−65	0.64	www.holliseden.com
55	N/A	(0.02)	177	1.23	www.mabxa.com
50	N/A	(0.04)	150	1.05	www.aastrom.com
47	N/A	(0.88)	78	1.5	www.bioject.com
46	N/A	(0.08)	235	0.2	www.cortexpharm.com

(Continued)

Company Name (Symbol)	Industry Sector	Tier
Neotherapeutics (NEOT)	Small molecules for nerve regeneration: Alzheimer's	4
Gliatech (GLIA)	Antibodies to control surgical scars	4
Trega Biosciences (TRGA)	Drug development services, information, chemistry	4
Aquila Biopharm. (AQLA)	Immune system drugs for HIV & other disorders	4
Cypress Bioscience (CYPB)	Devices to treat immune disorders	4
Cambridge NeuroSci (CNSI)	Drugs to treat nervous disorders & regeneration	4
Genetronics (GEB)	DNA delivery through electropororation	4
Endorex (DOR)	Drug delivery	4
Epimmune (EPMN)	Vaccines for cancer, viruses, malaria	4
Cyanotech (CYAN)	Nutraceuticals	4
Alfacell (ACEL)	Cancer therapy through ribonucleases	4
Protein Polymer (PPTI)	Biomaterials for surgery & wound healing	4
Hybridion (HYBN)	Antisense technology: cancer, viruses, eye diseases	4
ProCyte (PRCY)	Cosmeceuticals for aging & hair loss	4
Amarillo Bioscience (AMAR)	Drugs discovery for fibromyalgia & hepatitis	4
Oxis International (OXIS)	Therapies to limit damage done by free radicals	4

Cap (mils)	P/E Ratio	EPS	Performance/12 mo.	Beta	Web Site
44	N/A	(5.10)	−63	1.6	www.neotherapeutics.com
41	N/A	(0.70)	−59	0.9	www.gliatech.com
37	N/A	(0.54)	30	0.6	www.trega.com
33	N/A	(0.17)	210	0.71	www.aquilabio.com
33	N/A	(0.16)	−66	0.5	www.cypressbio.com
31	N/A	(0.19)	85	−0.85	www.cambneuro.com
30	N/A	(0.38)	−62	N/A	www.genetronics.com
25	N/A	(0.59)	6	−1	www.endorex.com
21	N/A	(0.50)	5	0.3	www.epimmune.com
19	N/A	(0.26)	95	1.1	www.cyanotech.com
15	N/A	(0.02)	74	N/A	www.alfacell.com
13	N/A	(0.23)	228	−2.5	www.ppti.com
12	N/A	(0.83)	0	−0.56	www.hybridion.com
11	N/A	(0.26)	−9	0.17	www.tricomin.com
8	N/A	(0.80)	83	−0.17	www.amacell.com
8	N/A	(0.41)	73	1	www.oxis.com

* Indicates unusual accounting circumstances.
Source: Data from WindowsOnWallSt.com as of November 2000.

Company Name (Symbol)	Industry Sector	Tier
Tier One Companies		
Agilent (A)	Biochip & equipment maker	1
Allergan (AGN)	Established eye care company	1
Alza (AZA)	Pharmaceuticals & drug delivery technology	1
Amgen (AMGN)	Major drugs on market & protein discovery	1
Biogen (BGEN)	Drug discovery & sales worldwide	1
Chiron (CHIR)	Vaccines for cancer, infectious & CV disease	1
Elan plc (ELN)	Drug discovery & delivery	1
Genentech (DNA)	Engineering therapeutic proteins	1
Genzyme General (GENZ)	Gene therapy, multiple disease targets	1
IDEC (IDPH)	Antibodies & isotopes for cancer & immune disease	1
Immunex (IMNX)	Antibodies & immune control for arthritis	1
Invitrogen (IVGN)	Genomic & biological research supplies & services	1
Medimmune (MEDI)	Antibacterials, antibodies & antiangiogenesis	1
Applera (ABI)	Instruments, software for genomics & proteomics	1
Quest Diagnostic (DGX)	Leader in diagnostic & information services	1
Tier Two Companies		
Abgenix (ABGX)	Monoclonal antibodies, transgenic mice	2
Affymetrix (AFFX)	Leading maker of biochip microarrays	2
Alpharma (ALO)	Generic drug maker	2
BioChem Pharma (BCHE)	Drug discovery	2
Celera (CRA)	Genomics	2
Celgene (CELG)	Drug development for cancer includes Thalidomide	2
Cell Therapeutics (CTIC)	Novel cancer & leukemia therapies	2
Celltech (CLL)	British biotech-specialist in antibodies & genomics	2
Gilead (GILD)	Novel therapies for infectious diseases	2
Human Genome S. (HGSI)	Drug discovery from genes to proteins	2
ICOS (ICOS)	Small molecules, antibodies, anti-inflammatories	2
Imclone (IMCL)	Antiangiogenesis, cancer vaccines, growth blockers	2
Medarex (MEDX)	Monoclonal antibodies for cancer & immune disease	2
Millennium (MLNM)	Vertically integrated: genomics to drugs	2
Protein Design Lab (PDLI)	Specialist in humanized monoclonal antibodies	2
QLT Inc. (QLTI)	Photodynamic therapy for eyes & immune disease	2
Sepracor (SEPR)	ICE pharmaceuticals: "improved chemical entities"	2
Shire Pharam. Plc (SHPGY)	International specialty pharmaceutical developer	2
Vertex (VRTX)	Small molecule drugs in-house & contract	2
Tier Three Companies		
Alexion (ALXN)	Immune system treatments	3
Alkermes (ALKS)	Drug delivery	3
Aurora Bio (ABSC)	Genomic materials & equipment	3
Aviron (AVIR)	Vaccines to fight viruses	3
Caliper (CALP)	Biochips & high throughput analysis systems	3
Cell Genesys (CEGE)	Cancer vaccines & gene therapy	3
Cephalon (CEPH)	Neurologically active drugs	3
COR Therap. (CORR)	Cardiovascular disease specialist	3
Corixa (CRXA)	Immune therapies for cancer & infectious disease	3
Cubist (CBST)	Specialist in fungal & microbial infection therapy	3
CuraGen (CRGN)	Genomic discovery & drug development	3
CV Therapeutics (CVTX)	Cardiovascular disease specialist	3
deCODE Genetics (DCGN)	Genomics based on Icelandic population	3
Diversa (DVSA)	Industrial genomics & gene shuffling	3
Enzo Biochem (ENZ)	Antisense therapy for viruses & immune regulation	3
Genencor (GCOR)	Industrial, agric., healthcare biotechnology	3
Guilford (GLFD)	Nerve regeneration, cancer, drug delivery, prodrugs	3
Immunogen (IMGN)	Antibodies & prodrugs for cancer	3

Cap (mils)	P/E Ratio	EPS	Performance/12 mo.	Beta	Web Site
$ 2,100	28	$1.68	26%	N/A	www.agilent.com
11,000	56	0.41	73	0.32	www.allergan.com
9,000	60	0.23	72	0.61	www.alza.com
67,000	58	0.33	32	0.85	www.ext.Amgen.com
7,900	25	2.12	−30	0.7	www.biogen.com
8,400	49	0.88	32	0.9	www.chiron.com
14,000	91	0.56	78	0.56	www.elan.ie/home/.com
38,000	N/A *	(0.41)	62	N/A*	www.gene.com
7,000	30	2.61	114	0.8	www.genzyme.com
8,000	226	0.78	154	1.4	www.idecpharm.com
2,200	183	0.22	71	1.7	www.immunex.com
3,900	2100	0.04	163	N/A	www.invitrogen.com
13,000	150	0.41	41	1.3	www.medimmune.com
19,000	N/A	0.94	124	N/A	www.pecorporation.com
5,000	84	1.30	263	0.2	www.questdiagnostics.com
1,500	N/A	(0.25)	110	1.33	www.aastrom.com
3,300	N/A	0.01	24	1.5	www.affymetrix.com
1,300	22	0.48	2	0.07	www.alpharma.com
2,300	11	2.06	1	1.18	www.biochem-pharma.com
2,500	N/A	(1.78)	54	N/A	www.celera.com
4,300	N/A	(0.13)	217	1.1	www.celgene.com
1,300	N/A	(2.49)	1141	−0.1	www.cticseattle.com
9,000	N/A	0*	17	N/A	www.celltech.co.uk
3,290	N/A	(0.81)	42	1.6	www.gilead.com
8,200	N/A	(2.27)	136	0.21	www.hgsi.com
2,200	N/A	(1.01)	30	0.73	www.icos.com
3,100	N/A	(0.83)	131	0.05	www.imclone.com
2,700	N/A	(0.28)	575	0.5	www.medarex.com
1,100	N/A	(3.59)	138	0.3	www.mlnm.com
4,290	N/A	(0.15)	376	0.9	www.pdl.com
3,900	N/A	(0.06)	6	1.2	www.qltinc.com
5,600	N/A	(2.71)	55	0.6	www.sepracor.com
4,800	N/A	0.00	76	0.4	www.shire.com
4,300	N/A	(0.53)	465	0.7	www.vpharm.com
1,100	N/A	(1.47)	304	1.13	www.alexionpharm.com
1,700	N/A	(0.19)	39	0.55	www.alkermes.com
725	65	0.55	210	−0.05	www.aurorabio.com
1,180	N/A	(4.94)	203	0.96	www.aviron.com
959	N/A	(1.74)	18	N/A	www.calipertech.com
764	6	3.39*	147	0.36	www.cellgenesys.com
1,900	N/A	(1.57)	112	0.7	www.cephalon.com
2,000	N/A	(0.44)	287	0.2	www.corr.com
738	N/A	(2.83)	103	0.5	www.corixa.com
950	N/A	(1.22)	225	0.7	www.cubist.com
1,600	N/A	(0.71)	210	1	www.curagen.com
1,300	N/A	(1.71)	395	−0.36	www.cvt.com
761	N/A	(0.23)	Since IPO −37	N/A	www.decode.com
800	N/A	(0.81)	Since IPO 26	N/A	www.diversa.com
940	148	0.25	44	0.75	www.enzo.com
1,100	N/A	(0.54)	Since IPO −21	N/A	www.genecor.com
460	N/A	(1.53)	30	0.7	www.guilfordpharm.com
1,100	N/A	(0.14)	700	0.02	www.immunogen.com

(Continued)

Company Name (Symbol)	Industry Sector	Tier
Immunomedics (IMMU)	Antibodies targeted at cancer with radioisotopes	3
Incyte (INCY)	Genomics & functional genomics data	3
Inhale (INHL)	Oral drug delivery specialist	3
Ligand Pharma. (LGND)	Drugs for specialty uses, wide range of targets	3
Maxim Pharma (MAXM)	Cancer therapy by immune system management	3
Maxygen (MAXY)	Molecular breeding or gene shuffling	3
Molecular Devices (MDCC)	Bioanalytical devices, combinatorial chemistry	3
Myriad (MYGN)	Genomics & proteomics for cancer therapies	3
Praecis (PRCS)	Developer of cancer & pain drugs, Ligand-based	3
Titan Pharma (TTP)	Drug development for Parkinson's, schizophrenia	3
Transkaryotic (TKTX)	Gene therapy, gene activated proteins, proteins	3
Trimeris (TRMS)	Vaccines to prevent viral infection from HIV/AIDS	3

Tier Four Companies

Company Name (Symbol)	Industry Sector	Tier
AVI Biopharma (AVII)	Novel antisense antibiotics, cancer antibodies	4
Aastrom (ASTM)	Stem cells	4
Aclara (ACLA)	Biochips, micro-fluidics	4
Adv. Tissue Sci. (ATIS)	Tissue replacement & regeneration	4
Alfacell (ACEL)	Cancer therapy through ribonucleases	4
Alliance Pharma (ALLP)	Blood substitutes, specialty chemicals	4
Allos Therapeutics (ALTH)	Small molecules for cancer	4
Amarillo Bioscience (AMAR)	Drugs discovery for fibromyalgia & hepatitis	4
Amer. Biogenetic (MABA)	Nerve cell regeneration	4
Antigenics (AGEN)	Immune system therapies	4
Aphton (APHT)	Anticancer vaccines using antibodies	4
Aquila Biopharm. (AQLA)	Immune system drugs for HIV & other disorders	4
Ariad Pharmaceutic. (ARIA)	Gene regulation, stem cell, small molecules	4
Aronex (ARNX)	Therapies for cancer & infectious disease	4
ArQule (ARQL)	Combinatorial chemistry & genomics	4
Atrix (ATRX)	Drug delivery	4
Avant Immunother. (AVAN)	Immune therapies for cardiac & viral disease	4
AVAX (AVXT)	Cancer vaccines from patient tumor	4
Avigen (AVGN)	Gene delivery technologies, gene therapy	4
Axonyx (AXYX)	Alzheimer's and memory therapies	4
Axys Pharma. (AXPH)	Drug discovery	4
BioCryst (BCRX)	Drug development for influenza & immune system	4
Bioject (BJCT)	Needle-free drug delivery	4
BioMarin (BMRN)	Enzymes for genetic disease	4
Biomatrix (BXM)	Cosmeceutical, biomaterials	4
Biopure (BPUR)	Blood replacement	4
Biosite Diagnostic (BSTE)	Emergency diagnostics	4
Bio-Technology Gen. (BTGC)	Drug development & marketing	4
Boston Life Sciences (BLSI)	Broad scientific platform, 11 products in pipeline	4
Cambridge NeuroSci (CNSI)	Drugs to treat nervous disorders & regeneration	4
Cell Pathways (CLPA)	Novel anticancer drugs	4
Cellegy (CLGY)	Cosmeceuticals & prescription drugs	4
Collateral Therap. (CLTX)	Gene therapy for cardiovascular disease	4
Connectics (CNCT)	Therapeutics for dermatology	4
Cortex Pharma (CORX)	Drugs for brain dysfunction & degeneration	4
Corvas (CVAS)	Cardiovascular disease specialist	4
Coulter (CLTR)	Cancer Therapies based on antibodies & isotopes	4
Curis (CRIS)	Cell regeneration specialist	4
Cyanotech (CYAN)	Nutraceuticals	4
Cypress Bioscience (CYPB)	Devices to treat immune disorders	4
Cytoclonal (CYPH)	Drug development from genomics	4
Cytogen (CYTO)	Drug discovery in antibodies and proteomics	4
Dendreon (DNDN)	Immune therapies for cancer	4

Cap (mils)	P/E Ratio	EPS	Performance/12 mo.	Beta	Web Site
1,000	N/A	(0.20)	890	2.33	www.immunomedics.com
1,900	N/A	(0.47)	94	0.5	www.incyte.com
2,000	N/A	(2.03)	212	0.45	www.inhale.com
803	N/A	(1.31)	39	1.7	www.ligand.com
800	N/A	(5.17)	150	-0.14	www.maxim.com
1,100	N/A	(1.73)	Since IPO -9	N/A	www.maxygen.com
857	N/A	(0.20)	73	1.6	www.moldev.com
1,600	N/A	(0.41)	395	-0.2	www.myriad.com
1,100	N/A	(0.90)	Since IPO +67	N/A	www.praecis.com
970	N/A	(0.74)	169	0.2	www.titanpharm.com
1,000	N/A	(1.90)	-2	1.5	www.tktx.com
1,000	N/A	(1.91)	203	-0.3	www.trimeris.com
124	N/A	(0.52)	-8	-0.68	www.antivirals.com
50	N/A	(0.04)	150	1.05	www.aastrom.com
314	N/A	(0.28)	Since 2000 IPO -71	N/A	www.aclara.com
243	N/A	(0.09)	26	0.77	www.advancedtissue.com
15	N/A	(0.02)	74	N/A	www.alfacell.com
444	N/A	(0.29)	116	0.32	www.allp.com
196	N/A	(10.00)	Since 2000 IPO -22	N/A	www.allos.com
8	N/A	(0.80)	83	-0.17	www.amacell.com
55	N/A	(0.02)	177	1.23	www.mabxa.com
342	N/A	(0.94)	Since 2000 IPO -13	N/A	www.antigenics.com
444	N/A	(0.92)	103	0.75	www.aphton.com
33	N/A	(0.17)	210	0.71	www.aquilabio.com
196	N/A	(0.12)	390	0.19	www.ariad.com
127	N/A	(0.16)	41	0.81	www.aronex.com
370	N/A	(0.35)	275	0.44	www.arqule.com
231	N/A	(2.45)	178	-0.04	www.atrixlabs.com
429	N/A	(0.24)	267	0.25	www.tcell.com
70	N/A	(0.89)	58	0.74	www.avax-tech.com
588	N/A	(1.03)	20	0.75	www.avigen.com
108	N/A	(0.07)	Since 2000 IPO -13	N/A	www.axonyx.com
160	N/A	(1.12)	14	-0.04	www.axyspharm.com/index.html
170	N/A	(0.13)	-59	0.6	www.biocryst.com
47	N/A	(0.88)	78	1.5	www.bioject.com
326	N/A	(1.02)	-36	N/A	www.biomarinpharm.com
450	26	0.21	-19	0.27	www.biomatrix.com/index.htm
663	N/A	(1.71)	147	N/A	www.biopure.com
426	82	0.13	160	2.2	www.biosite.com
431	49	0.16	-35	1.4	www.biogenerica.com
105	N/A	(1.08)	17	0.29	www.bostonlifesciences.com
31	N/A	(0.19)	85	-0.85	www.cambneuro.com
160	N/A	(0.99)	-39	-0.8	www.cellpathways.com
93	N/A	(0.83)	67	0.33	www.cellegy.com
379	N/A	(0.94)	60	1.2	www.collateralthx.com
151	N/A	(0.47)	-14	1	www.connectics.com
46	N/A	(0.08)	235	0.2	www.cortexpharm.com
500	N/A	(0.54)	554	0.7	www.corvas.com
660	N/A	(3.18)	100	1.8	www.coulterpharm.com
400	N/A	(15.00)	Since IPO -13	N/A	www.curis.com
19	N/A	(0.26)	95	1.1	www.cyanotech.com
33	N/A	(0.16)	-66	0.5	www.cypressbio.com
125	N/A	(0.51)	31	0.59	www.cytoclonal.com
332	N/A	(0.27)	169	0.5	www.cytogen.com
326	N/A	(9.03)	Since IPO -12	N/A	www.dendreon.com

(Continued)

Company Name (Symbol)	Industry Sector	Tier
Digene (DIGE)	Pharmacogenomics & diagnostics for women	4
Emisphere (EMIS)	Oral drug delivery specialist	4
Endorex (DOR)	Drug delivery	4
EntreMed (EMED)	Antiangiogenesis cancer treatments	4
Epimmune (EPMN)	Vaccines for cancer, viruses, malaria	4
Gene Logic (GLGC)	Genomics & functional genomics data	4
Genelabs Tech. (GNLB)	Small molecule drugs bind to RNA of viruses,lupus	4
Genetronics (GEB)	DNA delivery through electropororation	4
Genome Therap. (GENE)	Genomics-based drug discovery	4
Genset (GENXY)	Genomics, pharmacogenomics, drug discovery	4
Genta (GNTA)	Antisense therapy for cancer	4
Genzyme Oncology (GZMO)	Vaccines, antiangiogenesis, cell path. for cancer	4
Genzyme Surgical (GZSP)	Devices, materials & therapeutics for surgery	4
Genzyme Transgen. (GZTC)	Humanized Proteins from transgenic animals	4
Geron (GERN)	Anticancer & anti-aging stem cell therapy	4
Gliatech (GLIA)	Antibodies to control surgical scars	4
Hemispherx (HEB)	RNA-based drugs for HIV & CFS	4
Hollis Eden Pharma (HEPH)	Novel AIDS & antiviral therapies	4
Hybridion (HYBN)	Antisense technology: cancer, viruses, eye diseases	4
Hyseq (HYSQ)	Genomic discovery & drug development & biochips	4
Ilex Oncology (ILXO)	Contract cancer research	4
Immtech Int'l (IMMT)	Pneumonia & antiparasitic drug development	4
Immune Response (IMNR)	Immune therapies for HIV, gene therapy	4
Interneuron (IPIC)	Drug dev. for neural disease: stroke & anxiety	4
Isis Pharmaceuticals (ISIP)	Antisense drug development for cancer & viruses	4
Kos Pharmaceutical (KOSP)	Drug discovery, development, drug delivery	4
La Jolla Pharma. (LJPC)	Humanized antibodies for lupus, thrombosis	4
Large Scale Bio (LSBC)	Gene expression analysis & drug development	4
Lexicon Genetics (LEXG)	Genomics & functional genomics, mouse clones	4
Lorus Therapeutics (LORFF)	Antisense & antiangiogenesis for cancer	4
Lynx Therapeutics (LYNX)	DNA Analysis technologies & equipment	4
Magainin (MAGN)	Antiangiogenesis, respiratory genomics, infection	4
MGI Pharma (MOGN)	Cancer & rheumatology drug development	4
Miravant Medical (MRVT)	Photodynamic therapy, multiple targets	4
Nanogen (NGEN)	Biochips integrating chemical & electric function	4
NeoPharm (NEOL)	Cancer diagnostics & treatment, drug delivery	4
NeoRx (NERX)	Cancer therapies: internal targeted radiation	4
Neotherapeutics (NEOT)	Small molecules for nerve regeneration: Alzheimer's	4
Neurobiological Tech (NTII)	Drug development for neurological disorders	4
Neurocrine (NBIX)	Psychiatric, degenerative, inflammatory, cancer drugs	4
Neurogen (NRGN)	Drugs to regulate cellular communication	4
Nexell Therapeutics (NEXL)	Stem cells from immune system to fight disease	4
Onyx Pharma (ONXX)	Developer of "armed virus" technology for cancers	4
Orchid Biosciences (ORCH)	Bioinformatics, SNP analysis & SNP products	4
Organogenesis (ORG)	Living & connective tissue replacement	4
Oxis International (OXIS)	Therapies to limit damage done by free radicals	4
Pain Therapeutics (PTIE)	Developing novel drugs for pain management	4
Pathogenesis (PGNS)	New Antibiotics & inhalable drug delivery systems	4
Pharmacopeia (PCOP)	Lead discovery for drugs & high throughput analysis	4
Pharmacyclics (PCYC)	Photodynamic therapy, cancer & vascular disease	4
Pharmos (PARS)	Drug discovery in steroids, angiogenesis	4
ProCyte (PRCY)	Cosmeceuticals for aging & hair loss	4
Progenics (PGNX)	Developing drugs for cancer, HIV & other viruses	4
Protein Polymer (PPTI)	Biomaterials for surgery & wound healing	4
Regerneron (REGN)	Antibodies & designer proteins, genomics	4
Repligen Corp. (RGEN)	Drugs for autism, organ transplant, cancer	4

Cap (mils)	P/E Ratio	EPS	Performance/12 mo.	Beta	Web Site
561	N/A	(0.48)	85	1.1	www.digene.com
488	N/A	(1.92)	64	1.9	www.emisphere.com
25	N/A	(0.59)	6	−1	www.endorex.com
440	N/A	(3.24)	7	0.47	www.entremed.com
21	N/A	(0.50)	5	0.3	www.epimmune.com
434	N/A	(1.01)	162	0.9	www.genelogic.com
251	N/A	(0.29)	42	0.2	www.genelabs.com
30	N/A	(0.38)	−62	N/A	www.genetronics.com
284	N/A	(0.13)	230	1.5	www.genomecorp.com
323	N/A	(1.05)	16	0.8	www.genxy.com
370	N/A	(1.19)	78	1.1	www.genta.com
177	N/A	(1.74)	132	N/A	www.genzyme.com
102	N/A	(2.89)	34	N/A	www.genzyme.com
136	N/A	(0.70)	136	0.44	www.genzyme.com
446	N/A	(1.93)	75	0.36	www.geron.com
41	N/A	(0.70)	−59	0.9	www.gliatech.com
200	N/A	(0.28)	−22	−0.69	www.hemispherx.com
64	N/A	(2.09)	−65	0.64	www.holliseden.com
12	N/A	(0.83)	0	−0.56	www.hybridion.com
261	N/A	(1.56)	168	0.76	www.hyseq.com
680	N/A	(0.83)	61	0.85	www.ilexoncology.com
68	N/A	(1.57)	−55	N/A	www.immtech-international.com
122	N/A	(0.52)	−1	0.7	www.imnr.com
65	8	0.19	25	1.5	www.interneuron.com
417	N/A	(1.69)	−29	0.9	www.isip.com
456	N/A	(2.23)	360	−0.13	www.kospharm.com
168	N/A	(0.53)	560	−0.3	www.ljpc.com
325	N/A	(1.66)	Since IPO −49	N/A	www.lsbc.com
660	N/A	(0.88)	Since IPO +35	N/A	www.lexicon-genetics.com
175	N/A	(0.06)	344	0.5	www.lorusthera.com
142	N/A	(0.31)	9	0.35	www.lynxgen.com
119	N/A	(0.40)	168	0.5	www.magainin.com
330	N/A	(0.12)	66	0.5	www.mgipharma.com
310	N/A	(1.25)	48	1.4	www.miravant.com
253	N/A	(0.98)	71	1	www.nanogen.com
325	N/A	(0.07)	Since IPO +41	1.6	www.neophrm.com
214	N/A	(0.55)	367	0.01	www.neorx.com
44	N/A	(5.10)	−63	1.6	www.neotherapeutics.com
90	N/A	(0.22)	Since IPO +60	N/A	www.ntii.com
732	N/A	(1.07)	121	1.2	www.neurocrine.com
493	N/A	(1.09)	100	0.85	www.neurogen.com
87	N/A	(1.95)	−17	−0.6	www.nexellinc.com
287	N/A	(0.44)	85	1.1	www.onyx-pharm.com
421	N/A	(0.27)	Since IPO +20	N/A	www.orchid.com
275	N/A	(0.75)	−10	1.6	www.organogenesis.com
8	N/A	(0.41)	73	1	www.oxis.com
517	N/A	(2.90)	Since IPO +19	N/A	www.paintrials.com
640	N/A	(0.13)	164	1.2	www.pathogenesis.com
572	N/A	0.03	46	0.8	www.pharmacopeia.com
690	N/A	(1.80)	26	0.8	www.pcyc.com
138	N/A	(0.11)	64	0.45	www.pharmoscorp.com
11	N/A	(0.26)	−9	0.17	www.tricomin.com
324	N/A	(0.17)	−7	1.6	www.progenics.com
13	N/A	(0.23)	228	−2.5	www.ppti.com
960	N/A	(0.45)	239	−0.04	www.regeneron.com
132	N/A	(0.20)	14	−0.59	www.repligen.com

(Continued)

Company Name (Symbol)	Industry Sector	Tier
Ribozyme Pharma. (RZYM)	Ribozyme therapy to destroy viruses, & cancer	4
SangStat (SANG)	International transplant medicine specialist	4
Sequenom (SQNM)	Genotyping & SNP analysis for industry & drug dev.	4
Skye Pharma plc (SKYE)	Leading company in drug delivery	4
SuperGen (SUPG)	Acquires & develops promising drugs from innovators	4
Targeted Genetics (TGEN)	Gene therapy for multiple targets	4
Techniclone (TCLN)	Targeting methods for cancer therapy	4
Trega Biosciences (TRGA)	Drug development services, information, chemistry	4
Triangle (VIRS)	Specialist in developing antiviral drugs	4
Tularik (TLRK)	Gene expression control via small molecule drugs	4
Unigene (UGNE)	Oral delivery of therapeutic peptides	4
Valentis (VLTS)	Gene delivery & therapy to stimulate cytokines	4
Vasogen (MEW)	Devices to treat immune system disorders	4
Vasomedical (VASO)	Mechanical counterpulsation angina therapy	4
VaxGen (VXGN)	Developing AIDS vaccine	4
Vical (VICL)	Gene delivery "naked DNA" for cancer	4
Vion (VION)	Cancer drugs, prodrugs, drug delivery	4
Viropharma (VPHM)	Antiviral pharmaceuticals target RNA viruses	4
Visible Genetics (VIGN)	Genotyping, pharmacogenomics, gene sequencing	4
Vivus (VVUS)	Sexual dysfunction treatments	4
Xoma (XOMA)	Drug production technologies & drug development	4

Cap (mils)	P/E Ratio	EPS	Performance/12 mo.	Beta	Web Site
250	N/A	(0.98)	106	0.69	www.rpi.com
148	N/A	(2.58)	−62	1.4	www.sangstat.com
473	N/A	(6.34)	−10	N/A	www.sequenom.com
481	N/A	(0.71)	6	−0.7	www.skyepharma.com
664	N/A	(1.15)	−39	0.5	www.supergen.com
389	N/A	(1.05)	215	0.29	www.targetedgenetics.com
247	N/A	(0.16)	418	−2.67	www.techniclone.com
37	N/A	(0.54)	30	0.6	www.trega.com
239	N/A	(3.04)	−67	0.2	www.tripharm.com
1,500	N/A	(1.02)	42	N/A	www.tularik.com
70	N/A	(0.24)	126	0.39	www.unigene.com
255	N/A	(1.24)	75	−0.02	www.valentis.com
275	N/A	(0.15)	40	N/A	www.vasogen.com
181	N/A	0.02	221	0.6	www.vasomedical.com
339	N/A	(1.70)	111	N/A	www.vaxgen.com
356	N/A	(0.30)	−15	1.1	www.vical.com
204	N/A	(0.57)	43	1.4	www.vionpharm.com.com
282	N/A	(2.46)	−23	−0.16	www.viropharma.com
391	N/A	(2.53)	68	0.84	www.visgen.com
89	5.4	0.51	29	1.8	www.vivus.com
709	N/A	(0.46)	286	0.83	www.xoma.com

* Indicates unusual accounting circumstances.
Source: Data from WindowsOnWallSt.com as of November 2000.

Resources

BOOKS

Bains, William, *Biotechnology from A to Z*
Oxford University Press, 1998, 2000, ISBN 0-19-963693-1
An excellent detailed reference to industry terminology

Barnum, Susan R., *Biotechnology: An Introduction*
Wadsworth Publishing, 1998, ISBN 0-534-23436-4
An excellent overview of biotech science and the industries that have evolved from it

Cantor, Charles R., *Genomics: The Science and Technology behind the Human Genome Project*
John Wiley & Sons, 1999, ISBN 0-471-59908-5
Advanced scientific overview

Fogeil, M., *The Genetics Problem Solver: A Complete Solution Guide to Any Textbook*
Research and Education Association, 1995, ISBN 0-87891-560-5
A problem-solving text for students of genetics in a question-and-answer format

Grace, Eric S., *Biotechnology Unzipped: Promises and Realities*
Joseph Henry Press, 1997, ISBN 0-309-05777-9
An easily comprehensible overview of the science behind the business

Kornberg, Arthur, *The Golden Helix: Inside Biotech Ventures*
University Science Books, 1995, ISBN 0-935702-32-6
A look at the developing years of the largest firms in the field from a scientist/businessman and Nobel Prize winner

Oliver, Richard W., *The Coming Biotech Age: The Business of Bio-Materials*
McGraw Hill, 2000, ISBN 0-07-135020-9
A very optimistic view of the future

Rensberger, Boyce, *Instant Biology: From Single Cells to Human Beings and Beyond*
Byron Preiss Visual Publications, 1996, ISBN 0-449-90701-5
A quick digest of the mechanisms at work in biological processes

Ridley, Matt, *Genome: The Autobiography of a Species in 23 Chapters*
HarperCollins/Perennial, 2000, ISBN 0-06-019497-9
A brilliant explanation of the roles of genes in human life

Roth, Cynthia Robbins, *From Alchemy to IPO: The Business of Biotechnology*
Perseus Publishing, 2000, ISBN 0-7382-0253-3
An inside report on the founding of the industry and speculation about its future

Tagliaferro, Linda and Mark Bloom, *The Complete Guide to Decoding Your Genes*
Macmillan, 1999, ISBN 0-07-135020-9.

Watson, James D., *The Double Helix: A Personal Account of the Discovery of the Structure of DNA*
Mentor/Penguin Putnam, 1969, ISBN 0-451-62787-3
One of the codiscoverers of the DNA molecule gives a fascinating, quirky account

Wolfe, Stephen L., *Molecular and Cellular Biology*
Wadsworth Publishing, 1993, ISBN 0-534-12408-9
A primer for biology students, but very difficult for the layperson

Also note:

Dodson, Bert, and Mahlon Hoagland, *The Way Life Works*
Times Books, 1995

Kolata, Gina, *Clone, the Road to Dolly and the Path Ahead*
William Morrow, 1998

Levine, Joseph S., and David T. Suzuki, *The Secret of Life: Redesigning the Living World*
W.H. Freeman, 1998.

Ridley, Matt, *Genome: The Autobiography of a Species in 23 Chapters*
HarperCollins, 2000, ISBN 0-06-019497-9.

ONLINE REFERENCES

The National Biotech Register. An industry Yellow Pages can be ordered at www.biotech-register.com.

BioSpace. A site to visit daily or to receive e-mail bulletins from on weekdays. These e-mail alerts cover the most interesting news and features of the day and linking to the daily news archive will provide most press releases and links to the most important news articles of the previous 24 hours. The Web site is crammed with links to every facet of the industry. BioSpace e-mail alerts are usually transmitted at midday, which is too late to get ahead of the news curve and too early to be a comprehensive review of the entire trading day. Go to www.biospace.com.

For an authoritative database of clinical trials, company research, and alliance profiles go to www.recap.com; also affiliated is www.signals-mag.com, which provides in-depth analysis in magazine format.

BioWorld Online. An excellent reference source that provides news, corporate financials and background, industry overviews, stock quotes, and reports on the status of Phase III trials. Go to www.bioworld.com.

Chemscope. One of the biggest and most detailed information resources an investor could want. Again, regular newsletters are available. Go to www.chemscope.com.

PR Newswire. Day traders should begin the day by inspecting the morning's announcements from the PR Newswire Health & Biotech sector. Go to www.prnewswire.com.

Raging Bull and BigCharts have a free graphic charting site for stocks. Go to www.BigCharts.com; see also www.quote.ragingbull.com.

Charting services. Available at WindowOnWallStreet.com.

BioABACUS. A database of biological terms, acronyms, and abbreviations. Go to www.nmsu.edu/~molbio/bioABACUShome.htm.

Industry. Beck on Biotech provides reports on the industry and its segments. Go to www.beckonbiotech.com; also see www.bioventureconsultants.com.

UCSF Links Page provides links to the industry, organizations, directories, and news broken down by sectors. Go to www.mdi.ucsf.edu/Biotech_links.html.

Biotechnology Industry News from Yahoo, a comprehensive listing of the day's industry news, organized by time of release. Go to www .biz.yahoo.com/news/biotechnology.html.

Biotech Sage provides a monthly newsletter and industry links. Go to www.biotechnav.com.

CancerNet from the National Cancer Institute provides a wealth of information about coping with disease as well as links for clinical trials. Go to www.cancernet.nci.nih.gov.

"DNA from the Beginning" is an animated instructional site. Go to www.vector.cshl.org/dnaftb/index.html.

Drug Discovery Online provides free e-mail news and industry information. Go to www.drugdiscoveryonline.com; see also www.qxhealth.com.

Industry and general financial analysis is available at www .desresources.com; see also www.smartmoney.com; www. marketguide.com; and www.multex.com.

Earnings estimates are available at www.whispernumbers.com; www .earningswhispers.com; and www.streetIQ.com.

DrugInfoNet provides information for healthcare consumers and professionals. Go to www.druginfonet.com.

The Biotech Yellow Pages provide company contact information, from Network Science. Go to www.netsci.org/Resources/Biotech /Yellowpages.

The National Biotechnology Information Facility (NBIF): A major database with links to 7,000 biotechnology resources. Go to www.nbif.org /indxbdy.html.

National Center for Biotechnology Information, part of the National Library of Medicine and the National Institutes of Health as a public resource. Information about gene and molecular sequences and structures. Go to www.ncbi.nlm.nih.gov.

The Biotechnology Industry Organization acts as a lobby group in Washington. Its Web site offers news, press releases, and links to member Web sites. Go to www.BIO.org.

The Pharmaceutical Research and Manufacturers of America represents Big Pharma. The site provides overviews of the industry and drugs in the pipeline. Go to www.phrma.org.

The Institute for Biotechnology Information provides information to the industry and contacts for biotech firms in the United States. Go to www.biotechinfo.com; in the United Kingdom, go to www.bioindustry .org.

Windhover Information produces several magazines on the industry. Go to www.windhover.com.

University of Pennsylvania Bioengineering. A Web site full of links to industries in every field of bioengineering. The capsule descriptions for the listed companies are useful. Go to www.seas.upenn.edu/be /misc/bmelink/cell.html.

Lippincott, Williams & Wilkins Internet Publishing Systems provides a list of Web sites that are specific to the various fields of genetic, biotech, and traditional medicine. I intended to reproduce the list but am restrained by copyright. Please go to www.cvtherapeutics.com.

The Brutlag Bioinformatics Group, a central bioinformatics Web link resource. Go to www.dna.stanford.edu/motif.

Informagen provides daily pharmaceutical industry news releases. Go to www.informagen.com/News/Pharmaceutical.html.

Medical Technology Stock Letter for the newsletter by one of the industry's best known observers. Go to www.bioinvest.com; see also www .ctsl.com.

Should you ever run out of biotech companies to research, check out the list of Innovative Drug Development Companies who have participated in that organization's meeting since 1992. Go to wwwcmuis.com /pastemer.htm.

Also worth browsing is www.bioportfolio.com/bio (United Kingdom), which lists 5,500 biobusinesses worldwide.

Also note: www.genengnews.com—A genetic engineering news-letter; www.techvestllc.com—A technical newsletter for the industry; www.bloomberg.com; www.kiplinger.com; www.morningstar.net; www.smallcapsonline.com—For investment info and tracking; www .biotech.icmb.utexas.edu—For a biotech dictionary; www.cellsalive .com—For graphic depictions of biological processes; www.aibs.org /core/index.html—American Institute of Biological Science; www.worldyinvestor.com—News and commentary.

For updated news, commentary, and web links, please visit the author's website at www.biowolff.com.

APPENDIX C

Glossary

adenine   One of the four basis units making up DNA (A). It binds to (T). In RNA adenine binds to Uracil (U). Therefore, the DNA pairing is AT and RNA pairing is AU.

adjuvant   A compound that increases the effectiveness of another drug or antibody.

amino acids   Biological molecules that serve many functions. Most importantly, these molecules form the basic building blocks of proteins. Protein structures are built from combinations of 20 different amino acids.

amniocentesis   The drawing of fluid from a mother's womb to diagnose genetic disorders.

amplification   Increasing the number of copies of a gene.

aneuploidy   The addition or deletion of parts of a chromosome.

angiogenesis   Used in reference to an agent that promotes the growth of new blood vessels. This is being used experimentally to improve oxygen supply to the heart, perhaps eliminating the need for some surgeries.

antiangiogenesis   Use of an agent to block the formation of new blood vessels. A growing tumor requires an increasing supply of blood and will call for the creation of new supply vessels. Blocking this process will starve a tumor.

antibody   Proteins produced by the immune system to fight infections in response to an antigen.

antigen   A molecule on the surface of an invading organism that the body identifies as alien and then uses to target an immune system attack.

antisense   An antisense therapy is a short, single strand of DNA or RNA that has a sequence complementary to the target. Its components bind tightly to genetic strands including messenger RNA and DNA to cancel out the mRNA instruction. It is antisense in that the "sense" or meaning of the target is canceled out.

apoptosis   Genetically programmed cell suicide, a natural process that biotechnology is attempting to harness in order to induce the death of cancer cells.

assay   Laboratory technique to search for a biological response to an agent.

attenuated   A reference to weakened infectious agents, able to stimulate an immune response without causing disease. Used in vaccines.

autoimmune disease   An attack by the immune system on the body's own tissues.

autoradiography   The imaging of radioactive labeled substances that are placed in the body and targeted to regions of interest.

autosome   A chromosome that has no role in sex determination.

bacteriophage   Also known as a phage, this is a virus that attacks bacteria.

base   A part of the DNA molecule. DNA bases are adenine (A), thymine (T), cytosine (C), and guanine (G). These bases combine in countless variations and sequences of variations to create a genetic code.

base pair   Two bases that bond together to form one rung in the spiral (or twisted ladder formation) of DNA. Base Adenine can only pair with Thymine. Cytosine can only pair with Guanine (the pairs are joined by weak bonds).

base sequence analysis   A system to determine the sequence of bases.

B-lymphocytes   These are attack cells that are produced to combat invading organisms. They are produced in lymph nodes, in blood, and the spleen.

biochip   What the microchip is to electronics, the biochip is to this field. Using technology borrowed from semiconductor makers, these tiny chips have become the crucible for research into many genetic diseases. Because of their small size, they are called microarrays, also DNA arrays, chip arrays, and DNA chips. They are a fundamental tool in "high throughput screening," which has greatly accelerated biological analysis and discovery. A new generation of biochips is being developed to analyze proteins.

bioinformatics   High-speed, high-volume analysis, and management of genomic and biological data.

biolistics   Also called gene gun or particle gun technology, biolistics involves firing a tiny metal particle bearing DNA into a cell. The technology is capable of transferring DNA into the cells of humans, plants, animals, and fungi.

bioluminescence The emission of light by a biological material, useful in genetic analysis and high throughput screening.

biomass Any large accumulation of biological matter. The term is often used to refer to quantities of cellular materials to be used for food or energy.

bioprospecting The search for new genetic and protein materials among unusual life forms, including species living in extremely hostile environments. These materials can be used for biotech processes that may be conducted in equally extreme conditions of temperature, pressure, and acidity.

bioreactor A tank used for large-scale fermentation of biological materials such as bacteria that have been engineered to produce a medicinal protein.

bioremediation The use of biological systems or organisms to clean up pollution.

blood brain barrier One of the great hurdles in medicine delivery. Larger molecules are prevented from reaching the brain through this defense system. It protects the brain from toxins but it also stops drugs from reaching important targets. Crossing this barrier is a major threshold in delivering medicine to the brain.

cancer cells Cells that multiply and do not respond to the body's usual instructions to regulate cell division. These can appear as solid tumors and nonsolid tumors (cancerous cells that proliferate in the body through blood or lymph systems).

carrier A carrier holds one copy of a mutant gene that may cause inherited disease. The carrier may not manifest this disease because two copies of a "recessive" mutant gene must be combined to create a disorder. Offspring of the carrier may develop disease from this "recessive gene" if both parents are carriers.

catalyst A chemical agent that facilitates a reaction without undergoing change.

cDNA (complementary DNA) DNA synthesized from mRNA (messenger RNA); often used in DNA probes to find complementary strands.

cell cycle The stages of cellular reproduction.

cell fusion The fusion of a sperm cell and an egg.

cell line Cells that grow in a lab rather than in a living organism.

cell membrane The outer shell of a cell, which regulates everything entering and leaving the cell.

cell trafficking   The method used by the body to move cells where they might be needed. An array of molecules on a cell wall functions like a zip code, instructing bodily mechanisms where to send the cell in question.

centromere   A portion of the chromosome that anchors spindle fibers during cell division. (It is centered between two telomeres that mark the end of a chromosome.)

chimera   An organism that carries information from two different organisms, created by grafting part of an embryo from one species onto an embryo from another.

chirality   The molecular equivalent of being right- or left-handed. Chemically, left-handed and right-handed proteins may be exactly the same but they behave differently because of their chirality, just as left and right hands are essentially the same but often cannot perform tasks in the same way.

chorionic villus sampling (CVS)   The same as amniocentesis except the cells to be examined come from the mother's placenta.

chromatid   A strand created by the duplication of a chromosome (in mitosis or meiosis).

chromatin   The basic material of chromosomes, created when strands of DNA are joined in a matrix by organic compounds.

chromosomes   The structures in a cell nucleus that contain genes. (They can be seen under a microscope during cell division.)

clone   An exact copy of an organism or part of an organism such as a length of DNA.

cloning vector   A DNA molecule that has been genetically engineered to allow the insertion of cloned DNA. Using a cloned vector, it is possible to make enormous quantities of cloned DNA.

codon   A grouping of three nucleotides in RNA that codes for a specific amino acid.

coenzyme   A molecule needed by an enzyme to trigger its action.

collagen   The protein that gives fullness or firmness to skin cells. As it breaks down, wrinkles form.

combinatorial chemistry   A method to test many variations of a chemical compound for effectiveness en-masse.

complementary sequence   A sequence of DNA base pairs that will match with and join with another DNA sequence. In a sense, it is a molecular mirror image.

conserved sequence A sequence of base pairs in DNA that has remained stable throughout the evolutionary process, for example, a sequence that is the same in a fruit fly and a human.

contig Pieces of cloned DNA that overlap, and give a picture of the whole chromosome.

cosmid A vector, or delivery vehicle, that allows for the insertion of large amounts of DNA into a target.

crossing-over During reproduction (meiosis), chromosomes from the mother and father line up in pairs and the two chromosomes may swap genes. Some paternal genes may wind up on the mother's chromosome and vice versa.

cytokine The name for a family of immune system proteins, including interleukins, interferons, tumor necrosis factor (TNF), and colony-stimulating factors (CSF).

cytoplasm The internal contents of a cell excepting the nucleus.

cytosine (C) One of the four bases of DNA and RNA. Cytosine always pairs with guanine (C-G).

diploid An organism or cell having two sets of chromosomes.

DNA (deoxyribonucleic acid) The master (double-helix) molecule that contains operating instructions for the body.

DNA probes Small sequences of the base units (A,T,C,G). They are tagged with a radioactive or fluorescent label and merge with complementary DNA sequences. Because the sequence of the probe is known, the sequence of a DNA fragment that pairs with it can be inferred.

DNA profiling Also called DNA typing or DNA fingerprinting, this test can link DNA samples to a specific person at a crime scene or settle maternity and paternity issues.

DNA replication Use of existing DNA to synthesize multiple copies.

DNA sequence The exact order of nucleotides (or bases) in a given stretch of DNA.

domain Any part of a protein that has a discrete, identifiable function.

dominant disease If a disease is dominantly inherited, only one copy of the gene is needed to express the disease in the child who receives the mutation (recessive diseases requires two copies).

dominant gene Unlike a recessive gene, a dominant gene from either parent is always expressed in the next generation (one copy is enough).

With recessive genes, two copies are needed to express this gene in off-spring.

electrophoresis (or gel electrophoresis) The system that creates the familiar DNA fingerprint, a ladder of bars of varying thickness. A gel containing DNA fragments is electrically charged and the smaller pieces move toward the attracting pole faster than the bigger ones. They spread out in a consistent way and a characteristic pattern is laid out.

electroporation The use of pulsed electrical charges to open pores in cell walls, allowing drugs or genetic material to be inserted.

embryo twinning A developing embryo (bigger than one cell but not too big) physically split at an early age. These two embryos or zygotes may grow into distinct but identical creatures.

enzyme A protein that may speed up (or catalyze) reactions in cell mechanisms.

eukaryote Any cell with a self-contained nucleus. Cells that store DNA without protection from the wall of a nucleus (like bacteria) are called prokaryotes.

exon The section of a gene that codes for (or helps express) a given protein (see intron).

expressed sequence tags (ESTs) One of the creations of Celera Genomics: a part of a gene that can be extracted with synthetic DNA.

Factor VIII and Factor IX Proteins for blood clotting. A shortage results in hemophilia.

gamete A complete reproductive cell: sperm or egg.

gene A length of DNA that provides the code for a specific bodily function, usually the production of a specific protein. Its sequence of base pairs and its position on a chromosome provide the code for the making of specific proteins or mRNA.

gene expression The complex process which a gene's code is expressed (or converted) into chemical structures such as proteins or mRNA.

gene family A group of genes believed to be related by their ability to make similar products in the body.

gene gun (see also biolistics) Mostly used in agricultural genomics. Think of a small BB coated with genetic material. It is shot into a plant cell and some information is transferred.

gene machine A high-tech automated genetic typewriter. A researcher types in the gene fragment he wants (e.g., ATCG), and it is delivered.

gene mapping   Establishing the positions of genes on DNA molecules.

gene pool   The grand total of all genetic information held by all members of a breeding population.

gene product   The final materials that a gene expresses (or codes for). When a gene has been associated with a product, it's easier to determine if the gene is overactive or underactive.

gene therapy   Changing the body' genes to delete sections of DNA and insert corrected versions to cure disease. May also involve switching genes on or off.

genetic code   A trio of nucleotides (codons) used by messenger RNA to guide the production of amino acids, the building blocks of proteins.

genetic drift   Random fluctuations in gene frequency in a small population.

genetic equilibrium   A gene pool with no mutations or outside influences.

genetics   The study of patterns of inherited traits.

genome   The sum total of all genetic information contained in an organism.

genomic library   A collection of DNA clones used for reference and analysis.

genomic sequence   The exact order (or sequence) of nucleotides that make up any given section of DNA.

genotype   The actual genetic composition of a patient. Discovering a patient's genotype may provide valuable information about the nature of disease and the kind of medicine most likely to be safe and effective (see also phenotype).

germ cells   Reproductive cells that, when mature, can participate in fertilization.

germ line gene therapy   Genetic manipulation of germ cells.

ghost gene   A stretch of DNA that once functioned as a gene but is dormant. Also "pseudogenes."

globulins   Blood proteins that do not dissolve in water: Alpha, Beta, and Gamma types.

guanine (G)   One of the DNA base units. Guanine pairs with cytosine (GC).

haploid Any organism that has only one complete set of chromosomes.

hedgehog protein An important protein that appears to stimulate nerve regeneration.

hemoglobin The blood protein responsible for carrying oxygen.

high throughput screening (HTS) The highly mechanized and computerized process of checking thousands of different molecules to see which interact with a target molecule.

histocompatibility complex The spot on Chromosome 6 that allows the body to distinguish between self and nonself.

hormones Chemical messengers that direct bodily processes. According to type they can influence the growth of various cells and organs (i.e., beard, breasts).

human growth hormone One of the first proteins created artificially by the biotechnology industry, used to stimulate growth in hormone-deficient children. May also have properties to slow down the aging process.

hybridization The creation of a double-stranded DNA molecule by joining two complementary strands of DNA (or a strand of DNA with an RNA strand).

imprinting A peculiar phenomenon of inheritance. A gene mutation received from the father can cause one disease and the same mutation from the mother causes another. Positioning of the gene in the genetic sequence of offspring is believed to be the cause.

inducer Any substance that stimulates an increase in the amount of enzymes required to metabolize the substance (e.g., sugar stimulates insulin that leads to metabolization of sugars).

in situ hybridization Finding the location of DNA or cDNA in a tissue sample to locate which part is expressing a certain gene or harboring a virus. Probes perform this function by binding to complementary targets only.

insulin The well-known hormone that regulates blood sugars.

interferons Three proteins called Alpha, Beta, and Gamma defend the body against disease such as viruses and tumors. Once hailed as the key to human diseases, they disappointed investors when it turned out they were part of a more complex system.

interphase The period between cell divisions when a cell performs its intended functions.

intron A segment of a gene that does not code for a protein. See exon.

inversion   Reversing the order of genes in a chromosome.

in vitro   Literally meaning "in glass." Usually referring to a biological process outside an organism.

keratin   An inert protein that makes up hair and nails.

kilobase (kb)   Shorthand for 1,000 nucleotides. Used as a unit of DNA length.

ligand   A name for a molecular structure that binds to another molecule (such as the antigens that antibodies are designed to attach themselves to).

ligase   An enzyme that can break down fats.

linkage   A prediction based on the distance between two (or more) units such as genes on a chromosome. The theory holds that the closer together these units or "markers" are, the greater the likelihood that they will be inherited together.

lipids   A family of fatty molecules.

liposome   A very small sphere made of lipid molecules. Currently being studied as a drug delivery device that can encapsulate a protein and carry it safely through the digestive tract. Lipids tend to move toward inflamed tissues, a characteristic that could make them even more effective as drug delivery devices.

locus   The position of a gene or other point of interest on a chromosome.

lymphocytes   White blood cells.

lymphokines   Substances produced by T-cells to assist in immune reactions to foreign agents.

lysis   The destruction of a bacterium by a bacteriophage (virus).

mapping   Charting the position of a gene or marker along the chromosomes.

marker   A genetic variation found on a chromosome. This variation points the way to a specific gene that may show an important mutation.

megabase (Mb)   One million nucleotides. Used as a standard of measure.

meiosis   A form of cell division. The chromosomes in sex cells are duplicated, and then the resulting structures are split in half. The result: four sex cells, each with half chromosomes.

messenger RNA (mRNA)   A molecule shaped by DNA that directs the creation of proteins.

mitosis   The full version of cell division. When chromosomes are duplicated and the cell is divided, each resulting cell has a full copy of genetic
information. There are five important phases of mitosis: Interphase,
prophase, metaphase, anaphase, and telophase. These describe the process
after interphase (normal cell life) when a cell replicates its information,
confirms its suitability, organizes itself into position, and splits in two.

monoclonal antibody (MAb)   A custom-designed attack protein from
the immune system. Antibodies are shaped in the immune system's B cells
to bind to antigens on the surface of an invading organism. The invader
may have many antigens on its surface, and many antibodies will be created in search of the one that binds most tightly to the invader. Biotechnology attempts to discover the most effective antibody and then clone the
B cell that generates it. The cloned B cells produce only one antibody and
are therefore called monoclonal.

monogenic disease   A disease caused by a mutation in a single gene versus polygenic disease, multiple mutations that are expressed as disease.

mutagen   An environmental element that can cause mutation, for example, some elements of cigarette smoke.

mutation   An abnormal variation in the letters or sequence of a gene.

non-Hodgkin's lymphoma (NHL)   Unregulated growth of the de-
fenders, called B-lymphocytes, which usually repel invasion by foreign
organisms.

nuclear transfer   The process of cloning Dolly the sheep that began by
placing chosen DNA matter in an empty (nucleus removed) egg casing.
This egg, after growing, was implanted into a host sheep that gave birth to
Dolly (see embryo twinning).

nucleic acid   A chain of nucleotides.

nucleotides   The basic units of DNA. As discussed earlier, the DNA
molecule is composed of groupings of four basic nucleotides: A,C,T,G.
The RNA molecule is also composed of nucleotides that are somewhat different chemically.

nucleus   The sac inside a cell that carries genetic material.

nutraceuticals   Foods that have a health benefit beyond simple nutrition.

oligonucleotide   A short, custom-made strand of DNA.

oncogene   A gene that helps regulate cell growth but may cause cancers.

pathogen   An infectious agent, usually a virus or bacteria that causes
disease.

peptide Small protein molecules, usually composed of fewer than 20 amino acids. They are easily synthesized and have a wide variety of uses including medicinal applications.

phages Viruses that attack bacteria.

pharming Genetically engineering animals to produce desired substances, usually humanized proteins.

phenotype The characteristics of a genetic trait as expressed or are observable in a living organism. See genotype.

plantibodies Antibodies made by genetically modified plants, including corn and tobacco.

plasmid A circular DNA molecule, found in bacteria but not a part of the bacterial chromosome. Plasmids can be self-replicating and may be used as tools for cloning. A "Ti plasmid" is an abbreviation for tumor inducing.

point mutation These occur when one nucleotide ATCG is incorrectly copied.

polygenic diseases Caused by several gene mutations working together. See monogenic.

polymer A long molecule characterized by a repeating pattern of components. Plastics are the best-known polymers but biotechnology is now joining proteins together to form polymer chains.

polymerase An enzyme essential to copying DNA.

polymerase chain reaction (PCR) A technique to create millions of copies of a DNA sequence (gained fame in the O.J. Simpson trial).

polymorphism A variation in the sequence of a segment of DNA among individuals.

preimplantation genetic diagnosis The testing of a single early-stage embryo cell for genetic disease.

primer A short sequence of nucleotides (ATCGs) that kick-start or prime the copying of DNA, allowing polymerase to go to work.

probe A known single-stranded DNA or RNA molecule that can be used to probe or search for complementary sequences in a given sample. For example, a probe for a genetic mutation would signal the presence of a complementary strand of DNA or RNA, indicating the sample in question contained the mutation in question.

prokaryote An organism with no cellular nucleus.

promoter   Think of an on/off switch. It's a region at the front end of a gene that promotes its expression: It turns on, or off, the gene's unique functions. Expressed another way, it is a control point on DNA that instructs the RNA molecule to attach itself at that point and begin copying. If it is "on," the gene's function will be manifested through the RNA molecule.

proteases   A form of enzyme that breaks up proteins.

proteins   A large class of large and important molecules, including antibodies, hormones, and enzymes. The structure of these molecules will govern their operation.

purines   The "two-ringed" base units of DNA: adenine and guanine.

recessive gene   A variation that appears in offspring only when two copies are present—both the mother and father must contribute the recessive gene. Recessive disease is expressed or suppressed based on this criterion. See dominant gene.

recombinant DNA technology   A term that covers many techniques, all of which serve the purpose of cutting and splicing strands of DNA to alter their genetic codes.

restriction enzymes   A tool in genetic engineering. Derived from bacteria, they are the organism's defense against viral invaders that act by cutting up the DNA of the invader. For the genetic engineer, these enzymes allow precision cutting of targeted DNA sequences.

retrovirus   A virus, such as HIV, that contains RNA rather than DNA in its genome. This viral RNA promotes the making of specialized DNA, which is then inserted into the cellular nucleus of the host organism, dramatically altering its function to promote the survival of the virus.

reverse transcriptase   A viral enzyme that sparks the synthesis of DNA from a retrovirus's RNA pattern.

ribonucleic acid (RNA)   Similar to DNA in structure but more directly active in processes outside the nucleus. Primarily known for directing the synthesis of proteins, there are several types including messenger RNA (mRNA), which copies information from DNA and uses this information to construct proteins; ribosomal RNA (rRNA), which helps build the ribosomes that physically assemble proteins; and transfer RNA (tRNA), which brings required amino acids to a ribosome for assembly.

ribosomes   Cellular factories that synthesize proteins as directed by RNA.

ribozymes   These are RNA molecules that can destroy other RNA molecules. They may be useful against RNA-dependent retroviruses.

selective breeding   Crossbreeding pairs of organisms with desirable traits.

sequence tagged site (STS) A short DNA sequence that appears only once in the genome. Because its location is known, it serves as a landmark for gene mapping and other tasks. Expressed sequence tags (ESTs) are much the same but are derived from complementary DNA (see cDNA).

sequencing The process of determining the nucleotide sequence of a DNA or RNA molecule. Shotgun sequencing involves the reduction of a genome to fragments, learning their structure, and determining how the tiny pieces fit back together. Directed sequencing involves the sequencing of DNA from adjacent stretches of DNA.

silent mutations Usually dormant mutations in DNA. They have no apparent effect and can go unnoticed.

single nucleotide polymorphisms (SNPs) A variation in a single nucleotide in a DNA sequence.

small molecule Denotes a molecule that is small enough to be absorbed by the body in pill form. Larger molecules must be injected or delivered by novel systems.

somatic cell Any cell in the body other than the gametes (sexual reproductive cells).

spacer DNA DNA that has no apparent function in protein expression. It is found between genes.

SPRY gene The "sex-determining region-Y gene" that plays a role in the creation of human males.

stem cells The most basic cell of human life. It can grow into any human cell, from bone to brain. It is especially important to the generation of specific new human tissue in medical research (e.g., stem cells could be grown into new liver parts or spinal cord).

tandem repeats DNA sequences that repeat again and again. They have been compared to a stutter.

telomeres The tips of chromosomes. Telomeres are key to the replication of DNA molecules. They may be important factors in aging and in the uncontrolled replication of cells characteristic of cancer.

testosterone The male sex hormone.

thymine (T) One of the base nucleotides, which pairs with adenine (TA).

tPA A protein that promotes the flow of blood and dissolves clots.

transcription The creation of new messenger RNA by copying selected letters from DNA. The copying of a gene from DNA by RNA begins the process of gene expression.

transgenic animal   An animal that has received genetic material (inserted into its DNA) from another organism. For example, a goat with human DNA might express insulin in its milk. A transgenic animal can also be used to test therapies that act on a specific portion of inserted DNA.

transgenic plant   As above.

transgenic organism   An entirely original creature that can be created by mixing novel DNA parts from various sources.

translation   The making of proteins from amino acids according to the direction provided by mRNA nucleotide sequences.

transposons   (jumping genes)   These DNA segments move from one position on a chromosome to another. They are incapable of self-replication.

tumor necrosis factor   A so-called "biological response modifier," produced naturally in small amounts to enhance response to disease.

uracil   A base that is part of the makeup of RNA but not DNA. It pairs with adenine (UA).

vector   A way of delivering genetic information or codes to target cells. For example, a patient requiring gene therapy may be infected with an engineered virus (the vector) that will deliver new DNA sequences to cells. As much as possible, the viral vector will be rendered harmless before the subject is infected with it.

virus   An extremely small carrier of genetic information. In the presence of a host, it takes over the genetic machinery and instructs the host to reproduce new viral copies. If the host develops resistance to this infection, the virus will evolve its surface to become undetectable.

X chromosome   The chromosome believed responsible for sex determination during reproduction. A female usually carries two of them and a male only one.

xenotransplantation   The use of animal organs for transplantation.

Y chromosome   Usually joined with an X chromosome in males.

yeast artificial chromosome (YAC)   A vector (tool) to clone large DNA pieces.

zygote   The original cell formed by the union of two sex cells, sperm and egg, the gametes. A zygote is sometimes used to describe the very early stages of an embryo when a few stem cells are all that exist.

Notes

Introduction

1. Oscar Gruss Conference on Genomics and Bioinformatics, New York, April 14, 2000.
2. *Beck on Biotech Newsletter*, 2, 12, December 1999.
3. James D. Watson, *The Double Helix*, Mentor Science, 1969.
4. Richard W. Oliver, *The Coming Biotech Age*, McGraw Hill, 1999.
5. Cynthia Robbins Roth, *From Alchemy to IPO—The Business of Biotechnology*, Perseus, 2000.
6. Author's investment records.
7. James Welsh, Mutual Funds Columnist, www.wordlyinvestor.com, Lipper Company Report and Commentary, June 7 and 14, 2000; also Jesse Schulman, *FT Market Watch*, May/June 2000.

Chapter 1

1. Biotechnology Industry Organization (BIO) Annual Report, 1999.
2. James D. Watson, *The Double Helix*, Mentor Science, 1969.
3. Pharmaceutical Research and Manufacturers Association (PhRMA) Annual Report, 1999.
4. Incyte's 500th Gene-Related Patent, news release, www.incyte.com, August 17, 1999.
5. Naomi Aoki, "New Alchemy: Patents Aim to Turn Genes into Biotech Gold," *Boston Globe*, August 30/September 1, 2000.
6. Data from U.S. Patent Office, October 2000.
7. Pharmaceutical Research and Manufacturers Association (PhRMA) Annual Report, 1999.
8. *Wall Street Journal*, Online Edition, March 2000.
9. "Mid-2000: The Post Genomics Era," CIBC World Markets, Biotech Handbook.
10. PhRMA Annual Report, 1999.
11. Biotechnology Industry Organization (BIO) Annual Report, 1999.
12. Thomas Klopack, *Drug Discovery Today*, 2000.
13. Arthur Kornberg, *The Golden Helix, Inside Biotech Ventures*, University Science Books, 1995.
14. Biotechnology Industry Organization (BIO) Annual Report, 1999.

15. Department of Commerce/International Trade Administration, U.S. Industry and Trade Outlook, 1999.

16. Estimates derived from Heart Association Web site.

17. Quoted from PhRMA Annual Report, 1999.

18. U.S. Department of Health and Human Services, CDC release, November 1998.

19. CBC National News, June 13, 2000, www.Forbes.com.

20. Feldman, BIO release July 5/July 21, 2000.

21. Michael Murphy, California Technology Stock Letter.

22. Kerry Dooley, "Lilly Shares Drop 31%," Bloomberg, August 9, 2000.

23. Author's calculations using statistics from various industry sources, including Bloomberg.

24. IBM/Reuters, WindowsOnWallStreet.com, November 26, 2000.

Chapter 2

1. From *Wall Street Week with Louis Rukeyser*, PBS, July 14, 2000.

2. *Windhover Health Care Strategist*, Vol. 2, 2000.

3. From a telephone interview with Christopher J. Reinhard, president and COO, Collateral Therapeutics, June 13, 2000.

4. Figures from Celera 1999 Annual Report available through Celera.com.

5. Venter interview with Charlie Rose, PBS, June 26, 2000.

6. From recap.com.

7. Conversation with the author, April 24, 2000, New York.

8. Figures as of November 2000 from charting services including WindowOn WallStreet.com.

9. Background with research from Multex.com.

10. WorldlyInvestor.com, CBS MarketWatch.com May 26/June 1, 2000.

11. Bloomberg.com.

12. Fred Barbash, *Washington Post*, June 11, 2000.

13. From collected reports including CBS MarketWatch.com; Stephanie O'Brien, Jeff Clabaugh, Shawn Langlois, "The 'Buys' in Biotechs, Brokerages Soothe Genomics Concerns," *Clueless Investors*, March 15, 2000; Nadine Wong, WorldlyInvestor.com, "Biotech Sell-Off an Overreaction," *Wall Street Journal*, March 14, 2000; various reports; Jan Licking, "Smart Companies, Dumb Investors," Commentary, *Business Week*, March 27, 2000; "Maturing Biotech Sector Heats Up," *USA Today*, March 24, 2000.

14. sfgate.com, Tom Abate, November 14, 2000.

15. *New York Times* magazine, 2000.

16. PhRMA Annual Report, 1999.

17. Various author interviews, calculations, March/July 2000.

18. Collateral Therapeutics Annual Report, 1999, and telephone interview with Christopher J. Reinhard, president and COO, Collateral Therapeutics, June 13, 2000.

19. dbusiness.com, Charlotte, North Carolina, June 1, 2000.

20. Juan Enriquez and Ray A. Goldberg, "The Life Science Revolution," *Harvard Business Review*, March/April 2000.
21. PhRMA Annual Report, 1999.
22. Randy Scott, Incyte Genomics, *Wired News*, June 30, 2000, reported by Kristen Philipkoski.
23. Interview with the author, La Jolla, June 27, 2000.
24. *Financial Times*, August 7, 2000.
25. Celera.com press releases.
26. *Worth Magazine*, Spring 2000.
27. Jan Licking, "Smart Companies, Dumb Investors," Commentary, *Business Week*, March 27, 2000.
28. Interview with the author, Irvine, California, June 21, 2000.

Chapter 3

1. PhRMA Annual Report, 1999.
2. Bloomberg, BioSpace.com, Gliatech, September 27, 2000.
3. Telephone interview: Author and Vical investor relations, September 2000.
4. Frank Kilpatrick, Healthcare Communications Group, El Segundo, California.
5. PhRMA Annual Report, 1999.
6. www.pharma.org.
7. www.mlnm.com.
8. Data published regularly by qxhealth.com to encourage subscription to its database.
9. PhRMA Annual Report, 1999.
10. Interviewed on CNBC.
11. Tom Jacobs, "Lilly Trades Biotech Deals," The Motley Fool, September 6, 2000.
12. Biospace.com, Sepracor, Bloomberg, and Inhale Therapeutics press releases, The Motley Fool, September 6, 2000.
13. www.mlnm.com.
14. Commentary, *St. Petersburg Times*, Editorial Pages, March 2000.
15. U.S. Patent Office, November 2000.
16. Craig Venter, Celera CEO, Interview with Charlie Rose PBS, June 26, 2000.
17. Oscar Gruss Conference on Genomics and Bioinformatics, April 14, 2000.
18. BioSpace.com, CNBC.com, Reuters, July/August 2000.

Chapter 4

1. *Denver Post*, September 5, 2000.
2. Reuters, March 11, 2000.
3. Interview, July 17, 2000.
4. The Motley Fool (TMF).com.
5. Ken Hoover, "Analysts' Ratings Can Be Late, Misleading and Wrong," *Investor's Business Daily*, August 4, 2000.

6. Barron's, Bloomberg, Oscar Gruss Co, November 11, 2000.
7. Medical Technology Stock Letter, promotional information, www.bioin-vest.com.
8. Salomon Smith Barney, Private Client Equity Strategy, Biotechnology 2000, March 2, 2000.
9. Analyst Ashok Kumar of U.S. Bancorp Piper Jaffray lowers his rating on Dell from "strong buy" to "buy," Reuters, August 7, 2000.

Chapter 5

1. From Biospace.com.
2. Information from Corporate Annual Reports, *Signals Magazine*, BioSpace.com.
3. Telephone interview with Affymetrix investor relations staff, June 28, 2000.
4. *British Medical Journal* as reported by BioSpace.com.
5. Nihon Keizai, Tokyo, news releases, Corning and Motorola, Bloomberg, September 28, 2000.
6. Oscar Gruss Conference on Genomics and Bioinformatics, New York, April 2000.
7. CuraGen 1999 Annual Report and Press Kit.
8. Oscar Gruss Conference on Genomics and Bioinformatics, April 14, 2000.
9. Interview with the author, La Jolla, June 27, 2000.
10. www.vasogen.com.
11. See Avax press releases at www.avax-tech.com.
12. From a presentation at the First Security Van Kasper Growth Conference, San Diego, June 23, 2000.

Chapter 6

1. Data from Hoovers, Yahoo Finance, The Motley Fool, RagingBull.com, BigCharts.com.
2. John Campbell, PhD, Massachusetts Institute of Technology, Martin Lettau, Federal Reserve Bank, Burton Malkiel, PhD, Princeton, Yexioa Xu, PhD, University of Texas, summarized by Michael Hulbert, August 20, 2000, strategy@nytimes.com.
3. William J. O'Neil, *24 Essential Lessons for Investment Success*, McGraw-Hill, 2000.
4. *Chicago Tribune*, August 8, 2000; Andrew Leckey, "Biotechs Caught Fever while Many Others Froze Up," *New York Times*, October 8, 2000; Mutual Funds Report.
5. News releases and background are available at www.onyx-pharm.com.
6. News releases and background are available at www.entremed.com.
7. Clint Willis and Emily Hall, Morningstar, "Funds: Big Profits and Risk in Biotech Funds," Reuters News Agency, August 24, 2000.
8. Kathleen Pender, "Biotech Stocks Make for a Thrill Ride—If You Can Stomach It," August 4, 2000, www.sfgate.com.

9. See FAQ at www.foliofn.com.

10. Peter Ginsberg, U.S. Bancorp—Piper Jaffray, September 5, 2000.

Chapter 7

1. Edited from www.cytoclonal.com news releases, *Toronto Star*, Sepember 9, 2000.

2. *Toronto Star*, September 9, 2000.

3. www.geron.com.

4. From www.cellpathways.com, Yahoo Finance and Multex.com.

5. Posted by "njb143," September 23, 2000, RagingBull.com.

6. Yahoo Finance Corporate Profiles, Rating History, Medimmune.

7. Ben Hirschler, Reuter European Pharmaceuticals Correspondent, "Analysis—Biotech Triple-Whammy Highlights Sector Perils," September 26, 2000.

8. PhRMA Annual Report, 1999.

9. Vasogen third quarter investor's conference call, September 27, 2000.

10. William J. O'Neil, *24 Essential Lessons for Investment Success*, McGraw-Hill, 2000.

11. See releases at www.genecor.com and www.diversa.com.

12. Larry Feinberg, "Oracle Partners Hedge Fund," *Barron's*, November 18, 2000.

13. See www.cticseattle.com.

14. Bloomberg quotes Irv DeGraw of World FinanceNet.com and Richard Peterson of Securities Data to support this claim.

Chapter 8

1. Identities are kept confidential by agreement with the involved parties.

2. Statistics from Gomez Advisors, Forrester Research, *Time* magazine, *Boston Globe*, *Investor's Business Daily*.

Chapter 10

1. Karolinska Institute, November 2000, www.mic.ki.se/Diseases/index.html.

Chapter 12

1. Anna Snider, "Mining the Icelandic Genome," SmartMoney.com, July 10, 2000; Press releases, www.decode.com.

2. "Watching a Protein Fold," Pittsburgh Supercomputing Center, 1998, www.psc.edu/science/kollman98.html.

3. Sparrer et al., "Evidence for the Prion Hypothesis," *Science Magazine*, July 28, 2000; *Science Daily*, August 24, 2000; Reuters and Associated Press, various reports.

Chapter 13

1. First Securities Van Kasper Biotech Conference, San Diego, June 2000.
2. Faiz Kermani, "The Application of Drug Delivery Systems: Current Practices and Future Strategies," CMR International, United Kingdom.

Chapter 14

1. Data from National Institutes of Health.
2. The children suffered from severe combined immune deficiency—X1, which was publicized and dramatized in the United States in the well-known story of the "boy in the bubble," a child who could not have contact with the outside world without risking fatal infection. About 1 child in 75,000 suffers from the condition and the afflicted are usually boys.
3. www.onyx-pharm.com.
4. From a personal interview with Arthur Benvenuto, Chairman Advanced Tissue Sciences, La Jolla, California, June 2000,

Chapter 15

1. Vasantha Nagarajan, *Trends in Biotechnology*, 2000, www.Dupont.com.
2. Michael Hinman, Justin Jones, and Randolph Lewis, *Trends in Biotechnology*, Vol. 18, University of Wyoming, September 2000, www.silk@uwyo.edu.
3. Harry Eccles, *Trends in Biotechnology*, 1999.
4. U.S. Food and Drug Administration, www.fda.gov.
5. Carlo Montemagno, *Science Journal*, November 25, 2000.
6. "Two Drug Companies Accused of Stifling Competition," *New York Times*, August 7/September 7, 2000; "Investigation into Possible Anti-Competitive Conduct, September 7, 2000, www.qxhealth.com.
7. Sheryl Gay Stollberg and Jeff Gerth, "How Companies Stall Generics and Keep Themselves Healthy," *New York Times*, July 23, 2000.
8. Carol M. Ostrom, "Lower Drug Prices in Canada Prescription for Outrage in U.S.," *Seattle Times*, September 5, 2000.
9. David S. Cloud and Laurie McGinley, "How Drug Makers Influence Medicare Reimbursements, *Wall Street Journal*, September 2000.
10. David Tuller, "Battling the Pharmaceutical Microsoft," August 22, 2000, www.Salon.com.
11. "Drug Industry Raises Spending for Ads, Lobbyists to Fight Critics," *Wall Street Journal*, September 22, 2000.
12. Kristen Philipkoski, "Are Pharmas Doomed?" *Wired News*, March 2, 2000, www.wired.com.

Index

Abgenix, 51, 93, 100, 124, 218, 243
Accelerated evolution of genes,
    198–199
Adenoviruses, 222, 223
ADMET analysis (absorption-
    distribution-excretion-
    metabolism-toxicity), 204–206
Advanced Tissue Sciences, 235–236,
    248
Advisors/brokers (*vs.* going it alone),
    85–87, 138–139
Aethlon, 51
Affymetrix, 36, 93, 96–97, 124,
    147–148, 195, 212, 213, 214
Agilent, 214, 255
Aging/degeneration, 181, 185, 229,
    247–248
Agricultural biotechnology, 18,
    238–240
AIDS/HIV, 15, 32, 51, 61, 94–95,
    178–179, 255
Alkermes, 43
Alliance(s)/partnerships, 52, 63–65
Alliance Pharmaceutical, 108–110,
    308
ALS (Lou Gherig's disease), 178
Alzheimer's disease, 15, 22, 49, 62, 99,
    203, 232
American Bioscience, 252
Amersham Pharmacia Biotech (NYE),
    212
AMEX Biotech Index (BTK), 7, 40,
    114, 120, 127
Amgen, 11, 18, 21–22, 28, 30, 31, 37,
    67–68, 86–87, 88, 89–90, 91, 94,
    96, 131, 132, 141, 201, 202, 209,
    222, 234

Angiogenesis, 12, 224–225
Angiogenesis inhibitors, 225–226
Antisense therapy, 223–224
Applera Corp., 30, 212
Armed viruses. *See* Virus(es)
ARPAnet, 3–4, 199
Arthritis, 15, 59–60, 61, 143, 218
Assay development, 13, 207
Asset allocation, 121
Augouron, 28
Aurora Bioscience, 45
Autoimmune disease. *See* Immune
    system
AVAX Technologies, 51, 107–108
Aventis, 65, 96, 208
Avonex, 18, 34
Axcan Pharma, 229
Axys Pharmaceuticals, 36

Bacterial infection, 61, 178
Barnscomb, Elbert, 255
Bayer, 65, 307
Bayh-Dole Act of 1980, 68
Becker, Michael, 82
Beck on Biotech, 85
Benvenuto, Arthur, 248
Beta, 79, 115
Bexxar, 210
BigCharts.com, 84, 120, 135
Big Pharma. *See* Pharmaceutical
    industry
BioCapital, 253
Biochips, 14, 44, 96–97, 185, 213–214,
    255
Biocomputing, 14
Biogen, 18, 28, 34, 37, 86, 94, 96, 183
Bioinformatics, 13, 204–207

309

Biological computers and machines
    (wetware), 249–250
Biometrics, 14
Biomira, 230
BioSpace.com, 50, 51, 62, 85, 135
Biotech funds (pure/mixed), 126
Biotech Insight Stock News Letter,
    124
Biotechnology:
    approach to drug development, vs.
        traditional, 10–12
    classification of companies (see
        Tier(s))
    convergence/synergy in, 41–45
    future of, 22–23, 237, 254–256
    growth imperative, 155–158
    history of ("one of world's oldest
        emerging industries"), 9–14
    industrial, 17–18, 244–246
    market measurement/assessment,
        18–19, 26–49
    patents, 14–17, 52, 65–68, 253, 256
    PC paradigm (parallels in industry
        history), 3–8, 24–25
    in perspective, 155–159
    realms ("who's doing what"),
        193–203
    resources, 282–286
    revenue potential, 19–22
    science of (see Science of
        biotechnology)
    sector classified as separate from
        pharmaceutical industry, 12
    special sectors, 238–256
    terminology, 287–300
    tools/instruments, 204–215
    uniqueness of driving forces, 7–8
    worldwide (estimated number of
        companies), 18
Biotechnology companies (specific),
    data about:
    by market cap, 266–273
    by name (alphabetically), 258–264
    by tier, 274–281 (see also Tier(s))
Biotechnology companies (specific)
    involved in following areas,
    257–281
    accelerated evolution of genes, 199

    agricultural biotechnology, 240
    angiogenesis inhibitors, 226
    angiogenesis therapies, 225
    antisense therapy, 224
    assay development, 207
    biochip production, 214
    bioinformatics and software, 206
    combinatorial chemistry, 215
    cosmeceutical development, 248
    drug candidate development, 209
    drug delivery, 212
    drug enhancement, 210
    functional genomics, 197
    gene therapy, 223
    genomics, 196
    growth factors for tissue
        regeneration, 235
    instrument manufacturers, 213
    monoclonal antibody development,
        219
    nutraceuticals, 242
    pharmacogenomics, 208
    photodynamic therapy, 229
    protein therapies, 220
    proteomic analysis, 201
    ribozymes, 227
    stem cell research, 234
    tissue replacement, 236
    transgenic research, 244
    vaccines, 231
Biotechnology Industry Organization,
    16
Biotechnology investing/investment
    factors:
    alliances, 52, 63–65, 160–161
    analysts/brokerages-75–78, 85–87,
        159
    analyzing sample company
        (Millennium Pharmaceuticals),
        59–60
    bubble phenomenon/crash, 35–38,
        40, 69, 71, 117
    buying decisions, 141–142
    cautions about, 7–8, 139–141
    checklist, 160–166
    clinical trials/phases, 52, 54–56
    competition assessment, 161
    corporate factors, 163

decision making, 135–154
differing from dot-coms, 48–49
environment (business/regulatory), 165
exponential acceleration, 45–47
financials/metrics, 78–81, 162–163
first step, 135–136
formulas/charts/waves/patterns, 81–84
going it alone (*vs.* using broker), 85–87, 138–139
headlines/news and, 136–138, 148–149
integration (vertical *vs.* horizontal), 68–73
investor revolution, 158–159
IPOs, 150–152
key factors, 50–74, 160–165
key tests of investment profile, 52
lessons for, 133–134
making investment choices, 75
management, 163
margin, 128–129
market factors, 26–49, 52, 60–63, 159, 162
market timing, 144–145, 147–148
mutual funds, 126–128
new drug application (NDA) (to FDA), 56–59
patents, 52, 65–68
perspective on science, 190–192
pipeline, 52, 53–54, 160
portfolio planning, 113–134
price drivers, 26–29
profit taking, 149–150
research, 164
risk, 29–35, 38–41, 47–48, 119–125, 163–164
selling, 144–145, 148–149, 164
speculation, 158, 159
strategies:
    alternative, 126–128
    new *vs.* old, 113–114
target diseases, 61
technology assessment, 161
tier analysis, 122–125, 161–162
time horizons ("waiting for returns"), 78, 152–153
trend watching, 129–133
valuation, 27–28, 29–32, 87–88
volatility, 6–7, 114–121, 128–129
warning signs for getting out early, 38
what to look for in biotech companies, 50–54, 75
Biotechnology realms (therapies/ approaches/products), 12–14, 193–203, 204–215, 216–237
accelerated evolution of genes, 198–199
agricultural biotechnology, 238–240
angiogenesis, 12, 224–225
angiogenesis inhibitors, 225–226
antiangiogenesis, 12
antisense therapy, 223–224
assay development, 13, 207
biochips, 14, 44, 185, 213–214, 255
biocomputing, 14
bioinformatics, 13, 204–207
biological computers and machines (wetware), 249–250
biometrics, 14
combinatorial and ADMET chemistry, 13, 215
computer modeling, 13
cosmeceuticals, 14, 246–249
curative vaccines, 13
deadly protein (prion-based disease), 202–203
discovery industries, 193
DNA vaccines, 231
drug candidate development/ optimization, 208–209
drug delivery, 13, 210–212
drug improvement, 209–210
functional genomics, 196–198
gene shuffling, 13
gene therapy, 12, 220–223
genomics, 13, 193–196
growth stimulants, 234–235
high throughput machinery, 13
hybrids, 238
immune system modulators, 12
industrial biotechnology, 17–18, 244–246
microrobotics, 14

Biotechnology realms (therapies/
    approaches/products) *(Continued)*
  monoclonal antibodies, 12, 216–219
  nutraceuticals, 14, 240–242
  pharmacogenomics, 13, 207–208
  pharming, 13, 242–244
  photodynamic therapy, 13, 228–229
  promising approaches, 12–13
  protein therapies, 12, 219–220
  proteomics, 13, 199–202
  research fields, 13–14
  ribozymes, 227
  signal transduction and pathways,
      13, 236–237
  stem cells and tissue regeneration,
      13, 231–234
  strategies, 216
  telomeres, 13
  therapies, 216–237
  tissue regeneration/replacement, 12,
      13, 231–234, 235–236
  tools/instruments, 204–215
  transgenics, farming, and pharming,
      242–244
  vaccines, 229–231
  viruses, armed/smart, 13, 124,
      227–228
  "who's doing what," 193–203
BioTech Sage report, 86
BioVenture Consultant Stock report,
    85
"Blue Gene," 44, 176. *See also* IBM
Boger, Joshua, 95
Bollinger Bands, 84
Bollon, Arthur P., 136
Brennan, Michael J., 68, 69, 70, 72
Bristol-Myers Squibb, 252
British Biotech, 142
Brokerages:
  assessing analyst ratings, 75–78
  vs. going it alone, 138–139
  paying for advice, 85–87
Bubble, 35–38, 41, 140
Buffett, Warren, 28, 135
Burroughs Wellcome, 59

California Technology Stock letter,
    85

Cambridge Antibody Technology
    Group, 218
Campath, 59–60, 62, 307
Cancer, 15, 22, 32, 51, 61, 99, 100, 142,
    180, 192, 210, 223, 230, 237, 252
Capiello, Frank, 26
Cardiovascular disease. *See* Heart/
    cardiovascular disease/stroke
Celanese, 146
Celera Corporation, 6, 14, 29, 30,
    31–32, 36, 39, 41, 66, 71, 72, 79,
    85, 100, 129, 147, 172, 173, 193,
    195–196, 202, 255
Celgene, 75–76, 226
Cell(s):
  division (mitosis), 187–188
  living, 177–178
  signaling, 236–237
Cell Genesys, 101–102, 107
Cell Pathways, 99, 139–141, 142, 148,
    251
Cell Therapeutics, 142, 148–149, 226
Centocor, 28
Chart patterns, 81–84, 145
Chiron, 91
Chromosomes, 175
Cisco Systems, 5, 98, 114
CJD (Creutzfeldt-Jacob) disease,
    202–203
Clinical trials, 52, 54–56
  Phase I, 54–55
  Phase II, 55–56
  Phase III, 56
  success in, and valuation, 30
Coca-Cola, 27, 104, 113
Coenzyme Q10, 241
Collateral Therapeutics, 41, 43, 225
Collins, Francis, 67, 256
Colony stimulating factors (CSF), 184
Combinatorial and ADMET
    chemistry, 13, 215
Compaq, 5, 214
Competition, assessing, 161
Computer analogy (gene machinery),
    176
Computer-biotech convergence/
    modeling/analysis, 13, 43–45,
    204–207

Computer industry paradigm for
  biotechnology, 3–8, 24–25, 48
  important difference, 48
  lessons from PC revolution, 24–25
Computer *vs.* neural networks, 250
Congress Watch, 252
Convergence/synergy, 41–45
Corning, 98, 147, 214, 255
Cosmeceuticals, 14, 246–249
Coulter Pharmaceuticals, 210
Cray, Seymour, 3, 32
Cray Supercomputer, 200, 201
Crick, Francis, 4, 44
Cristanti, Andrea, 190–191
Crohn's disease, 218
CuraGen, 47, 75, 100, 101, 194, 197,
  206, 207, 307
Curis, 235
Cystic fibrosis, 45, 51, 223
Cytoclonal Pharmaceutics, 136–138
Cytogen, 230
Cytokines, 36, 183
CytoTherapeutics, 233

Danisco A/S, 146
Dauchot, Michael, 122
Decision Resources, 226
deCode Genetics, 196–197
Defense Advanced Research Projects
  Agency (DARPA), 3–4, 199
Delivery devices, 13, 21, 51, 210–212
Delivery vectors, gene, 42
Dell Computer, 5, 87, 150, 157
Diabetes, 20–21, 61, 143, 180, 216
Discovery industries, 193
Disease(s)/disease processes, 15, 22,
  61, 143, 178–181, 184–185
  aging/degenerative, 181
  AIDS/HIV, 15, 32, 51, 61, 94–95,
    178–179, 255
  Alzheimer's disease, 15, 22, 49, 62,
    99, 203, 232
  arthritis, 15, 59–60, 61, 143, 218
  asthma, 61
  autoimmune, 143
  bacterial infections, 61, 178
  biotech approach to treatment,
    184–185

cancer, 15, 22, 32, 51, 61, 99, 100,
    142, 180, 192, 210, 223, 230,
    237, 252
  CJD (Creutzfeldt-Jacob) disease,
    202–203
  comprehensive database on, 178
  Crohn's disease, 218
  cystic fibrosis, 45, 51, 223
  depression, 61
  diabetes, 20–21, 61, 143, 180, 216
  endocrine, 180
  fungal, 179
  genetically inherited defects, 178
  graft versus host disease (GVHD),
    143, 183
  heart/cardiovascular disease/stroke,
    15, 19–20, 22, 41, 51, 61, 99,
    143, 181
  high blood pressure, 61
  high cholesterol, 61
  immune system, 143, 179
  infectious, 178–179
  inflammatory, 143
  ischemia, 143
  lymphoma, non-Hodgkin's (NHL),
    62–63, 210
  macular degeneration (AMD), wet
    age-related, 229
  major families of, 178–181
  mental illness, 181
  metabolic, 180
  multiple sclerosis, 61, 143
  obesity, 61
  pain, 61
  parasitic, 179
  Parkinson's, 45, 61, 83, 203, 243
  schizophrenia, 61
  targets, major, 15, 61
  thrombosis, 61
  trauma, 181
  viral, 178
Distribution (ADMET analysis),
  205
Diversa Corporation, 45–46, 102–105,
  125, 145, 146, 151–152, 243,
  308
Diversification, 24, 121, 125
Dividends, 155–157

DNA, 4, 10, 43, 44, 66, 97, 170–175, 186, 188–189, 212, 222, 231
  analysis, 188–189
  base pairs (CG or AT), 170
  chromosomes, 175
  code of all human beings 99.9 percent same, 172
  complementary (cDNA), 173
  discovery of, 4, 10, 44
  errors, 171
  expressed sequence tags (ESTs), 173–174
  fingerprint, 189
  "fishing rod," 173–175
  four-bit (A,C,T,G) language of genome, 43, 97, 170–173
  gel electrophoresis, 188–189
  genes, 172
  junk, 172, 186
  misspelling of a single letter, 171
  naked, 66, 222
  patents and, 66
  PCR, 188
  sequencing machines, 212
  single nucleotide polymorphism (SNP), 30, 44, 46, 171–172, 195
  stuttering, 172–173
  "ultimate software," 170–173
  vaccines, 231
Doss, Monica, 43
Dot-coms (vs. biotech companies), 48–49
Double-blind trials, 56
Double Twist, 42
Dow Chemical, 103, 146, 243
Dresdener RCM Biotechnology Fund, 118, 122, 126, 127
Drug delivery, 13, 21, 51, 210–212
Drug development:
  biotech approach vs. traditional, 10–12, 45
  enhancement, 209–210
  lead generation and optimization, 208–209

"me-too" drugs, 17
number of products currently undergoing human clinical trials, 16
DuPont, 243

Earnings seasons, 87
EarningsWhispers.com, 87
Elan Pharmaceuticals of Ireland, 62
Eli Lilly, 24, 64, 92–93, 113, 250
Emisphere, 43
Endocrine diseases, 180
Energy, 17, 246
Enriquez, Juan, 19
Entremed, 125
Environment (business/regulatory), 165
Environmental cleanup products (genetically engineered bacteria/enzymes), 18, 245
Enzymes, 176
Epidermal growth factor (EGF), 235
Epitope, 217
Epogen, 11, 21–22, 67, 131, 209, 234
Excretion (ADMET analysis), 205
Exons/introns, 186–187
Expressed sequence tags (ESTs), 173–174
Ex vivo method, 222

Farming/transgenics/pharming, 242–244
Feinberg, Larry, 146
Feldbaum, Carl, 22
Fibers, 17
Fibroblast growth factor (FGF), 235
Fidelity Management and Research, 81
Financials/metrics, 78–81, 162–163
Fischer, Alain, 223
Fitzpatrick, Richard E., 248
Folio, 127, 128
Folkman, Judah, 226
Food(s), genetically modified, 239, 240
Food and Drug Administration (FDA), 16, 56–59, 99, 246–247
  approval times, 16, 56–59, 150

cosmeceuticals, 246–247
new drug application (NDA),
    56–59, 142
Franklin, Rosalind, 44
Franklin Biotechnology Discovery
    Fund, 7
Functional genomics, 10, 196–198
Funds, mutual, 7, 81, 126–128

Garren, Ronald, 124
Gene(s), 172. *See also* Gene therapy;
    Genetics
  biochips, 14, 44, 96–97, 185,
    213–214, 255
  defined, 172
  delivery vectors (converging
    technology), 42
  gun, 222
  jumping, 187, 222
  language of, 186–192 (*see also* DNA)
  number of (in human body), 172
  shuffling, 13
GeneLogic, 36, 42, 68, 69–70, 71, 72,
    129, 197, 198
Genencor, 105, 125, 145, 146, 243
Genentech, 18, 28, 91, 123, 202, 218,
    250–251
General Motors, 91, 92, 113
Gene therapy, 12, 42, 220–229, 237.
    See also Gene(s)
  angiogenesis, 224–225
  angiogenesis inhibitors, 225–226
  antisense therapy, 223–224
  branches of, 223–228
  converging technologies and, 42
  methods (and attendant challenges),
    221–222
  photodynamic therapy, 228–229
  power of, relative to other sectors,
    237
  ribozymes, 227
  smart viruses, 227–228
Genetics:
  genomics and, 186–187
  inherited defects, 178
  privacy of information, 255
  testing, 97, 255

Genome:
  defined, 172
  revolution, and privacy problem,
    255
Genomics, 10, 13, 29, 129, 172,
    186–187, 193–198, 204
  companies, 129
  decoding the software, 193–196
  functional, 10, 196–198
  genetics and, 186–187
  information overload, 204
  valuation of companies in, 29
Genotyping, 23, 185
Genset, 36, 198
Genta corporation, 223
Gentronics, 43, 211
Genzyme General, 51, 125, 153, 218
Genzyme Surgical, 236
Genzyme Transgenics, 124, 218, 243
Gerber baby foods, 240
Geron Corporation, 138, 233
Gilboa, Eli, 138
Gillette, 37, 113, 114
Ginsberg, Peter, 124, 129
Glasky, Michelle, 48–49
Glaxo, 252
Goldbert, Ray A., 19
Goldin, Daniel, 4
Graft versus host disease (GVHD),
    143, 183
Granulocytes, 183
Greenspan, Alan, 26, 157–158
Grey, Michael, 204, 206
"Growth imperative," 155–158
Growth stimulants/factors, 234–235
Guilford Pharmaceuticals, 57

Hall, Emily, 126
Harrell, Douglas, 45
Haseltine, William, 65, 66, 169
Headlines/news:
  interpreting (a sample story),
    136–138
  selling before, 148–149
Healthcare/biotech combination
    funds, 7
Healthcare market potential, 19

Heart/cardiovascular disease/stroke, 15, 19–20, 22, 41, 51, 61, 99, 143, 181
Hemispherix, 43
HGS. *See* Human Genome Sciences (HGS)
High throughput screening (HTS), 13, 207
Hill, Charles, 77
HIV. *See* AIDS/HIV
Home pregnancy test, 213
Hoovers, 78
Hormones, 177
Hulbert, Mark, 121
Human beings:
    DNA code of all human beings 99.9 percent same, 172
    number of chromosomes, 172
    number of genes, 172
Human Genome Project, 39, 67, 172, 255, 256
Human Genome Sciences (HGS), 14, 19, 30, 31, 41, 58, 65, 66, 70, 71, 72, 79, 80, 81, 86, 93, 114, 115, 116, 117, 118, 123, 141, 169, 202, 208, 251
Hungerford, Larry, 82
Hungerford, Steve, 82
Huntington's, 203
Hybrid industries, 238
Hybridization, 97
Hyseq, 98

IBM, 3, 5, 24, 44, 46, 131, 132, 176, 201
IDEC Pharmaceuticals, 5, 28, 34, 91, 218
Immune system, 181–183
    disease, 143, 179
    language of, 183–184
    modulators, 12
Immunex, 34–35, 91
Incyte, 3, 29, 37, 42, 66, 70, 71, 72, 129, 131, 132–133, 198
Industrial biotechnology, 17–18, 244–246
Infectious diseases, 61, 178–179

Inflammatory diseases, 143
Information overload, 204
Inhale Therapeutic Systems, 43, 64
Initial public offerings (IPOs), 23, 41, 145, 150–152
In silico testing (*vs.* wet-bench science), 205–206
Instrument manufacturers, 213
Insulin, 20–21, 176, 180, 190, 250
Insurance, and genetic testing, 255–256
Intangibles, 29, 49, 83, 87, 159
Integration, vertical *vs.* horizontal, 68–73
Intel, 5, 25, 87, 98, 113, 114, 116, 117, 118, 120, 150, 157, 158, 159, 214
Intellectual property, 29, 49, 87
Interferons (IFN), 183
Interleukins/interferons, 35–36
Introns/exons, 186–187
Invesco, 81
Investment. *See* Biotechnology investing/investment factors:
Invitrogen, 103
"Irrational exuberance," 157
Ischemia, 143
IVAX, 252

Janus, 81
Jenner, Kris, 34
Johnson & Johnson, 28, 131, 209, 218
Jumping genes, 187, 222
Junk DNA, 172, 186

Kam, Ken, 23
Kernen, Joe, 155
King, Michael, 36–37
Klopack, Thomas, 204
Kollman, Peter, 200–201
Kornberg, Arthur, 50

Label expansion, 209
Lai, Henry, 191
Lasker, Mary, 50
Leschly, Jan, 47

Leukemia, 59
Ligands, 211
Ligase, 189
Lilly, 24, 64, 92–93, 113, 250
Liposomes, 211
Lymphoma, non-Hodgkin's (NHL),
    62–63, 210
Lynx, 197

Macrophage, 183
Macular degeneration (AMD), wet
    age-related, 229
Mad cow disease, 202
Malaria breakthroughs, 190–191
Margin, 128–129
Market cap/research & development
    spending (MC/RD ratio), 82–83
Market cap yardstick, 89–90
Market factors, 18–19, 26–49, 52,
    60–63, 159, 162
Marketguide.com, 83
Market timing, 144–145, 147–148
Maxim Pharmaceuticals, 51, 307
Maxygen, 42, 198, 199
Mayer, Steven, 71
McCamant, Jim, 85
McDonald's, 240
MC/RD ratio (market capitalization/
    research & development
    spending), 82–83
Medarex, 46, 51, 218
Medical Technology Stock Letter, 85
Medimmune, 5, 28, 34, 91, 119, 123,
    141, 218
Mendel, Gregor, 43–44, 186
Mental illness, 181
Merck, 91–92
Messenger RNA (mRNA), 175–176,
    223
Metabolic disease, 180
Metabolism (ADMET analysis), 205
Metcalfe's Law, 46, 47
Metrics/financials, 78–81, 162–163
Microrobotics, 14
Microsoft, 5, 24, 150, 156
MIKA Pharma GmbH of Germany,
    248

Millennium Pharmaceuticals, 14, 19,
    26, 27, 36–37, 41, 59–60, 62–63,
    64–65, 71–72, 93–94, 96, 123,
    124, 130, 131, 141, 208, 251,
    307
Miravant, 229
Mitosis, 187–188
Mitsubishi, 147, 214
Moltz, Jim, 63
Monoclonal antibodies (MAbs), 12,
    59, 216–219
Monsanto, 240, 243
"Moonshots," 34–35
Moore's Law, 45, 46, 47
Morgan Stanley, 76
Morningstar.com, 127
MorphoSys of Germany, 218
Motley Fool, 77, 84, 85
Motorola, 98, 147, 214, 255
Multicenter trial, 56
Multiple sclerosis, 18, 34, 61, 143
Murphy, Michael, 81–82, 85
Musical chairs metaphor (stock
    market), 26, 37
Mutual funds, 7, 81, 126–128
Mycoplasma Genitalium, 194
Myriad Genetics, 46, 197

Nanogen, 98, 214
Naqvi, Faraz, 122, 126, 127
Nasdaq, 155
Nasdaq Biotech Index, 6, 7, 40, 129,
    130, 153
Neotherapeutics (NEOT), 48–49, 62
Network(s):
    Metcalfe's Law, 46, 47
    neural (vs. conventional computers),
        250
Neupogen, 22
New drug application (NDA) (to
    FDA), 56–59, 142
Newfound Genomics, 197
Newsletters, 85
Nexia, 245
Nicholas Applegate Global Health
    Care Fund, 126
Niké Investments, 128

Novartis, 96, 103, 146, 240
Nutraceuticals, 14, 240–242

Oil/energy, 17, 246
O'Neil, William, 121, 144–1
Onyx Pharmaceuticals, 124, 227–228
Orchid Biosciences, 151, 215, 308
Osiris Therapeutics, 233
Osteoporosis, 180
"Outperform" (analyst rating), 159

Papadopoulos, Stelios, 253
Parkinson's disease, 45, 61, 83, 203, 243
Partnerships/alliances/collaborations, 52, 63–65, 160–161
Patents, 14–17, 52, 65–68, 253, 256
PC paradigm (parallels in industry history), 3–8, 24–25
PCR (polymerase chain reaction), 188
PE Applied Biosystems, 212
P/EG (price/earnings-to-growth), 83, 84
PEGylation, 209–210
P/E ratio, 78
Periodontix, 243
P/GF ratio (price to growth flow), 82
Pharmaceutical industry, 10–11, 24, 28, 46, 58, 68–69, 126, 127, 144, 238, 250–254
  challenged by biotech companies, 24
  creating public relations nightmare, 251–252
  differences, 10–11
  drug candidate time line, 46
  role in development of biotech industry, 144, 250–254
  takeovers of leading biotech firms, 28
Pharmaceutical Industry Association, 142
Pharmaceutical Research and Manufacturing Association (PhRMA), 14, 45, 54, 58
Pharmacia, 229
Pharmacogenomics, 13, 207–208

Pharming, 13, 242–244
Phased clinical trials. See Clinical trials
Phenotyping, 185
Philip Morris, 156
Photodynamic therapy, 13, 228–229
Photofrin, 228, 229
PhRMA. See Pharmaceutical Research and Manufacturing Association (PhRMA)
Pipeline, 52, 53–54, 160
Piper Jaffray, 124, 129, 158, 159
Plastics, 17, 245
Pluripotent stem cells, 177
Point mutation, 186
Pollution control, 245–246
Polypeptide, 175
PPL Therapeutics, 243
Prices, drivers of, 26–29, 87–88
Privacy, 255
Procter & Gamble, 146
Prodrugs, 227, 228, 229
Product pipeline, 52, 53–54, 160
Profits, taking, 149–150
Progenics Pharmaceuticals, 32–33
Proof of concept, and valuation, 30, 33, 83
Protein:
  deadly (prion-based disease), 202–203
  final product, 176
  folding, 44, 176
  machines, 176–177
  with a purpose (antibodies), 217
  ribosome (cellular protein factory), 175, 176, 200
  therapies, 12, 219–220
Protein Design Labs, 78, 93, 119, 120, 123, 124, 141, 202
Proteomics, 13, 199–202, 204
Prusiner, Stanley, 202, 203
Pulp/paper, 17
Purdue, Edward, 194

QLT Phototherapeutics of Canada, 228
q ratio, 83
Qxhealth.com, 50, 62–63, 135

Raging Bull.com, 135
Recap.com, 51, 60, 62, 65, 85
Recombinant DNA, 187–190, 250
Regulation. *See* Food and Drug
    Administration (FDA)
Reinhard, Christopher, 41, 43
Remicade, 218
Resources, 282–286
Restriction enzymes, 189
Retrovirus, 221
Reynaud's disease, 106
Rhone-Poulenc Animal Nutrition,
    103
Ribosome (cellular protein factory),
    175, 176, 200
Ribozymes, 227
Risk, 29–35, 38–41, 47–48, 119–125,
    163–164
    credibility and, 38–41
    four tiers, and, 122–125
    of ignorance, 47–48
    managing, 119–125
    portfolio design, 121–122
    and rewards, 32–35
    tolerance, 122, 163–164
    uncertainty and, 29–32
    valuation and, 29–32
    volatility and, 119–121
RNA, 175–176, 223
Robbins-Roth, Cynthia, 125
Roche, 18, 28, 251
Rothberg, Jonathan, 75, 100

SAANDs (selective apoptotic
    antineoplastic drugs), 139
Salomon Smith Barney, 86–87, 128
Schering-Plough, 251
Science of biotechnology, 169–185
    biotech approach to treatment,
        184–185
    disease processes, 178–181
    DNA, 170–176
        error correction operations, 176
        fishing rod, 173–175
        ultimate software, 170–173, 176
    gene machinery (computer analogy),
        176
    immune system, 181–184

living cells, 177–178
    messenger RNA (mRNA), 175–176
    polypeptide, 175
    protein machines, 176–177
        enzymes, 176
        hormones, 177
        insulin, 176
        nerves/muscles/blood cells, 177
    ribosome (cellular protein factory),
        175, 176
    RNA, 175–176
    stem cells (pluripotent/totipotent),
        177
    what you need to know, 169–170
Scientific achievement, and valuation,
    32
Scientific specialties, 10
Scotia Holdings, 142
Scott, Randy, 66
Selling considerations, 145–149, 164
Semiconductor index (SOX), 120
Sepracor, 64
Sewage handling, 245
Shaoul, Michael, 78
Sharpe ratio, 82
SignalGene, 197
Signals Magazine, 85
Signal transduction and pathways, 13,
    236–237
Silent mutations, 186
Silk milk, 245
Single technology companies, 125
Skin cells, and cosmeceuticals,
    247–248
SkinMedica, Inc., 248
Smart viruses. *See* Virus(es)
Smith Kline Beecham, 47, 210
SNPs (single nucleotide
    polymorphisms; "snips"), 30, 44,
    46, 171–172, 195
Social/ethical dilemmas, 255–256
Software/bioinformatics, 13,
    204–207
Somatic cell nuclear transfer (SCNT),
    233
Soros, George, 26, 37
Spider silk, 245
Spinal cord, 232

Stem cells, 13, 177, 231–234, 256
  ethical debate, 256
  pluripotent, 177
  tissue regeneration and, 231–234
  totipotent, 177, 232
StreetIQ.com, 87
Synagis, 218
Synergy/convergence, 41–45

Takeovers, 28
Tax(es), 127, 128, 147
  capital gains exposure, 127, 128
  selling and, 147
T cells, 182
Technical analysis (formulas/charts/
  waves/patterns), 81–84
Technical indicators, 84
Technology, assessing, 161
Telomerase, 136–138, 230
Telomeres, 13
Theakston, Hillary, 46, 103
Therapeutic genes (converging
  technology), 42. *See also* Gene
  therapy
Therapeutic proteins, 12, 219–220
3M, 214
Tier(s), 89–112, 161–162
  analysis (investor's checklist),
    161–162
  choosing investments among,
    111–112
  defining four levels, 90–91
  market cap yardstick, 89–90
Tier 1 companies (majors), 90, 91–93,
    111–112, 123, 153, 274–275
  choosing investments, 111–112
  defined, 90
  discussed, 91–93
  list of, 274
  risk management, 123
  waiting for returns, 153
Tier 2 companies (big cap, small
    revenues), 90, 93–99, 111, 123,
    141, 153, 274–275
  choosing investments, 111
  defined, 90
  discussed, 93–99

list of, 274–275
risk management, 123
waiting for returns, 153
Tier 3 companies (mid cap, high
    expectations), 91, 99–105, 111,
    123, 153, 274–277
  choosing investments, 111
  defined, 91
  discussed, 99–105
  list of, 274–277
  risk management, 123
  waiting for returns, 153
Tier 4 companies (micro cap, macro
    risk), 91, 105–111, 123–124,
    142–144, 152–153
  choosing investments, 111
  defined/discussed, 91, 105–111
  list of, 276–281
  profile of a contender, 142–144
  risk management, 123–124
  waiting for returns, 152–153
Tissue replacement/regeneration, 12,
    231–236, 248
  companies developing growth
    factors for, 235
  companies involved in tissue
    replacement, 236
  cosmeceutical therapy and, 248
  stem cells and, 231–234
Toolmakers, 212–213
Totipotent stem cells, 177, 232
Toxicity (ADMET analysis), 205
Transgenics, farming, and pharming,
    242–244
Transkaryotic Therapies, 67–68
Transposons, 187, 222
Trauma, 181
Treatment, biotech approach to,
    184–185
Trega Biosciences, 204, 206, 207
Trends, 129–133
Tumor necrosis factor (TNF), 183

UbiQgel, 241
Uncertainty, 29–32
Unit investment trusts (UITs),
    127–128

Universities, role of, 10, 46, 68
U.S. Bancorp-Piper Jaffray, 124, 129, 158, 159

Vaccines, 13, 20, 229–231, 241
  companies developing, 231
  DNA vaccines, 231
  in food, 241
  new vaccines, 229–231
  savings due to, 20
  for viral infections, 230
Valuation, 29–32, 87–88
Value investing, 28
Vascular endothelial growth factor (VEGF), 225–226, 234
Vasogen, 106–107, 142–144
Vectors, 221
Vegetables, 239
Venter, Craig, 30, 39, 71, 173, 255
Vertex Pharmaceuticals, 78, 93, 94–96, 123, 124, 141, 251
Vezeau, Claude, 253
Vical, 43, 57
Virus(es), 13, 124, 178, 221, 222, 223, 227–228, 230
  adenoviruses, 222, 223
  armed therapeutic, 13, 124

DNA delivery by, 221
  retrovirus, 221
  smart, 227–228
  vectors, 221
  viral infections, 178, 230
Visible Genetics, 255
Volatility, biotech, 6–7, 114–121, 128–129. See also Risk

Warner-Lambert, 28
Waste management, 18
Watson, James, 4, 10, 44
Wet-bench science, 205
Wetware (biological computers/machines), 249–250
Whisper number, 87
Whitfield, Roy, 3
WindowOnWallStreet.com, 84, 135
Wolinsky, Steven, 216

Xenomouse, 243
Xerox, 24

Yahoo Finance/Multex, 51, 78, 83
Yeast, genome of, 194